IN DEFENCE OF CANADA

In Defence of Canada

FROM THE GREAT WAR
TO THE GREAT DEPRESSION

◈

JAMES EAYRS

UNIVERSITY OF TORONTO PRESS

Reprinted 1967
Printed in the U.S.A.

To the dear memory of Stefan Stykolt

STUDIES IN THE STRUCTURE OF POWER:
DECISION-MAKING IN CANADA

Editor: JOHN MEISEL

1. *In Defence of Canada: From the Great War to the Great Depression.* By JAMES EAYRS
2. *The Vertical Mosaic.* By JOHN PORTER
3. *In Defence of Canada: Appeasement and Rearmament.* By JAMES EAYRS

STUDIES IN THE STRUCTURE OF POWER: DECISION-MAKING IN CANADA

The series "Studies in the Structure of Power: Decision-Making in Canada" is sponsored by the Social Science Research Council of Canada for the purpose of encouraging and assisting research concerned with the manner and setting in which important decisions are made in fields affecting the general public in Canada. The launching of the series was made possible by a grant from the Canada Council.

Unlike the books in other series supported by the Social Science Research Council, the studies of decision-making are not confined to any one of the disciplines comprising the social sciences. The series explores the ways in which social power is exercised in this country: it will encompass studies done within a number of different conceptual frameworks, utilizing both traditional methods of analysis and those prompted by the social, political, and technological changes following the Second World War.

In establishing the series, the Social Science Research Council has sought to encourage scholars already embarked on relevant studies by providing financial and editorial assistance and similarly to induce others to undertake research in areas of decision-making so far neglected in Canada.

J. M.

◈

PREFACE AND ACKNOWLEDGMENTS

This book covers the period from the end of the Great War to the ending of the Great Depression. The reader will quickly discover that this is no rigorous analysis of the national security policy of Canada, if only for the reason that there was little national security policy of Canada rigorously to analyse. Nor is it a comprehensive history of the nation's military affairs. I have instead chosen to concentrate on that which I found interesting to follow up and which the available material allowed me to follow up. Thus I have pursued the politics of rehabilitation immediately after the Great War, and the role of the Army in running unemployment relief camps during the Great Depression, without worrying unduly whether these subjects have any place in a study of national security policy properly so called.

I hope this book will turn out to be the first of several. All being well, later volumes will be concerned with Canadian national security policy as it unfolded to meet the threat of the dictatorships from the Manchurian crisis to the outbreak of the Second World War, and the very different threats of the long-range bomber and the intercontinental missile in the nuclear age, as well as of para-military skirmishing along the periphery of the Great Powers' spheres of influence. The emphasis of this volume is mainly on the military. This is partly because of the richness of the materials in the military archives to which I was privileged to obtain access, partly because the diplomacy of Canada during the decade and a half with which it is concerned was, to say the least, under-developed. In the later volumes, the emphasis will shift to external affairs, foreign policy coming into its own as the tempo and importance of Canadian diplomatic activity steadily increase. If the study as a whole has any thesis, it is that the military and diplomatic components of national security policy are, and ought to be, indissolubly combined, in study and analysis as well as in formulation and execution.

◈

I began to write this book during 1962–63, while on sabbatical leave from the University of Toronto. I gratefully acknowledge the aid of a grant from the Canadian Social Science Research Council for this period, one of several awarded for studies of "decision-making" in Canada. I am indebted to the director of this project, Professor John Meisel, for construing its terms of reference so liberally as to include me in and for his valuable editorial advice. I finished writing this book during 1963–64, while on leave of absence from the University of Toronto. I gratefully acknowledge the aid of grants from the Social Science Research Council of New York, and from the Canada Council, enabling me to bring the present work to completion as well as to undertake research for future volumes.

This book is based mainly on the written materials described in the Note on the Sources. I have had as well the benefit of valuable interviews. I am grateful to Rear Admiral Walter Hose, C.B.E., R.C.N., General A. G. L. McNaughton, C.H., and Lt. General Maurice Pope, C.B., M.C., for generously giving me their time and for sharing their knowledge of the history they helped to create. Admiral Hose and General McNaughton made available documentary material without which much of the book could not have been written. General McNaughton was also good enough to search his files for suitable photographs, three of which appear in the book. The portrait of General J. H. MacBrien was made available through the courtesy of Mr. W. A. H. MacBrien.

For permission to make use of the various collections of private papers on which much of the book is based, I am grateful to their various custodians (who are listed in the Note on the Sources). Most of these collections (with the exceptions noted in the following paragraph) are deposited at the Public Archives of Canada. The partnership between historian and archivist, as Sir Keith Hancock has noted, "is on the face of it . . . so one-sided; the historian is such a selfish person, the archivist such a selfless one . . .";* I acknowledge my debt, incurred over many years, to the Dominion Archivist, Dr. W. Kaye Lamb, and his staff,

*W. K. Hancock, *The Smuts Papers*. The Creighton Lecture in History, 1955 (London, 1956), p. 17.

particularly Miss Jean Ballantyne, Mrs. Eileen Bond, and Mr. J. Atherton.

As recorded in the Note on the Sources, I have been privileged in writing this book to make virtually unrestricted use of the official files of the Armed Forces. Without the guidance of the custodians of this immense resource, I should have been unable to exploit it. I am therefore indebted to Colonel G. M. C. Sprung, Director of the Historical Section, Army Headquarters, and members of his staff, particularly Mrs. Alice Sorby, M.B.E., Staff Sergeant Adrien Plamondon, C.D., and Sergeant Paul R. Marshall, C.D.; to Mr. E. C. Russell, the Naval Historian, and his staff, particularly Mr. T. Thorgrimsson and Mr. P. A. C. Chaplin; and to Wing Commander R. V. Manning, the Air Historian, and his staff, particularly Mr. R. V. Dodds. I am grateful as well to Mr. J. Cardillo, who patiently explained to me the mysteries of Central Registry, Department of National Defence; and to Mr. A. Willms and Mr. H. Logan, who offered round-the-clock hospitality at the Public Archives Record Centre.

Colonel C. P. Stacey, formerly Director, Historical Section, Army Headquarters, and now a colleague in the Department of History, University of Toronto, was good enough to read my manuscript in its entirety. He shared with characteristic generosity his unrivalled knowledge of its subject, correcting many errors of fact and challenging several points of interpretation. If factual errors and perverse interpretation remain, it is certainly not his fault.

It is a pleasure once again to express my appreciation to the University of Toronto Press, friendliest of publishers, and to Miss Francess Halpenny and Mr. R. I. K. Davidson, of its Editorial Staff, for help and encouragement all the way.

J. E.

July 1964
Toronto

◈

CONTENTS

IN DEFENCE OF CANADA

INTRODUCTION

Views from a Fire-Proof House

THE NEW WORLD AND THE OLD

In 1918 Canadians turned away from Europe, leaving behind their dead. However misguided isolationism might appear to a later generation, drawn as their fathers had been drawn into the vortex of militarism, it was a natural response to the brutal years at the Western front. Major gains were measured in yards, millions of lives exchanged for desolated acres of mud: how could such a conflict affect the traditional reassurance of geography? The Great War brought Canadians to Europe, but left Europe remote to Canadians. The world was still wide. To the protection of the oceans—Admirals Atlantic and Pacific—might be added that of the Monroe Doctrine. What more was required? Where, indeed, was the enemy? "There is no world menace," declared the Leader of the Opposition during a debate on the militia estimates in 1920. "The Minister says that this expenditure is needed for the defence of Canada—defence against whom? There is no answer; there is no answer to be made. . . ."[1] As Prime Minister of Canada, Mackenzie King reiterated this conviction eighteen years later: "At present," he declared in 1938, "the danger of attack upon Canada is minor in degree and second-hand in origin";[2] and nothing that happened during the six years of war to come made that prediction inaccurate. It was true that German U-boats torpedoed shipping in and about the Gulf of St. Lawrence, and that Japanese balloons of mulberry-bark, armed with smallish charges of explosive, fell upon the West coast and as far inland as Manitoba. But this was hardly what the embattled residents of East London would have recognized as *Blitzkrieg*. The words of the Canadian delegate to the League of Nations Assembly in 1924, however galling to their audience, stated the simple truth. Canada was like "a fire-proof house, far from inflammable materials." And so it would remain, until the age of the long-range bomber and the intercontinental missile.

Isolationism in Canada was the product of geography; it was shaped by a crucial circumstance of history. Canadians in 1918 were only just emerging from the cocoon of colonialism. When newly independent nations enter the world arena for the first time, they characteristically believe themselves to be above and beyond its rivalries and quarrels. Not for them the sordid power politics of older nations. Conflict is seen as a disease from which the ancient and degenerating may suffer but to which the young, if they keep their distance and their principles, may remain immune. George Washington proclaimed his determination to shelter the infant American republic from the entangling alliances of the European powers; Trotsky confidently assumed that, as revolution swept the globe, there would be nothing for his Commissariat of Foreign Affairs to do except, as he said, "shut up the shop"; in our own time the leaders of newly independent states in Asia and in Africa are united at least in their belief that power politics are an alien importation from the decadent West, carried in the cargo of the imperialists along with the firearms and the whisky.

Among North Americans, it might be felt, such attitudes are justifiably held only by Mohicans and other decimated tribes. Anti-imperialist attitudes are not necessarily the product of detached research and mature reflection. They are as often ideological as historical. In 1918 they were the basic component of the Canadian ideology. Nor did they wholly lack justification. Canada's distrust of Europe derived from the Great War, and was being powerfully reinforced by the Paris Peace Conference. "It was European policy, European statesmanship, European ambition, that drenched this world with blood": so the Canadian delegate told the First Assembly of the League of Nations. That was more than half true; and he might have added, with more truth, European generalship. "Fifty thousand Canadians under the soil of France and Flanders," he did go on to say, "is what Canada has paid for European statesmanship trying to settle European problems. I place responsibility on a few; I would not distribute it over many; but nevertheless it is European."[3] These bluntly accusing words, an official of the Canadian delegation wrote privately at the time, "hurt and stung many people," and in his view "marred the performance."[4] But they conveyed, however tactlessly, the way Canadians felt; and the Prime Minister himself wrote to their author to express his "appreciation of the stand you took in stating to the Conference, as frankly as you did, the price the world has paid for the European diplomacy of the last hundred years."[5]

Nor, did it seem, had the trauma of the trenches changed Europe for the better. Ancient enmities and grievances arose from the ashes; the scope for intrigue and for disaster seemed if anything greater than before. "Everywhere there are signs of trouble," wrote one of Canada's representatives at the Paris Peace Conference: "Asia Minor and Turkey are disorganized—Roumanians threatened on three sides by Bolshevists and Hungarians—Russia poisoned and poisoning—Hungary communist and Germany in near chaos. 'Tis surely a sad mess out of which to evolve a new Europe."[6] "The 'war drunk lunatics' . . . of Europe," wrote a distinguished Canadian jurist to his Prime Minister on the eve of the latter's departure for an Imperial Conference in 1923, "have learnt nothing and never will. . . . *One* man in Downing Street still has the power to hurl us into the shambles of war! They simply, *one and all*, cannot be trusted."[7] "When I see the miserable little struggles for petty personal triumphs and, except on the part of the British, the lack of ideals," the Canadian High Commissioner in London wrote in 1926, "I don't wonder the U.S. keeps out of this European menagerie."[8]

Distrust of European statecraft and European statesmen passed easily into an assertion of North American moral superiority. In Canada, as in the United States, there was nourished the conviction that the New World in its national life and international behaviour exhibited standards above and beyond those of the Old. Like Mr. Herbert Hoover, Canadians returned from the Great War steeped in the idea "that through three hundred years [North] America had developed something new in a way of life of a people, which transcended all others of history," transcending especially that "boiling social and economic cauldron of Europe, with its hates and fears."[9] Rare was the Canadian, addressing himself to the theme of his country's place in the world, who did not elaborate this contrast. "As one who had the great privilege of listening only a few weeks ago to the noble and inspiring message of peace and international goodwill that the late lamented President Harding delivered to the people of Canada," one of Mackenzie King's correspondents wrote to him in 1923, "I cannot help contrasting it with the continued hypocrisy and savage . . . utterances of European national leaders."[10] Mackenzie King himself inflicted Harding's homilies upon his fellow Prime Ministers in London. He quoted, approvingly, the presidential peroration—"It is the public will, not force, that makes for enduring peace, and peace can always be kept, whatever the grounds of controversy, between peoples who wish to keep it"—and added: "I place these words on record largely because I think they help to illustrate the new-world point of view that is in very striking contrast to the old-world attitude of the past, if not of the present, that force is always essential in the preservation of peace."[11] "We think in terms of peace," declared the Canadian delegate at the Fifth Assembly of the League of Nations, "while Europe, an armed camp, thinks in terms of war."[12]

Such moralizing led logically not to isolation but to engagement. Ought not the practitioners of the New World's standards help, by more active participation in its affairs, to uplift the standards of the Old? That is not what happened. Fear of contamination proved a stronger impulse than any missionary zeal. The less North America's contact with Europe, the better; the more, the greater the danger of succumbing to what Herbert Hoover described as "miasmic infections which might . . . harm or even destroy . . . the hope of the world."[13] Accordingly, the first duty of the missionary was to stay out of the cannibal's pot. "We in Canada have the opportunity and the power, if we rightly insist upon it, of removing ourselves from the horrors and paralyzing burdens of further European wars. Surely *we* at least who have got nothing out of the war . . . except graves, pension lists, and grinding debt and taxation, should have learned our lesson once and for all time?"[14]

National policy quickly reflected the isolationist outlook. Up went the barriers to immigration, so that no "miasmic infection" might invade the healthy body politic. "Bolshevism," wrote the editor of the *Canadian Annual Review* in 1918, "had a basis wherever Russians and Jews and other foreigners gathered together";[15] to keep out Bolshevism, keep out foreigners. "We are told there are enormous numbers of people on the continent of Europe who want to come here," remarked a former Minister of Immigration in 1922. "I want to say I regard it of the dimensions of a national menace that there is any danger whatever of the bars being let down."[16] They were not let down.

No less discouraged were foreign contacts and commitments. Questioned in 1920 on Canada's readiness to accept a mandate for Armenia, the Leader of the Opposition replied that the proposal "would provoke general protest from one end of the Dominion to the other . . . A sort of reaction has set in . . . with respect to interference by the Governments of this Continent with European Affairs."[17] In 1922 the Canadian Government refused to grant an interest-free loan for the relief of famine in Russia and turned down a Soviet request for credit to buy seed wheat. In 1924 it ignored an appeal to contribute to the relief of famine in Albania. In 1925 Canada declined to sign the Geneva Protocol: "She is realizing today," her delegate remarked in conveying the decision to the League of Nations Assembly, "more intensely than she did at the time of the Great War, what it has cost her; she therefore naturally hesitates to undertake in advance rigid obligations which would render her liable to intervene in conflicts so far removed from her shores."[18] Later that year it was largely at Canada's insistence that a clause was inserted in the text of the Locarno Agreements, specifically exempting the dominions from their provisions. "I do not see," a member of the Government observed, "that Canada should assume obligations in connection with the boundaries between France and Germany . . . [or] guarantee any boundaries in central Europe or elsewhere."[19]

THE LEAGUE AND THE NATION

Isolationism likewise coloured Canada's attitude towards, and policies within, the League of Nations. If other countries entered the League in something of the spirit expressed by General Smuts—"the tents have been struck and the great caravan of humanity is once more on the march"—Canada may be said to have been mainly concerned lest she be called upon to do more than her share of the work in breaking camp, or be compelled to march without the consent of her Parliament.

"The Members of the League"—so runs the celebrated Tenth Article of its Covenant—"undertake to respect and preserve as against external aggression the territorial integrity and existing political independence of all Members of the League. In case of any such aggression, or in case of any threat or danger of such aggression, the Council shall advise upon the means by which this obligation shall be fulfilled." Before the text of the Covenant entered in its final draft that of the Treaty of Versailles, the delegates of Canada at the Paris Peace Conference had profound misgivings about this undertaking. In a memorandum of February 1919, C. J. Doherty, Minister of Justice in Borden's Government and one of three Cabinet ministers accompanying Borden to Europe for the tasks of peace-making, argued that the Article guaranteed all existing territorial arrangements, however unjust; that it placed unequal responsibilities upon member states; that Canada, particularly, would be unfairly loaded by virtue of its immunity from external aggression, its exclusion from the understandings by which the frontiers of Europe had been shaped, and above all, by the certain unpopularity of action under Article 10 among the Canadian public. It was, in his words, "a mutual guarantee where the risks run and the burdens imposed are not equal between the nations entering into it, and where the inequality is particularly striking in the case of countries in Canada's position, and works specially to their detriment."[20] The Prime Minister entirely agreed. The Article, in Borden's words, called upon the signatories to declare "(*a*) that all existing territorial delimitations are just and expedient, (*b*) that they will continue indefinitely to be just and expedient, (*c*) that the signatories will be responsible therefor." In these terms the undertaking was unwise, if not absurd; the Article, in Borden's view, "should be struck out or materially amended," his own preference being deletion.[21] But while there were others at Paris concerned as he was (even so dedicated an apostle of collective security as Lord Robert Cecil thought the Article should be amended to allow for "peaceful change"), none was prepared to challenge France and those other nations to whom Article 10 was as vital as to Canada it was expendable. So it passed into the Covenant intact.

The Canadians had lost a battle, but not yet a war. At the First Assembly, and again at the Second, the implacable Doherty pressed for an amendment of the Covenant to delete Article 10. Though unsuccessful, his persistence inscribed upon the agenda of the Third Assembly the question of "Amendment to Article 10 of the Covenant," and it fell to the new Liberal Government to decide what to do about it. Mackenzie King and his colleagues were no more sympathetically disposed towards Article 10 than their Conservative predecessors. Yet to press on with Doherty's demand for deletion might prove more trouble than it was worth; it was becoming obvious that it would never receive the unanimous approval of the Assembly required for adoption; and the two Cabinet ministers representing Canada had no great zeal for the cause. "Mr. Lapointe and myself," W. F. Fielding wrote to Mackenzie King from Geneva,

> would have been quite content if we had not been called upon to do anything about it. However, it was there and we had to deal with it in some shape. We concluded, after some study of the matter here, that there was no possibility of striking out Article Ten, even if we had been anxious to do so. Vague and indefinite as to many it seems, it was regarded by the smaller nations as some sort of guarantee for their protection, and therefore they were not willing to have it deleted. . . . Thus, when nobody seemed to favour the proposal to delete Article Ten, there was a very decided hostility in many quarters to that motion. Mr. Lapointe and I decided that no good purpose could be served by adhering to the Doherty motion. . . .[22]

Instead of deletion, the Canadian delegates hit upon the idea of modification. Lapointe outlined the proposal to a committee of the Assembly on 14 September. He stated (according to the official records of the League of Nations in which speakers were quoted indirectly)

> that, as a result of conversations which he had held since his arrival in Geneva, he was convinced that it would be impossible at the present moment

to secure the deletion of Article 10. . . . He thought it desirable that the Committee on Amendments, if it was unwilling to propose its deletion, should at least make suggestions with regard to its modification. . . . He thought such a step was dictated by international honesty and candour. . . . He proposed that they should affirm their approval of the principle recognized . . . last year, by adding at the end of Article 10 the following words: 'Taking into account the political and geographical circumstances of each state'.

Further, in order to give due weight to the sovereign authority of Parliament in the various states Members of the League of Nations, the Canadian delegate proposed the following amendment:

'The opinion given by the Council in such cases shall be regarded as a matter of the highest importance, and shall be taken into consideration by all the Members of the League, which shall use their utmost endeavours to conform to the conclusions of the Council; but no Member shall be under the obligation to engage in any act of war without the consent of its Parliament, legislature or other representative body'.

The motive of the Canadian delegation in taking this step was a sincere desire to further the interests of the League of Nations. They were the pioneers of the idea of the League of Nations in North America, and as such they wished to remove all the obstacles which barred its progress.[23]

No immediate action was taken, nor did the Canadians expect or seek it. "The marvellous capacity which the machine has for jollying things along," Fielding wrote to his Prime Minister, "will be used in this case, and nothing will be done. We are not worrying over that, for we were not very anxious to have anything done and only took up the case because it had been left on the order paper."[24] It was still on the "order paper" a year later. The Canadian delegate to the Fourth Assembly, Sir Lomer Gouin, Minister of Justice in Mackenzie King's Government, dropped the demand for formal amendment in favour of the device of an "interpretive resolution" which, while expressing the substance of the Lapointe amendments, would, it was hoped, not offend those members reluctant to acquiesce in any tampering with the fundamental constitution of the League. Its text was as follows:

The Assembly, desirous of defining the scope of the obligations contained in Article 10 of the Covenant so far as regards the points raised by the Canadian delegation, adopts the following resolution:

'It is in conformity with the spirit of Article 10 that, in the event of the Council considering it to be its duty to recommend the application of military measures in consequence of an aggression, or danger or threat of aggression, the Council shall be bound to take account, more particularly, of the geographical situation and the special conditions of each state.

'It is for the constitutional authorities of each Member to decide, in reference to the obligation of preserving the independence and the integrity of the territory of Members, in what degree the Member is bound to assure the execution of this obligation by employment of its military forces.

'The recommendation made by the Council shall be regarded as being of the highest importance and shall be taken into consideration by all the Members of the League with the desire to execute their engagements in good faith'.[25]

This resolution failed by one vote—that of Persia*—to secure the unanimous consent necessary for formal adoption. But, as Sir Lomer Gouin wrote afterwards to Mackenzie King, "we know now that the Great Powers and all the Members of the Council shall interpret that famous Article 10 in the sense of the amendment proposed by our colleague, Mr. Lapointe."[26] So, unhappily for the peace of the world, it was to prove.

It has been customary to attribute the reserve with which Canadians watched the Geneva experiment to the coercive characteristics of the Covenant, and to suppose that as long as the League of Nations confined its activities to conciliation and friendly persuasion it could count on Canadian approval and support. This interpretation is misleading. It implies a degree of attachment to the League as a non-coercive agency for peaceful change which, whatever might be said in public, no Canadian policy-maker, and few Canadian opinion-makers, really felt. For Canada's suspicion of Geneva derived not only from concern lest through Articles 10 and 16 the newly independent Dominion be placed at "the beck and call of a Council not responsible to the nation for its actions" or, even worse, it become involved "in conflicts in some far-away section of Europe, or in some distant portion of South America";[27] it derived as much, or more, from the New World's hostility to the Old. It was as a European institution, and therefore as an alien institution, that the League of Nations appeared to Canadians. "The League was born ostensibly as a world League," commented a former official of the Department of External Affairs in 1926, "but really is a European League with the non-Europeans tacked on. The most distinctive and powerful New World people went out of it." A Canadian had no more legitimate concern "with the administration of Danzig or of the Saar

*Whose delegate, Prince Arfaed-Bolveh, declared: "In insisting on maintaining Article 10 in its entirety, Persia is influenced neither by caprice nor by obduracy, nor by any want of respect or sympathy for Canada. There is, however, a strong contrast between the political and geographical situation of Persia and that of Canada. Canada is situated on the shores of the Atlantic Ocean and is part of the Great British Empire; Persia is situated in Asia and is surrounded by States which are not members of the League. No one would ever dream of attacking Canada, for this would imply an attack upon the British Empire. From this standpoint, the position of Persia is entirely different. . . ." *Records of the Fourth Assembly*, 1923. 13th Plenary Meeting, 25 Sept., p. 81.

Valley"* than had "a Nova Scotian . . . [with] the municipal government of Vancouver."[28] "Let us . . . conciliate Quebec and Ontario," remarked a member of Parliament in 1923, "before we start conciliating Roumania and Ukrainia."[29] Sir Joseph Pope, Under Secretary of State for External Affairs until 1925, dismissed the Covenant as "not worth the paper it is written on," and wrote in his diary: "Our reps. are making a great stir at the League of Nations, advertising Canada and incidentally themselves. I think it all absurd, and am convinced that Canada's true policy right now is to develop her resources and to leave European questions such as the Bessarabian frontier &c to our Imperial statesmen and the trained experts of Downing Street."[30] His successor, O. D. Skelton, while holding imperial statesmen and the trained experts of Downing Street in somewhat lesser regard, was no less convinced that Canadians should cultivate their garden. In his first major paper prepared when Under Secretary of State for External Affairs—"Notes on the Protocol of Geneva" which, he wrote apologetically to the Prime Minister, "I fear are longer than the Protocol"[31]—Skelton reiterated the now familiar contrast "in the angle from which questions of armament and security are approached by a country like Canada, fortunate in its comparative isolation and its friendly neighbours, and by many of the countries of Europe, heirs to centuries of feuds and fears. . . ." The Protocol itself he described as "A League of European Victors . . . , distinctly a European affair. It would not protect Canada an iota. It is designed to safeguard the territorial gains of the winners in the world war. . . .[32] Other prominent Canadians were capable of even more sweeping condemnation. "The League of Nations," wrote Sir Clifford Sifton in 1920, "is a preposterous and expensive farce, and amounts to nothing more than a part of a machine designed to involve us in European and Imperialistic complications. Canada ought to call a halt on this business."[33] Five years later he wrote, again to the editor of his newspaper:

> You will remember that I never was very keen on the League of Nations. Twenty-five years of more or less constant intercourse with people over there have given me a pretty good idea of their point of view. . . . I am suspicious of the bunch of second-rate professors that are congregating around Geneva; busy-bodies who think in small dimensions, but long-winded sentences. . . .[34]

Few people in Canada regarded the development of the League with less sympathy and greater misgiving than the man who was Prime

*A Canadian, R. D. Waugh, a former mayor of Winnipeg, had been a member of the Saar Valley Commission; a decade later another Canadian, Mr. Vincent Massey, was offered (and declined) the post of Administrator of Danzig.

Minister throughout the greater part of its history. Mackenzie King, as his biographer remarks, "was the type of uplifter who might have been expected to give the League his full and enthusiastic support,"[35] and his public attitude, during its early years at least, was generally one of gushing endorsation. Thus, during a speech in Montreal in 1925, having failed to rouse his audience by his remarks on the tariff, railways and immigration, he reportedly "turned his notes on these subjects into discard, and plunged into a panegyric of the League of Nations, of Canada's part in the future of civilization."[36] But this was clearly a case of any port in a storm. Mackenzie King's true opinion of the League was disclosed during its time of testing in the Abyssinian crisis of 1935; and his activities throughout the crisis ensured in no small degree that it did not emerge triumphant.

STATUS AND STATURE

Not all the Old World was reviled by all the New. Some of those whose ancestors or who themselves had crossed the sea from England or Wales, Scotland or Ireland, retained for their mother country an affection so fierce as to cause them to exempt her from any of the villainies of Europe. They exhibited in this an attitude markedly different from that of French-speaking Canadians, encouraged by ecclesiastical guardians to distrust the anti-clericalism and decadence of the Third Republic. Love of Britain was strongest in pockets of United Empire Loyalists scattered here and there throughout the Maritime Provinces and in the Eastern Townships, old-fashioned folk who had earlier fled the republicanism brought to America by the Revolution and whose regard for England would not have been seriously shaken had Edward VII been succeeded by George III. But it was strong elsewhere, in the pleasant fastnesses of middle-class English Canada in Quebec City, in Montreal, in Toronto—above all, in Toronto—and in Victoria, as well as in those not so pleasant fastnesses—Lowertown and Cabbagetown—where English-speaking proletarians, seeking scapegoats for their squalor, were wont to fasten on the neighbours with the odd accents and unfamiliar names. Upon this curiously assorted following politicians and publicists would call to support their schemes for federating the Empire and preserving the hegemony of Britain against those Canadians, misguided or even treasonable, who sought to weaken the ties and to subvert the old traditions. Nor was there silence when they were called. In 1922, the refusal of the Canadian Government to help Lloyd George and Churchill hold the line at Chanak caused Arthur Meighen to declare, in a speech made famous by its peroration: "There are those who write and talk as though Britain were not our good partner and friend but our chief antagonist, an imperious, designing mistress, seeking to lead us to our ruin. . . . Let there be no dispute as to where I stand. When Britain's message came then Canada should have said: 'Ready, aye ready; we stand by you'."[37] Five hundred members of the Toronto Liberal-Conservative Businessmen's Club rose to cheer their leader for these sentiments, and cheered and cheered again.

But the majority of Anglo-Canadians were more disposed to ask what the cheering was all about. It was true that theirs was an attitude of ambivalence. The most case-hardened Anglophobe knew well enough how much his country owed to Britain. He might detest the English visitor, even more the English immigrant (that, more likely than not, he had been an English immigrant himself some years before did not prevent his posting, or applauding the posting of, "No English wanted" signs outside the employment offices of mining towns and logging camps); but he could only admire English institutions. The young Mackenzie King, for all his liberal nationalism, "was greatly moved when he stood on the streets of London and saw the Coldstream and Grenadier Guards leave for South Africa. The British had something that Canadians could scarcely know, 'something of pride & glory, something which makes a people one . . . common heirs to the enjoyment of its liberties, its historic past and its present greatness'."[38] These were sentiments more easily held at the beginning of the Boer War than at the end of the Great War. Yet even in 1919, and for many years after that, Canadians of British descent might wish that something of the excellence of England—its Parliament and Press, its universities and theatre—might grace the wilderness which they had made their home.

But this heritage of excellence, which might have inspired Canadians left to discover it for themselves, lost much of its lustre when thrust upon them by its heirs. That too often happened. "The culture of London seemed so polished," an historian of the Colonial Office has observed, "that it was hard to treat with perfect seriousness the aspirations of Toronto or Auckland, Lagos or Belize. To the men of Whitehall, the civilisation of the colonies, whether newly contrived by expatriated Britons or the child of the primordial jungle, was not merely different to their own, it was inferior to it. Colonial peoples were like children and were to be treated with all the kindness and severity of the Victorian parent."[39] This was hard to take. Canadians exposed to the Englishman's sense of effortless superiority, his condescension, his ignorance of other peoples' ways of doing things, developed anti-Anglo-Saxon attitudes in some cases not far from the neurotic. These were hard to overcome. "It is amazing," wrote Mackenzie King early in the Second World War, "how these people . . . from the Old Country . . . seem to think that all they have to do is to tell us what is to be done."[40]

If a Canadian Prime Minister could think this in 1939, what did a Canadian Prime Minister think in 1919? "You know how placable a man Sir Robert Borden is," J. W. Dafoe wrote to a mutual friend, "but I spent an evening with him in London when he spent most of his time raging against a document which had been submitted to the war cabinet that day by a very high official of the Foreign Office, in which the Dominions were put in their place. . . . He said that he had about come to the conclusion that they were hopeless."[41] That was the conclusion come to by most of the Canadians—businessmen, journalists, politicians —who did much negotiating with the British during the next few years. Dafoe himself affirmed that, "with rare exceptions, the permanent officials of the departments with which we have to do, the Foreign Office, the Army, the Navy and the Colonial Office, haven't the slightest conception of the relationship which exists today between the various British nations and what is more I do not think it is possible to teach them."[42] "If the Empire holds together," wrote a former member of the Department of External Affairs after a year or two in Lombard Street, "it won't be the Englishman's fault. They are hard traders, as one sees in the City, and as far as I can see the only thing to do is to trade as stiffly as possible with them all along the line."[43] It was perhaps no accident that the most unfavourable impressions were recorded by the Canadian who, more than any other, carried the burden of negotiation with British officials on a variety of subjects during the years from 1922 to 1929. This was the High Commissioner for Canada in the United Kingdom. His letters to his Prime Minister over that period disclose his mounting disillusionment:

> There has never been any doubt in my mind that the average Englishman, especially the insular minded one, thinks himself inestimably better than the Colonial. . . . When I have had the pleasure of meeting the different Ministers on the [cattle] embargo question . . . I leave them with the conviction that in their hearts they have the same feeling towards me that they would have towards a child. . . .
>
> I have not gone any further with the Treasury in regard to their debt to us. . . . The more I think of the position they take up in regard to that debt the more provoked I am about it. It is absolutely unconscionable. It is not honest. . . . [P. C. Larkin to Mackenzie King, 16 May 1922]

I am perfectly helpless in these people's hands. They seem to take such an extraordinary and irresponsible view of a plain business matter. It appears that they owe money long overdue but they only pay it "to meet the wishes of the Canadian Government" and they can write a letter making some statement at some time and then all responsibility ceases and they can discontinue payments. How can you treat with people like these? They are either absolutely ignorant of the first principles of business . . . or what I think [are] trying to tire us out. . . . [Larkin to King, 22 November 1923]

. . . I see that Mr. Otto Niemeyer of the Treasury has been raised to the dignity of a Knighthood. That title has been earned by a cost to Canada of twenty-three million dollars! . . . I cannot help thinking that the sentiment is all on our side. . . . There is no sentiment in Government or Government Departments in this Country. . . . If you were living over here as I have been for the past two years, you would fall, as I have, from the clouds. [Larkin to King, 3 June 1924]

One of the great mistakes Canadians labour under is that sentiment cuts any figure. There is a great deal of waving of flags and talk of Imperial sentiment and all the rest of it, but when it comes down to business the sentiment, if any existed, vanishes quickly. . . . [Larkin to King, 14 June 1924]

. . . It is quite apparent that any courtesies or concessions made to Canada by Ministers and others here will have to be drawn from them by forceps. . . . They have very little more respect for Canada to-day than they have for the Gold Coast. . . . [Larkin to King, 26 November 1926]

. . . What a joke it is for the Dominions to call themselves Sister Nations when we know in our hearts that the last word is always with the man who is acting as Colonial Secretary or Secretary of State for the Dominions here. . . . I do not think it is quite unkindness but they feel in the same way as George III felt towards the thirteen Colonies—they were rebellious children and must be whipped into obedience. . . . [Larkin to King, 6 July 1926]

. . . What particular distinction or capacity has any man in the present British Government shown that makes him superior to the average Canadian Minister? I have watched this closely for the past six years, read their speeches in and out of Parliament, looked carefully into their different measures and their conduct of the Government, and I would be sorry indeed if I did not think that Canadian affairs were not in more competent hands—men with, on the whole, more serious minds. We have, certainly, during the past few years, made some strides forward—the strides that a capable son should and must make if he is to obtain and keep the respect of his parents, but I will never be satisfied until they look upon Canada, if not with the deference they show our neighbours, at least with as much respect as they show to a South American Republic.

The statesmen here will find a hundred reasons, if necessary, to keep us in what they consider our proper position; reasons that obtained a hundred years ago. It accords better with their dignity that we should continue in the eyes of the world as dependents. . . . [Larkin to King, 23 January 1928]

II

Amidst these rancorous prejudices and conflicting conceptions of nationhood and imperialism, there had to be worked out, sometimes by error, more often by trial, the constitutional position of Canada as a member of the Commonwealth of Nations. The subject has not lacked historians; but these, being for the most part actors in the events they describe, have only perpetuated the passions of the moment. No part of Canadian history needs more urgently to be rescued from both the misleading versions in which it has been cast.

In one of these—the "Authorized Version," as it has been called—the development of Dominion status is depicted as a simple conflict of right *versus* wrong. Autonomist saints confront and put to flight centralist sinners: the former are said to have resided (after December 1921) at the East Block in Ottawa (more accurately, at Laurier House and Kingsmere, the Prime Minister's town and country homes), the latter at Downing Street and Whitehall. From document to document the stately pageantry unfolds: colony becomes nation in triumphant vindication of what we are asked to accept as the Grand Design of Mr. King.* In the competing, less authorized, version, Mackenzie King's imperial policies are made to figure as the malign servants of his personal ambition; or else (or as well) are presented as a betrayal of the British connection to American continentalism—a process begun in the infancy of a long career and culminating in August 1940 on a railway siding near Ogdensburg, N.Y.

A revisionist interpretation will not be attempted here. But in order to understand the defence policies of the Dominion during the period from the Great War to the Great Depression (and, indeed, much later), it will be necessary to examine briefly the changing relations of Canada and the British Empire, conducting the examination, so far as a Canadian may do so, free from the misconceptions of the "Authorized Version" and its enemies.†

*"Mr. King" as in "Mr. Gladstone"; such was the hold of the late Prime Minister upon official Ottawa that it was (and remains) its custom to refer to him in this way long after his death in 1950.

†Interested readers may find in the lengthy introduction to R. MacGregor Dawson's collection of documents entitled *The Development of Dominion Status* (Toronto, 1935) the most self-confident and uncomplicated expression of the "Authorized Version" in scholarly form. (I exclude as unscholarly the oversimplified treatment in J. W. Pickersgill, "Mr. Mackenzie King and the Development of the Commonwealth," an Address to the Empire Club of Toronto, 10 December 1953; it is not, however, without interest for the connoisseur.) The

The degree to which self-governing dominions were or ought to be free to conduct their external affairs as they saw fit had for many years stirred controversy. By 1919 their responsibility for commercial relations with other states—control over tariffs and trade agreements—had been established, as had responsibility for local defence. But what part they were to play in shaping the Grand Strategy of the Empire, embracing both foreign policy and imperial defence, remained something of an enigma. Their contribution to the Allied victory removed once and for all any possibility of returning to the status of colonial subordination (a status which, in Canada's case, had been defunct since the 1840's). But what sort of status was to replace it? That was very much an open question.

The absence of any authoritative answer was due in part to the studied reluctance of the authorities to subject dominion status to any kind of searching examination. Lloyd George declared that dominion status defied definition, and stressed the danger of "limiting our Constitution by too many finalities."[44] Yet though this shying from precision may have owed something to what a German writer called "the Englishman's unsystematic genius" in imperial affairs, it stemmed as well from a harder-headed consideration. Any definition that was not to be divisive demanded agreement on fundamentals; and on such fundamentals the self-governing dominions were not agreed. There was no consensus within the Commonwealth about the nature of the Commonwealth.

What, broadly speaking, was orthodoxy in Australia and New Zealand was held by important politicians in Canada to verge on heresy. Whereas William Hughes and W. F. Massey were content to allow imperial strategy to be worked out by the imperial government, with only occasional advice and assistance from dominion prime ministers convened in conference at London, Canadian governments could not and did not accept this procedure without far-reaching reservations. As early as 1885, when Sir John A. Macdonald refused to send troops to the Sudan to "get Gladstone & Co. out of the hole," it had been apparent that Canadian governments would reserve for themselves the right to decide to what extent they might associate their country with Britain's imperial adventures. Such a reservation was basically incompatible with the ideal of a single, unified imperial policy in foreign

principal exponent of the rival version is D. G. Creighton, in the following essays: "Canada in the World," in *Canada's Tomorrow* (Toronto, 1954); "Towards the Discovery of Canada," *University of Toronto Quarterly*, vol. XXV, no. 3, April 1956; and "Sir John A. Macdonald," in C. T. Bissell, ed., *Our Living Tradition* (Toronto, 1957), esp. pp. 51–52.

affairs as in defence. On this rock the "group unit concept of Empire," as Hertzog of South Africa disparagingly called it, was eventually to founder.

It was thus sheer necessity, as well as a certain curious pride in imprecision, which delayed definition of dominion status and postponed investigation of the limits, if any, to autonomy. Instead, a shroud of ambiguity was laid over the most vexing questions, as in the celebrated Resolution IX adopted by the Imperial War Conference in 1917 which recognized "the right of the Dominions and India to an adequate voice in foreign policy and in foreign relations." There being no agreed index of adequacy, no one could complain, no one could rejoice. The veneer of unanimity was preserved, to be marred, inevitably, at a later date. For the moment, the meaning of the protean Resolution IX depended upon the interpretation the imperial government chose to place upon it.

The Imperial Conference convened at London in the summer of 1921 enabled the British Prime Minister to expound to the assembled dominion premiers his "general conception of the mutual relationship in which we meet." For their wartime achievements, "the British Dominions have now been accepted fully into the comity of nations by the whole world." They were signatories of the Peace Treaties; they were members of the League of Nations; "in other words, they have achieved full national status, and they now stand beside the United Kingdom as equal partners in the dignities and responsibilities of the British Commonwealth."[45] This exposition, however, offered no clues as to how those "dignities and responsibilities" were to be shared. None were offered because, in Lloyd George's view, none were required. It was unnecessary to state what surely all would take for granted: that while the dominions might justly claim autonomy and equality of status, these attributes of nationhood did not imply that each of them would now embark upon distinctive foreign policies. That would be tantamount to breaking up the British Empire; and no one present, the British Prime Minister felt sure, wanted that to come about.

Canada was represented at the Imperial Conference of 1921 by her Prime Minister. Arthur Meighen was not one to press dominion status to the point of disrupting the Empire. And yet he was no less reluctant to accept a theory of imperial control by which Canadian external affairs could be adversely affected. Foremost in his mind at that time was the problem of the impending renewal of the Anglo-Japanese Treaty, on which the imperial authorities were determined but to which, as Meighen knew, the United States was adamantly opposed. Canada was caught in the Anglo-American cross-fire and Meighen's mission was obviously to bring the United Kingdom and the United States together again. He sought to do this by offering his own interpretation of the infinitely malleable Resolution IX. He put to the Imperial Conference three propositions:

> There should be regular, and so far as possible, continuous conferences between the responsible representatives of Britain and the self-governing Dominions and India with a view, among other things, of determining and clarifying the governing principles of our relations with foreign countries, and of seeking common counsel and advancing common interests thereupon.
>
> That while in general final responsibility rests with the Ministry advising the King, such Ministry should, in formulating the principles upon which such advice is founded and in the application of those principles, have regard to the views of His Majesty's Privy Council in other Dominions and of the Representatives of India.
>
> That as respects the determination of the Empire's foreign policy in which any Dominion is peculiarly concerned the view of that Dominion must be given a weight commensurate with the importance of the decision to that Dominion. Speaking for Canada, I make this observation with particular reference to our relations with the United States.[46]

Meighen's propositions provoked a storm of controversy at the Conference. Hughes of Australia led the attack. He declared that they were "incompatible with a United Empire—with an Empire that will endure," and demonstrated with little difficulty the practical objections to implementing successfully Meighen's principle of peculiar concern. How could it solve the principal problem of foreign policy then confronting the Conference? Canada, as the custodian of imperial policy towards North America, might recommend the abrogation of the Anglo-Japanese Alliance; but Australia, as the custodian of imperial policy in the Far East—for "we are vitally concerned in China and Japan—very much more so than Canada or South Africa"—would recommend its renewal. It could lead only to deadlock. Meighen responded mildly to the onslaught of the Prime Minister of Australia by saying that he had not thought himself to have "been the father of any constitutional proposals" but that he had merely stated what he "believed to be the present position." It seems unlikely that Meighen did not recognize his own innovation for what it was—unless one of his critics was correct in asserting that the Canadian Prime Minister "was out of his depth in the Conference . . . dealing with matters about which he had no real knowledge."[47] A more plausible explanation is that Meighen intended his proposals not so much to provide an enduring solution to the imperial dilemma as to safeguard Canada's interests in the immediate foreign policy problem before the Conference. In that it proved successful, for the Anglo-Japanese Treaty, largely on account of Meighen's objections, was not renewed.

So the group-unit concept of Empire emerged unscathed from the Imperial Conference of 1921. The Empire, it was now recognized, was composed of partners who on major issues of high policy would move as one, all partners contributing to the final decision. "There was a time," said Lloyd George, "when Downing Street controlled the Empire; to-day the Empire is in charge of Downing Street."[48] But how was the Empire to take charge of Downing Street when some of the partners were 12,000 miles from the scene?

To this question the Conference devoted much thought. It canvassed a wide range of proposals, from the slightly fanciful suggestion of the Prime Minister of New Zealand that an imperial yacht—"a vessel of some 25 knots"—be placed at the disposal of dominion governments whose leaders could then be rounded up rather more rapidly than usual "at Vancouver, Victoria, Sydney, Melbourne, Auckland, Wellington, or the Cape, when necessary,"[49] to a revival of the idea of stationing resident dominion ministers at London. The most practical suggestion came from the British Foreign Secretary. "What you want," Lord Curzon told the dominion prime ministers, "is greater knowledge . . . on matters which concern you as parts of the Empire, and in which you yourselves, your Parliaments, your troops, may be involved. . . ." Such intelligence, he suggested, could be conveyed by the British Government sending "out to you, to the Prime Ministers of the Dominions, once a month, or, if necessary, once a week, a selection of those extremely confidential Foreign Office Papers which are now seen only by the Cabinet and circulated to our representatives . . . abroad." At this juncture Curzon was interrupted by the Prime Minister of Australia. "You are speaking," asked William Hughes, "of sending it by post?" "Yes," Curzon replied, "and a great crisis leading up to war does not develop in a week or two. A war or any great affair in which you are concerned is the result of a process that has been going on for several weeks or months."[50]

Less than a year later, the great crisis of Chanak brought the Dominion of Canada to the brink of war not in several weeks or months, but in a matter of hours. The group-unit concept of Empire bobbed like flotsam in its wake. New Zealand eagerly, Australia less eagerly, had responded affirmatively to Winston Churchill's call to help defend the "soil which is hallowed by immortal memories of the Anzacs"; Smuts in South Africa pretended not to hear the call; while Mackenzie King in Canada replied sharply that only Parliament could decide. As if the disarray were not great enough, those members of the British Government who had sought to involve the dominions in their excursion were themselves dramatically repudiated by the British public in the election of November 1922. In an editorial attempt to salvage something from the wreckage, *The Times* of London suggested that perhaps, after all, the existing machinery of consultation had not been at fault; the machinery was not perfect, to be sure, but neither was it automatic, requiring a "genuine and sustained effort by all parties concerned to bring it into full operation." Had that effort really been made? The dominions' prime ministers, it suggested, might not have carefully perused the precious information conveyed to them in Foreign Office despatches.[51] That made galling reading in Ottawa: the fact was that not a single cabled despatch on the situation in the Near East had been received by the Dominion Government before 15 September, when Churchill's "invitation" arrived unheralded at Government House.

From these events very different conclusions might be, and were, drawn. For the extreme autonomist, the logical conclusion was that, a single Grand Strategy for the Empire being so evidently incompatible with the national interests of its component parts, each of the dominions should henceforth shape its own policy in foreign affairs, relying upon common tradition, common sense and, above all, a common fund of information, to prevent them from striking out on too sharply divergent paths. This development commended itself, interestingly enough, to a former exponent of imperial federation, Philip Kerr, who had been in Ottawa during the Chanak crisis and set down his reactions in a letter to his Canadian friend Vincent Massey:

> The essential thing is that the Dominions should equip themselves with the best possible information about foreign affairs, either by having ambassadors or High Commissioners of their own, or by having a better system of consultation & information in London, or both, so that they have an intelligent policy *on its merits* about international questions as they arise. . . . Mackenzie King's policy, which was Laurier's, of pleading ignorance, i.e., the ostrich policy, is the most fatal of all. . . . The only way is that Canada should have a mind of its own about every issue. . . .[52]

That was a view more easily held if one were not Prime Minister of a country whose people preferred to have no mind at all about any issue of international affairs. Mackenzie King did not go so far. At the conclusion of a restrained account of the Chanak crisis in the House of Commons, he permitted himself the following comment: "We have felt, and feel very strongly, that, if the relations between the different parts of the British Empire are to be made of an enduring character, this will only be through a full recognition of the supremacy of Parliament, and this particularly with regard to matters which may involve participation in war."[53] This statement was a half-way house. It repudiated the group-unit conception of Empire: the decision to go to war or to remain at peace is the supreme decision of external policy; that much granted, autonomy in foreign affairs must necessarily follow. But the statement did not assert the right of each dominion to formulate and conduct its own foreign policy. That involved the acquisition of intelligence, the forming of opinions, the taking of decisions, on matters that the Prime Minister knew his countrymen for the most part would rather leave alone. He was prepared to allow them to remain in ignorance.

As for Australia and New Zealand, their Prime Ministers showed up at the Imperial Conference of 1923 with their faith in the feasibility of a single imperial policy wholly unimpaired. It should not on this account be thought that governments at Canberra and Wellington were any less moved by what they conceived to be their national interest than governments at Cape Town or at Ottawa. If Hughes and Massey responded quickly to the call to help hold the line at Chanak, it was because they felt it vitally important that the line be held: a Moslem insurrection in the Middle East would cut the chain of communications on which Australia and New Zealand depended. If Bruce and Massey echoed the Admiralty's description of the Oceanic Commonwealth and defended the concept of a single Empire strategy at the Imperial Conference of 1923, it was because their countries stood to gain by the construction of an imperially financed base at Singapore and by any improvements in the fighting strength of the Royal Navy. In the Pacific dominions, nationalism required that imperial ties be tightened; in Canada and South Africa, nationalism demanded that they be loosened. Nationalism was no less nationalism for that. The tenacity of nationalism, not for the last time, was seriously under-rated by those who thought more of unity than of diversity.

The British, too, spoke as if nothing had changed; it was not surprising that they did, for they had much to lose by change. Austen Chamberlain, in his first speech as Foreign Secretary, confided to his audience at a Guildhall banquet that "the first thoughts of any Englishman on appointment to the Office of Foreign Secretary must be that he speaks in the name, not of Great Britain only, but of the British Dominions beyond the seas, and that it is his imperative duty to preserve in word and deed the diplomatic unity of the Empire. Our interests are one. Our intercourse must be intimate and constant and we must speak with one voice in the Councils of the World."[54] It was not altogether easy for a British Foreign Secretary to speak this way after Chanak; evidently, it was not too difficult, either.

What made it much more difficult was the United Kingdom's participation, in the autumn of 1925, in the Locarno Agreements, a complex of treaties, conventions and declarations of which, for Britain, the crucial portion was the Treaty of Mutual Guarantee between Belgium, France, Germany, Great Britain and Italy—the so-called Rhineland Pact—having the effect of binding the United Kingdom Government to come to the aid of either France or Germany if one attacked the other.* To this undertaking the dominions, especially Canada, were strenuously opposed but, notwithstanding their opposition, the United Kingdom persisted in its policy. For the first time since the Great War, a British Government had asserted the national self-interest of the United Kingdom against the larger interest of imperial concern.

The effect of this assertion upon those still convinced of the merits and feasibility of a single Empire strategy was daunting and in some cases shattering. Loring Christie, the Canadian diplomatist who had as much as anyone to do with the shaping of the group unit concept of Empire in its post-war form,† was severely shaken. "Locarno," he wrote to his friend Philip Kerr,

> has left me wholly at sea. What is to be the new Imperial working hypothesis? We had the theory of trusteeship. That was replaced by a theory of partnership and diplomatic unity, common foreign policy. That has broken down. What next? . . .

---

*At the time it seemed more likely that France would attack Germany than Germany would attack the French of whom, under Poincaré, the British Government took a gloomy view. France, Lord Curzon informed the Imperial Conference of 1923, "is pursuing a policy that, in our view, at any rate, is far from being favourable to the recovery of the world." (Imperial Conference, 1923. Stenographic Notes of Proceedings, Third Meeting, 5 October 1923, King Papers.) This was also the view of some English-speaking Canadians, e.g., Sir John Willison: "Is there much to choose between a Hohenzollern in Berlin and a Poincaré in Paris? For a generation we denounced Germany for the seizure of Alsace and Lorraine. That, after all, was not a great thing in comparison with what France is now doing [in the Ruhr]." Willison to Sir Joseph Flavelle, 22 Oct. 1923. Willison Papers.

†Christie, as the trusted adviser and confidant of both Sir Robert Borden and Arthur Meighen, had been largely responsible for whatever intellectual coherence Canadian external policy possessed during the period 1918–1921. The propositions put by Meighen to the Imperial Conference of 1921 were contrived and drafted by him. Because his views at the time ran counter to those of Mackenzie King, Christie was virtually forced to resign from the Department of External Affairs in 1923. He re-entered the Department in 1935 and, at the time of his premature death in 1941, was Canada's Minister to the United States.

> It seems to me certain that the Liberal Party in Canada will say at once that this event does away with the case for [a common foreign policy] . . . And what about the Conservative Imperialist? . . . Where will he come out? Will he in the end say, "Well, it looks as though we must look out for ourselves; as in London it must be Britain first, so in Ottawa it must be Canada first"? . . .

This, indeed, was precisely where the Conservative Imperialist, in the person of R. B. Bennett, was to come out four years later. But for the moment Conservative Imperialists were reluctant to abandon Empire strategy for Canadian strategy. Sir Robert Borden, to whom Christie had confided his misgivings over Locarno, insisted that the old ideal was still attainable. Though, he wrote,

> the project of continuous consultation seems to have broken down for the time being, it does not necessarily follow . . . that it has wholly broken down or that its failure is due to inherent defects. A very difficult period ensued and, unfortunately, political conditions in the Dominions failed to give such initiative and leadership as might have contributed to carrying out the original project. Mr. King was continually looking over his shoulder at Quebec, and sought evasion of responsibility in a futile and nebulous verbosity which must have been most exasperating to British statesmen.[56]

But Arthur Meighen was not as certain as his chief that Empire grand strategy had failed only because there was a shortage of Empire grand strategists. "It would not seem to me impracticable," he wrote to Christie, "to get a plan which would place in the hands of the Dominion representatives respectively the right to say what matter is of consequence to demand the interest of their respective Dominions in it, and the right to a voice in its disposition." But, he conceded, "there is more difficulty . . . in evolving a plan in which the voice of the Dominion, after its right to be heard is conceded, may sound in the ultimate decision. . . . The whole situation is disturbing, and I feel myself more or less in the position of a man who does not know whether or not his idols have been shattered, but who fears."[57]

No comparable fears disturbed the mind of the Prime Minister of Canada. The Chanak affair had engraved upon it, as upon that of his principal adviser, O. D. Skelton, the unshakable conviction that projects for imperial policy, however fashioned, were practically unworkable and politically dangerous. Locarno vindicated that conviction, leaving him free in the years to come to fight his sturdy autonomist's fight against that increasingly unreal adversary, "Downing Street domination," gaining in the process the support of prairie radicals with whom anti-imperialist attitudes offered better prospects of harmony than did

Liberal policies on the freight rates and the tariff. Nothing was more distinctive about Mackenzie King's external policies than their insistence that the Commonwealth should not collectively do anything which might detract from the individual responsibilities of its members; and that, to be on the safe side, it had better not do anything at all. To Canada's "everlasting no" there were two exceptions. One was its membership of the Imperial War Graves Commission; the other was its endorsement, at the Imperial Conference of 1937, of the policy of appeasement of Nazi Germany. The historian may record, leaving others to moralize upon, the melancholy fact that only in burying the dead of the First World War, and causing more dead to be buried in a Second, would Canada combine with other members of the inter-war Commonwealth in any sort of purposeful activity.

I

The Strange Siberian Interlude

"The world has drifted far from its old moorings." So, portentously, Sir Robert Borden wrote in his diary for 11 November 1918, after the purser of the *Mauretania*, bound for Britain, brought to his cabin the news that Germany had surrendered. The military policy of the Canadian Government at the armistice might now be stated very simply. It was to return, with all possible speed, more than 300,000 troops overseas to their home and native land; and to re-establish them there, with a minimum of fuss and grievance, in the lives and careers disrupted by the Great War.

The policy of the fastest possible demobilization was complicated at the outset by the pre-Armistice decision to send Canadian forces to Russia. During the summer of 1918 the British authorities had turned, in some desperation, to Canada to help provide men for expeditionary forces to be sent to North Russia and Siberia. The objectives of these interventions were never unambiguously defined, even at their earliest stages, and the Canadian Government could not be sure whether it was being asked to open a new front against the Germans or to assist in a counter-revolutionary drive against the Soviets. In such circumstances it might well have hesitated before complying, and did in fact hesitate; but Sir Robert Borden, anxious to be helpful, and dazzled by prospects of trade and mercantile opportunities with and in Russia, overcame his own doubts and those of his colleagues and gave the orders to proceed. An artillery brigade of roughly 500 men sailed for Archangel, arriving on 30 September 1918. But the most important Canadian contribution was to the Siberia expedition. On 27 October the first contingent of what were soon to be 4,000 Canadian troops landed at Vladivostok under the command of a Canadian officer, Brigadier-General J. H. Elmsley.[1]

The Armistice with Germany removed the ostensible military motive for the intervention, and Elmsley's despatches soon disabused Borden of his hopes for economic opportunities. The pressure to bring the Canadians back from Russia, and to cancel the scheduled embarkations from Canada of those destined for Russia, became intense. "There is considerable dissatisfaction and anxiety all over the country," noted the *Hamilton Daily Times*, "regarding Canada's expedition to Siberia. . . . What do we propose to do now? Overthrow the Bolshevists? And for what purpose? Are we sacrificing our soldiers . . . to validate bonds held by foreign nations?"[2] And the *Farmers' Sun*, speaking not only for farmers but for many returning soldiers, declared:

> Canada sends one military force to Siberia, via Vladivostok, and another to the Valley of the Dwina, via Archangel, to wage war against the armies of the Russian Government and people. . . . It is an amazing episode, the meaning of which becomes clear. Imperial federation or imperial consolidation becomes a fact, and the people of Canada, devoted to an assured self-government, as they thought, pass under the sway of the Imperial War Cabinet. . . . The Round Table has had its way. . . .[3]

The prospects for prompt and sensible decision in this situation were not improved by the division of the Canadian Cabinet—a division not only of opinion but of geography. The Prime Minister and three of his colleagues—C. J. Doherty, Sir George Foster, and A. L. Sifton—were in London attending meetings of the Imperial War Cabinet. A lengthy exchange of cables between them and what was left of the Government at Ottawa discloses very clearly the difference of opinion on the issue:

> *Sir Thomas White [Acting Prime Minister] to Sir Robert Borden, (22 November 1918)*: Many members of Council strongly opposed to our sending troops now ready to sail to Siberia and continuing expedition. Mewburn [Minister of Militia] has delayed ship sailing on Monday. . . . Some protests have been received against further participation by Canada from persons whose sons are in the Expedition and who claim that as the war is over we have no right to send them. This argument seems strong to me as applied to draftees.

> *Borden to White (24 November)*: Telegram received. In my judgment we shall stand in an unfortunate situation unless we proceed with Siberia Expedition. We made definite arrangements with British Government on which they have relied. They could reasonably hold us responsible for great inevitable delay in making other arrangements. Canada's present position and prestige would be singularly impaired by deliberate withdrawal from definite arrangements under these conditions. When that arrangement was made prospective demand upon our man power was much greater

than at present. Draftees sent to take part in terrible fighting in France have much more right to complain than draftees sent to Siberia where no fighting is anticipated beyond possible quelling of some local disturbance and where the chief duty will be to assist the new Russian Government to train Russian [troops]. However I leave the matter to judgment of Council with the strong feeling that withdrawal from our deliberate engagement will have extremely unfortunate effect. Foster, Sifton, Doherty concur.

White to Borden (25 November): Very strong feeling in Council against continuance Siberian Expedition, Ballantyne, Crerar, Calder and Reid most strongly opposed. Crerar has written me letter of protest. So far as I can judge public opinion will not support further action on any large scale if at all. Great Britain and France are immediately interested by reason of Russia's large indebtedness to them and the desirability of retaining stable government in order that such indebtedness may be met. Canada has no such economic or business interest as will justify the employment of a Canadian force composed of young men whose parents and friends desire should return at once to their ordinary occupations. Even if composed of volunteers the expense to Canada would meet with strong criticism in the House and country. My own view after hearing many discussions in Council is that Canada should, now that the war is over and no necessity exists for the re-establishment of the Eastern front, discontinue further participation and expense. It seems clearly a task for nations more immediately interested in the finances of Russia. There is an extraordinary sentiment in Canada in favour of getting all our men home and at work as soon as possible.

Borden's telegram to White crossed that of White to Borden. To the former, White replied on 26 November:

Your cable respecting Siberia will be fully considered in Council today. Needless to say we all desire to meet your wishes. Please cable whether you know any modification possible whereby Canada should send only those now ready to sail and immediately required. *Globe* has strong editorial against Canada aiding in interfering in Russian internal affairs and assisting to set up any particular form of government. I think question has considerable political importance at this time. Could time of service in Russia be limited to, say, next summer with voluntary forces to relieve them if necessary.

Borden replied in a no less conciliatory fashion to White's cable of 25 November: "If feeling both in Cabinet and among public is so strongly opposed we leave question to your own determination." On 28 November White responded: "We have decided to proceed with Siberian expedition as originally planned. Arrangements will be made for the return within one year from the conclusion of peace of any who may desire to return to Canada. This will substantially meet the views of the troops participating in the Expedition. You may regard the matter as closed."

What tipped the scales in this direction? The decisive factor seems to have been the rump Cabinet's anxiety not to break faith with the British Government. The key figure in its decision was T. A. Crerar, the Minister of Agriculture. Crerar spoke for the prairies, and he spoke in the accent of prairie radicalism. He, more perhaps than any other member of the Union Government, might be regarded as custodian of the nation's conscience, and the Government's proposed intervention in the affairs of Soviet Russia had sorely troubled him. "I am absolutely opposed to sending any additional forces to Siberia," he had written to White in the letter mentioned by White in his cable to Borden, "and . . . in my judgment, the Forces at present there, or on the way there, should, as soon as convenience will permit, be brought home."[4] When Borden appeared to favour proceeding with the expedition, Crerar's opposition became crucial, and White immediately wired to him in Winnipeg: "We have important cable from Borden stating that himself and all colleagues overseas favour continuance Siberian expedition. He urges strongly that Britain relies upon this force and that to discontinue would be breach of faith with British Government. . . . I am concerned about your letter and shall be glad if you will wire me in cypher whether you will concur in decision of Council after full consideration of Sir Robert's cable."[5] Crerar replied: "If [it] can be clearly shown withdrawing forces is breach of faith with British Government this would certainly modify my view."[6] On the strength of this assurance, White notified Borden that the expedition would proceed as planned. The event may have reinforced Crerar's decision to resign from Borden's government in February 1919.

The operational role of the Canadians in Siberia almost immediately became the subject of controversy. The Cabinet at Ottawa, in agreeing with extreme reluctance to allow those troops already there to remain and to be reinforced, was determined that they should suffer no casualties, and therefore should take part in no fighting; otherwise Canadian public opinion, already ill-disposed towards the Russian adventure, would be inflamed. So unbelligerent a role was not at all to the liking of the British authorities who, ever since the Armistice, had been veering round to Churchill's view that the objective of Allied troops in Russia was "to strangle the infant Bolshevism in its cradle." The head of the British Military Mission in Siberia, General Knox, protested to the Canadian Overseas Minister of Militia in London:

> . . . I understand that the Canadian Government proposes that the Canadian troops should be used as the Americans are now being used, with this possible difference that they may occupy barracks somewhat further West.

This is not intervention but irritating occupation and is unlikely to satisfy either Russians or Czechs. The Americans here are not a standing eyesore to the fighting men at the front, but well fed and well clothed Canadians near the front will find it difficult to explain why they leave the fighting to men half armed and equipped.[7]

The Canadian Commander, General Elmsley, shared this appreciation. "Policy of every support to Russia other than with troops," he cabled to his headquarters in London and Ottawa, "a half measure which undoubtedly dangerous course pursue this critical period."[8]

The ministers at Ottawa, confronted with this distressing intelligence, their public aroused, their leader absent, and their troops on the way, became more and more apprehensive. Borden was bombarded with messages: "Telegrams from White," he noted glumly on 27 November, "thick as autumn leaves in Vallombrosa." "We must be able to give public statement on this matter," Rowell pleaded on that date, "also with our reasons for continuing to send troops. . . . Could you cable us statement such as we might make public?"[9] This brought little satisfaction: "There was no public announcement," Borden replied, "because publicity would have defeated the purpose. . . ."[10] White repeated the request for a statement that could be made public in a cable of 3 December "as to the reasons why it is desirable that Canadian forces should be kept in Siberia at this time and for the next six months or year. We have many inquiries as to reason and feel we have not sufficient information as to the true position. Think the Imperial Government might well keep us informed as to developments."[11] Borden replied to this as follows:

British Government with our approval undertook obligations to well disposed persons in Russia with a view to re-establishing Eastern Front. Although necessity for such front no longer exists obligations must be fulfilled. Canadian troops peculiarly effective for work of character required. Have asked Foreign Office to cable you more fully. . . .[12]

This was hardly the kind of explanation that White and his colleagues at Ottawa had hoped for or required. They now tried a somewhat different tack: a direct approach to the War Office. On 4 December, Major-General W. G. Gwatkin, the Chief of the General Staff of the Canadian Army, signalled as follows:

. . . When it finally decided to proceed with despatch of expedition Dominion Government not only guaranteed that men would not be kept against their will in Siberia longer than one year after signing of armistice, but also expressed hope that before next summer entire force might be recalled. Is there no chance of that hope being fulfilled? Political difficulties foreseen: people war weary, nervous, irritable and even qualified reply, in affirmative sense, would have quieting effect. My Ministers know that this message has been sent.[13]

Two days later, having been supplied with further ammunition by the Canadian political officer at Vladivostok,* General Gwatkin sent the following message to the Chief of the Imperial General Staff:

My Minister, with whose knowledge this message is sent, has received from his political officer at Vladivostok a report indicating that arrangements in Siberia lack coordination and control; that the railway system is in a condition seriously disorganized; that among Allies there is no general agreement; that Americans are inactive; that Japanese bent on commercial penetration are subsidizing insurgent elements. Stop. The inference is that Elmsley and his Canadian command will be placed in a difficult position; and the Dominion Government feels increasing disinclination to involve itself in an undertaking which may terminate disaster. To enlighten and reassure the Dominion Government it is of the utmost importance that the British Government pronounce fully on the general situation, state definitely its policy with regard thereto and indicate the measures it proposes to adopt. Stop. Meanwhile the despatch of troops to Vladivostok will not be interrupted; but the Dominion Government does not wish them to move inland until situation, policy and intended action are clearly understood and it may be necessary to recall them to Canada unless their mission is made clear.[14]

Here was at least plain speaking. But the Canadian demand for a clear statement of policy was not and perhaps could not be met. To the first message, the War Office replied that it, too, hoped that by summer-time the Siberian situation would so improve that all foreign troops, British no less than Canadian, might be withdrawn. "Precisely similar difficulties will face us as regards keeping British troops," it observed; "naturally we should not ask you to call on Canadian troops to do more than British ones are expected to carry out."[15] The second of Gwatkin's messages brought a lengthy statement of British policy towards intervention in Russia. The Government did not consider that it had a mission to upset the existing Bolshevik regime or impose any special form of political system. But that did not mean it could follow Russian affairs disinterestedly. Anti-Bolshevik regimes had sprung up within territory under Soviet jurisdiction under the shelter of Allied troops; the British

*Col. John F. Lash, a Canadian Army officer. He had been stationed at Vladivostok as the personal representative of the Canadian Minister of Militia, Gen. Elmsley's representative at Allied Headquarters, Siberia, and the Canadian channel of communication between Ottawa and General Elmsley. "What I have felt all along," the Minister had written to his Chief of Staff, "is that we should have somebody at the Base, to whom Elmsley, in the event of him going away from the Base, could communicate, and to whom we could send communications regarding strictly Canadian matters. . . ." S. C. Mewburn to Gen. Gwatkin, 1 Oct. 1918, Canadian Army Records, Ottawa.

Government was in a sense responsible for their existence, and did not intend to desert them now.[16] Gwatkin was less than satisfied with this exposition. "It is a damned, cold-hearted, facing both ways effusion, inspired by cowardice," he wrote bluntly. "It says nothing. It does not withdraw; it does not go forward. . . . It is an annoying phase."[17]

II

"Annoying" was not too strong a word by which to describe the increasingly tangled affair which the Canadian involvement in Siberia had now become. For its complication the Canadian Prime Minister must be held largely responsible. It was Borden's personal commitment which had got Canada into the affair; it was his distaste at having to take hold of a troublesome nettle which now made extrication so difficult. Preoccupied at Paris with strategy of the grandest kind—the Treaty of Versailles (which filled him with misgiving) was just then under consideration in the Imperial War Cabinet—and far removed from the petty distractions of the domestic political scene in the Dominion, he had no inclination whatever to provide the leadership in the matter which his colleagues at Ottawa so evidently desired. "Eight cables yesterday and ten today," he wrote with obvious irritation in his diary on 9 December. "Cabled Reid to have fewer sent if possible."

Among the eight messages for the Prime Minister on 8 December was a telegram from Mewburn, the Minister of Militia, repeating the text of the cable which had been sent to the Chief of the Imperial General Staff, and urging on Borden a policy of no commitments in Siberia. There was also a plaintive communication from Sir Thomas White:

Official advices to the Militia Department from Vladivostok state that all military reason for allied military intervention is gone and that the matter is one of purely political expediency. There is a good deal of feeling in labour and other quarters here against our continued participation and my personal view is that a serious political situation may arise later unless some definite statement can be made as to the return of the expedition within a reasonable time. Relatives and friends of those forces to go are naturally restive. Might I suggest that you take the matter up in a confidential way with the Imperial authorities and make such definite arrangements as you think will meet our situation here.[18]

To Mewburn's message Borden replied:

. . . Have asked Balfour to advise you regularly as to political and economic conditions. War Office advises you as to military conditions. Canadian political officer at Vladivostok is in touch with you. Under these circumstances Council is in a better position to judge than we are at this distance and we leave matter entirely to judgment of Council as we feel as you do that no disposition should be made of Canadian troops which might lead to disaster. Please dispose of matter without further reference to us.[19]

And to White's:

I telegraphed you earlier . . . respecting Siberian expedition and have nothing to add. Question should be settled by Council without further reference to me. . . . We have taken matter up repeatedly with War Office and I do not see advantage of any further discussion with them.[20]

These, Borden hoped, would prove to be "final messages re Siberian situation." But he was wrong.

The Ottawa ministers now had responsibilty for decision thrust upon them and, however reluctant they might be to do so, now had to act. White wrote to Mewburn: "In view of what Sir Robert says, I am of opinion that we should at once cancel further sailings and arrange for the return of our forces at as early a date as possible. . . . Please bring the matter up in Council for discussion."[21] The Cabinet's concensus on 21 December was once more that those troops scheduled to sail should sail, but that they should undertake no action in Siberia which might place them in jeopardy. The War Office and the Canadian Commander at Vladivostok were informed of this decision by cable the next day:

. . . Situation everywhere changed since Canada undertook to furnish contingent; policy of allied and associated powers not yet defined; and public opinion strongly opposed to further participation.

Therefore, although despatch of Canadian troops will for present continue, they must all return to Canada next spring.

Meanwhile Dominion Government cannot permit them to engage in military operations nor, without its express consent, to move up country; and Elmsley should not leave Base until Bickford his infantry brigadier reaches Vladivostok.

This message sent by my Minister's direction, and in substance repeated to Elmsley. C. G. S.[22]

Meanwhile, out in the field, the Canadian and British military commanders were having their differences about the extent of the operational role of the Canadian forces. Knox had asked Elmsley to move his troops further inland. Elmsley had cabled to Ottawa for permission to comply with this request, but had warned Knox that if his troops were allowed to move forward, they could only do so if the Allied Council at Vladivostok were "severally and collectively to guarantee the safety of my L. of C. [lines of communication] from our base at

Vladivostok to our railhead, and further guarantee, in so far as it is in their power, to expedite the transmission of all our ammunition and stores between the above places. . . ." He had added:

> To you, Knox, this demand might appear unreasonable, futile, and non-productive of results. To me, however, it appears reasonable and must, first, because it affects the lives and welfare of my men, and, secondly, I am a firm believer that in military matters "He who is not with me is against me" . . .
>
> Perhaps I am a false prophet—I hope so—but I feel certain that when the time comes for my troops to move west I shall find that the foundation of all military operations, viz., a secure L. of C., is wanting.
>
> However anxious we may be to assist a good cause, I would feel that I was breaking faith with my own Government if I moved a single unit from Vladivostok under these conditions. . . .[23]

While Knox was pondering this communication, the new instructions from Ottawa to Elmsley arrived, and their contents were transmitted to him. He wrote at once to Elmsley:

> I am afraid it would not be of the slightest use to suggest to the Allied War Council that its members should guarantee the safety of your L. of C. To begin with neither the Americans nor the Japanese wish us to go on, the first because President Wilson is advised by Jews who sympathise with Bolshevism and the second because they want a weak Russia rather than a strong one.
>
> At the same time I think that both you and Lash with whom I have had frequent conversations on the subject, exaggerate the risk. It will be nothing approaching the risk run by your Brigade in France every time it went over the top. Your men will be in exactly the same boat as regards dependence on their L. of C. as are the French, Italian, Czecho-Slovak, Rumanian, Pole and Serb contingents. The commanders of these contingents have accepted the risk.
>
> You take I understand three months' supplies with you and you can live as regards bulky essentials on the country. You will not have many guns and you are not going to loose off shells as you did in France. . . .
>
> Of course you will say that it is all very well for me to buck since the responsibility rests with you. I can only reply that I undertook a similar responsibility by telegraphing immediately railway communication was opened in early September for permission for the Middlesex to go West. . . .
>
> After all you cannot do anything without risk. Our Government is bound to carry on with its policy now it has started, and the Hampshires have followed the Middlesex. I will try to carry on with my job even if every British or Canadian soldier is withdrawn, but each of our men in western Siberia is worth his weight in gold.
>
> Frankly I am quite beat by this last telegram from Ottawa. They seem to have made up their minds to do nothing. If so, why don't they say so at once?[24]

The Canadian Government, acting on the basis of intelligence from Elmsley and Lash, refused to allow the Canadian forces to move west from Vladivostok. The War Office then began to exert pressure of a different kind. Since the Canadians in Siberia were apparently not to be allowed to be used for any operational purpose, it stated in a message to the Canadian C.G.S. on 4 January 1919, there was no longer any point to their presence, and they might as well be withdrawn. In that event, however, the two British battalions which had moved inland would be dangerously exposed, and it was proposed that they should pull back to Vladivostok.[25] This proposal shocked the Canadian military. "Clio is writing a chapter which, I fear, will disgrace humanity," the Chief of the General Staff commented at Headquarters;[26] an officer at the Canadian Ministry of Overseas Military Forces advised Loring Christie: "Naturally, if the Canadian troops which form the major portion of the British Force in Siberia are withdrawn, the British Government have no course open but to recommend the withdrawal of the two British battalions, which would otherwise be isolated. If the British are withdrawn, then the field is left open to Japan."[27] General Elmsley was so distressed at the turn of events that he now addressed himself directly to the War Office in his own personal appeal:

> . . . Action suggested by you, if concurred in by Canadian Government, may have disastrous effects on a situation which is already critical: and may neutralize any decisions arrived at by Peace Conference for assistance to Russia based on military, economic or humane grounds. I request from whole Allied point of view that you ask Canadian Government to hold in abeyance your cable regarding withdrawal Canadian troops, pending decision of Peace Conference . . .[28]

On 10 January the Cabinet at Ottawa considered the new situation which had arisen. As a result of its discussion, the Chief of the General Staff was instructed to cable the War Office yet another statement of why the Canadian Government would not allow its forces in Siberia to become embroiled in the political and military uncertainties that awaited them further west of Vladivostok. The Government did not propose to make any immediate alteration in the disposition of its Siberia forces; the 1,100 men then in Vladivostok would remain there for the time being; the 2,700 then at sea, bound for Vladivostok from Vancouver, would proceed to their destination; the remaining 1,200 still in Canada "will stand fast and until reply is received to this cable no decision will be reached regarding their demobilization." The Canadian Government, the message concluded, "is prepared to let matters stand as they now are, provided that there is any hope of a very early decision respecting the Siberian problem on the part of the Allied and Associated Powers."[29]

To this the War Office replied: "Much appreciation your sympathetic attitude. We fully understand your difficulties which are largely our own. . . . We earnestly hope matter will be given early consideration at Peace Conference and some agreement come to by the Allies. We will communicate with you as soon as a decision is reached and trust it may be such as to enable you to adhere to arrangements contemplated prior to the Armistice." The War Office shared Elmsley's appreciation of the importance of the Canadian and British forces standing fast. Its message ended on a note which was doubtless intended to be reassuring but could only have been disquieting: "Regarding Bolshevism, public opinion here is becoming more enlightened and begins to realise it is no longer a Russian domestic problem but a menace to civilisation."[30]

General Elmsley, whose intervention had been partly responsible for the Canadian Government's decision not to take up the War Office's invitation to withdraw Canadian troops from Siberia, now began to have second thoughts about his earlier reluctance to have his forces take up positions further inland. His military representative at Omsk cabled on 14 January that, in his view, "good effect would be produced by presence Canadians between Irkutsk and Omsk, even if only for next three months"; the risks involved, he added, would be negligible as "British troops already here treated with great deference and respect by all class Russians."[31] Lash, the Political Adviser at Vladivostok, concurred. On 16 January General Knox requested in haste that a small Canadian detachment be sent immediately to the town of Orenburg (now Chkalov), over two thousand miles inland along the Trans-Siberian railway. This request was referred to the Canadian authorities in London, who turned it down. Knox was furious. "Please ascertain," he cabled to his deputy, "whether Elmsley has had to refer home . . . question about detaching one officer and six men to Orenburg. If he has, this is the limit, and you should wire it home as a typical instance of the difficulties under which we are working."[32]

A few days later, Colonel Lash supplied the Minister of Militia at Ottawa with a reasoned plea for allowing the Canadian forces to move up the line:

> The enormous effect produced by even a small number of British troops has much impressed me, and their withdrawal at this critical time would probably result in disaster to the Government and the anti-Bolshevik efforts of the country for the Russians, who would take withdrawal as desertion of the anti-Bolshevik cause, with the attendant encouragement to Bolsheviks, with such decrease in strength and influence of Government and better elements. . . .
>
> I understand that the co-operation of the Canadian troops depends solely on concurrence of Canadian Government in Allied policy as a whole.

This cannot be calculated from here, as it must be settled at Allied Capitals, and so far there is no evidence of the combined policy by all Allies, especially as policy of Japan and America is not known.

I presume that the statement that Canadian troops will return next Spring means that they will leave here May or June; meanwhile, they are no use at Vladivostok.

Japanese troops are along the Railway from Vladivostok to Irkutsk, and Canadian troops could be of great assistance doing garrison duty in towns between Irkutsk and Omsk.

I am certain that the steadying influence of their presence on the whole area would be prodigious. . . . The withdrawal of Canadian troops would be inviting serious risk.

This expedition, in view of the Armistice, has become peculiarly a Permanent Force task. . . .[33]

Despite Borden's previous injunction that Siberian questions should be settled by the Cabinet at Ottawa and not by himself and his colleagues in London or Paris, the Acting Prime Minister felt that in the light of Lash's communication he had better refer the problem to his Chief overseas. "We are unwilling to send our troops alone into interior," White cabled Borden on 24 January. "High Commissioner at Omsk reports great danger if troops not sent forward and line established. . . . Your advice would be helpful."[34] Borden replied: ". . . troops now at Vladivostok . . . should not be sent forward pending further developments which I believe will result in decision that they should be returned to Canada at an early date."[35] The "further developments" to which Borden referred were chiefly his own plan for a conference between the warring Russian factions and the states with troops in Russia. Such a conference did not materialize, and Borden thereupon advised the British Government that, unless there were good reasons for not doing so, the Canadian forces in Siberia would be withdrawn in April, sooner if weather permitted.[36] Winston Churchill and A. J. Balfour attempted to dissuade Borden from this decision, arguing that if the Allied forces at present in Russia remained at their posts "Bolshevist power will probably crumble," while if they were evacuated, the Bolshevik regime would soon control all of Russia, would presently combine with Germany, and then be in a position to "menace the world and especially the British Empire exposed to attack in India and elsewhere."[37] To this strategic projection (in some respects not inaccurate), Borden turned a blind eye:

I replied that these considerations would not carry judgment of Canadian people in favour of further military effort. Russia must work out her own salvation which may take years. If Bolshevist power crumbles other Governments will probably fight each other for some time to come. Bolshevists are no more likely to combine with Germany than any other Russian

Government. Moreover Bolshevist policy and action are becoming more moderate. . . .[38]

In any event, whatever the fortunes of the Russian Bolsheviks, the Canadian Government was primarily interested in getting its soldiers home. Churchill finally, though with evident reluctance, gave in. "In view of the very decided attitude taken up by Canada regarding the withdrawal of her troops from Vladivostok", he wrote to Borden on 17 March, "the War Office have no option but to acquiesce, as they have felt it impossible to continue to urge the Dominion Government to share, against its will, in a task of much difficulty and anxiety."[39]

There was now no longer any question of Canadian forces being sent beyond Vladivostok into the Siberian interior, and very little of their uneventful sojourn being extended beyond the break-up of the ice which would permit their returning home. There was still some time to elapse before their departure, however, and it had not yet been settled what, if any, role they were to play in the event that Vladivostok itself, or nearby points essential to its defence, were brought under Bolshevik attack. On 13 April Elmsley reported to Ottawa that a small Russian force at Shkotova, across the bay from Vladivostok, had become "seriously threatened by insurgents," and that at the urgent request of the Allied Commander-in-Chief he had placed "one company of infantry at his disposal, to co-operate with a small detachment of Italian and French troops, together with Japanese battalion. . . . Urgency would not permit my consulting you before taking the above action. . . .[40] The Allied force reached the scene to find that the insurgents had retreated; they camped in the vicinity for about a week without any molestation; and then returned to Vladivostok. "All, for the time being, is well," the Chief of the General Staff wrote to his Minister in Ottawa, "but it is really rather remarkable that, at this stage of the proceedings, there should be an insurgent force 30 miles, or more, this side of Vladivostok."[41] With the exception of this solitary and bloodless foray, the 4,000 Canadian soldiers in Siberia took part in no action whatsoever. Embarkation began in May; the last of their number left Vladivostok harbour for home on 5 June.

After their departure, the only Canadians left in Russia were the 500 members of the 16th Canadian Field Artillery Brigade who had been landed at Archangel the previous September. Unlike the Siberian contingent, the Canadian forces in North Russia were several times in close combat with the Bolsheviks—their most memorable engagement, the battle at Tulgas, took place on the very day of the Armistice in the West—and sporadic artillery duels were fought by them throughout the hard winter. Despite their ferocity, these operations attracted slight attention in Canada compared with the activities—or inactivities—of the Siberian force. There were, of course, fewer men involved; there was no question of their reinforcement; and their morale, at least until spring, was remarkably high. The Canadians in Siberia, nearly all draftees, had been from the first reluctant starters: some had to be put aboard ship at bayonet point.[42] The Canadians in North Russia, however, according to one of their officers, "although most of them had seen service in France and were civilian soldiers, were more anxious to stay on in Russia and fight Bolsheviks, than to return to their pre-war peaceful occupations."[43] Nor was their employment beset by the same complications of international policy. In March 1919, the War Office promised the Canadian Government that its forces at Archangel would be withdrawn as soon as the port was open for navigation, but on 30 April Borden was informed that they could not leave until late summer or Autumn. On 18 May Borden wrote a stiffly worded letter to Winston Churchill: "I insist," it concluded, "that the Canadians shall be withdrawn immediately,"[44] and, to Lloyd George: "It will be most unfortunate if the War Office persists in its apparent determination to extend the period of service for the Canadians at Archangel. I must insist that they shall be withdrawn without the slightest unnecessary delay."[45] "I am very glad indeed," wrote the Minister of Militia to his Prime Minister, "to see that you have taken this stand."[46] The Brigade left Archangel on 11 June; a Cunard steamer named *Czaritza* took them off.

II

The Politics of Re-establishment

ANGER OF THE "OTHER RANKS"

Between the Armistice and June 1919, repatriation of Canadian troops was far from fast enough to suit those whom a shortage of shipping had compelled to be left behind. Soldiers barracked at the cheerless concentrations in Kemmel Park, in Epsom, and in Witley were exposed to the chill discomforts of a severe English winter, to the dangers of influenza and to the perils of *ennui*. They became restless and resentful, and demonstrated their dissatisfaction by rioting. Those returning knew they were lucky to have returned at all, but the frame of mind of the homecoming Canadian soldier was not exactly placid. In March 1917 Sir Robert Borden had spoken to those of the Expeditionary Force about to take part in the Battle of Vimy Ridge. "You men," he declared, "are about to enter one of the most serious engagements that ever faced the Canadian corps. . . . As the head of the Government I give you this assurance: . . . that no man, whether he goes back or whether he remains in Flanders, will have just cause to reproach the Government for having broken faith with the men who won and the men who died."[1] But many of those who came back felt that faith had been broken. What indeed had been bought by all those lives and limbs, seemingly so recklessly squandered?

It was not hard to find people to blame. "The British generals one and all," wrote a Canadian from British Columbia, "are the most incompetent lot of bloody fools that have ever been collected together for the purpose of sacrificing armies. . . ."[2] If British generals were so singled out, it was not because they were British, it was because they were generals. Few Canadians rose high enough to have borne fairly responsibility for the strategic direction of the war, but this did not prevent the anger of the "other ranks" of the Canadian Expeditionary Force from being directed at officers of any rank. "No one seems to know," the historian of the Royal Canadian Legion has commented, "where such a feeling began and, indeed, it is almost impossible to believe it when one recalls the loyalty and devotion the Canadian soldier displayed towards his officers in the field and the fact that from 1916 onward most of the officers came from the ranks."[3] Be that as it might, from 1918 onward, loyalty and devotion to those who had formerly been his officers were not the most clearly recognizable characteristics of the Canadian soldier.* The basic reason for his animus was his wartime experience. That the slaughter was greatest among second lieutenants did not alter the fact that, as one officer wrote after it stopped, "we were in clover compared with the men." Even in that "continuous ditch of hidden men" (as H. M. Tomlinson described the Western front), the principle of the equality of sacrifice seemed to many of the men to be marred by the officers' better rations, better pay, better everything.

Officers' wives have pudding and pies,
Soldiers' wives have skilly.

To the lingering resentment over the privileges of war was joined an even fiercer reaction to the privileges of peace. In December 1919, the President of the Comrades of the Great War wrote indignantly to the Prime Minister of Canada to complain of favouritism towards officers in appointments to the Land Settlement Board and the Soldiers' Civil Re-establishment Board:

> . . . Are you aware of the fact that the private is nowhere and that it costs more in salaries for the said officers and administration of the staff than is given in vocational training and assistance to the men desiring them? . . .
>
> You will admit, I am sure, that re-establishment has not yet arrived to the soldiers. You will also admit that they are very bitter when they see the ex-officers running things, and trying to run them the way they did in Canada, England and France. . . . So many of the officers got their appointments through political pull, and would have starved to death in the years gone by if it had not been for the same paternal government which you head. Imagine, too, how many of these Sam Browners ever had a man clean their belts and their boots of them ere they received their commission? No, Sir Robert, this is the day of the private soldier and when the poll comes up he will be seen there as solid as he protected this country during the war that has passed. . . .[4]

*Nor of the British soldier. See Graham Wootton, *The Politics of Influence: British Ex-Servicemen, Cabinet Decisions and Cultural Change (1917–1957)* (London, 1963), pp. 41–6.

Specific grievances included the creation of what seemed an overloaded bureaucracy to deal with veterans' affairs and discriminatory appointment of ex-officers to lucrative positions within it. "This Convention deprecates the building up at Ottawa of a huge Civil Service Machine particularly in Departments of Administration touching the interests of ex-soldiers and sailors, as not being in the best interests of the country."[5] "The Dominion Executive of the G.W.V.A. does protest most emphatically against the present discriminating practice of giving preference to officers in appointments of a non-military nature, and demands that in all such appointments equal consideration shall be given to men of the rank and file who possess the necessary qualifications."[6] But perhaps the most rankling practice of all was the discrepancy in scale of pension between officers and men of the ranks. "I had my pension fixed at $600," a blind veteran told his comrades in 1920. "I want to know how it is that the eyes of a brigadier general in Canada are worth $2700, and my eyes are worth only $600. . . ."[7]

It was only a matter of time before men in such a mood, returning to a country not noticeably transformed for the better in their absence, resentful of those who had prospered while staying behind, would vent their anger—now more rationally—against the Government which had broken Borden's pledge at Vimy.

THE G.W.V.A. AND ITS RIVALS

The returning soldiers did not lack organizations through which to formulate their demands and express their grievances. The veterans' associations formed before or soon after the Armistice included: the Great War Veterans' Associations of Canada, the Army and Navy Veterans, the Imperial Veterans in Canada, the Grand Army of United Veterans, the Comrades of the Great War, the Tuberculous Veterans' Association, the Royal North West Mounted Police Veterans' Association, the Canadian Pensioners' Association, the Amputations Association of Canada, and the Canadian Legion of Ex-Servicemen. Such a plethora of special pleaders inevitably weakened their potential influence. "If the various organizations representing returned soldiers in this country," declared a representative of the Grand Army of United Veterans invited to attend a conference of the G.W.V.A.,

> can merge . . . into one grand body for the purpose of taking care of the ex-service men and women and their dependents, there will be no need for political action or partizan work of any description, for if 500,000 comrades

scattered throughout this Dominion were to become enrolled under one grand banner just as we fought overseas, then what political party or what political force or any other force could refuse a joint request from the organization that represents the veterans? . . .

We made a request to Ottawa and also to the Provincial and Municipal Governments. When we went before Premier Drury of Ontario a little while ago, he asked the delegates of the different organizations: "Q. Whom do you represent? A. The Army and Navy Veterans. Q. Whom do you represent? A. The Naval Veterans. Q. Whom do you represent? A. The G.A.U.V. Q. Whom do you represent? A. The G.W.V.A." Then the Premier just smiled, because he knew he did not have to do anything; we were all broken up. . . .[8]

Even more than their numbers, the turbulent rivalry which beset the various veterans' associations greatly diminished their influence as a political force, and unnecessarily retarded the formation of what became, in 1925, the Canadian Legion. This was marked on occasion by extraordinary bitterness and even by bloodshed. The faithful always treat the heretic worse than the infidel. "Members of our Association," a delegate of the G.W.V.A. told its convention in 1921, "have been assaulted not only verbally but physically on the streets by officers of other associations—we have had lawsuits and slander actions and have had accusations made by representatives of other associations. . . . The sore is still too raw to say the word 'comrade' to some men who have said what they have said against us. . . ."[9] But the price of separatism proved high. "If the returned men do not get together soon," commented their wartime commander privately in October 1921, "they will, as a body, cease to have any influence in Canada. The politician has kept them apart in the past and according to my impression he is just as active today as ever. Either some of the returned men cannot see what is going on under their noses, or they have become politicians themselves."[10]

The most important of these associations was the Great War Veterans' Association of Canada (G.W.V.A.). It had been formed at a veterans' convention in April 1917; its initial membership of 18,000 reached perhaps ten times that number soon after the Armistice. Its earliest resolutions were directed not only towards securing benefits for veterans but towards government policy in the conduct of the war, advocating such measures as conscription, confiscation of wealth for the war effort, government operation of factories and utilities for the duration.[11] From the beginning an effort was made to abolish differences in rank between officers and men: all members were "comrades," and among the recommendations of the G.W.V.A. was a proposal that pensions for all ranks should be made the same. Yet its founders were anxious that its members be thought neither grasping nor radical in their approach to reconstruction. "Please believe," a recruiting pamphlet beseeched its readers, "that we are not a collection of disgruntled, dissatisfied, unhappy men; but that we are an orderly gathering of returned soldiers, seeking again to become civilians, hoping that we may yet be allowed to serve our country in a civilian capacity as truly as we tried to do when we proudly wore our khaki. . . . This Association is clean now, and you can help to keep it so."[12] A "Declaration of Principles" adopted by the G.W.V.A. in 1919 emphasized the moderate and constitutional nature of its objectives:

1. We stand unalterably opposed to the introduction of the doctrines of Bolshevism and anarchy in this country, and we are not in accord with the underlying principles of the "One Big Union", which expresses itself as being in full accord with the Russian Bolsheviki and the German Spartacan, and whose principles seek by "massed action" of labour to enforce their power upon the majority of the people, and have as one of its possible results the menacing of our institutions of Government, and the threat of their replacement by Soviet rule.

2. We desire and will endeavour to ensure that all members of our Association will, whenever occasion demands, lend active assistance in upholding constitutional authority, the laws of the Country, and Good Order. . . .[13]

In 1921 a member of the G.W.V.A. spoke proudly, and to an approving audience, of the restraint and moderation demonstrated by the G.W.V.A. during the past years, when it was confronted with demands for militant and even violent action. "In the face of that the G.W.V.A. has held its head high and appealed to the best in the returned soldier and has never stooped to anything sordid or mean. We have never appealed to the man on the street in any manner that we could not give him a fair deal upon. We have never appealed to his pocket or his prejudice, but only in a way that has been noble and honourable. . . ."[14]

The moderation of the G.W.V.A. commended it to the Government, of which it became an obvious favourite among its rivals. This favouritism (which in 1921 earned it the lion's share—$50,000—of profits of wartime military canteens) the wilder spirits among the other ranks strongly resented, as they did what they regarded as the commanding position within the G.W.V.A. of the despised "officer class."* "Don't

*That, while all veterans were "comrades," some were more comradely than others, may be deduced from an extract from a letter of a militia commander to the Officer Military District No. 2: ". . . the attitude of the returned soldiers to the militia and labor question . . . is a matter to which I have given a great deal of attention, as I have interested myself very largely in the Great War Veterans' Association, whose President at Sault Ste. Marie is Capt. David Kyle, M.C., the Vice-President of the Algoma Steel Corporation, and I do not think it could be in better hands, his influence being very strong, particularly as he is the direct employer of from 3,000 to 4,000 men. . . ." Maj. P. B. Wilson to Brig.-Gen. J. V. Gunn, February 15, 1919. Army Records.

take all the guff that the G.W.V.A. representative at Ottawa throws into the Government to give it temporary peace," the President of the Comrades of the Great War wrote inelegantly but forcefully to the Prime Minister of Canada in December 1919.

> The G.W.V.A. is a joke—and it is a wonder that the government has failed to recognize the fact, even though the officers who control its destinies claim that they are the only organization that is recognized by the government and that they represent 80% of the returned men. That's all bosh—and the heads secretly recognize the fact. At the present time in Vancouver there are two organizations, besides the Comrades, who will not have anything to do with the G.W.V.A.—and all of us are numerically stronger. . . .[15]

VETERANS AND ALIENS

Never far from the mind of authority was the thought that men returning from the Front to a civilian life not much better than that of the trenches would seek to remedy their lot by unconstitutional means. "Bolshevism," cried a speaker at the meeting of the Socialist party of Canada held at the Walker Theatre in Winnipeg on 22 December 1918 (and his words were duly recorded by the local police agent in attendance), "Bolshevism is the only thing which will emancipate the working class. . . . There are thousands of men coming back who went over to fight. They will say, 'We have fought for this country and by the gods, we are going to own it.' "[16] That was not an unreasonable expectation. But it neglected a crucial component in the returning soldier's outlook. Hostile as he might be towards big business, bossism, and the officer class, his resentment of what were loosely described as "aliens" was far fiercer. That soon became apparent in Winnipeg, several months before the General Strike. Towards the end of January 1919, the Socialist party planned a second meeting, in the form of a memorial service for Rosa Luxemburg and Karl Liebknecht, who had just been murdered in Berlin. Deprived by the city authorities of the use of a hall for the purpose, the Socialists decided to hold their meeting out of doors. The ensuing situation was described by the officer commanding the Military District (No. 10) in a report to the Militia Council at Ottawa:

> At 2.00 p.m. on Sunday the 26th of January, some 1500 to 2000 Veterans assembled in the City Hall Square and the Socialist Meeting was not held, but some of the Socialist fraternity in the neighbourhood were rounded up by the Veterans and made to kiss the Union Jack, and roughly handled. The Veterans then split up into three different columns and visited the

various known Socialist headquarters, which they wrecked. . . . One of these [columns] visited the Alien Quarter in the North End of the City, another proceeded to Elmwood, paying a visit to the Edleweis Brewery, the proprietor of which is a naturalised German. This place was badly smashed up. The third party of Veterans visited the establishment of S. Blumenburg, the . . . noted anti-conscriptionist and Socialist. . . .

On Monday the 27th of January, three large parties of Returned men again assembled, and the situation began to look somewhat serious. The feeling of the Returned soldiers against aliens and firms employing them was running high, and some irresponsibles amongst the Returned soldiers attempted to inflame the others by proposal that all establishments, such as the Swift Canadian Company, the Canadian Pacific Rlwy., Shops, and the Canadian National Rlwy., Shops, should be raided and wrecked and the aliens employed thereat beaten up and chased out of town.

About 2.00 p.m. I was informed . . . that this had actually been determined on by the Veterans and that a large body of them were on the way to the Swift Canadian plant, to carry out these intentions. I was shortly afterwards telephoned by the Mayor of Winnipeg, asking if I would go down to this mob and address them. . . . The Secretary of the Great War Veterans Association . . . called on the men and stated I had come to speak to them. I pointed out to them that they were destroying their hard earned record in the Field, and advised them to go about getting their aims brought about in a proper and constitutional manner, in which they would be given every possible assistance and support. . . . The result was that the Returned soldiers, deciding to follow our advice, quietened down and began to disperse. . . .[17]

Whatever appeal Bolshevism might have had for the veterans was lost because of their hatred for those "aliens"—Canadians of German and Central and Eastern European origin—suspected of being Bolshevik. "The alien," declared Comrade F. W. Law of the G.W.V.A. in May 1919, "has been one of our first objects you might say, since the return of the men. . . . We are opposed to the alien and will be opposed to him until such time as he gets out of the country. . . ."[18] A resolution forwarded by the St. Catharines, Ontario, branch of the G.W.V.A. to its Central Executive, proposed the "dismissal from their employment of all foreigners and single men who have not served in the present war."[19] "The foreigner who does not conform to British ideals," declared Comrade Wilson of Toronto at the G.W.V.A.'s Vancouver Convention in 1919, "is a cause of unrest. He is undesirable, and our resources and wealth should not be accessible to him, neither should the job a Great War Veteran could fill. . . .[20] And so Sam Blumenberg, who had appealed to the returned soldiers to overthrow the established order, found instead that they had wrecked his dry-cleaning shop on Portage Avenue.

Bolshevism had surprisingly little attraction for the great majority of the returning Canadian forces. But the Cabinet—what remained of it at Ottawa—was none the less acutely apprehensive about the immediate future. On 16 April 1919, the Acting Prime Minister cabled to Borden in Paris:

> Council much concerned over situation in British Columbia. Bolshevism has made great progress among workers and soldiers there. We can not get troops absolutely dependable in emergency and it will take long time to establish old militia organization. Plans are being laid for revolutionary movement which if temporarily successful would immediately bring about serious disturbances in Calgary and Winnipeg where Socialism rampant. We think most desirable British Government should bring over a cruiser from China Station to Victoria or Vancouver. The presence of such ship and crew would have steadying influence. Situation is undoubtedly serious and getting out of hand by reason of propaganda from Seattle and workers and soldiers.[21]

Borden thought the remedy proposed by his Ottawa colleagues most unwise. "We are still at a loss," he cabled White after an exchange of telegrams, "to know of any use to which the British Cruiser could be put in case of trouble. Surely it would be most unfortunate to have the crew of a British ship called upon to suppress purely local Canadian riots, or insurrection. As far back as 1885 we have attended to our own rebellions." However, he did agree that if the situation seemed to warrant it, it might be desirable to invite the British Government "to send squadron to Vancouver and Halifax not later than June 1st, in order that Canada may have opportunity of demonstrating appreciation navy service during war."[22] Such a visit could not be arranged at short notice, and White was soon again appealing to Borden: "Several members Council think presence British cruiser desirable at Vancouver or Victoria. Strike in Winnipeg of all workers including Tramways and Post Office. About thirty thousand out and serious rioting may occur. Situation in British Columbia very grave. Returned men will not rejoin Militia or North West Mounted Police."[23] Borden's return on 25 May exerted a steadying influence upon his ministers, whose physical and mental resources had been strained to the point where their judgment was evidently no longer reliable*; at any rate, nothing more was heard about asking for British cruisers. But fear of imminent Bolshevik revolution persisted, fed by alarmist cables from the Colonial Office warning, among much else, "that the Russian Soviet Government has a plan for resuscitating the revolutionary movement in Canada, and has put two million Roubles in foreign money at the disposal of the Communistic sections at Ottawa,

*Half of the Cabinet, one of its members noted privately, "are worn out—tired or ill actually." Diary of Sir George Foster, 6 Dec. 1919.

Calgary, Lethbridge, Edmonton, Regina, Victoria, Vancouver, Toronto and Montreal."[24] And all the authorities were in dread of what might happen later in the year, when the majority of returned soldiers would experience their first taste of unemployment throughout a Canadian winter. The demands of those veterans' associations committed to law, order, and moderation were accordingly assured of full and sympathetic consideration. "Received the representative of the Great War Veterans' Association," Sir Robert Borden noted in his diary on 9 June 1919. "The President spoke in a discursive manner for an hour and twenty minutes. . . ."

J. HARRY FLYNN AND HIS GRATUITY MEN

By far the most pressing issue of the politics of re-establishment was the soldiers' gratuity. Much had already been done for the returning members of the Canadian Expeditionary Force—more, certainly, than any government had done in any previous war, and more (so the Borden Government insisted) than any other government was doing at the end of the Great War. Gratuities upon discharge, intended to tide the veteran over until his re-entry into civilian life, had already been paid; pensions were provided for the disabled and the bereaved; a system of retraining was available to some, though not to all, who stood in need of it. The most remarkable feature of the Government's re-establishment programme was the Soldiers' Land Settlement scheme. The Act of 1917 by which it had been established provided that Dominion land to the extent of a quarter section could be purchased by returning soldiers; this offered no great inducement, and by the summer of 1919 only slightly more than 2,000 men had taken advantage of it. The Government then introduced a number of changes, intended to make the scheme more attractive, the chief of which was the provision of credit to enable the veteran to make his living from the land. To have represented this plan as a grateful nation's reward to its returning heroes was tempting, but it could not be done without placing in jeopardy the Government's fundamental principle, that no special category of veteran—farmer, technician, university student—was to be singled out for favour. Accordingly, the plan was introduced and defended as a land colonization measure rather than a soldiers' re-establishment measure. Its object, Arthur Meighen declared in the House of Commons, was not "to afford a gratuity or reward to the soldier . . .; the primary and great principle of this Bill is to secure settlers on the land of this country. . . . We believe that we cannot better fortify the country against the waves of unrest and discontent that now assail us, as all the rest of the world, than by making the greatest possible proportion of the soldiers of our country settlers upon the land."[25] The measure, in keeping with the rest of the Government's re-establishment programmes, was frankly paternalistic; to one of its critics in Parliament, it was "paternalism gone mad."[26]

These various measures of re-establishment cost the country more than $100 millions a year. Even so, virtually all the returned men believed them to be inadequate. They differed only on the degree of their inadequacy and, more importantly, on the principle of their inadequacy. In what way ought the nation to discharge its debt to those who had fought for it? By providing for the individuals concerned as comprehensive a system of social security as it was possible to devise and feasible to finance? Or by a cash settlement on the grounds that those to whom it would be paid knew best the nature of their needs and how these could be satisfied? The Government remained committed firmly to the more paternalistic of these principles. So, at first, did the G.W.V.A. and other veterans' groups. But by the autumn of 1919 there had developed significant opposition to the existing programme of re-establishment; and by the spring of the following year the "gratuity men" were in the saddle, threatening to ride away with the whole veterans' movement and (the Government feared) to make their own bid for political power.

The gratuity issue made its first appearance at a general meeting of the G.W.V.A. in Calgary on 23 February 1919, which passed, with what went on the record as a unanimous vote, the so-called Calgary Resolution: a cash grant of $1,000 should be paid to each member of the Canadian Expeditionary Force who had served in Canada, $1,500 to each serving overseas, and $2,000 to each serving in a theatre of war, all in addition to existing pensions for disability. The Calgary Resolution, whatever its appeal to the rank and file, did not unreservedly commend itself to the officers of the G.W.V.A.; its official organ, *The Veteran*, declared in May 1919 that the proposed gratuity would cost the country $1,000 millions, which it could not afford, and advocated instead improvement in existing pension and rehabilitation measures. On 16 May a G.W.V.A. deputation was told by the Minister of Finance, Sir Henry Drayton, that gratuities on the scale proposed would bankrupt the nation, and that the Government could not therefore grant them.

The Calgary Resolution was the centre of interest and discussion at the G.W.V.A.'s third annual convention at Vancouver in July 1919. Its officers had hoped to head off demands that the Association reaffirm the Calgary Resolution, but they underestimated the strength of feeling among the membership in its favour:

Comrade Woods (*Calgary*): What has overshadowed us since the war? It is the spectre of Bolshevism; that spectre threatens us, Sir; and I have personally, and so have my comrades, put up a fight to keep our returned men quiet, by giving them promises of what we will do for them at this Convention: that we will express your wishes, boys, at this Convention. It is a shame that the boys who went over in 1914 should be disappointed; and there is no doubt about it, that there is a feeling of disappointment. . . . If the soldier is repatriated, and is given the opportunity to be contented by being helped to his feet, then Bolshevism will disappear, disloyalty will disappear. . . . Before I sit down, I would like to convey to you gentlemen assembled here the danger of delay, the danger of storm. Don't let us go back and say we want an expression of your opinion, because we know their opinion. . . . I tell you, gentlemen, when I think of next winter coming, with a possible crop failure, any scheme that we can get together that can avert this catastrophe that is coming for us, will be good. We all admit that a repatriation bonus is necessary, that it will dispel this Bolshevistic tendency throughout the Empire. . . .

Comrade Gibson (*Regina*): . . . To my mind, there is no doubt whatever, Mr. President, that the rank and file—please accept the term I use absolutely without any meaning of disparagement, because some of my best friends are among the officer class—there is no doubt that from the extreme East to the extreme West the voice of our locals is voiced here at this Convention. . . . There is no doubt whatever but that the rank and file will be solid in the Dominion upon the principle of some gratuity. . . .

Comrade Axon (*Victoria*): . . . I am not leaving this Convention without voicing the opinion of my comrades, as they have instructed me to do it. . . . As a workingman, and meeting not one but a dozen workingmen, the boys have been asking me, "Have you got us that two thousand dollars yet, Axon?", and I said "No, but I am going to try and get it for you" (*Applause*) . . .

Comrade [unidentified]: . . . I am from the Crow's Nest Pass district . . . If I went home and did not support the Calgary Resolution, or a resolution that embodies the Calgary Resolution, I might as well go out to the bug-house here. It would not be safe for me to go back. . . .[27]

Confronted by a divided Convention, the G.W.V.A. leadership hastily contrived a compromise and, by strenuous argument and pleading, obtained its acceptance. The resolution adopted demanded gratuities but refrained from specifying how large they should be: "such bonus should be on an equitable basis limited only by the country's ability to pay, with classification, distribution and administration to be agreed upon and decided by a Joint Parliamentary and G.W.V.A. Commission. . . ."[28] The Liberal Party held its leadership convention in Ottawa the following month; so easy an opportunity of winning the support of returned soldiers could not be resisted, and the convention unanimously approved the following plank for its platform: "That this convention declares that the adoption of a system of cash grants to the soldiers and dependents of those who have fallen is the most satisfactory and effective means of Civil Re-establishment, such grants to be in addition to the present gratuity, and to any pension for disability resulting from service." But the Government remained adamantly opposed. On 5 September Sir Robert Borden received a G.W.V.A. deputation to which he handed a letter declaring that the country's financial condition "precluded any larger or further gratuity."

Two days later a meeting of disaffected veterans at Queen's Park, in Toronto, formed themselves into the United Veterans' League, and installed as their president a 37-year-old ex-sergeant named John Harry Flynn. Their objective, as later defined by Flynn, was "to form all the soldiers and sailors into one grand body for political purposes, not necessarily a political party, but to use our political power to dictate the platform of one political party, and put that political party forth to represent us, and only those who will represent returned men to be upheld by this political power."[28] "The G.W.Vs. have broken loose," Sir George Foster wrote in his diary on the day following these events, "and are on the hunt for $2,000 gratuity to each." And on 11 September:

> The G.W.Vs. are flooding Govt and M.P.'s with telegrams—branches are passing resolutions—extremists are talking like Hun Spartacans [*sic*] and the senior men in the organization are howled down. Some wonderful financial arguments are being made. Smith of Montreal carried the Vets meeting with the slogan "Take it out of the Ger. Ind. [German Industrialists?]" and Flynn of Toronto would lead his men to [word illegible] and take it. From whom?

In response to this volatile situation, the House of Commons decided, on 18 September, to refer the Government's amendments to the Department of Soldiers' Civil Re-establishment Act to a Special Committee of twenty members drawn from both political parties. The Calder Committee, as it was known, began its work the following day. Technically it had no reason to deal with the gratuity issue; practically there could be no escaping it. "The deliberations of the Committee," it was warned at the outset of its hearing by the counsel for the G.W.V.A., C. G. MacNeil,

> must be conducted in such a way as to command the confidence of a very critical and suspicious audience, suspicious because of preceding events,

and critical because they are facing the prospects of a very uncertain and gloomy future. . . . For months and months we have approached the Government in various ways; we have interviewed the Prime Minister and members of the Cabinet, and I venture to say that if our principal recommendations had been received with less perfunctory consideration, the extreme demands that have risen in many quarters would not have been made. . . .[29]

The Committee during more than forty sessions heard the evidence of sixty-eight witnesses, including eight representatives from the G.W.V.A., twenty-five officials of the departments, commissions, and boards concerned with various aspects of civil re-establishment, the President of the University of Toronto and the President of the Trades and Labour Congress. The central, and certainly the most publicized, figure at the inquiry was John Harry Flynn. During the course of many hours of testimony before the Committee on 1 October, Flynn argued that the sum $1,000, $1,500, and $2,000 be paid to each member of the Canadian forces who had served in Canada, Britain, or France, respectively. Flynn's proposal was given a rough time by members of the Committee, but its passage was tranquil compared to that of Flynn himself. Most of his testimony, as he complained at its conclusion, was taken up in cross-examination of his earlier career as an American citizen and teacher of commercial studies at a number of little-known educational institutions; his war record was subjected to particularly intensive scrutiny by several members of the Committee evidently persuaded that the best way to discredit the gratuity proposal was to discredit its leading supporter:

Q. How long were you in England? — A. I was ten days in the camp and I slept constantly in mud puddles.
Q. At what camp? — A. At what they called the segregation camp near Westerhanger. . . .
Q. Were they huts or tents? — A. Tents part of the time without any floors. . . .
Q. In what year? — A. 1917.
Q. What season of the year? — A. April.
Q. Did you leave Canada in April? — A. I left Canada in April.
Q. When did you arrive in England? — A. I arrived in the latter part of April, or the first part of May. . . .
Q. Do you not remember that we had beautiful weather then? — A. I remember that we had rainy weather. . . .
Q. Who were your comrades in the tents? — A. Do you want the names?
Q. Yes? — A. It is impossible to give the names of all the companions I served with in France.

Q. I am speaking of England? — A. Even in England, I would not be able to give the names of all those who were my companions.

Q. Could you not give us one name? — A. Yes, Sergeant Johnston was one, of Hamilton, Ontario.

Q. Who else? — A. I am unable to give you the names now. . . .

Q. Who was the officer in charge?. . . .[30]

Flynn's cross-examination only made him a martyr in the eyes of his supporters, so much so that another witness, Colonel A. T. Hunter, took it upon himself to warn the Committee against its tactics:

. . . Our Originals Club is composed of as level-headed men as any. . . . They think concretely, and while I am at it I wish to say that they brought up another thing at out last meeting. During your proceedings you investigated the record of an individual soldier. That, I may say, is intensely irritating for the returned man. . . . The rank and file of the soldiers will be entering more and more into public life, and the whole body of returned men will be bitterly hostile if any attempt is made, particularly by those who have not themselves served, to bore and pick holes in the military record of any soldier. . . . It produced an intense irritation, the perhaps well-intentioned ideals of the Committee in looking up the record of a sergeant.

A member of the Committee thereupon observed: "Perhaps, Colonel Hunter, if you had heard the witness to whom you refer giving evasive answers, telling the deliberate lies that he told, you would sympathize with the attitude of some members of the Committee?" Hunter replied: "I understand that the Committee is long-suffering. Of course the general attitude, I may say, of the public is to say, 'These parliamentarians receive three times as much as a Superior Court Judge for the time they employ, and it is fair game to take it out of them.' "[31]

At the conclusion of Flynn's testimony, the counsel for the G.W.V.A. and the representative of the Imperial Veterans in Canada (who had favoured improved pensions but opposed cash gratuities) formally dissociated their respective organizations "entirely from the statements made by Mr. Flynn, which seriously reflect upon British institutions and sense of fair play, and are not in accord with the ideals for which Canada's citizen soldiers have served and now seek to maintain." Flynn, permitted by the Committee to reply, rose to the occasion:

The statement has been made here that I am representing my own views, and not the views of the returned men. The returned men in Canada will prove to the Committee that I am so representing them, and that the means I have adopted is an absolutely constitutional way of putting forth our demands, and the constitutional way is to use our franchise and to put out of office men who will cry out "No, no," when a man whose evidence has been attacked asks to be allowed to reply. I will announce from my platform that my religion has been brought into this question and that more attention has been paid to that and to other personal matters in connection with myself than to the re-establishment of soldiers. I want to make that clear to the returned men from my platforms. I want it understood that when I came here I came on the demand and at the request of a majority of the returned men in the cities I have been in in Ontario, and, so it will be, throughout the Dominion as I visit the different places. I say that the representatives of the Great War Veterans' Association . . . are not representing the views of the men who sent them here, and that I will prove. . . .[32]

The gratuities proposal never stood much chance of adoption by a Committee the majority of whose representatives supported a Government several times on record as opposed to it; but whatever slight chance it may have had was doubtless removed during the course of Flynn's advocacy.

The tenor of the Committee's findings and recommendations is conveyed in the following paragraphs from its Report:

Summing up the whole situation, your Committee are convinced that as regards the problem of re-establishment generally, the Canadian people and their representatives in Parliament, as well as the Government, have always shown an earnest desire to meet any real need that has arisen or may exist. Parliament heretofore has not been parsimonious in voting money whenever and wherever the expenditures were shown to be necessary. Frequently, however, the opinion was expressed in Parliament that the greatest care should be taken to avoid any action that would tend to deprive the soldier of his self-reliance and self-respect. It was thought to be against the best interests of the soldiers themselves that they should rely unduly upon the State in the period following discharge. Your Committee concur in these views. After hearing all the evidence, they agree that the best policy towards the soldier is to surround him with conditions that will tend to strengthen his self-confidence and self-reliance. . . .[33]

In reference to the question of making further provision for cash grants, gratuities or other financial assistance to be distributed generally on any basis to all ex-members of the C.E.F., your Committee desire that there should be no misunderstanding as to their views.

Your Committee having fully discussed and considered the financial position of Canada including the further large sums of money that must be borrowed to carry out the work to which the country is committed cannot see their way clear to recommend to Parliament any proposal that would provide for a further general distribution of grants or gratuities either in cash or credits. . . .

Your Committee are of the opinion that nothing would be gained by entering upon a detailed analysis of the general scheme for re-establishment presented by Mr. Flynn. His proposals if carried out would involve the raising and distribution among returned men of over one billion dollars, a sum equivalent to two-thirds of our entire war debt and that, for interest charges alone, would entail the raising of a sum of approximately fifty-five million dollars annually. Apart altogether from the suggested basis of distribution, the Committee unhesitatingly agree that the sums of money involved are so huge as to render the scheme absolutely impracticable, and for this reason cannot recommend the same for the consideration of Parliament.[34]

Before the Report was made public, it was considered by the Cabinet. "Council 8 to 10 p.m. on Calder's Comm. report," Sir George Foster wrote in his diary on 11 October.

We are up against a very grave situation and shall disappoint very sadly the gratuity grabbers. But the country will approve the stand we take [which] is to help the disabled, and the individuals who lost chances of education and training in enlisting at early age to the utmost to rehabilitate themselves and to look after the widows and orphans. The schemes proposed by the soldier plans run into an expense of 250 to 850 millions. Neither one nor the other can be raised nor should be. . . .

A week later:

Council meeting in evening. The subject chiefly discussed was the Report of Committee on Soldiers' settlement. The proposed findings of Committee were considered. The line is 1. Against all gratuities further to soldiers. 2. In aid and extension of help in training and educating disabled soldiers and making or helping to make up to the student and mechanic whose studies were interrupted by war service by way of loan and further training. The added expense will amount to millions but moderate in comparison to the schemes proposed. . . .

And on 24 October:

. . . The report of Committee on Soldiers' Settlement is now ready practically—Monday will see it laid upon the table and then we shall hear something—the recommendations are just but the temper of the minority of the Returned Soldiers is not receptive to facts—the impulse to take the money is natural and it is hard for the better class to keep the lead.

It soon became not just hard but impossible for the "better class"—the old-guard officials of the G.W.V.A. and the other moderate veterans' associations—to keep their followers from breaking ranks and rallying to John Harry Flynn and his gratuity men. "The G.W. Vets. . . . now face the possibility of political action urged by the extreme section," noted Sir George Foster, ten days after the terms of the Committee's Report became known. "It is doubtful if they can withstand."[35] A month later he was more optimistic: "The returned soldiers are quieting on the increased gratuity question and the better element are I think gaining gradually a controlling influence. The application of needed relief to those actually in need will approve itself to the people of

Canada and to the majority of returned soldiers."[36] But this sanguine prediction insufficiently reckoned with the force of Flynn's oratory and the mood of his growing band of followers. In January 1920, Foster recorded: "The G.W.V. Association is verging gradually to political action, the master heads are not strong enough to prevent the trend of the mass which in part has a vague idea as to what benefits may be gained by political action and the large number of irresponsibles who are out for the stuff and believe they can get it thro' political action."[37]

The G.W.V.A.'s Fourth Annual Convention, held in Montreal in March, 1920, coincided with the climax of Flynn's campaign. This time the leadership could not repeat their successes of the previous year in holding the gratuity resolution to a vague expression of principle. Quickly it became apparent that the members were out for the cash. The argument that the country could ill-afford it was brushed aside. "A short time ago," related Comrade Howe of Kingston,

> I had an interview with the present Finance Minister, Sir Henry Drayton, and asked him what he thought of the problems of the returned soldier, and particularly that part of it dealing with the question of re-establishment. . . . He replied that if the country was expected to pay or was compelled to provide the money to enable the re-establishment plan of the G.W.V.A. to go through, that Canada would represent a squeezed orange, that there would be nothing left but the rind. . . . I took exception to that and pointed out to Sir Henry . . . that if the G.W.V.A. plan were adopted by the Government, Canada would not represent a squeezed orange but would represent an orange perhaps with the financial pips taken out of it and the juice equally distributed throughout the orange, and that is what we want in Canada (*applause*). . . .[38]

Spurred on by such oratory, the Convention adopted a lengthy resolution embracing the gratuity principle in terms no less specific than those of the Calgary Resolution a year earlier:

> 1. That proper re-establishment of the returned soldier can more efficiently and more economically be accomplished by means of a cash bonus payable to 100 per cent. of the forces, which should be based on length of service.
>
> 2. That we urge upon the Government the necessity of a cash re-establishment bonus based upon an additional $1.00 *per diem*, for the total period of their enlistment, to men who have seen such service on a belligerent front. The minimum amount to be paid shall be $1,000, or such other amount as may be agreed upon, and a proportional bonus be paid to those who saw service in Great Britain, Canada and Siberia. . . .[39]

"They voted for gratuity," Foster commented in his diary on 27 March, "and passed a mass of resolutions. Altogether it was I should say not a very successful meeting. The extremists won out."

On 30 March a G.W.V.A. deputation presented the Convention's resolution to the Government at Ottawa. (Flynn was not a member of this deputation, having been refused an audience because, as a contemporary account put it, "of his violent language towards members of the Government personally; any other representative would be welcomed."*) However, it was not a warm welcome. "The aftermath of the G.W.V. Montreal Convention is weakness and discouragement," Sir George Foster wrote following his reception, as Acting Prime Minister, of its deputation. "The Resolutions were crude—the management has gone into extremist and weak hands—the membership has fallen. . . . 'Ne'er do wells' and English rads and roustabouts will persist and give trouble but in the end come to naught. . . ."[40] On 9 April Foster reiterated in the House of Commons the Government's previous refusals to countenance any further cash payments to the returned men:

> The Government is not and never has been of the opinion that the best way to reconstitute, readjust, and re-establish the returned soldier is by placing in his hand a sum of money over which there should be no government supervision, and without any reference to the peculiar and differing conditions and circumstances of each returned soldier.[41]

That, Foster thought, ought to settle the matter: ". . . Made a statement in the House as to gratuities or bonus in cash to soldiers, and turned that request down finally."[42] A week later he commented:

> The declaration of Govt. re soldiers' cash gratuity has been approved by the country but Flynn and his following are pressing a campaign and the extremists will follow them. The Pensions Committee [of Parliament] have declined to take up gratuity question. So the issue is now joined and we shall see. If the U.S. grants a cash bonus of a billion or two it will make it harder for us, but will not deflect our policy. The yearly push for increased indemnity [for M.P.s] is being made. To do this and to raise Judges' salaries and ministers' salaries will be feed for the Flynn men and be hard to counteract in the country. . . .[43]

And on 25 April: "Flynn is doing the abusive and sensational, and surely must be disgusting the better portion of soldiers and the most of the general public."

By the summer of 1920 the agitation for soldiers' gratuities had begun to subside. The dreaded winter had come and gone without unemployment and hardship on the scale that had been feared; the

*J. Castell Hopkins, *Canadian Annual Review, 1920* (Toronto, 1921), p. 453. "The Ottawa newspapers say," Sir Robert Borden noted in his diary for 25 April (he was then recuperating in South Carolina), "that a scoundrel named J. Harry Flynn has been saying damaging things about me."

United States Congress did not see fit to reward returning servicemen with further cash payments; and, most importantly, much of the wind had been taken out of the sails of the gratuity men by the Government's acceptance of the proposals of the Parliamentary Pensions Committee, resulting in substantial increases in the incomes of the disabled and the bereaved. "Soldiers' Gratuity agitation seems dying down in Canada and in U.S.," Sir George Foster noted on 16 May. "It has met I think its quietus." And on 20 June: "Soldiers' Pensions to get a boost of about $10m—increased indemnities faded out."

In these circumstances, the G.W.V.A. annual convention met, this time in Port Arthur, to consider its position. A general election was only weeks away, and this caused some of the comrades, notwithstanding the discouraging history of the gratuity proposal, to insist that the Convention endorse once more either the Calgary or Montreal resolutions. "I do not think in the history of the G.W.V.A.," Comrade Walker of Alberta declared,

> we have ever had such a favourable scheme as we have had now. I think the G.W.V.A. built its reputation and membership on what they were going to get by re-establishment, and it is up to them to maintain it now. That is why our membership has dwindled, because they believed the G.W.V.A. has avoided the onerous issues that bring us here. . . . It looks very much to us in the West as though as soon as it got to Ottawa, [the gratuity proposal] was dropped like a hot potato. If we do not put it through now, we are not going to have a member in the G.W.V.A. in twelve months' time. . . .[44]

The charge that the officers of the G.W.V.A. had been lukewarm in their efforts to place the Association's demands for a cash bonus before the Government brought indignant denials both from themselves and from the membership. "Let me pay this tribute to Comrades Waistell, Maxwell, Dace and MacNeil," C. G. Power got up at once to say. "They bothered the life out of every member of Parliament for a period of six weeks, and I can assure you that the G.W.V.A. made itself felt in the halls of Parliament at Ottawa. I was one of those members who had a resolution from my local branch against the $2000 or any other gratuity, so they did not bother me, but most members of Parliament's lives were made miserable during that period."[45] The Secretary-Treasurer of the G.W.V.A., C. Grant MacNeil, arose to defend himself against the charge that he had pressed the case for gratuities with insufficient vigour:

> I resent the inference that we dropped it like a hot potato at Ottawa (*hear, hear*), and I want to say that I went with that proposal before two sessions of Parliament and have been heaped with abuse from within the

Association as well as without it because I tried honestly to serve the mandate of the Montreal Convention (*hear, hear*).

The officials of this Association have not wavered from the mandate from that Convention. The Dominion officials were left alone to press the fight with the Parliamentary Committee. There are three reasons why it was not possible to gain consideration of that proposal. . . .

One reason was that there was not a member of the Government, of the Unionist Party, of the Opposition, who would champion what we considered was right at that Convention. They would not touch it, not one of them was prepared to sincerely advocate that proposal. Why? Because there was a strong, influential section of public opinion against it.

We reached the stage in our negotiations where we did not dare take any more spectacular tactics without risking the danger—and it was a great danger—of reaction of public opinion which would have damned us from ever bringing it forward again, and we had to keep it alive in fairness to the men whom we felt we represented.

Another reason we could not advance it was because there was not sincere support from our Association. The men who openly advocated that resolution came to me and said "Forget that—to Hell with that. That is just camouflage."

If the members of this Association have that conception of their re-establishment proposals, then for Heaven's sakes tell me. I took it seriously. If the Association takes it seriously, very well, let us get into the fight. But every man has to line up and stay with the question until there is unanimous agreement, and then there has to be wholehearted and full support. . . .[46]

That was well said, and skilfully said. For, as the Secretary-Treasurer knew better than anyone, not all the members of the G.W.V.A.—perhaps by that time not even a majority of the members—took their gratuity demands seriously. This they forthwith proved. A succession of speakers arose to disabuse the Convention of the idea that the cash gratuity, in either the Calgary or Montreal versions, was any longer a matter of practical politics:

Comrade Grant (*Ottawa*): I want to go on record, Comrades, as saying there is no possibility—get that into your heads—of the country at large receiving our proposition for a money vote. Why? Because we are not at one amongst ourselves. The Ottawa Branch is on record against Cash bonuses. The public know these things. You talk about men who have left the G.W.V.A. because they couldn't get these things done for them. I can tell you of hundreds who won't come in as long as there is that plank in our platform. . . .

Comrade Margesson (*Ottawa*): I will not raise my voice again in favour of the cash grant, because we cannot get it. It cannot be done. The country is in no shape to do it. The people are groaning now under taxation and public opinion is against it. All political parties are crying economy. The Farmers' cry is "Economy—spend less money—the country is going to the dogs" . . .

Comrade Loughnan (Ottawa): . . . if this Convention decides upon a cash gratuity—because that is what it will come to no matter how you wrap it up—you reopen the whole question and bring back the whole matter we have been trying to live down through the Flynn episode from coast to coast, and you will kill this Association (*hear, hear*). . . .

We have suffered more from that infernal cry of Flynn's as returned soldiers in Canada than from any other cause . . . It was very nearly the death-knell of the G.W.V.A. and if you insist now in resuscitating this question you are going to put yourselves down and out. . . .[47]

Encouraged by this support, MacNeil spoke again:

. . . I do not want to see men any longer voting in convention because they are afraid of the crowd at home. I know there are men in this convention that do believe it is not possible to get a cash bonus, and they tell me this on every hand. They vote this, that and the other way at the meeting, and they come around to me and say, "We know all that stuff, MacNeil, but you know we cannot get it; it is impossible!" That is the sentiment that is paralysing our efforts. You put in "as outlined in the Montreal Resolution" and you will again throw the Association into a deadlock, which is poor strategy and which throws you solidly against all three parties. Let us be honest about this. There is not a party as a party in the Dominion of Canada, and I speak of the Labour, National, Liberal, Conservative, Progressive and Independent Parties, that can say they will come out for a cash gratuity. You throw yourselves directly into opposition to the financial interests and the C.M.A. [Canadian Manufacturers' Associations]. . . .[48]

That was enough. By this time the opponents of gratuity were preaching to the converted, with the exception of a handful of die-hards. A skilfully drafted resolution made no mention of the Montreal Resolution, nor of gratuities as such:

This convention reaffirms the necessity for the adequate re-establishment of all ex-service men, and pledges itself to continued efforts towards the attainment of the same, as such re-establishment will not be complete until such time as all ex-servicemen are placed, as far as possible, in the economic position which they would have attained but for war service.

So the gratuity issue dropped out of the politics of re-establishment. Its disappearance rid the veterans' organizations of the main cause of their bickering and disagreement; and in 1925 their struggle for unity ended victoriously with the creation of the Canadian Legion.

III

The Military and its Missions

AIDING THE CIVIL POWER

The Canadian military establishment, surveying the world in 1919, found much to justify the reconstitution of the land forces of the Dominion. It discerned two types of threat to the integrity of the nation, as a counter to which a strong militia was urgently required.

The most pressing threat was judged to be that of internal subversion. Senior Canadian officers believed most fervently that the welfare of their country was being placed in jeopardy by the activities of communist agitators, sustained ideologically and materially by Soviet Russia. "The principal peril confronting us at the present moment," a General Staff memorandum proclaimed in 1919,

> is the danger of the overthrow of Law and Order in our own Country. In the period preceding the War, immigration was unrestricted, with the result that we have taken into Canada large numbers of foreigners, who in many instances have preserved their original nationality; who have not absorbed our civilization and national ideals; and who see in a *bouleversement* an opportunity for personal gain. In certain districts in the West the number of aliens exceeds the citizens of Canadian nationality. The Bolshevik revolution in Russia and such institutions as the I.W.W. have created large funds and organizations for the propaganda of ideals and aims contrary to our own, and they find this foreign element a fruitful soil on which to work. . . . The contagion begun on the foreign element spreads to the less intelligent of our citizens and is creating a very dangerous and unhealthy state of affairs. . . .[1]

The Inspector-General of the Canadian Air Force, who in 1919 had been Chief of the General Staff, wrote in 1922 to one of his officers who had protested the zealous investigation of his men by the Royal Canadian Mounted Police:

> I dare say you regard us here as alarmists; but it is well to be on the safe side, and certain it is that there are revolutionaries—fewer in Canada

than in other countries—who are bent on serious mischief. Tomorrow, if they could, they would set up what in their jargon they call "the dictatorship of the proletariat"; and part of their deliberate policy is to tamper with Departments of the Government by introducing their agents into them: this is what they call their "germ-cell" method. We know that they have tried to corrupt the Militia; and what is more natural than that, if they had a chance, they would corrupt the C.A.F., wherein they could do, particularly by sabotage, an infinite amount of mischief. . . .*

The alarm of the General Staff at the prospect of Bolshevik insurrection was shared by commanding officers throughout the country, whose reports during the immediate postwar years reflect their apprehension. "As far as the strikers themselves are concerned," the General Officer Commanding Military District No. 10 wrote from Winnipeg in May 1919, "I do not consider that they have the slightest intention of disturbing the peace or causing trouble in the way of disturbances, but unfortunately behind all this trouble there is a well defined element of socialistic and bolshevist tendencies, who may at any moment cause a bad outbreak of rioting and general unruly conduct in the City."[2] From Vancouver, a fortnight later, the G.O.C. of M.D. No. 11 observed: "Looks as if majority of workmen did not desire strike but forced into striking by Central Committee who have been advocating One Big Union."[3] In December 1920 the G.O.C. of M.D. No. 2 wrote from Toronto to the commander of a Hamilton regiment to say that "information, apparently from very reliable sources, would tend to show that the Soviet forces are very active in Hamilton," and urged "the paramount importance that . . . weapons on charge to your brigade . . . should not fall into hostile hands."[4] Toronto was regarded as a focal point of revolution, "owing to labour unrest, unemployment, and Soviet activities."[5] The military authorities of the city were kept in a state of anxiety by weekly "situational reports" furnished by paid informers; the kind and quality of intelligence with which they were supplied may be judged by the following specimen:

Toronto. There are no signs of anything unusual at present, with the exception of, A Little Agitation amongst the Irish Section.

---

*Sir Willoughby Gwatkin to Sqn.-Ldr. Maclaurin, 16 May 1922. (Air Force Records, C. 3812).

The Department of External Affairs took a less alarmist view than did the General Staff. Asked by the Prime Minister what ought to be done about the circulation of subversive materials, O. D. Skelton, soon to become Under Secretary of State for External Affairs, replied: "This certainly is hot stuff, but it is not quite as alarming as it may seem at first glance. . . . These movements . . . if allowed to blow off steam and to scrap with one another . . . do not do anything like as much harm as they would like to do." Skelton to King, 19 Dec. 1924. King Papers.

Commencement of A propaganda scheme Is expected at an early date.

THE RED AGENTS, seem to be keeping In the background at present.

It is surmised that, should any serious movement be premeditated, Signs of Activity will be noticeable at, (28. WELLINGTON STREET.—TOP FLOOR)

From, Information received, It is suspected that endeavour's are made to tamper with the, MILITARY MAIL. In this District . . .[6]

Some effort was made to distinguish between cases of ordinary labour unrest and cases where, to quote a General Staff memorandum circulated among Military Districts late in 1921, there were "organized attempts on the part of the Red element to seize the reins of government." Tactics should be varied accordingly. "If it can be clearly defined that it is a labour trouble pure and simple," the memorandum declared, "with no 'Red' backing or revolutionary tendencies, the police, backed by the Permanent Troops of the Garrison, should be able to handle the situation. . . . In this case no reliance can be placed on the Active Militia as they would refuse to turn out." But where the situation was created or exploited by Bolsheviks,

it will probably be very well staged and will require a careful plan and prompt measures to defeat it. The failure of the Winnipeg Strike and the consequent defeat of their plans will probably have taught our Soviet agitators a lot, and it must be anticipated that their next effort will at least be free from any of the mistakes they made in the West in 1919. The development of such Soviet plans can only be overcome

(i) . . . by having a reliable military force to maintain law and order and to protect public and private property by dispersing any crowds that the police fail to handle;

(ii) . . . by having an organization to re-establish and maintain all food, fuel, and necessary transportation services with military authorities in a position to back up the police in providing adequate protection to these services. . . .[7]

Complying with the recommendation of this memorandum, the military authorities of M.D. No. 2 met in Toronto in December 1921. In the words of one of those present:

we went very thoroughly into the question of the military plans and operations in the event of serious rioting or other disturbances, and I append a defence scheme drawn up which covers, as far as we can foresee, all the preventive measures which we can take.

. . . there are some 18,000 men and women jobless in Toronto at the present time, and a large number of these are under the baneful influence of agitators and would when the time was ripe for mischief throw discretion to the winds and take an active part in any demonstration or riot that was started by the agitators. . . . The Communist Party are bent on making use, if at all possible, of the unemployment situation. . . .[8]

The threat of riots and subversion, whether exaggerated or not, led the General Staff logically enough to its recommendations on the size and nature of Canada's postwar land forces. If the Dominion was considered to be endangered by Bolshevik-inspired disorder, armed force was necessary if only to keep the country free from internal disturbances, or to put these down as they arose. A voluntary militia would hardly deter disorder; in any case, experience had shown that its members could neither be relied upon to turn out when ordered nor to obey orders when turned out. "It is unsound," an officer of the General Staff wrote to the G.O.C. of M.D. No. 2 in August 1919, "to issue military arms to civilians, even though they should be ex-soldiers."[9] A permanent force was essential for what was known legally and euphemistically as "aid to the civil power," known more bluntly by those engaged in it as "strike duty."*

In June 1919, the Minister of Militia and Defence, Major-General S. C. Mewburn, placed before the House of Commons an amendment to the Militia Act authorizing the increase of the permanent militia from 5,000 to 10,000 men. "It is not the intention," he declared, "to increase up to that number at present, but it may be necessary in the near future to add to the present permanent force in a reasonable way. . . ."[10] The reason, he explained, was so that it might better come to the aid of the civil power when circumstances required:

> . . . a permanent force is absolutely necessary for the preservation of law and order in every country. I regret to have to say that I am confirmed in that belief by events that have been happening all over the world: the troubles arising to the south of us and the troubles that are arising in different parts of Canada. Judging by many letters I have had from all parts of Canada, it would appear as if in some cases people are getting stampeded. I have even been told that the Government are negligent in that they have not a permanent army of at least 100,000 men in Canada. I received a letter from Winnipeg urging that the Government should have a permanent force that can deal with the situation there. The stand I take in connection with all these troubles is, I think, the right one. . . . I take the stand that in any municipality where there is trouble and where the militia have to be called out in aid of the civil power for the preservation of law and order, every citizen of Canada has the duty to perform to the State [*sic*] and he should link up with the militia and do his duty. . . .

---

*"Giving aid to the Civil Power or, to give it its more popular name, 'Strike Duty,'" wrote an authority on the subject, "is the most unpopular duty that the militia can be called upon to perform. Happily they are seldom asked to do it but in these restless days one never knows. . . ." Major T. V. Scudamore, "Aid to the Civil Power," *Canadian Defence Quarterly*, vol. IX, no. 2, Jan. 1932, p. 253.

I do not feel pessimistic about the future but I think that without any doubt I would be negligent in my duty as Minister of Militia if I did not propose that we should have some force that would be available for the preservation of law and order in the country. Taking into consideration the great extent of territory of Canada, I do not think it an unreasonable request to ask Parliament for a mandate to increase the force to 10,000 and leave it to the Governor in Council to determine as to when that force should be increased.[11]

This proposal touched off a lively debate. Those members imbued with the spirit of prairie radicalism were bitterly opposed. "I say to this Government," cried A. R. McMaster, "trust the people! The heart of the Canadian people is as sound as our No. 1 Hard Manitoba wheat. . . . If there is unrest and discontent in the country, an attempt to overawe the discontented by a 100 per cent increase in our military establishment is definitely not the proper procedure. . . . It is not the size of your military establishment, it is not the number of your soldiers; it is the ready obedience which the people give to constituted authority that is necessary."[12] T. A. Crerar and Michael Clark argued similarly. "I am profoundly convinced," declared the future leader of the Progressive party, "that the maintenance of law and order and the bringing of happiness to the people lies not so much in creating armed forces as it does in endeavouring to strike at the causes which lead to unrest. . . . I believe that the vast majority of the foreign element of our population . . . are law-abiding. . . . That being the case, let us appeal to the good that is in our citizens rather than to the establishment of large armed forces to overawe them."[13] And, finally, the member for Red Deer: "So far from the unrest being an argument for increasing the military forces, the unrest in Winnipeg is exactly the other way . . . I cannot think that the step is a wise one. I do not think it is needed; I do not think it is necessary to double the standing army in Canada; for I have supreme confidence in the common sense and sanity of the Canadian people."[14] These arguments did not prevail. The Militia Act was amended as the Minister desired. But at no time during the next few years did the actual strength of the Permanent Force exceed the total of 4,125 to which it was brought in 1920, let alone approach its authorized total of 10,000.

On several occasions between 1919 and 1923 this small force came to the aid of the civil power: once in Quebec City in June 1921, twice in Sydney, Nova Scotia, in 1922, most spectacularly in the summer of 1923, when as many as 1,100 members of the Permanent Force were called in, mainly from other Military Districts, when the miners of Cape

Breton again went out on strike. The intrusion of the military on such a scale perplexed and angered the Prime Minister. "The demonstration of force seems to have exceeded all bounds of necessity or prudence," Mackenzie King wrote to the Minister of National Defence[15]; and, a few days later (to the former Minister of National Defence), "I am unable to understand wherein it has been necessary to send to Cape Breton the numbers of troops that are there at the present time."[16] The authority by which they had been requisitioned was that of a judge of the County Court; in 1924 the Militia Act was amended so that henceforth troops could be called out only on the authority of the Attorney-General of the province concerned.[17]

Aiding the civil power was not required of the military during the later 1920's. But with the advent of the Great Depression this once again became the Army's principal assignment. On 15 August 1931, the officers in command of the Military Districts of the Dominion were advised by the Chief of the General Staff that it was their responsibility to "keep National Defence Headquarters informed of any conditions in their respective military Districts as may, from time to time, possibly lead to, or actually result in, threats of violence or violence or rioting and breaches of the peace, and whether such disturbances or threats of same are likely to result in calls for aid to the civil power."[18] Troops were called out to quell disturbances at Oshawa, Ontario, in April 1932; at St. Catharines, Ontario, in May to July 1932; and at Stratford, Ontario, in September and October 1933. The Permanent Force in M.D. No. 11 was constantly prepared for action in Vancouver throughout 1934 and 1935, though its services were never actually employed.* The likelihood of clashes between the Army and the unemployed in which lives might be lost and the military brought into disrepute led to the promulgation of the most stringent procedures in the event of soldiers being used to maintain order. District Officers Commanding were reminded, in March 1934, that "the justification which the Criminal Code confers . . . is dependent upon the existence of a certain set of circumstances—namely, a riot, and this means a riot in fact and not a mere anticipation that such is likely to occur." Officers were enjoined to obtain in writing a full record of conversations between themselves and civilian authorities in which the use of troops was discussed, and to exercise the utmost discretion in deciding whether the occasion warranted their being armed.[19] It was not to be wondered, in view of these requirements, that the District Officer Commanding Military District No. 11 wrote

*See below, pp. 137–46.

to the Chief of the General Staff during riots in Vancouver: "I will extend any and every facility to prevent our troops being requisitioned."[20]

II

The threat of subversion, in the estimation of the Canadian military establishment in 1919, demanded more than the availability of a strong permanent force to put down or to deter resort to violence. There was another, and in the long run a more effective, method of maintaining peace, order and good government in the Dominion, and that was by inculcating its people in the practice and principles of good citizenship. For this purpose, training in a non-permanent militia on the most extensive scale was believed to be as good a device as any. In the words of a General Staff memorandum prepared ten years after the Armistice, "A considerable and widely distributed Militia organization, around which the loyal and stable elements could rally, and which would, in addition, provide to its members valuable education in the duties and privileges of citizenship, was strongly indicated."[21]

This conclusion raised almost immediately the issue of the manner in which the non-permanent militia should be recruited. Was the Dominion to revert to the pre-war, rather, the pre-1917, method of voluntary enlistment? Or was it to acquire its reserves by means of some scheme of compulsory military service? A strong case could be made—indeed, was made*—for conscription. In addition to the usual arguments (fitness of the nation's youth, equality of sacrifice), an especially cogent reason for proceeding by compulsion presented itself. Volunteers were likely to be few and far between. Certainly this was true of the returning veterans. "A young ex-Patricia officer, invited to join a militia unit, declined tersely. 'I have formed my last four', he said"; and spoke for thousands like him.[22] "The returned man for at least two years to come will not put on his uniform," a non-permanent officer testified before the Otter Committee in December 1919. "I tried to get them to come to the review for the Prince of Wales, but they would not come. I have asked the G.W.V.A. when the men will put on the uniform and they replied, on one occasion only—for the funeral of one of our comrades."[23] "The fact remains," a G.W.V.A. member declared at its annual convention in 1921, "we are pretty sick of war. . . . I do not believe that if you

*See, for example, H. M. Mowat, "A Citizen Army," *Queen's Quarterly*, Oct.–Dec. 1918; C. F. Hamilton, "A Military Policy," *University Magazine* (McGill), Feb. 1920.

took a plebiscite vote you would find the G.W.V.A. in the frame of mind to say that they wanted anything in the line of militarism. They will tell you that there are men who had better jobs and more money while the war was on, and these are the men who desire to perpetuate this kind of thing."[24]

If, moreover, the value of the non-permanent militia lay in its capacity to transmit to its members the ideals of Canadian citizenship, it was better to expose conscripts to its influence: preaching to a force of volunteers would be preaching to the converted, whereas it was precisely those who would ordinarily have nothing to do with such a force for whom militia service would have the most benefit. "A voluntary system," observed a General Staff memorandum of 1919, "while it will probably provide the requisite force to meet and overcome the offenders, gives no chance of eliminating the root cause by education. Just that element in the country which needs the education in citizenship the most is the one which is not reached."[25] For this reason, above any other, the General Staff was in 1919 a firm supporter of compulsory service in a non-permanent militia. "I advise that a scheme for universal training should be submitted to Parliament at the approaching Session," the Chief of the General Staff wrote to the Deputy Minister of his Department on 20 November 1918. "If it is decided to submit such a proposition, I will be prepared with the details."[26]

But if policy is the art of the possible, defence policy is above all the art of the practicable. Canada in 1919 (so its leaders believed) was not far from revolution. The returning soldiers were interested in jobs, pensions, and gratuities. They were supremely uninterested in adding further to their locust years in uniform. If ordered to report to barracks they would have simply disregarded the orders: *quis custodiet ipsos custodes*? Conscription was in fact out of the question, as the politicians very quickly realized. "The Minister," minuted the Chief of the General Staff early in 1919, "is inclined to think that it would be premature to introduce legislation on the subject of universal training, at any rate until after demobilization, when the influence of the returned soldier (should he favour the scheme) will tell."[27] Another senior officer was more realistic. "I strongly advise that the whole proposal be postponed until the beginning of the fiscal year 1920," wrote Major-General Sir Eugène Fiset. "The scheme is more or less a dream. I foresee tremendous difficulties to any scheme in practice, and nothing should be done until the officers overseas have had a chance to discuss same."[28] But the returning veterans, both officers and men, had no taste for further compulsory military service. "We must all agree with the theory of Universal

Military Service when the Country is at War," declared a resolution of the G.W.V.A.'s Parkdale (Toronto) branch in January 1920:

It is only equity, when Susan's son is called out for rough work, that Dorothy's darling shall also be ready as well as willing to answer the bugle. But our people abhor compulsion even in matters of health and it is not necessary at this moment to shove our boys and youths where they can be led. . . . There is enough of the spirit of the volunteer left in the Veterans, if the politician will get out of the road. . . .[29]

That was about the end of it. Little more was heard in Canada about conscription for the next twenty years—after which the country for a time heard about little else.

REPULSING THE AMERICAN INVADER

The military planner's primary task is to identify his enemy. Its identification, known in the parlance as "strategic intelligence," involves the strategic intelligencer in a two-fold assessment, that of intention, and that of capability. Would Ruritania attack if it could? Could it attack if it would?

There was not much of an intelligence community in Canada in 1919. The right of legation, granted in 1920, was not exercised until 1926, though quasi-diplomatic establishments had functioned in London and in Paris since before the turn of the century. The Department of External Affairs consisted of two elderly gentlemen and Loring Christie, the latter forced into retirement in 1923. But, not for the only time, the dearth of professional intelligence officers did not prevent policy-makers, responding intuitively to their environment, from drawing the correct conclusion. These were all agreed that, for a decade at least, Canada would have no enemies; and that, of all the nations on earth, the least likely to attack the Dominion was her great neighbour.

In the whole of the public service, only one individual frontally challenged this conclusion. He happened, however, to be the only public servant whose main job it was to formulate strategic intelligence for the military establishment, the Director of Military Operations and Intelligence (D.M.O. & I.), Colonel J. Sutherland Brown. "Buster" Brown occupied this crucial position from 1920 to 1927. He once described its responsibilities in these words:

Nobody can occupy my post satisfactorily unless he is a glutton for reading, not only of the daily press and periodicals to keep abreast of the current events, but he must pay studied attention to the Service journals, he must keep abreast of military thought by reading military publications and in addition follow all questions of policy of the various countries in the world. Added to this there is a volume of routine reading such as that contained in the files dealing with Disarmament and the League of Nations. . . .[30]

It was no sinecure to be the General Staff's one-man "thinking Directorate," as the D.M.O. & I. was fond of describing his job. "I find," he wrote, "that I can never get away from professional thoughts and I have not read more than three novels in the last six years."

Between December 1920 and April 1921, the "thinking Directorate" was engaged in the preparation of Defence Scheme No. 1. For more than a decade this 200-page document held sway as official strategic doctrine for the armed forces of the Dominion. Its central assumption, on which all military planning was based, held that the principal external threat to the security of Canada lay in the possibility of armed invasion by the forces of the United States. (Extracts from Defence Scheme No. 1 are reproduced in Document 1, pp. 323–28 below.)

In his assessment of intention, the strategic intelligencer can make only two kinds of error: he can mistake his enemies for friends; and (less commonly) friends for enemies. It was "Buster" Brown's distinction to have committed the more unusual of the strategic intelligencer's sins. To his peculiar assessment he had been led by anti-American prejudice acquired early in life and from which he did not deviate throughout the remainder of his career. "I have studied the United States and the United States' citizens since I was a youth," he wrote in 1927 in defence of the thesis that war between the United States and the British Empire was still a possibility seriously to be reckoned with, "and I flatter myself that I know something about them. I am firmly convinced that it is from no humanitarian point of view that the United States has not had wars with Great Britain."[31] To this belief, which he fortified by bits and pieces of evidence culled from reports of the Imperial General Staff, he remained faithful to the end.

Defence Scheme No. 1, with its instructions for offensive action ("advance into and occupy the strategic points including Spokane, Seattle and Portland"; "converge towards Fargo in North Dakota . . . and then continue a general advance in the direction of Minneapolis and St. Paul") and its disparaging comments on several civilian groups ("Members of Parliament . . . are drawn from various sources of life, most of them with no War Service and no knowledge of the vast machinery required for War. . . . Such men need education"; "French Canadians . . . took little interest in the Great World War. . . . the main reason for lack of interest was lack of proper political control and leadership from Ottawa"), was nothing if not a sensitive document. Every precaution was taken by its author to ensure that its circulation was as limited, and its contents as secret, as possible. Fortunately for him, the politicians of the day had little interest in what the military was up to. It is almost certain that no Canadian Prime Minister ever read Defence Scheme No. 1, and not unlikely that none knew of its existence. It had necessarily to be shown to the officers commanding the various Military Districts; with their copies they received orders that the existence of the Scheme was "to be unknown to anybody in your District except yourself. Only such parts as are necessary will be communicated, either verbally or by very secret letter to the members of your staff and Heads of Services and Departments, that are necessary to help you mature your plans. The necessity of absolute secrecy must be impressed upon them."[32]

Several of the District commanders protested that this restriction would make effective planning difficult if not impossible, and asked permission to show the Scheme to their senior staff officers. Permission was granted after a certain amount of soul-searching, but once again "the absolute necessity for secrecy" was stressed, "not only to prevent the scheme becoming known to possible enemies of this country, but so that certain parts of it, which have a political touch, may not become known to people who would put it to political use."[33] A number of District commanders, fired with enthusiasm by the plan, proposed to undertake field trips into their potential battlefields for the purpose of observation and reconnaissance. "You will recollect a conversation which we had concerning a little trip . . . into the area to the south of here," the G.O.C. Military District No. 12 wrote from Regina to the Chief of the General Staff in May 1921.

> I have received an "invitation" from Judge Wood of Weyburn for Colonel Parsons and myself to take a trip in his car. I have accepted this invitation, and will supply gasolene, etc. . . . Could a special arrangement be made whereby I would be allowed travelling expenses for the Judge who will be our chauffeur? The expense to the Public . . . will be very small.[34]

But General MacBrien disapproved—not so much of the expense as of the whole outing. "We have had similar requests from most of the General Officers Commanding," he wrote in reply,

> and as a matter of policy the Minister thinks that such trips should be postponed for the present for fear of something going wrong at this critical time.
>
> After the Training season, I think, would be time enough, and then our scheme would be further advanced. [*] For the present, we have plenty to do in working out all the preliminary arrangements leading up to mobilization: the next step would be Concentration.

*Then, too (with any luck), a general election would have been held.

Were you to go in company with Judge Wood, it would be difficult to keep him from getting an inkling of the duty which you were on. As you realise, great care must be taken in this respect. No matter how well disposed outsiders are, it is unwise to let them know very much about this matter. . . .[35]

With this sentiment, another commander was disposed to agree: "Our plans, in any event and such as they are, are not likely to prove of considerable interest to possible enemies. I rather suspect that the enemy in contemplation is the enemy 'within our gates', the pacifist, the anti-conscriptionist, and the so-called anti-militarist and others in the House of Commons and without the House."[36]

II

The occupational disease of the military planner is a malady which might be described as "strategist's cramp," and its symptoms as a kind of creeping paralysis of the imagination when it comes to assessing the influence of a changing political and technological environment upon the fortunes of his country. It is therefore to be expected that Defence Scheme No. 1, the central assumption of which might charitably be said to have been stillborn, lasted longer than events justified. That it lasted for more than a decade is a measure of the lethargy and isolation of the Canadian military. Early in 1922 the results of the Washington Conference on Naval Disarmament were made public. Their ultimate significance—awarding Japan naval supremacy in the Pacific and feeding those imperialist ambitions which so over-reached themselves at Pearl Harbor—may be seen in retrospect; at the time the achievement at Washington appeared to be the ending of Anglo-American naval rivalry and of the last remnant of possibility of an Anglo-American war. A strategist not afflicted with strategist's cramp might well have construed these developments as requiring the scrapping of Defence Scheme No. 1 along with the capital ships the British and Americans were ready to consign to the acetylene torch and the bottom of the sea. That was not the reaction of J. Sutherland Brown. "The decisions arrived at by the Washington Conference," he wrote in a circular letter to officers commanding Military Districts in January 1922, "have materially improved the relationships between Great Britain and the United States. This makes it more than ever necessary that all matters connected with Defence Scheme No. 1 must be treated with the utmost secrecy."[37]

Nearly two years later, the thought of the D.M.O. & I. was not to abandon Defence Scheme No. 1 but to bring it up to date and to define its operational directives. For this purpose, the criticisms of Military District Commanders were solicited. They were asked, in Colonel

Brown's letter of 9 November 1923, to "consider the Scheme as a whole and not be too much carried away by local desires and difficulties. . . . Where strategy is objected to, definite and full reasons for such objection should be submitted, together with alternative plans." The letter concluded on a note of cautious optimism:

> More wars, campaigns and battles have been lost by extreme caution, lack of initiative and lack of sound organization, than by any other causes. Given good commanders and staffs and a reasonably trained peace establishment, our Non-Permanent Militia can meet any foreign troops attempting the invasion of Canada with a fair prospect of success.[38]

Considering that in that year the militia vote had been cut to $9,668,671 (it had been $11,016,939 in 1921–22), permitting the training of only 38,000 officers, N.C.O.'s, and specialists for about eight or nine days of the year (its authorized strength was 130,000 men trained for a full month), this conclusion was perhaps after all more optimistic than cautious.

None of the military district commanders saw fit to dispute the central assumption of Defence Scheme No. 1, and to argue that the eventuality for which such daring preparations were to be made would never come about. Perhaps they believed it might; perhaps they thought it imprudent to express their doubts. The most fundamental criticism came from the Commander of M.D. No. 5 (Quebec), who took exception to the task imposed upon him: "It would appear a logical truth that Commanders of Districts are not *au fait* with the political and strategical questions throughout Canada sufficiently to analyse a Scheme drawn up and expressed as 'considered military opinion' at National Defence Headquarters, where presumably the members of the Defence Council have concurred in the draft."[39] The Commander of M.D. No. 4 (Montreal) bridled for a different reason. "I consider that the most difficult point in the Scheme," he wrote, "is the fact that it is drawn up for forces which are to a certain extent non-existent."[40] But most of the commanders seem to have been swept along by the *panache* of Colonel Brown's strategic conception. "Insofar as the Defence of this District is concerned," wrote the Commander of M.D. No. 12 (Regina), "an energetic and dashing thrust must be immediately made to control the area lying between the junctions of Snake Creek with the Missouri River. . . . If the above described area were under Canadian control it is considered that without detriment to our interest sufficient steel could be obtained to complete the Hudson Bay Railroad which is most urgently needed for the defence of Canada. . . ."[41] And the Commander of M.D.

No. 10 (Winnipeg), his enthusiasm getting the better of his syntax, offered these comments:

> If retirement is forced by overwhelming numbers, it is considered that the lines on which the action of our troops is based, viz., a bold, active and vigourous defensive, employing Defence Tactics, made up largely of offensive elements, combined with an aggressive harrassing of the enemy columns and communications, and with the continued endeavour to establish the tactical conduct of the Campaign on such lines as to enable us, even on the defensive, to impose our will on the enemy, and to keep our own freedom of decision and of action, thus forcing the enemy practically to accommodate himself to our will, would delay and hold up his advance indefinitely. . . .[42]

III

The central assumption of Defence Scheme No. 1 not only ran counter to the central assumption of Canadian foreign policy; it challenged most of the assumptions held by others within the military establishment. In the first issue of the *Canadian Defence Quarterly*, the authors of the section given over to Air Force matters dismissed the hypothesis of military action between Canada and the United States as "a contingency too remote from practical politics and too impossible of solution to be considered. The history of the United States and Canada," they concluded, "the common civilization of the two countries, the intimacy of their economic and social ties, and the impossibility of making adequate preparation for the defence of the border, all make war with the United States too remote a possibility for serious consideration."[43] But the author of the Scheme remained unrepentant, and the Scheme itself unrevised. "Aggression by a Foreign Power," Brown wrote in the fourth issue of the *Canadian Defence Quarterly*, "may cause the defence of Canada to be Direct or Indirect. In the Great War just passed, it was Indirect. The next trouble may be nearer home. Let us hope that we are reasonably prepared."[44] In 1927, shortly before vacating the post of Director of Military Operations and Intelligence, he attempted a full defence of his Scheme. "It will be argued by many people who should know about international affairs," he began his memorandum of 11 November for the Chief of Staff,

> that war between the United States and the British Empire is unthinkable. . . . Great Britain has borne patiently insults from the United States on many occasions. She has taken these insults, I am fully convinced, on account of the weakness of the Canadian frontier.
>
> The United States has forced the hand of Canada on many occasions and is now attempting to force her hand with reference to the development of the St. Lawrence.

The day may come when the United States may think she is strong enough to bluff the British Empire with a threat of war. It is necessary then for the Empire to be in a strong position to meet this threat.

Canada is slowly, but surely, molding a national feeling which stands for looking after her own interests and she will show a strong front to any demands from the United States. If the United States knows that the Canadian Military Forces are a factor that cannot be lightly considered and that the whole Empire is behind us they will think before they take any action against us.

This all above is an argument that the United States may be a possible enemy, but to look at it from the academic point of view a defence scheme that provides for the defence of our frontiers will cover, with but slight variations, every military problem with which we will be faced. All the great soldiers that have ever considered Canadian defence have laid that down as an axiom on which to base Canadian defence.

I think it desirable that we should pursue the very sound course of organizing the Canadian Militia for the primary duty of Home Defence and I therefore recommend that as soon as you can get the Honourable the Minister's concurrence, Defence Scheme No. 1 should be re-written and brought up to date.[45]

This advice did not find favour with the new Chief of the General Staff, Major-General H. C. Thacker; nor did the new D.M.O. & I., Colonel H. H. Matthews, share the peculiar views of his predecessor. The Defence Scheme was not rescinded; nothing was done, however, to keep it up to date. This policy produced some bewilderment among the District Commanders who bore the responsibility of carrying its daring operational directives into effect. "In looking over the Defence Scheme here," wrote the Officer Commanding Military District No. 10 in July 1928, "I find that very little has been done with regard to it. No District Defence scheme seems to exist and amendments and appendices don't seem to be complete. . . . The Defence Scheme as we have it is by no means up to date. Is it the policy of the Department to keep it so? . . ."[47] Colonel Matthews replied:

. . . With regard to the Defence Scheme I think that it would be better to let the matter stand as it is for a while longer. As you say, the whole thing is very much out of date and the only satisfactory solution would be to rewrite it. There may be an opportunity to do this during the coming Fall and Winter though it is difficult to get the powers that be to take any real interest in anything beyond the organization of an Expeditionary Force. . . .[47]

One of the first acts of General A. G. L. McNaughton upon becoming Chief of the General Staff early in 1929 was to look into the status of Defence Scheme No. 1. On 9 January he minuted upon Colonel Brown's memorandum of 11 November 1927: "What action, if any, was taken by General Thacker in this matter?" Colonel Matthews told him:

> . . . no action was taken. . . . General Thacker informed me verbally, on several occasions, that he considered Defence Scheme No. 1, as it stands, to be chimerical, to say the least, and stated that he did not wish me to attempt to bring it up to date. He frequently expressed the opinion that it would be better, with the means at our disposal, to first concentrate on the practical organization and equipment of an Expeditionary Force, and some progress was made in this direction during his regime. . . . He thought it most important that the Government should lay down a policy as to whether or not the direct defence of Canada is to be considered and provided for.[48]

Early in 1931, the Canadian Government was informed of the World Disarmament Conference to be convened at Geneva a year or so later. For this purpose it was required to submit to the League of Nations, under whose auspices the Conference was to meet, its own estimate of future defence requirements for the Dominion. A committee, consisting of the Chief of the General Staff, the Chief of Naval Staff, and the Under Secretary of State for External Affairs, met during 1931 for this purpose, and in the course of its meetings the strategic assumptions underlying Defence Scheme No. 1 naturally came up for review and, just as naturally, for criticism. In May 1931 orders were sent to all Military District Commanders cancelling the Scheme.[49] Later in the year, General McNaughton presented a new appraisal of Canada's strategic situation from the army point of view—the first in ten years. Since the General Staff considered it in the immediate aftermath of the Great War, he noted,

> there has been an important political and strategical evolution in the world positions occupied by the United States, Canada and the United Kingdom. Strategically, the situation was completely altered by the Washington Treaties, 1921–22, whereby naval parity between the United Kingdom and the United States was agreed to, and in consequence, security of Canada's sea communications in the event of war with the latter country was voluntarily waived. Politically, Canada's position vis-à-vis the United States has been immeasurably stabilized. . . . So, as a result of these changes, it can no longer be held that the conclusions referred to above should continue as the basis of Canadian military organization.[50]

In October 1933, the General Officers Commanding Military Districts were ordered to destroy by fire "the various chapters, instructions, amendments, appendices, etc., in connection with Defence Scheme No. 1."[51] And so J. Sutherland Brown, then commanding Military District No. 11, put the torch to the project of his career. It is not known whether he abandoned as well his periodic forays into "enemy" territory around Portland and Seattle, where he had been wont to carry out, *incognito* and on his own, reconnaissance in depth.

PREPARING AN EXPEDITIONARY FORCE

Planning for "the organization and the despatch of an Expeditionary Force to help the Empire in case of a European Combination or a Minor Crisis"—to quote from the formulation of Defence Scheme No. 1 —throughout the 1920's had a lesser priority than planning for "the Defence of Canada against the United States." Since all planning was the work of the tiny group in the Directorate of Military Operations and Intelligence, not much progress could be made on the problems of an expeditionary force. The Chanak crisis in September 1922 caused a momentary flurry of interest in the project. On 18 September, two cables were received at Ottawa from Winston Churchill, appealing to the Canadian Government for an expression of willingness to send a contingent to help hold the line against Mustafa Kemal in the Neutral Zone. The Cabinet met three times throughout the day; Mackenzie King "found all present strongly against participation by Canada in sending of a contingent."[52] This attitude notwithstanding, the Chief of the General Staff was instructed by the Minister of Militia and Defence "to prepare in concrete form a memorandum showing what troops are available for despatch *in the event* of same being necessary."[53] In General MacBrien's absence, this instruction passed directly into the hands of J. Sutherland Brown who before the day was out had prepared the following memorandum:

> General MacBrien is away, but all these questions have been put before him and although he may not agree with all the details, this has his general agreement. . . .
>
> There is no information at present in the hands of the General Staff as to whether [the Chanak crisis] is a struggle for the existence of the Empire, which well it might be if Germany or Russia should take a hand in this movement, or whether it is only a minor crisis which will call for the full authorised forces of the Crown or only for a portion of those forces. It is difficult to give concrete information unless a concrete problem is cited.
>
> If only a small contingent is necessary, it is recommended that the Permanent Force be used as the basis of this. The strength of the Permanent Force on the 31st August is . . . Officers: 402. Other ranks: 3,191. . . . It is considered that an Expeditionary Force using the Permanent Force as a basis could be recruited and equipped and ready for despatch in two weeks.

If a force of larger size is required, the following considerations should be reviewed before considering the sources from which the troops will be drawn:

The General Staff have been busy reviewing the regulations for the Defence of Canada from the "direct" standpoint, and have not yet had time to consider fully the question of the despatch of an Expeditionary Force, but some consideration has been given to this and we have the lessons and the mistakes of the mobilization of the Expeditionary Force of 1914–18 to teach us. . . . [*]

Complete training returns for the present year are not yet available, but so far, 5,000 officers and 45,000 other ranks have been trained. It is considered that there would be no difficulty in raising by voluntary enlistment, within a few months, a force of 200,000 Officers and men.[54]

The difficulty, indeed, arose in another quarter. For if the Chanak crisis gave an impetus to planning an expeditionary force within the Canadian military establishment, within the Canadian Government it produced undisguised hostility to anything smacking of Canadian participation in what Colonel Brown had described as "minor crises" of the Empire. Something of its attitude was disclosed by Mackenzie King at the Imperial Conference in 1923. At its Eleventh Session, on 22 October, he made the following observations:

There is one point, I think, I ought to speak of with care. Lord Derby mentioned that one thing the Government here would like to be sure of was the number of men, or rather the extent of the forces, that could be counted upon. If that has reference to what at any time the personnel may be, what the equipment and general organization may be, of course that is always available; but if it has reference to what the numbers of men or extent of forces may be available at any given moment for participation in war, I think I ought to make it clear that as to what extent Canada would participate in a war at any time must be considered a matter which her own Parliament will wish to decide. . . . In any crises affecting the honour and integrity or the common interest of the Empire, Canada may be expected to do in the future as she has in the past, and be ready to play her part. It would be wrong, however, to have it assumed that any Department of Government here could feel that it had—if I might use the expression—a blank cheque from the Dominion to be filled in at a moment's notice without reference to any particular situation that might arise. . . .[55]

*Of these lessons and mistakes of mobilization of the C.E.F. in 1914, Col. Brown wrote elsewhere: "Years of thought and preparation were thrown away by Sir Sam Hughes, who took hold of mobilization himself. . . . The Military Districts were not consulted and in fact were ignored. They had no knowledge of the military movements that were taking place. . . . The first few days in camp was chaos. Bodies of men arrived before arrangements were made to receive them. . . . There was as yet no Divisional Staff, nor was one appointed until embarkation was in progress. . . ." "Military Policy of Canada, 1905–1924, and Suggestions for the Future," *Canadian Defence Quarterly*, vol. I, no. 4, July 1924, pp. 27–8.

This clarification evidently took the Secretary of State for War somewhat by surprise. "I made two assumptions," Lord Derby explained after Mackenzie King had spoken, "and I appeal on two assumptions which I hope are not ill-founded. First of all, that, if any part of the Empire, wherever it is, is attacked, the whole Empire will rally to the support of the part so attacked. Secondly, that it will rally to the fullest extent of its powers. . . ." The Canadian Prime Minister then proceeded to make clear that neither of these War Office assumptions was warranted:

> So much depends on what is meant by saying that—if the Empire is attacked at any particular point. My mind goes back to the situation as it was a year ago at the time when there was a certain difficulty with the Turks. If that had resulted in actual hostilities, I cannot say at the moment what the Canadian Parliament would or would not have ultimately done; but I would say this, I think there is very grave doubt whether the Parliament of Canada would at that particular time, with the information it had on that question, have undertaken to supply troops, at any rate at the beginning of the War. It is quite conceivable that trouble beginning with Turkey might have come in course of time to assume proportions where Christendom itself was in danger—a Moslem-Christian conflict—in that event there is scarcely doubt that Canada would have felt a certain responsibility to the Empire as a whole. I cite this because I think similar cases may arise, and I think it would only convey a sense of false security if one were to assume that in any situation which came about the merits of the emergency would not be looked into and examined from the point of view of the direct interest and responsibility of the Dominion, and the extent of its participation, if any, determined thereby. . . .[56]

Derby tried again. "May I," he asked, "put it this way? If the actual invasion of any portion of the British Empire was threatened by a foreign nation, all parts of the Empire would wish to come to the rescue. . . ." Mackenzie King responded: ". . . having regard to the existing circumstances."[57]

Those to whom the unfolding of Mackenzie King's cautious revolution came as an unpalatable surprise could no longer with any realism cling to the fiction of automatic dominion participation in Britain's wars. They might, however, still suppose that occasions might arise when a Canadian Government would wish to participate in minor imperial crises. But what the Prime Minister of Canada was attempting to convey to his largely unsympathetic audience at the Imperial Conference was that minor imperial crises had ceased to be *casus belli* for any government of which he happened to be the head. That the imperial authorities were slow to grasp what was for them so hard a political fact is not particularly remarkable. What is more remarkable is that several years were to pass before Mackenzie King's own military advisers understood what lay in the mind of their political chief. And that is not to say they liked it.

As good an illustration as any of the diverging political conceptions of the Canadian Government, on the one hand, and the Canadian military on the other, is provided by a memorandum prepared by the Chief of Staff, Department of National Defence, in October 1926, as part of its preparation for the forthcoming Imperial Conference of that year:

> 1. Policy in order to be carried through to its logical conclusion must have behind it Force. To obtain the best results it is desirable to have a truly Imperial service. It does not appear that the autonomy of any Dominion would be in any way affected by making complete arrangements for the organization, the training and the equipping of a truly Imperial army. Thus it would be preferable that Quotas to be supplied by each part of the Empire should be laid down for the different hypothetical situations and that each Government in the Empire should then pursue its policy of organizing and training the forces. Whether the forces are to be committed to War would depend entirely upon the Government concerned, so there would be no surrender of autonomy by any of the self-governing Dominions.
>
> 2. The policy of mutual assistance throughout the Empire has been recognised for many years. The fighting organization has been made uniform throughout the Empire.
>
> 3. We have had no clear statement of military policy since 1905. Certain policies and conclusions arrived at between 1914 and 1918 were effective only for the War. It is desirable that the Canadian Government should decide on the size of the military force it is prepared to maintain in peace, which for sound military reasons should be of sufficient size to form a nucleus to absorb, command, organise, train and put in the field the man power of this country.
>
> 4. The respective staffs should study certain definite problems and work out tentative arrangements for the mobilization and despatch of certain forces, so that plans might be ready when the emergency arises. If the emergency arose the Government would then decide whether it would despatch the particular force in question. If they decided on the despatch of the force they would do so with the knowledge that immediate effect could be given to its decision, and that its troops would intervene in a more useful and effective manner than if arrangements were left to be improvised at the last moment.
>
> 5. Once a clear defence policy has been enunciated and the quotas of the three services to be provided by the different portions of the Empire in an emergency have been decided, there will be sufficient data on which to base a scheme for the provision of war material and other requirements, each of which will require consideration. . . .[58]

Soon after preparing this document, General MacBrien instructed the Director of Military Operations and Intelligence to give top priority to the preparation of a mobilization scheme "for a force intended for expeditionary purposes commencing with one Division plus one Army co-operation Squadron, R.C.A.F. The scheme should provide for the sending of four to six such Divisions." Colonel Brown's directive concluded with the observation that "your experience in your present appointment will enable you to much better carry out this work than your successor."[59] That was flattering, but at this juncture assistance was more important to the D.M.O. & I. than flattery. "Much has been done," Colonel Brown minuted on General MacBrien's instruction, "but any one of the above [tasks] will require further considerable work and reflection. . . ."[60] To General MacBrien he wrote on 15 October:

> The Directorate has been undermanned ever since it was re-created in December 1920. I have hesitated in asking for extra help for two reasons—the first was that the votes for militia purposes have been so small since the war that it did not appear to me politic to ask for further expenditures for the head when the body was so attenuated; the second reason was that the matter of military policy has apparently not been given the consideration that the General Staff think necessary and therefore many things have been held in abeyance for more influential and sympathetic days.

Those days, he felt, had at last arrived: "The present Imperial Conference, the appointment of the present Hon. Minister of National Defence, [*] and the memorandum of the Chief of Staff [quoted above] . . . indicate that a period of greater activity is now upon us." Those in charge of other directorates, Colonel Brown noted, had asked for, and received, additional assistance: "My request should be thoroughly considered along with the others."[61] General MacBrien concurred; but the new Minister, sensitive to public criticism that his department had too many brass hats already, thought it best to wait a while. "I understand," Colonel Brown wrote hopefully in May 1927, "that the Hon. the Minister's objection was only of a temporary nature. I am fully of the opinion that if the important work of Military Operations and Operational Intelligence is to be fully attended to that there should be an Assistant Director of Military Operations."[62] Once again General MacBrien sup-

*Col. J. L. Ralston. "It is safe to say," commented the *Canadian Defence Quarterly*, "that no appointment in the present Government has been hailed with more general satisfaction than that of Colonel the Honourable James Layton Ralston, C.M.G., D.S.O., K.C., LL.D., M.P., as Minister of National Defence. The appointment had some unusual features about it for it was not the Minister who sought the office but the office that sought him. . . . The confidence in Colonel Ralston almost universally expressed from the Atlantic to the Pacific, regardless of political affiliations, is a fine tribute to the worth of the man and is of good augury for the success of his Administration." *Canadian Defence Quarterly*, vol. IV, no. 2, Jan. 1927, p. 129.

ported his officer's request—"in my opinion," he wrote to Ralston on May 10, "if the various defence schemes and completion of the organization for defence are to be gone on with an Assistant Director of Military Operations is needed"—and this time with success. By the summer of 1927 the personnel of the Directorate of Military Operations and Intelligence had been doubled—to two officers. But for most of his final year in the post, Colonel Brown laboured on alone.

One of the officers closely involved in the planning of the Expeditionary Force was, fifteen year later, to assume command of it. In a memorandum of 25 October 1926, Brig.-General A. G. L. McNaughton stated for the benefit of the D.M.O. & I. the assumptions which the General Staff had agreed should form the basis of Defence Scheme No. 3:

In order to simplify arrangements in connection with the transportation, accommodation and initial tactical employment of a Canadian Expeditionary Force operating as part of an Imperial Army, it has been accepted that our contingent will be mobilized in accordance with the Britannic War Establishments. It has also been accepted that once our Force is in the field, Canada shall have the right to modify the establishments of her units in the light of experience and of any special conditions pertaining to reinforcements, etc., as her military authorities and Government may see fit.[63]

The first results of these efforts took shape early in 1927, stimulated by anti-British demonstrations in China which the General Staff believed might conceivably require the despatch of a Canadian force to the Far East. A memorandum of 26 January distinguished between the two contingencies which might occur:

(*a*) the emergency as it appears at present, which requires a force of only sufficient size to protect British interests in China. On account of Canadian nationals residing in China, on account of the increasing trade developments with the Far East and because of Canada's general interest in the Pacific Ocean, it may be desirable for the Canadian Government to send a small co-operating force. This force might consist of anything from an Infantry battalion to a Brigade Group.

(*b*) The conflagration in China might develop to such a great and threatening degree, possibly supported by Russia, that a much larger military effort would have to be made by the British Empire, and Canada might be called upon to supply an infantry division with, or without, mounted troops in addition. . . .[64]

Plans were developed in some detail for mobilizing the force required for the lesser of these two contingencies, and a draft scheme eventually reached ministerial (although almost certainly not Cabinet) levels. On 8 February the Chief of Staff reported to the D.M.O. & I. that it had "been handed to the Hon. the Minister of National Defence. This was discussed with him in some detail and he approves of it in principle, therefore work should proceed on the lines of the scheme submitted. Referring specifically to the Far East," General MacBrien added, "should it become necessary to despatch a Canadian force to operate there, it would be necessary to include pack rather than wheel transport."[65]

With the departure of J. Sutherland Brown from the Directorate of Military Operations and Intelligence, the task of completing Defence Scheme No. 3 passed to his successor, Colonel H. H. Matthews. In January 1930, Colonel Matthews produced the following progress report for the new Chief of the General Staff, General McNaughton:

> Early in 1927 the C. of S., General MacBrien, instructed the D.M.O. & I., Colonel J. S. Brown, to prepare plans for the mobilization of an expeditionary force. . . .
>
> The general idea of the scheme, known as Defence Scheme No. 3, was approved in principle by the C. of S. prior to his retirement in June 1927. Certain details, however, remained to be worked out, and the scheme was still unfinished when handed over to me by Colonel Brown in December 1927.
>
> In 1928, General Thacker personally examined the scheme, and by his direction some modifications to the original policy and numerous amendments were made to the text, and the plans were extended to provide for a force consisting of—
>
> 1 Corps of 2 Divisions
>
> 1 Cavalry Division with proportion of L. of C. [Lines of Communication]
>
> Corps and Army Troops, depots, etc., all based on organization and establishments laid down for B.E.F.
>
> But there still remained certain details to be completed . . .
>
> During 1929 the text and form of the Scheme was, at my direction, revised . . . but no changes were made to the policy as approved by General Thacker, nor was any attempt made to work out the unfinished details.
>
> The completion of the work could be conveniently carried out during the next two or three months, but before it is put in hand you may possibly wish to change, or add to, the premises on which the scheme is now based. . . .[66]

General McNaughton authorized Colonel Matthews to proceed to complete the scheme. Working closely with his new assistant, Lt.-Col. H. D. G. Crerar, the D.M.O. & I. had it ready within a year. On 11 January 1932, the Chief of the General Staff placed the final version before the Minister of National Defence in the Conservative Government. "Defence Scheme No. 3," he wrote, ". . . deals with the organization, mobilization and despatch of a Canadian Expeditionary Force to a trans-oceanic theatre of war. This Defence Scheme has been under consideration since 1927. It has been actively revised during the last year . . . and has been very confidentially examined by District Officers Commanding. . . . As now submitted, the scheme is in its final form."[67] It was approved by the Minister, D. M. Sutherland, on 20 January 1932.

Soon after the approval of Defence Scheme No. 3, work was begun on a document called Defence Scheme No. 4. "This Defence Scheme," its author noted in a provisional draft,

> deals with the military action which is required following a decision by the Canadian Government to despatch a Canadian Contingent for the purpose of taking part in a Minor Empire Crisis. It visualizes a situation in which His Majesty the King, on the advice of his Ministers, has declared that a state of war exists, or is imminent, between the British Empire and some minor State, or combination of minor States—or that a condition of rebellion or revolution, menacing the existence of the Empire as a whole, has broken out within its confines—that the area as a whole lies outside the North American continent, and that His Majesty's Government in Canada has decided to organize and despatch overseas a Canadian Contingent to co-operate with other Empire forces in suppressing this external or internal threat. . . .[68]

Defence Scheme No. 4 never got beyond the draft stage; it may be because the senior military authorities came to understand that the contingency for which it was preparing was not much less remote than that envisaged in the old Defence Scheme No. 1. (Defence Scheme No. 2, dealing with the eventuality of a war against Japan, was mainly developed during the later 1930's.)

EDUCATING OFFICERS

The military profession, like other professions, considers itself responsible for, and jealously retains control over, the education of its members.

Responsibility and control are most directly achieved in educational institutions operated by the military establishment. The leading institution of this kind in Canada, during the years between the two world wars, was the Royal Military College of Canada.* R.M.C. had been founded

*Until 1922, the Royal Canadian Navy had its own educational institution in the Royal Naval College of Canada, authorized by the Naval Service Act, 1910, "for the purpose of imparting a complete education in all branches of naval science, tactics and strategy," and established at Halifax in January of that year. When the buildings were severely damaged by the Halifax Explosion in 1917, the College was removed to Esquimalt. The curriculum was narrowly technical in its nature—Stephen Leacock referred derisively to "a Canadian naval college for instruction in Canadian naval tactics"—and its plant and operation ramshackle and improvised. In 1922, faced by the necessity of reducing expenditure, the Naval Staff unhesitatingly recommended that it be closed; and it was. "Of the

in 1875 "for the purpose of imparting a complete education in all branches of military tactics, engineering, fortification, and general scientific knowledge in subjects connected with, and necessary to, a thorough knowledge of the military profession, and for qualifying officers for command and staff appointments."[69] For its operations the Department of Militia and Defence (after 1922, the Department of National Defence) was responsible, and to its minister (president of the College) the commandant submitted his annual report. The commandant himself was a senior officer of the General Staff, usually in the sunset of his career. Close supervision over College administration and policy was exercised by a Board of Visitors, consisting of six or seven military dignitaries (including the Chief of the General Staff) and three or four prominent civilians; its chairman in 1920 was Sir Robert Falconer, President of the University of Toronto, in 1921, General Sir Arthur Currie, Principal of McGill University.

Cadets qualifying for admission to the College received four years of education and training, partly at government expense; upon graduation they were encouraged, though not obliged, to take up careers as commissioned officers in the permanent force as opportunity allowed. During the Great War the duration of the course had been cut back to three years; this, it was generally admitted, had not been successful, and in 1919 the Government reinstated the four-year course, as well as authorizing an increase in the number of places from about 150 to 300. R.M.C. graduates dominated the military establishment, contributing (as of 1920) no fewer than two lieutenant-generals, fifteen major-generals and twenty-six brigadier-generals. While not all of these continued on the strength of the permanent force after the Armistice, the influence of the College justified the claim of its Commandant in 1921 that it was "the corner-stone of the Canadian Militia."[70]

What was taught there, and how, thus became of crucial importance to the quality of the officer corps. From the outset the curriculum became the object of anxious scrutiny by those who, on the one hand, favoured a more rigidly specialized approach centring on recognized "military" subjects, and those who, on the other, favoured a general education in which the humanities and what were coming to be known as the social sciences would find their proper place. The generalist philosophy triumphed, not only because of the fact that in peacetime the majority of graduates entered civilian life, but also because it was conceded that the modern military officer ought to know more about

services," it has been written, "the Navy displays the least respect for intellectuals." Morris Janowitz, *The Professional Soldier* (Glencoe, Ill., 1960), p. 431.

the world than the techniques of bridge-building, map-reading and the care of men and horses. "The youth of Canada in attendance here," the Director of Studies reported in 1921,

> are of that age when they should have that education which will make of them first, good citizens, for a good soldier should be first and foremost a good citizen. The intelligence with which he is endowed should be developed as far as possible by keeping its possessor busy at the mental gymnastics best suited for the needs of his military vocation. He should be taught to read intelligently and write and speak coherently. He should be taught to reason logically and observe accurately. He should assemble his facts gained and deduce the general principles to which they lead. . . .[71]

In November 1920 the commandant of the College visited the United States Military Academy at West Point. "It was most interesting to learn of their systems of academic work," he reported, perhaps a trifle ungraciously for a guest, "although on the whole it is considered to be too rigid and inelastic."[72]

The quality of instruction left something to be desired. The milieu of the military academy was more likely to attract those interested in an early and substantial pension than in the free play of the mind. In 1920 the Commandant recommended that all members of the instructional staff not previously in the Service be given a commission on appointment. "The difficulties," he urged, "are not insurmountable, and further more [the proposal would] materially assist in maintaining the high standard of discipline at the College and will do away with the inconsistency of Civilian Professors receiving military salutes and being restricted in the giving of punishment and enforcing of discipline. It is only natural that a Gentleman Cadet at the College should have a higher respect for his superior if he is an officer in uniform who can instanter give certain military punishments rather than a gentleman in civilian clothes whom he addresses as 'Mr.' and looks upon merely as a School-teacher."[73] The proposal was not accepted; even so, as late as ten years afterwards, relations between staff and students were not exactly those of a community of scholars. "It might be mentioned in passing," the Professor of English wrote disparagingly in 1931, "that the odd student who does find time to form his own opinions on any subjects, and who has the temerity to try to express them in class, usually becomes an object of suspicion ('that lad's a bit of a Bolshie') not only to his classmates but, *mirabile dictu*, even to some of his teachers. . . ."[74] Matters were not helped by an acute shortage throughout the country of really qualified academic personnel. It was one thing for the Director of Studies to proclaim that "the time is past . . . when the Gentleman Cadets will be taught by members of the staff here whose scientific accomplishments are not up to the standards of first-class all-round educationalists";[75] it was another to find and keep them. During 1920 it was found necessary to make the fullest use of all hands without too much regard to their training: "Professor Bridger, Associate Professor of English, helped in Elementary Mathematics; Mr. Gelley, Instructor in English, lent a hand in the Department of French; Mr. Twiss, Instructor in Mathematics, gave very valuable services in the Laboratory work of the Department of Physics; Captain Gammans, Instructor in Artillery, helped out in the Department of Mathematics and that of French. In this way," the Director of Studies concluded optimistically, "the greatest good to the Gentleman Cadets was secured by the co-operation of the Staff in their educational effort."[76]

II

Once entering upon their military careers, officers of the permanent force had only limited opportunity for formal education. It consisted entirely in being posted to one or other of the British staff colleges—the Senior Officers School at Sheerness, the Staff College at Camberley, perhaps the Staff College at Quetta, India. (It was not until after the Second World War that comparable institutions were established for the Canadian services in the Dominion.) In 1928, four officers, of the rank of Captain or Major, were on course at Camberley, two at Quetta, one at Sheerness. A few very senior officers might attend the Imperial Defence College in London. Such a posting was as sure a sign as any of eventual high command, and was therefore much sought after and gratefully received; for those temperamentally suited to its curious amalgam of military and academic life it was a magnificent opportunity, as one of its Canadian graduates has dutifully recorded:

> . . . I am at a loss for words to describe the good fortune of those who are selected to attend the Imperial Defence College. Here I was, already in my forty-seventh year, once more relieved of all duty, in the company of quite senior sailors, soldiers, airmen and civil servants, enjoying the rare privilege of studying the strategy, as well as the wider aspects of defence, of the British Commonwealth and Empire. This was done by taking up a number of hypothetical wars that directed our minds to every continent and to every ocean. To assist us in the consideration of these problems we were addressed by members of the Government, ambassadors and Service attachés home on leave, the British chiefs of staff, senior civil servants, and not least,

heads of big corporations many of whose interests were pretty well world wide. In these studies I was much struck by the attention paid to the economic side of warfare, and by the remarkable knowledge possessed by British experts of the economies of our potential enemies. War, in our day, had considerably overrun the comparatively narrow province of the professional sailor, soldier or airman.[77]

A less formal method of broadening the horizons of Canadian officers than enrolment in British staff colleges—but no less educational for its informality—was that of attachment (or, as would now be said, secondment) to the British War Office. This practice, which had been begun in 1910 but lapsed in 1914, was revived in 1925, when Major H. D. G. Crerar began a tour of duty in the Directorate of Military Operations. In 1931, Major Maurice Pope was assigned to what had become known as "the Canadian chair" in a section of the Directorate of Staff Duties, which "for the greater part of the Long Armistice was judged to be the most appropriate posting for the Canadian interchange officer."[78] Of this experience General Pope (as he became) wrote later:

My tour at the War Office was to me quite as valuable as another Staff College course. The British colonial empire is extensive and a study of the problems besetting its Army brings one pretty well to every part of the world. The Directorate of Staff Duties had an interest in certain aspects of the security of defended ports abroad, of distant oilfields, and of protectorates. At the least, this interest taught me much in the way of strategy, and also of geography. I had occasion to think back to my days in S.D. 2 when, in 1941, we sent our troops to Hong Kong.[79]

The pattern of in-service training available to the fortunate few among the small Canadian military establishment of the 1920's and 1930's was designed to foster a sense of imperial solidarity among the officers of the parent country and the dominions. There is little doubt that it had the desired effect. "The war establishments of our units," General Pope has recalled, "and the composition of our formations were precisely those of the British Regular Army. All our manuals were British and so was our tactical training. Practically all our equipment had been obtained in the United Kingdom. . . . To qualify for higher rank our permanent force officers were required to sit for examinations set and marked by the War Office. . . . Our army was indeed British through and through with only minor differences imposed on us by purely local conditions."[80]

To most Canadian nationalists, so slavish an imitation of British military traditions and military practice savoured of an unwholesome colonial mentality; it undoubtedly added to the militia's difficulties in gaining and retaining public support for its activities. To the more militant nationalists, there was something even sinister in the intimacy of liaison between the Woods Building and Whitehall. "The close relations existing between our Department of National Defence and the equivalent military and naval departments in England," commented a published report of a study group of the Canadian Institute of International Affairs in 1934,

> were looked upon as highly suggestive of some sort of understanding [that in the event of war between the United Kingdom and a foreign power, Canada would allow Britain the use of certain ports and military stations]. . . . It was noted how members of the Canadian permanent forces are sent regularly to England for training, and how Canadian army regulations and equipment are coordinated with those of the British army. At critical moments on the eve of war the advice of the military authorities is apt to become only too influential, and in Canada this advice would be imperialist in its sympathies.[81]

This insinuation, whatever grain of truth it may have contained, was bitterly resented and emphatically rejected by the General Staff at Ottawa. Lieutenant-Colonel Kenneth Stuart wrote an indignant rebuttal to the author of the report:

> I can say definitely that no contractual military understanding exists between the Department of National Defence and the War Office, Admiralty or Air Ministry. The inference that such an understanding is suggested by the attachment of our officers in England is a false one. The main purpose of attaching officers in England is to give them a type of training which facilities in Canada do not admit of giving. The fact that we use similar training manuals, organization, etc., is a direct result of the acceptance of the principle of mutual support by successive Imperial Conferences as one of the principles governing the common defence of the Empire. I know of no soldier who regards this principle as other than a form of moral obligation, to be implemented or otherwise solely at the discretion of the Canadian Government. The final observation that military advice would be imperialist in its sympathies is a sweeping statement, and like all half-truths is most misleading. It completely ignores the fact that, though sentiment in Canada may be imperialist in character, there is a large and fast growing body of opinion within the Services whose views, though perhaps influenced by sentiment, will be governed by reason, and whose advice, if called for, will be motivated primarily not by Imperial but by Canadian requirements . . .[82]

But neither side really heard, much less understood, the other. The dialogue of the deaf continued throughout the 1930's until the coming of the Second World War put an end to it.

III

Canadian officers of the 1920's and 1930's did not have to attend staff colleges or be seconded to the War Office to gain knowledge of what their colleagues in other imperial services were thinking and doing. They were the beneficiaries of strategic intelligence as comprehensive in its coverage as any available to anyone on their side of the Atlantic Ocean. Under authority of a recommendation of the Imperial Defence Conference of 1909, a direct channel for interchanging military information was opened between the Chief of the Imperial General Staff and the Chiefs of the General Staffs or Commanders-in-Chief of the armies of the self-governing dominions and colonies. Through it there passed what was at first no more than a trickle but which soon became a torrent of documents, flowing out from London. By the 1920's, the General Staff at Ottawa were the recipients of what was for them an *embarras de richesses*. From the War Office came, first and foremost, the quarterly liaison letter from the Chief of the Imperial General Staff; a special monthly secret intelligence summary (despatched personally to the Chief of the General Staff); the monthly confidential "blue" intelligence summary; various reports and memoranda, as and when issued, dealing with technical matters and training; and a covey of secret documents from the Committee of Imperial Defence. From Army Headquarters in India were received a weekly secret intelligence summary; a quarterly review of important military events; and special secret intelligence letters issued at intervals varying from three to six months. In addition, the General Staff received monthly secret intelligence summaries from the British South China Command, based at Hong Kong, and the Malaya Command, based at Singapore; copies of the quarterly liaison letters sent to the War Office by the Chiefs of the General Staff in Australia, New Zealand and South Africa; and copies of Admiralty and Air Ministry intelligence documents sent to the naval and air intelligence officers at Ottawa. In return for all this, there went out from the military at Ottawa the quarterly liaison letter of the Chief of the General Staff to the Chief of the Imperial General Staff, together with certain semi-official liaison correspondence from the Director of Military Intelligence and Operations to his counterpart at the War Office and the British military attachés at Washington and Tokyo. "Neither in scope nor in value," General McNaughton conceded in 1929, "does this compare with what we receive in exchange."[83]

Although it seems unlikely that anyone outside the General Staff had any precise notion of the extent and variety of incoming intelligence of which it was custodian, the fact that a direct channel between it and the imperial military existed was generally known and in some quarters criticized. The same Canadian Institute of International Affairs study group whose report had deplored interchange of officers drew unfavourable attention to the intelligence exchanges. "The Department of National Defence at Ottawa," it noted in 1934, "is the only Canadian government department which has the right to communicate direct with its opposite number in London, without having to use the channel of the Department of External Affairs," a fact which, the Report claimed, "evoked considerable criticism" among the members of the study group. "Many of the members were of the opinion that, while direct communication on routine matters might be desirable, all communications involving defence policy should pass through the hands of the Department of External Affairs so that the civil authorities should be kept fully informed of all preparations and understandings."[84] (This procedure was put into effect in 1937, on the orders of the Prime Minister.)

The clear implication of the criticism was that the military, through its privileged channels of communication, sought to hoard and even to conceal intelligence from the civilian branches of government. There was no truth in this. In fact, soon after becoming Chief of the General Staff, General McNaughton expressed his concern lest the immense repository of intelligence at its disposal be insufficiently exploited, and proposed that it be shared among other government departments. "Most of the incoming information," he wrote to the Minister, "stops in this Department and while it is of great interest to our officers I do not think that we as a country are getting all the benefit out of it that we should. In particular, I think that much of it would be of use to the Department of External Affairs, and possibly also to the Commercial Intelligence Section of the Department of Trade and Commerce. I would like to have your authority to discuss the matter with Dr. Skelton and Mr. O'Hara with a view to seeing in what way we could make our information of use to them."[85] Whether the Department of External Affairs accepted and made use of the offer is not known, but it is evident that its later suspicion that the military was attempting to usurp its function as the centre of the national intelligence community was unjustified. In 1936, on the initiative of the General Staff, the intelligence reports received from the British attachés at Washington were sent out henceforth through the Canadian Legation there. This procedure, Colonel Crerar observed in requesting it of the Military Attaché at the British Embassy, "serves to torpedo the misconception, which is prevalent in certain official circles in this country, that our service personnel, in the process of keeping in technical touch with yours, are perhaps inclined to leave our Canadian diplomatic organization in the dark concerning matters on which the latter should be informed. This is very definitely a misconception—but any procedure which gives possible grounds for suspicion we would be wise to amend."[86]

A more cogent criticism of the intelligence system at the disposal of the General Staff would have been that it relied too exclusively upon imperial sources and too little upon its own. That, however, was not the fault of the military. In 1927, the Minister of National Defence took up with the Prime Minister the question of creating Canadian military attachés for the Dominion's legation at Washington and the High Commissioner's office in London. The newly appointed Canadian Minister to the United States, Mr. Vincent Massey, had strongly urged the appointment of a military attaché for the Legation, "to keep us advised as to the progress which was being made in that country in aviation and military matters," and to handle the already considerable volume of military correspondence. The War Office had indicated informally that it would welcome the appointment of a Canadian service officer in London, following the precedent already set by Australia.[87] But Mackenzie King and his Cabinet colleagues were, as King wrote to Ralston, unanimously opposed to the project.[88] In 1928, while attending the Imperial Defence College, Brigadier-General A. G. L. McNaughton was given a desk in the offices of the High Commission, but no duties to go with it. An officer of the R.C.A.F. served at the Air Ministry during the 1920's and early 1930's. In 1937, Colonel G. P. Loggie was assigned to Canada House as ordnance representative of the Department of National Defence. But it was not until February 1940, when Air Commodore W. R. Kenny took up his duties at the Legation in Washington, that Canada acquired a military attaché known formally as such.

IV

Of the fewer than four hundred officers of the permanent force, only a score or so had access to the store-house of information accumulating in the files of the General Staff. The rest, so far as their education was concerned, were on their own. They were exhorted by their commanders to improve their minds by independent reading and study:

It is realized that you have a fair amount of time on your hands. Is it employed in working up your efficiency, or is it wasted in Bridge, Mah-Jong or Poker? Do you read? . . . It is taken for granted, naturally, that Commanding Officers are aware that all text books which apply to the branch of the service they command, have been read, re-read and digested. It is unsatisfactory to think that many officers prepare for examinations, and often then do no reading whatever of military books until they are required to qualify for further promotion . . . No one is looking for geniuses [!], but all expect a good showing both in a military and intellectual way from men who choose soldiering as their profession. . . . [89]

Opportunities must be created to enable young officers of the Permanent and Non-Permanent Militia of Canada to develop their natural qualities, for no matter how great an asset their natural qualifications may be, further training is essential. Any officer interested can avail himself of the opportunities that exist in all large cities to study. Books on travel, works in geography and modern history will reveal the characteristics of races and will enable the student to gain most valuable information about foreign peoples. Articles in leading British and American magazines are invaluable, for they enable one to keep up to date on all phases of British and foreign politics. Too much attention cannot be paid to current events by the young officer who aspires to hold an appointment upon the Intelligence Branch of the Staff when the next war breaks out. . . .[90]

An officer cannot get very far nowadays unless he keeps abreast of the times, not only in military subjects but in world events generally. . . . It is suggested that *The Army Quarterly* and the *Journal of the Royal United Services Institution* should be perused by every officer. For general information the weekly edition of *The Times* is suggested, as few officers will find time to delve through the dailies. There are, unfortunately, few if any Canadian publications which give all the news of the world and it is practically necessary to rely on the English ones. This is perhaps a good thing as they are written in the best of English. . . .[91]

For the professional officer bent on self-improvement and promotion, there was much to read. The military literature was extensive; it was also forbidding, much of it falling into the category of volumes which, once put down, are not easily picked up again: "the mass of military writings," a present-day authority has described it, "poured out by peacetime officers in the Western world, bored by their routine commands, stultified by the hierarchy, condemned to live out their unheroic lives in a thousand wretched provincial garrison towns. One sees in the mind's eye that ocean of uninspired writing, laced with quotations from Clausewitz, Caesar, Napoleon, . . . the pages yellowed and brittle at the edges."[92]

A Canadian contribution to this literature began in 1923 when officers, and anyone else interested, acquired their own journal of military affairs. This was the *Canadian Defence Quarterly* (*C.D.Q.*). It was not the first Canadian military journal by any means. The *Canadian Volunteer Review* dated back to the founding of the voluntary militia system in the 1850's, developed into the *Canadian Militia Gazette*, which in turn became the *Canadian Naval and Military Gazette*. The *Canadian Naval and Military Gazette* served, when the *C.D.Q.* began publication, mainly as a vehicle for service news and occasionally for service complaints. The R.C.N. had a monthly *Naval News Letter*, distributed in mimeographed form to the Senior Naval Officer at Halifax and Esquimalt, all R.C.N. officers serving abroad, all Canadian naval ships and establishments and the editor of the unofficial journal *The Sailor*. It was edited by the Naval Secretary, who explained its aim as being "to keep all officers in as close touch as possible with the work carried out by the R.C.N. and R.C.N.V.R. on both coasts, and also that officers serving with the Imperial Navy may be able to keep in touch with R.C.N. matters in Canada." But despite an appeal to naval officers to contribute articles dealing with their "experiences and interesting events," the *Naval News Letter* did not achieve more than the modest promise of its title. It seems to have expired in the early 1930s, probably a victim to the economy measures of those years. The editor of the *C.D.Q.* thus did not exaggerate when, looking back on its first decade of publication, he remarked that " a service journal which would try to reflect military thought, examine critically the direction of military development, and study in some degree the trend of world movements, had not been seen in Canada" before it.[93]

Credit for its creation was given to Major-General J. H. MacBrien, the Chief of Staff when it first appeared. General MacBrien, the editor affirmed, had been "optimistic enough to believe that there was a field in Canada for a . . . service journal produced by Canadians, and, even more optimistically, he held that there existed a school of military thought in the Dominion that was capable of giving such a journal a distinctive character."[94] In 1923 a committee consisting of representatives from the Cavalry, the Infantry and the Artillery Associations, a fourth from the Air Force and a fifth from the Department of National Defence, assumed responsibility for producing a quarterly service magazine. There was no government grant to help it on its way, and no one connected with it (except its printer) was paid for his services. The costs were borne by the three founding Associations, which agreed to take a quota of copies for their members, and it was hoped that advertising and new subscribers would fend off too large a deficit.

The first issue appeared in October 1923. It was not much to look at, and there was not much to read. Six articles were reprinted, not always by permission, from other service periodicals; there were a few topical notes about Artillery activities and Camp Schools of Instruction. Only one original piece redeemed the issue, an unsigned article on "Air Policy" (the work of J. A. Wilson, the Secretary of the Air Board). The second number, out in January 1924, was no great improvement. Disheartened, the committee decided upon dissolution, but Colonel H. H. Matthews, the General Staff officer who had been on the founding committee in 1923, urged another try. Under his editorship, the size of the *C.D.Q.* increased and its quality steadily improved. The third issue (April 1924) contained an editorial section, which was to become the *C.D.Q.*'s regular and, in many ways, most interesting feature. In later years it conducted *tours d'horizon* with magisterial authority; its début was more diffident:

> Perhaps it would be well to take our readers in our confidence and outline briefly some of the hopes and fears which beset the path towards the goal of our ambition, viz., to produce, quarterly, a Service Journal which will not only be a credit to the Canadian Defence Forces but will also compare favourably with the Naval, Military and Air Service Magazines published in Great Britain and various Foreign Countries. . . .
>
> The Editorial and Managing Committee is anxious . . . to obtain original articles of general or special interest to the Naval, Military and Air Forces, and especially would appreciate stories of incidents of the Great War connected with units of the Canadian Expeditionary Forces; articles dealing with questions of strategical importance to the Empire; military and political geography; tactics and training; discussions on problems which confront the Defence Forces to-day, such as Tanks . . .; anti-aircraft Defence; the necessity for the maintenance of an efficient Air Force; Civil Aviation . . .; etc.
>
> . . . under existing circumstances it would appear to be necessary to let an Editorial and Managing Committee at National Defence Headquarters co-ordinate the work. The chief danger from too direct control of a publication of this nature by Departmental officials is that contributors are not always inclined to be so outspoken as they might be when dealing with present conditions, looking into the future, or deducing lessons from the past. In practice, however, we propose to allow all reasonable scope in the form and presentation of any ideas which may be embodied in articles submitted to us and which we select for publication. Our object is to encourage individual officers to think for themselves and to express their opinions on the many and varied problems which concern the Canadian Defence Forces today.[95]

By 1928, when Colonel Matthews handed over his editorial duties to Lieutenant-Colonel Kenneth Stuart, the *C.D.Q.* had hit its stride and had acquired a distinctive character. Its circulation was as high as 2,000; its contents a *pot-pourri* of serious articles on military affairs reprinted from other journals but to an increasing extent the work of Canadian contributors, battlefield reminiscences, cautionary tales, and adventure stories in the style of *Blackwood's Magazine*. In 1928 appeared the first (and, sad to say, the last) contribution in the French language.* In 1930 the first annual prize essay competition was announced; Major Maurice Pope and Lieutenant C. P. Stacey duly shared the prize.

Between 1928 and 1935 the editorial section was wholly the work of the Editor. Colonel Stuart was far from non-committal in his views, which faithfully reflected the prejudices of his fellow officers as these might be expressed in the mess or in their private correspondence. General disarmament was confidently declared to be at once unlikely and undesirable: "Complete disarmament might even increase the danger of war. Properly controlled armaments would help maintain a balance of power among the nations . . . Anything approaching complete disarmament would be decidedly unsafe at the present stage of the world's development."[96] The League of Nations was treated with contempt: "Not being universal it possesses neither the prestige to initiate the necessary measures nor the power to enforce its decisions." "Any tightening up of the obligations of the Convenant will savour of the 'Super State' idea which is, of course, anathema to the Anglo-Saxon mind."† The imperial ambitions of Japan were sympathetically portrayed: "Any threat to her interests in Manchuria is a threat to her very existence . . .;[97] "Japan is the policeman on duty at Manchuria corner . . . quietly content that once again he has justified his existence, not in the realm of aggressive conquest, but of conquest over those

*Maj. Ernest Legaré, "Le Français dans l'Armée canadienne," *Canadian Defence Quarterly*, January 1930, vol. VII, no. 2, pp. 228–34.

†Similar views were expressed by the Canadian officer at the World Disarmament Conference in Geneva. "My short experience of the L. of N.," wrote Lt.-Col. H. D. G. Crerar in 1932, "leads me to the conviction that we are attempting, as nations, something which we have no where near succeeded at attaining as citizens, or subjects. The theory which assumes that we are prepared to surrender, to an international organization, powers which we do not freely hand over to our several national governments is, to my mind, all wrong. It may appeal to sentiment, or even to intellect, but it can't to common sense. Perhaps I may be too close to the show, but I can't help feeling that it is becoming more like a keg of international dynamite, than a universal solvent. . . .

I don't like the way things are going, or not going, one little bit. Unless the miraculous happens in European political relations, this Conference is going to accentuate the present troubled situation. . . ." To Maj.-Gen. A. G. L. McNaughton, 25 May 1932. McNaughton Papers.

forces which tend to disrupt the peace of the world";[98] "If our sympathy appears to be with Japan, it is not because we do not appreciate the Chinese case, it is because we believe Japan has been treated shamefully by the Council of the League of Nations."[99] Pacifists, isolationists, "collectivists," idealists, were treated with scorn: "The origin and causes of war are so diverse and their ramifications so interwoven into the fabric of society that it is beyond the wit of man to devise an agency capable of ensuring everlasting peace; in other words, war is inevitable;"[100] ". . . the public refuses to study or even to think about war. In fact, any person who is so misguided as to devote any time to the study of war is deemed to be a prospective inmate of the nearest lunatic asylum. . . . As a direct result of this mental inertia, disarmament is looked upon as the panacea for the evils of war. . . . [But] it is the public . . . who make war. . . ."[101] And (a contribution from Captain E. L. M. Burns):

> . . . if a false idea about any subject is not confuted and replaced by a true one, the false idea will prevail in men's minds. For one man who has urged the necessity for national protection, for armies and navies and air forces, and given any reason other than that we have always had protective forces of some kind, a dozen have argued with eloquence and passion that war is a curse; that arms breed war; that all men are brothers and would live in concord if Krupp's, Schneider's and Vickers' plants were burned down; that international disputes could be settled by arbitration and would be so settled if it were not for the existence of guns and battleships; that if we threaten no one, no one will attack us; that the soldier is a murderer in a red coat—a hodge-podge of truisms and plausible fallacies. . . . Of course, war is no nearer to abolition for all the industry and fervour of the pacifists. Their reasoning all rests on false premises. They resolutely refuse to contemplate human nature as it is. . . .[102]

That the fare offered the readers of the *C.D.Q.* was anything but insipid, its editor fully realized; and more than once went out of his way to dissociate its contents from official policy. "We have reason to believe," an editorial in the July 1931 issue remarked, "that the notes which appear in these columns are regarded by some of our readers as a reflection of official or semi-official thought. We wish to disabuse any who harbour such an opinion. The views recorded here have neither an official nor a semi-official significance; they portray, solely, the wanderings of the very unofficial mind of the Editor, and have no connection whatever with Naval, General or Air Staff policy."[103] That was easier said than believed. It was not long before the *C.D.Q.* came under fire, appropriately enough from those who had more than once been exposed to its own withering editorial attack. The report of the study group of the Canadian Institute of International Affairs which, as previously noted, had taken exception to the exchange of officers and information by the Department of National Defence, also singled out for censure its sponsorship of the *C.D.Q.*:

> The Department of National Defence publishes a Defence Quarterly, presumably subsidized by public money, the editorials of which are opposed to the whole idea of the collective system and are of a strongly jingoist character. . . . There was a general feeling that a publication subsidized by the Dominion should not permit the members of the defence forces, who are one branch of the civil Service, to express their personal views on matters of high policy. . . .[104]

The National Secretary of the Institute sent a draft of the report to the Department of National Defence so that any factual inaccuracies might be corrected before publication, and in this form it came before the editor. Colonel Stuart thereupon wrote directly to the author:

> I find that practically every reference to the *Canadian Defence Quarterly* is either incorrect or misleading. . . . The Department does not publish the *Quarterly*. It is published by a Committee of Officers in Ottawa. . . . The majority are officers in the non-permanent active militia and are not connected with the Department of National Defence. The only definite connection between the *Quarterly* and the Department is the annual grant of $400.00 which is about seven percent of the annual cost of production. . . .
>
> The responsibility for the actual production of the publication is delegated by the committee, which meets quarterly, to two regular officers, myself as editor and another who acts as sec.-treasurer. We both have our normal work to do and all work in connection with the *Quarterly* is done after office hours in our own time and in our own homes. . . .
>
> I have written every editorial in the *C.D.Q.* for the past six years and I never have and never will challenge the *idea* of a collective system. It is the applicability of the idea to present conditions that I cannot credit, hence my belief that both the popular conception of the "collective system" and certain aspects of present conditions must be modified before the *idea* can be applied effectively. In this respect the views I have expressed in the *C.D.Q.* differ little from certain of the conclusions in your report.
>
> I refer to the latter part of the quotation with some hesitation as I am not sure of the sense in which the word "jingoist" is used. If it is meant to imply "support of a bellicose policy," then I deny the impeachment and maintain that no such policy has ever been advocated in the editorials of the *C.D.Q.* . . .
>
> . . . If "high policy" refers to that of one's own government then I think there is general agreement that no servant of the government should criticize or even discuss the matter. The *C.D.Q.* has been careful in its observance of this rule. On the other hand, what harm is there in discussing Imperial and Foreign Affairs, provided such discussion does not, either directly or indirectly, embarrass one's own government?

I feel that there is a vital need in Canada today to interest our public in imperial and world affairs. The tendency in Canada, on the part of individuals and small groups, is to blame the government in power for anything and everything which they may not like in respect to our imperial and international relations. You know as well as I do that it is not the government but the ignorance and apathy of the public in such matters that is to blame.

The efforts of the *C.D.Q.* in this educative task are perhaps minute but we have succeeded in making a fairly important cross section of Canadian public opinion think about imperial and international affairs. I refer to some 4,000 officers in the non-permanent militia, extending from coast to coast. Our effort may be a "drop in the bucket," but it is achieving results. My purpose is not to force my own views on any body, it is merely to promote thought within the Canadian defence forces. Experience has taught me that one of the best means of promoting thought is to provoke it, hence the somewhat aggressive style adopted in some of my editorials.

The *C.D.Q.* has been published for twelve years. During that time every number has devoted part of its editorial space to a discussion of imperial and international affairs. Yet the first serious criticism we have ever had, though we have had a lot of bouquets, is that contained in your report. I feel that the criticisms of the Study Group, for the reasons I have stated, are in large measure unjustified. Moreover, I doubt if those who made the criticisms have ever really really read the *C.D.Q.* because, in principle, there is little difference in our conclusions, namely, that before a "collective system" is applicable, both the system and present conditions must be modified. The implication in your report is that the *C.D.Q.* should be muzzled, not because it embarrasses the government, which, so far as I know it has never done, but apparently because some of the views expressed appear to have been in conflict with those held by some members of the Montreal Study Group. . . .[105]

Despite this elaborate justification, the Report in question was published largely unrevised and unrepented. The word "jingoist" was, in the published version, replaced by "militarist." The allegation of departmental control and subsidy was not withdrawn in the light of Colonel Stuart's explanation; indeed, there was added to the indictment the additional charge that the *C.D.Q.* "goes out under government frank."[106] This charge was incorrect; what had led to its being laid was the fact that it was mailed in envelopes of the Department of National Defence marked "O.H.M.S.," but these all bore proper postage paid for out of the journal's revenue.

The publication of the attack on the *C.D.Q.* aroused great concern at Defence Headquarters, and not only there. On 5 November 1934, General McNaughton was called to the telephone by the Prime Minister, and was obliged to explain to him what the matter was all about. He informed R. B. Bennett that the Department was preparing an official criticism of the Report, which the Canadian Institute of International Affairs had undertaken to distribute to its members. McNaughton added that in his view "this draft should be sent to Dr. Skelton, Under Secretary of State for External Affairs, and that further action, if any, should rest on his judgment. . . ."[107] Nothing further seems to have been done, and it may be presumed that Skelton applied to the affair the golden rule of his Department: "Never complain and never explain." It would have been in character.

From 1935 on, as a European war became more and more of a certainty and the inadequacy of Canadian preparations more and more obvious, it became more and more difficult to keep the contents of the *Canadian Defence Quarterly* entirely consonant with the letter and the spirit of government policy. "Our forces are poorly equipped and trained." So began a forthright assessment of "The Defence of Canada" published in 1936.[108] "A day or two ago I read Tommy Burns' article in the July number of the *C.D.Q.*," Maurice Pope wrote to its editor, "and I thought it remarkable that matters have so much improved that you were in a position to approve the publication of such a plain statement. Much water seems to have flowed under the bridge. . . ."[109] But such rejoicing was premature. The publication of "The Defence of Canada," and of at least one other contribution making its appearance in the *Quarterly*, were unfavourably regarded by the Government. When, in November 1936, it was suggested by a committee of the Conference of Defence Associations that the *Quarterly* be used as a vehicle for disseminating the views of the military establishment among members of the "attentive public," the Chief of the General Staff instantly demurred. "Gentlemen," Major General E. C. Ashton informed his audience,

> we are in a dubious position with regard to the Defence Quarterly. During the past year two cases have arisen where articles published in the Defence Quarterly have been questioned. Now the difficulty is this: at the present time that Quarterly is connected very intimately with the Department of National Defence and by a certain section of the public is looked upon as a means of propaganda carried on by the Department of National Defence. I told you that we have had two cases where we have had a little trouble. . . . It is felt that the Quarterly could do its job very much more freely if it was entirely the mouthpiece of the Non-Permanent Active Militia and that is what it should be. The Non-Permanent Active Militia can say what it likes, but at the present time the Minister has to take the responsibility for anything that appears in the Quarterly.
>
> One of these articles was over-looked by Colonel Crerar, unfortunately. We do not allow an article to appear in the Quarterly until it has been passed by the Department and it makes it very awkward and difficult for

the paper to do its job, and it would make it difficult to do the job you are suggesting to do. . . .[110]

The *Canadian Defence Quarterly* continued to be published under the auspices of the Department of National Defence until the outbreak of war, whereupon it expired and was never revived. Canada had no comparable publication until the autumn of 1956, when the *R.C.A.F. Staff College Journal* made an auspicious if belated first appearance.

V

What sort of military mind emerged in Canada as the result of its exposure to these various educative influences?

The concept of the military mind is used more often than it is used precisely. At one time it may refer to its level of intelligence, or competence, or ability; at another, to the distinguishing characteristics of its working; at still another, to the views it characteristically holds, the attitudes by which it is known, the prejudices to which it gives expression.* Little is known about the second of these aspects, and even less about the first. (Enough, it is hoped, has been said already to make further discussion of the third unnecessary.)

Whatever intelligence tests might reveal about the intellectual capacities of the military profession in relation to those of other professions (and whatever intelligence tests may reveal about intelligence), liberal democratic societies commonly believe that the military mind characteristically operates at a lower level of intelligence than, say, the legal mind or the medical mind. Such a belief was (and remains) widely spread among Canadians. (The existence of the belief cannot be proved, any more than the validity of the belief.) Parliamentarians were so prejudiced, and within the bureaucracy, particularly the Department of External Affairs, it became an article of faith. As members of the military establishment were drawn into civilian-dominated committees of policy-formation, and were allowed and encouraged to mingle, at staff colleges and elsewhere, with the non-military élites, prejudice against them diminished, but only in proportion to their acquisition of the civilian point of view. All this, however, is a development of the period after the Second World War.†

*This analysis is employed by Samuel P. Huntington. See his chapter on "The Military Mind" in *The Soldier and the State* (Cambridge, Mass., 1959), pp. 59–79.

†See my *The Art of the Possible: Government and Foreign Policy in Canada* (Toronto, 1961), chapter III, "The Military Establishment."

The working of the military mind, as distinct from its level of competence and the views that it holds, is commonly believed to be characterized by discipline, rigidity, logic, and the scientific method, and only slightly by flexibility, tolerance, intuition and emotion.* It may be that the former were the distinguishing characteristics of the mind of the Canadian military during the 1920's and 1930's; certainly their counterparts in the civilian bureaucracy believed them so. "It is the tendency of the professional soldier," the Minister at Washington wrote to the Under Secretary of State for External Affairs in 1929, "to think in terms of military exigencies with little regard for the intangible forces of public opinion."[111] Against that judgment may be set an evaluation of a member of the Department of External Affairs by a member of the General Staff: "I admire his brain, but his reasoning is cold and his conclusions, on such matters as I know about, always seem to ignore the human factors such as sentiment."[112] As always, generalization is as treacherous as it is necessary.

One characteristic of the military mind in Canada may be mentioned with more confidence. The military establishment was not noted, and indeed is still not noted, for a prevalence of military intellectuals. There were, to be sure, intellectual officers.† Major-General Sir Willoughby Gwatkin, Chief of the General Staff throughout the Great War and Inspector-General of the Canadian Air Force, relaxed by writing Latin poetry and macaronic verse, half Latin, half English, or half English and half French; his fugitive writings included studies in Canadian ornithology and on the traces left in Canada by the Basques, and he was awarded an honorary Doctor of Laws degree by the University of Toronto.[113] Other officers who might be described without inaccuracy and without insult as intellectual soldiers, though less relentlessly academic than the truly exceptional Gwatkin, were A. G. L. McNaughton, H. D. G. Crerar, Maurice Pope, and E. L. M. Burns. All rose to the

*Again the typology is Huntington's. *The Soldier and the State*, pp. 59–60.

†"In describing intellectual pursuits among officers, the intellectual officer can be distinguished from the military intellectual. The intellectual officer is the soldier who brings an intellectual dimension to his job. His intellectual quality is held in check by the needs of the profession. He sees himself primarily as a soldier, and his intellectuality is part of his belief that he is a whole man. The military intellectual is a markedly different type. Although he is a professional soldier, his attachments and identifications are primarily with intellectuals and with intellectual activities. He would have no trouble shifting from military to university life, for his orientations are essentially scholarly. He is generally denied, or unequipped, for the highest command posts, as would be the case with intellectuals in civilian society. His position is essentially advisory, but, in the military setting, the advisory post is institutionalized and accepted." Janowitz, *The Professional Soldier*, p. 431.

highest positions of command; three became lieutenant-generals (McNaughton became full general); and McNaughton, Pope and Burns assumed after their active military service important diplomatic responsibilities.

The military in Canada has thus produced its share of soldier-diplomats and soldier-intellectuals. But it has produced no soldier-strategists. There are no Canadian Douhets or Slessors, no Fullers or Liddell Harts, much less any Canadian Clausewitzes or Mahans. The reasons for this deficiency are complex: they have to do with the unimportance of Canada as a military power, the difficulty of defining a strategic role, the unattractiveness of the military profession for intellectuals and, above all, with the fact that the nation's non-military intellectuals, until perhaps very recently, might be numbered on the fingers of a severely mutilated hand.

PROSELYTIZING THE PUBLIC

The well-being of a peacetime military establishment in a liberal democracy depends ultimately on the public's confidence that its existence is essential to their safety. That attitude is not always automatic. Usually is must be created. Politicians prefer re-election to rejection. And so the military become propagandists in their own cause. To their other missions—maintaining internal order, deterring attack from abroad, educating their leaders—may be added that of proselytizing publics.

At National Defence Headquarters in Ottawa today, public relations is a highly developed craft requiring multitudes of craftsmen. Forty years ago, its techniques were primitive, its personnel non-existent, but the need none the less recognized. "These are days," an article in an early issue of the *Canadian Defence Quarterly* observed,"[114] "in which the soldier needs the public support of every possible citizen, and there are thousands of civilians who are without convictions one way or another on the whole question of defence. The judicious use of news can arouse the sympathetic attention and the interest of that civilian population which is fundamental to the maintenance of any military structure in a democracy." The medium of propaganda was of course the newspaper, and its distributor the newspaperman. Officers were advised to cultivate journalists. "The relationship is in no sense sinister. It is not preyed upon or abused; it is simply a guarantee of accuracy and fair presentation to the public." Moderation was of course essential. "It is not in accordance with the best military traditions to turn soldiers loose into any booster-go-getting publicity campaign, but legitimate news is a healthy stimulus, and the more news of military training, sporting events, promotions, transfers, movements of units or personnel or social affairs, the better for all concerned." "It may be said that the peacetime work of a military unit is not spectacular, but the fact remains that crowds will still turn out 'to see the soldiers,' and there is still the general impression that the army is the most virile of professions. It is this element in the public mind that should be played upon."

Whether this was in fact sound advice is certainly debatable. The mood of the moment was unreceptive to the martial spirit. "Newspapers," declared Agnes Macphail in the House of Commons in 1925, "have glorified the 'gentleman cadet.' This is a disastrous thing. . . . Empire Day is made the occasion for nothing but a strutty, silly, pompous, bombastic performance by military men and those who are backing them. Do you know—possibly the Government does not know—that the common people of Canada laugh heartily . . . they are moved to mirth by the speches and performances they hear and see on such a day as Empire Day. . . ."[115] Agnes Macphail may not have articulated the general will, but, all the same, too much publicity about military affairs was likely at that time to be counter-productive.

The author of "News Value" concluded his advice by commending the public relations activities of airmen. "The Royal Canadian Air Force has made judicious use of publicity and the results are notable. It is the branch that has touched the public imagination and newspapers find Air Force news very acceptable. Statements have been prepared for the local press at the various air stations outlining the work accomplished by the Force during the past twelve months. It is an excellent means of establishing the right sort of relationship between the civilian population and the Force, and does a great deal towards impressing the public with the practical utility of military flying." The ineluctable advantage of the Air Force in its relations with the public was, and remains, the fascination for the ordinary man (and his son) of its equipment, whether Avro Avians or Avro Arrows. "A young fellow . . . sees a machine going through the air," remarked the Minister of National Defence in 1931, "and he wants to be in it . . . in the old days he wanted to be an outlaw."[116] (Thirty years later, the effort expended by the R.C.A.F. upon public relations was thought by a Royal Commission on Government Organization to be distinctly excessive, and the Force was reprimanded on that account.)

The Navy, traditionally the "silent Service," adopted, as might be expected, a less strident approach. Nevertheless, it was by no means indifferent to its proselytizing role. Indeed, this was recognized as crucially important. In 1922, the Royal Canadian Navy had been reduced to what was almost a reserve force, its only sea-going duties being to train the reserves. That less-than-satisfactory status had been accepted by the Navy in preference to a severely curtailed mission afloat precisely because the Director and his senior officers had thought it essential to bring home to the inland publics the significance of sea-power, and the need for Canada to be strong on the oceans as on land and in the air. An effective public relations campaign was thus an essential precondition to the Navy's putting out to sea again.

The obvious technique, employed to good effect by the U.S. Navy, was to take influential friends for a "boat ride."* For the Royal Canadian Navy, however, it was unsatisfactory: when it came right down to it, only the Prime Minister was of sufficient influence to make the effort worth-while; and there was always the risk that he would prove prone to sea-sickness, so rendering the Navy's public relations programme counter-productive.† Moreover, until the early 1930's, the R.C.N. had no boats impressive enough—indeed, sea-worthy enough—to invite very important people to ride in. When *Saguenay* and *Skeena* entered Canadian service in 1931, the R.C.N. for the first time in a decade had ships worth showing off, but lacked funds for any "boat rides" worthy of the name. Still, there could be and there were opportunities for "open house" when the ships came into port.‡

But this was a technique of the 1930's. During the 1920's there was not much more the Navy could do than talk. And talk it did—not haphazardly but as the result of a deliberate campaign. The Director of the Naval Service was its tireless spokesman; he may well have wondered, as did on one occasion Admiral Jellicoe, whether it was to be his fate

*"Perhaps the most popular aspect of the [U.S.N.'s public relations] program was the . . . 'boat-ride.' . . . The industrialists proved no more immune than Congressmen to the allurement of short trips in naval craft; as a public relations device they have few equals. A general, glumly watching a cruiser sail away one day with a load of Congressmen, was heard to say plaintively . . . 'And all we can do is to take them for a walk'!" Robert Greenhalgh Albion and Robert Howe Connery, *Forrestal and the Navy* (New York, 1962), p. 30.

†As the First Lord of the Admiralty discovered in 1923. See below, p. 179.

‡See below, p. 161. The author recalls being invited when a small boy aboard either *Skeena* or *Saguenay* in Tadoussac Harbour, for a celebration the high point of which was throwing, with other children, cream-puffs and even tomatoes at ratings disguised as clowns. He cannot think that this experience led him, ten years later, to become a rating himself.

to "travel up and down, through eternity, along the Canadian Pacific Railway, making speeches at intervals to gentlemen of the Canadian Clubs."[117] A typical luncheon was that held in his honour at the Canadian Club of Quebec City on 22 April 1924. Nicely shaping his argument to the interests of his audience (being mainly composed of the local financial community), Commodore Hose told how useful the Canadian Navy had been to the Royal Bank of Canada. It seemed that the Royal Bank had experienced great difficulty "in a certain foreign capital to get its just claim recognized, despite the efforts of the British Consul stationed there. It so happened that a Squadron of the Canadian Navy was reported to be on the seas in that vicinity. There was no threat made, but . . . the arrival of the Squadron created just enough impression on the officials of the foreign capital to tip the scales in favour of the Royal Bank." He concluded in masterful fashion by declaring that "he had always considered the French to be the finest race of sea-going people of the world."[118]

In 1927 the retiring Naval Secretary reviewed the progress of the campaign, and indicated what ought to be done in future:

> The naval education of the people being the keystone of future naval development, it may be of interest to develop more fully what is being done in this respect.
>
> The education of the people in Canada means the education of (a) Parliament, (b) the Press, (c) business men.
>
> (*a*) Parliament should be educated by the Government. In practice . . . the present situation in Quebec prevents the Liberal Government from attempting to discuss naval affairs.
>
> (*b*) The Press can be educated by (i) personal conversations with Editors; (ii) making the Navy and naval defence sufficiently interesting to the public to justify leading articles and news items.
>
> (*c*) The support of business men can be enlisted by talks to Chambers of Commerce, Rotarian Clubs, etc.
>
> To educate Parliament, the Press, and business men, the story to be told must appeal primarily to common sense, and to commercial interest; secondarily to sentiment—the idea that Canada, as an autonomous nation within the Empire, should provide for the defence of her shore and territorial waters, and eventually should take her share in the defence of the Empire. The latter idea though it may appear to be an excellent argument carries least weight when advocating naval needs.
>
> The story must be a consistent story which will appeal in great or less degree to all. One cannot safely use one argument in the Imperialistic Centres (Toronto and Hamilton) and another argument in Quebec or the Prairie Provinces. . . . One must bring opponents and friends to a single line of thought . . .
>
> The story must avoid all political questions; it must be such that Liberal

or Conservative or Progressive can adopt it without prejudice to the policies of their respective parties.

To be able to impress on Parliament, the Press and business men a story which will appeal to all, one must have a policy for the Navy, and the policy adopted by the high authorities of the R.C.N. is to emphasize defence not offence—defence of Canadian shipping and territorial waters.

The story told hitherto relates how Canada has two million dollars worth of shipping on the ocean every day of the year; outlines the dangers to shipping at focal points of trade routes in time of war; gives a typical example of the effectiveness of stopping trade in a seemingly unimportant article (tin); and appeals to the business man's appreciation of the value of insurance against commercial risks.

It explains that the R.N. can only protect the trade routes vital to the Empire as a whole and leaves it to the imagination to picture what would be the situation if outgoing and incoming trade were stopped.

As given to the Government only, the story concludes with an explanation that an annual naval vote increasing gradually to 6 million dollars after five years would give Canada a naval force capable of providing for shipping in time of war safe egress and ingress within Canadian territorial waters.

For the past five years the Director of the Naval Service has told this story to Cabinet Ministers, to Members of Parliament, to Editors and to businessmen . . . There is very much still to be done. . . .[119]

II

During the 1920's, Canadians were weary of war; the proselytizing mission of the military was accordingly that of attempting to keep alive the public's interest in military affairs and its support of a drastically curtailed programme of military expenditure. During the early 1930's, Canadians had become frightened of war. Depression at home and crisis abroad divided and demoralized the nation, rendering it vulnerable to demagogues and their emotional appeals, a prey to conspiracy theorists and all manner of diagnosticians intent upon fastening blame for the malaise of nations upon the scapegoat of their choice. In these new circumstances, the proselytizing mission of the military had to be altered accordingly. No longer was it enough to keep the military in the public eye. The ideology of anti-militarism, in all its manifestations, had now to be met and put to flight by a reasoned and convincing justification of the role of force in keeping the peace.

The anti-militarist assault was led, as might be expected, by those on the political Left. Frank Underhill, Professor of History at the University of Toronto, was the most articulate and fearless of those attacking the problem of war from the standpoint of democratic socialism; his arguments were the more impressive coming from one who had served his country in the trenches. Underhill's villains were British imperialism and its capitalist lackeys:

> Skilful propaganda is already under way to suggest to us that we must draw closer to the other British nations for the protection of our common civilization. It is not yet quite clear who the common enemy is, but that will emerge in due course. We have already had Lord Lothian as a missionary from England preaching his gospel and we are, no doubt, in for a stream of English missionaries like him. They will all be individuals of the most perfect gentility and they will all present a beautiful idealized picture of British liberal imperialism. They will all stress its fundamentally peaceful aims. They will assure us that Canada cannot remain aloof from Europe and that we will inevitably be affected by what happens there. Anyone who is interested in historical parallels need only look up the speeches of the imperial missionaries of the pre-war decade—Earl Grey, Lord Milner, Mr. Lionel Curtis and their friends. We shall be hearing the same speeches again in the 1930's. In fact, the Round Table movement, which supplied the main impetus to the pre-war drive, has since the war been reincarnated as the Royal Institute of International Affairs, and has its Canadian branches consisting of a carefully selected group of the best people in each of our main cities. The Universities are the chosen field for this preliminary propaganda; their historians and lawyers and economists are so useful after a war has broken out in proving that we are fighting for the loftiest ideals. . . .
>
> It is not likely . . . that an attitude of mere aloof nationalism will be sufficient to keep us out of war entanglements once the propaganda of sentimental imperialism gets going at full force. The men who control Canada at present are practically all men who made their pile out of the last war. . . . They will be quite willing to preach war to us from the point of view of a proud, self-reliant nationalism; and they will find plenty of newspaper editors to assist them. It therefore behoves all Canadians who sincerely believe in peace to set themselves to expose the causes out of which wars really arise. They will not find much help from the University professors. But they may find masses of unexpected allies in the University undergraduates, who have begun to pass resolutions that they will in no circumstances fight for their King and Country. . . .[120]

When the next war breaks out in Europe, we shall be invited to join it by the British Foreign Office not only as a war for British freedom but also as a war for collective security as represented by the League Covenant to which we are signatories. Actually it will be a war for power and profits, for markets, and raw materials, for debts and investments, just as the war of 1914 was. That is what all wars are about. The idealist camouflage is for the purpose of getting suckers like us to bury 50,000 more Canadians in France and Flanders . . .

War is inherent in our present capitalist civilization. Until we have eliminated the domination of our national economies by private profit-seeking capitalist magnates we will not have eliminated war from the world. But this will be a long process. In the meantime we in Canada should make up our minds now, since the probability is another war in Europe, that we will not under any conditions send armed forces overseas to take part in it and that we will maintain our neutrality, regardless of what the pretexts for the war may be. . . .[121]

Anti-militarism was also rife among the young. One of their spokesmen was Escott Reid who, during most of the 1930's occupied the strategic opinion-forming post of National Secretary for the Canadian Institute of International Affairs. In 1927, when editor of the *Trinity University Review*, he wrote:

Preparedness for national defence has never yet brought a feeling of security to nations and it never will. It brings nothing but insecurity and fear and, as a result, war. . . . Preparedness for war will beget war; we must prepare for peace. . . .

Arbitration, security and disarmament are inseparable. There can be no disarmament unless the nations find security elsewhere than in national armies; there can be no security unless each nation binds itself to accept the decisions of arbitral courts. We believe in the creation of an informed public opinion which will put its full strength behind the principle of arbitration of international disputes; and which will refuse to support the national government when it has violated that principle. . .

If there is another war it is we, individually, who will be responsible for it. Not governments, not churches, not leagues, but we, ourselves. Governments and Leagues of Nations are not things apart from us; it is we who make them what they are. If they do not work, it is we who are to blame. To make war impossible, man must be changed. Yet we do not need to change millions; a few men changed will work wonders; and those few ourselves. For if *we* do not change, nothing will save us from a hell of self-contempt when, after the next war, we survey the ashes of a dead civilization. . . .[122]

The state of mind of the young seven years later is indicated in the results of a questionnaire conducted by the *McGill Daily* and published on 20 November 1934. (The questionnaire, it was claimed at the time, was "distributed without propaganda of any kind to undergraduates during the previous week;"[123] that week, it is relevant to note, was the week of Armistice Day remembrance.) Roughly five hundred students answered the questionnaire; men outnumbered women by four to one; fifty respondents were not Canadian.

A. Do you believe there will always be wars?—Yes, 197; No. 241; Indecisive, 59.

B. I will support the Canadian Government in any war which she may declare—83.

I will support the Canadian Government in certain wars which I believe to be justifiable—233.

I will not support my government in any war—134.
Indecisive, 47.

C. I believe war to be justifiable for Canada:
When Canada is invaded—331.
When Canadian life and property are endangered abroad—141.
When Great Britain is invaded—163.
When Great Britain declares any war—60.
When the League of Nations requests assistance—103.
When U.S.A. is invaded—62.
Under no circumstances—121.
Indecisive—18.

D. If the Canadian Government declared war, I would:
(I would encourage my brother or fiancé to:)
Enlist voluntarily—56
Serve when conscripted—79
Serve when the alternative is imprisonment—22
Refuse military but render humanitarian service only—134
Refuse all service—102
Actively oppose the continuation of the war by
(a) refusal to pay taxes—50
(b) organizing peaceful mass protests and petitions—179
(c) engaging in a general strike—107
Indecisive—22

E. For the purposes of peace, I endorse
A World Court—244; The League of Nations—266; An international police force—183; Strengthened National Defences—45; Nationalization of munition production—185; Abolition of armaments—222; Closer unification of the British Empire—149; Abolition of all military organizations—194; Investigation into the private manufacture of arms—317; World Federation of states—146; All movements for better understanding between nations and races—367; International language—109; Abolition of glamorous pictures of war in (*a*) schools, 347; (*b*) churches, 341; (*c*) theatres, 388.

Debates held at the University of Toronto and at McGill in November 1934 resulted in support of motions favouring a policy of pacifism for Canada—without, however, producing general agreement as to what was meant by pacifism.* Not all the undergraduates (as the McGill

*"What exactly pacifism was and how many different forms of it there were is a complex question," R. B. McCallum noted in his *Public Opinion and the Last Peace* (London, 1944), p. 173. Two main usages may be distinguished: the pacifist as a person who believes the abolition of war to be desirable and possible; the pacifist as a person who is not prepared to become an agent of force in the conflict of nations (or of classes), and so adheres to the doctrine of non-resistance in the Quaker, or Gandhian, tradition. The majority of the 500 students answering the *McGill Daily* questionnaire were pacifists in the former sense; a surprisingly large number (134) pacifists in the latter sense. Members of the Oxford Union declaring themselves opposed to fighting for King and Country were not necessarily pacifists in either sense.

questionnaire makes clear) were pacifists in any recognizable meaning of the term. "The radicals," wrote one tough-minded young student at the University of Toronto in 1936, "are a sorry lot of sentimental Student Christian Movement-CCFers who don't really know what the score is. Most of them merely see the socialist movement as an anti-war movement to save their own skins. Skin-saving is an all too prevalent ideal in all political parties down here. . . . There is more hope from Winnipeg."[124] That may have been a bit unfair to the Toronto socialists. But there *was* more hope from Winnipeg, where John W. Dafoe was waging, in the columns of the *Free Press*, his lonely fight against appeasement.

Of the various peace and anti-war movements of the time, none was more important than the League of Nations Society in Canada. This body was defined by its constitution as "a citizen's organization formed in 1920 to arouse public opinion on world affairs, and by every possible means to give effect to that opinion in the building of peace. The Society stands for . . . the maintenance of peace and security for nations by the collective action of them all."[125] Nothing was said about methods, and hence the Society's membership was open to Canadians of every shade of opinion, from passive non-resisters to militant sanctionists. The bulk of the membership probably occupied that middle ground between the two, hostile to sanctions and collective security, but favouring an extension of the League's domain in the settling of international disputes by friendly persuasion.

It was inevitable that the Society would be sought out by anti-militarists attempting to use it as a vehicle for their views. The ladies of the Toronto branch reported on 25 May 1934 that they had been busy throughout the preceding year distributing such pamphlets as "Essentials of Disarmament," "Salesmen of Death," and "Enemies of Peace" not only throughout Canada but "to South Africa, Australia and New Zealand, the United States and Great Britain, orders coming almost weekly." In addition, they announced, "we issued two coloured posters, 'Poison Gas Kills Babies Too', and 'Nations Build Tanks while People Starve.' . . . Our latest adventure is trying to interest people in an investigation of the manufacture of munitions similar to the one for which a Commission has been appointed by the United States Senate for the investigation of American manufactures."[126]

Activities of this sort, zealously and enthusiastically prosecuted in cities and towns across the nation, provoked the charge that, as Major-General W. A. Griesbach put it in a speech to the Senate on 1 May 1934, "the Canadian end of the League of Nations [Society] has fallen largely into the hands of pacifists or people pacifistically inclined."[127] The accusation was dealt with at the Society's Annual Meeting three weeks later, when Norman McLeod Rogers, a Queen's University professor at that time acting as an unofficial adviser to the Leader of the Opposition (he was to join the Government as Minister of Labour the following year when the Mackenzie King administration was formed), grappled with the semantics of pacifism:

> If General Griesbach is accustomed to use words with a scrupulous regard for their precise meaning no objection can be taken by this Society to his assertion. . . . Pacifism as defined by the highest Anglo-Saxon authority is "the doctrine or belief that it is desirable and possible to settle international disputes by peaceful means." . . . That belief is held with deep conviction by the National Council and members of the League of Nations Society in Canada and by members of similar organizations in other countries. Far from denying that we are pacifists in the sense indicated above, we welcome the designation and accept its implications without apology.
>
> If General Griesbach used the word "pacifists" in its more popular and looser sense as the equivalent of "conscientious objectors" it may be well to point out that a very substantial number of the Council and members of the League of Nations Society in Canada served overseas during the late war, and that this experience more than any other consideration has made them active supporters of the peace movement in Canada. The League of Nations Society in Canada is an autonomous organization which is bound to similar organizations in other countries by no ties other than a common devotion to the cause of peace and international co-operation. It imposes no oath or pledge upon its members as to the action to be taken by them in the event of war. That is a matter which has been left exclusively to the conscience of the individual concerned. . . . The League of Nations Society in Canada seeks to educate and organize public opinion in this country behind the obligations assumed by its government on behalf of peace. We believe that if we want peace we must prepare for it by cultivating the will to maintain it. We are convinced in this as in many other aspects of self-government public indifference is fraught with grave peril to the vitality of our institutions and the substance of our commitments for collective security. We acknowledge the possible necessity of sacrifice in the cause of peace. We regard this sacrifice as insignificant compared with the sacrifice certain to be required in the event of another war. . . .[128]

III

In the broad spectrum of anti-militarist sentiment there was no more powerful or pervasive idea than the notion that international conflicts were fomented and exacerbated by the great private enterprise armaments industries. The fevered condition of the European powers was attributed to the machinations of militarists, munitions-makers and others having a vested interst in discord and catastrophe. Upon the gross figure of the merchant of death was heaped responsibility for an astonishing variety of social ills. His was in any case a vulnerable figure, and the case to be made against him was so plausible that it seemed, at first sight, beyond rebuttal. Salvador de Madariaga had made it to the satisfaction of thousands in 1929:

> Armaments presuppose armament firms. There are no armament firms in the world which are established on the principle of pure and disinterested patriotism. They are all industrial enterprises which have in common with every other industrial enterprise in the world that their aim is to manufacture dividends. They only differ in that the intermediate products wherewith they manufacture dividends are guns and battleships, instead of motor cars or cheese. Now an industrial enterprise is essentially interested in its market. There is no mystery about that, no villainy. It is all above board. Let us print it in capitals, for it is blatant, open and obvious, in fact it is a platitude: ARMAMENT FIRMS ARE INTERESTED IN FOSTERING A STATE OF AFFAIRS WHICH WILL INCREASE THE DEMAND FOR ARMAMENTS.[129]

The remedy was no less plain than the diagnosis. Let the armaments industry be nationalized, let the munitions-maker be deprived of the profit motive, and an important cause of conflict among nations would disappear.

The directness and simplicity of the "devil theory of war," with the munitions-maker figuring as principal devil, assured for it in Canada, as in the United Kingdom and the United States, ready acceptance among a wide audience. Those already convinced of the inequity of capitalism eagerly embraced so dramatic an indictment of its inequities, arousing doubts amongst those not otherwise socialistically inclined. "Who is it that wants war?" the Reverend William Beattie asked rhetorically of his League of Nations Society audience in 1934. "There is but one group in the world, and that is those who are making blood money out of it. . . . I have been saying to my boys that . . . it is their duty to study the situation so thoroughly that if another war breaks out they will know whether that war was made in the business offices of munitions manufacturers or elsewhere. . . ."[130] But belief that wars made by the makers of munitions was by no means confined to those on the political Left. "The armaments manufacturers," declared General A. D. McRae in the Senate of Canada, "are the power behind the arming and counter-arming of nations and . . . dominate the governments of their own country."[131] Mr. Vincent Massey, President of the National Liberal Federation, casting about for some suitable theme for a speech to the International Convention of Kiwanis Clubs in June 1934, finally chose that of the "merchants of death." "I want," he wrote beforehand, "to avoid the usual 'good will' address. I want to deal with some things that really matter in the realm of foreign affairs, particularly disarmament and the problem of the private manufacture of munitions of war. . . . I feel that if public opinion could be aroused on this problem governments would be forced to act."[132] The speech, Mr. Massey noted afterwards, "was a genuine success"; no part of it was more successful than the passage in which he had declared: "We must put an end to the manufacture for private gain of weapons for the destruction of human beings. . . . So long as we have scattered throughout the world great and powerful corporations whose interest is to make profit out of war, there will be irresistible forces working against those who are trying to organize peace."[133]

The most influential statement in Canada of this thesis was that presented in *Maclean's Magazine* by George Drew, then a well-known officer in the non-permanent active militia and a rising young politician in Ontario, under the lurid title "Salesmen of Death: The Truth about War Markets." It was widely read to begin with and, reprinted in pamphlet form, earned its author a reputation as an outstanding authority on the subject. (It was to George Drew that Vincent Massey had written for information in order to prepare his own speech.) These extracts convey the flavour of the work:

> In spite of the League of Nations and the World Court, . . . the *danse macabre* of the armament builders goes on apace, and Canada should be prepared to take some practical part in an effort to restrict this deadly competition which recent history has proved inevitably leads to war. . . .
> Behind national competition in armaments and navies lies a vicious commercial competition of armament and shipbuilding companies which seek to promote international ill-will for the purpose of preserving a ready market for the death-dealing equipment they produce. . . . Private profit in the production of armament furnishes one of the most active sources of international friction, which can be removed only by some form of national ownership which would eliminate the personal advantages resulting from sales. . . .
> It is high time that the general public which suffers from a war should take some part in this question of disarmament and not leave it to those who have so conspicuously failed to face the realities in the past.[134]

Agitation in Canada against the merchant of death may have been partly responsible for the refusal of successive administrations to encourage the development of a munitions industry capable of creating for the armed forces their own weapons of war. It was certainly responsible for the feeling, strongly held by governments no less than by the public, that any munitions production as might take place in Canada ought to be undertaken by public enterprise, not private. It was the assumption throughout the 1930's, when the General Staff argued (without success) for self-sufficiency in all phases of weapons development, that any increase in capacity for munitions production would be brought about in government-owned plant. When the campaign for a new Dominion Arsenal which could produce cannon and automatic rifles as well as ammunition seemed to be getting nowhere, the Master General of the Ordnance informed the Chief of the General Staff that, in his view, the time had come for private enterprise to make up the deficiency. "I feel," he wrote, "that the scheme to manufacture *all* arms and munitions in government plants may be due in part to the agitation which has been carried on in this country, in Great Britain, the United States of America, and in France. But this agitation is being forgotten under the pressure of general insecurity and rearmament. Nothing has been heard of it in Canada for months. I suggest that we need not be frightened off investigating the possibilities of private manufacture in this country by this propaganda, which is now discredited in many particulars."[135] This assessment underestimated the force of the opposition.

IV

Lacking a fully-fledged munitions industry of their own, Canadians could not find many native-son merchants of death upon whom they could vent their anger. They did not, however, lack their own General Staff. It was accordingly upon its members, as much upon the munitions-makers of Europe, that the wrath of the Canadian pacifist community settled. The Great Depression sharpened the contrast between the situations of the permanent force officer and the unemployed citizen (or the citizen employed in one of the officers' relief camps at the rate of twenty cents a day). The General Staff was variously accused of being over-paid, over-manned, and preoccupied by trivia. "I was almost staggered," J. S. Woodsworth declared in February 1932, "when I compared the salaries received by people in the Department of National Defence. . . . We have no fewer than one hundred and thirty-nine people receiving between $4,000 and $4,900; thirty people receiving between $5,000 and $5,900; fifteen people receiving between $6,000 and $6,900."[136] The salary of the Chief of the General Staff, which was $10,000 per annum, came under fire in the House of Commons on several occasions. It was not just that, in the eyes of the critics, these salaries were high; it was that their recipients did not earn them. "We have here," J. S. Woodsworth remarked, "an army of swivelchair generals." "I cannot think what these generals or colonels or whatever they are can be doing," Agnes Macphail stated a few days later. "It seems to me we have a general staff capable of handling an army of half a million men."[137] The initial exemption of Service officers from the Bennett Government's across-the-board 10 per cent reduction in the salaries of civil servants did not enhance their public reputation. "If there are people who do not earn their salaries," Martial Rheaume, the Member for St. John-Iberville, stated in the House of Commons, "they are the army officers. . . . I wonder what is their occupation. I suppose they are busy doing pretty much the same thing as those in my county: a little riding jolt of one or one hour and a half in the morning, and the day's work is over."[138] "I think perhaps the greatest close corporations we have in Ottawa," remarked F. G. Sanderson (South Perth), in March 1935, "is the staff down at the Woods Building. . . . I go further. I say that the staff in the Woods Building is overmanned. You cannot get into the place; they are like an army of chocolate soldiers down there. . . ."[139] There had come into the possession of the Member for South Perth a copy of N.D.H.Q. Circular Letter No. 21 of 1934, setting out, in some detail, "the correct pattern and size of mess dress ties" to be worn by officers of the Canadian militia: "Ties with pointed ends," it prescribed, "should not be worn, and the edges of the bow should be straight and parallel. Particular attention should be paid to the dimensions of the tie, which should be about two inches wide at the ends and the length of the tie, in inches, should be twice the size of the collar, namely an officer wearing a 15½ collar should wear a tie approximately 31 inches long."[140] This intelligence, in the temper of those times, did not so much amuse as anger the House of Commons; C. G. Power spoke for more than the members of the Opposition when he declared with some bitterness: "Here we are with one-half the brains of the Department of Defence being utilized in order to ascertain just how long and wide a black tie must be worn with a mess jacket, and the other half designing stables in Calgary . . . , while thousands of men throughout the country are being employed at twenty cents a day. . . . It is a crying shame and a disgrace to our country and our civilization."[141]

The charge that the Canadian General Staff was frittering its time and the taxpayers' money in idle and useless pursuits was not on the face of it consistent with the charge that, as a sinister purveyor of militarism, it was leading the country closer to war. But that inconsistency did not prevent the latter charge from being laid, sometimes by the same people who accused it of frivolity. The notion that general staffs, by their mere existence, were causes of war was no less widespread than that of the merchants-of-death. "Armaments," wrote Salvador de Madariaga in 1929,

are not held by a nation in an inchoate form. Men and material are organized into a force, and put under the leadership of a general staff. The general staff, composed as it is of soldiers or sailors, has, as is traditional in the fighting profession, a high sense of honor. The military branch of any administration may therefore be expected to give full value to the state in exchange for its salaries and privileges. Now, what can a general staff do three hundred and sixty days a year at the rate of six hours a day but prepare for war? Here again the facts are above board. There is no mystery. Every important nation keeps a fully manned and fully endowed general staff which is expected to be fully occupied.[142]

To this view David Lloyd George added the weight of his authority, in a passage quoted in the House of Commons by J. S. Woodsworth:

In every country it is a part of the business of the fighting staff to work out plans for defence against all possible enemies. Their minds get absorbed in these brilliant schemes. They gloat over their efficiency, and like every inventor, yearn to put their machine to a test. In the secrecy of their department, the possible war soon becomes a likely war, and the likely gradually glides into the inevitable war. It is at first discussed in whispers behind locked doors. Then at clubs where gather together men whose patriotism is above any suspicion. . . . The next stage is always the after dinner speech. . . .[143]

This argument Woodsworth, and others, adopted as their own. "One of the greatest troubles about this military question," he remarked on one occasion, "is that we have professional militarists whose job is involved, men who are at the thing in season and out, trying in every way to use their influence to perpetuate it."[144] "I do want to say," declared F. G. Sanderson some years later, "that with a very few exceptions the officers are what I would call war lords, men who are attempting to create the feeling throughout the country that Canada must be prepared for another war. . . . Instead of the officers running the Department and running the Minister, the Minister should take a firm stand and control those who are under him, and if he cannot control them he should get rid of them."[145]

One specific remedy seemed clear. At the very least, governments interested in the peace and welfare of their peoples should keep their General Staff officers away from disarmament conferences, for their attendance would inevitably transform them into rearmament conferences. "We in Canada," J. S. Woodsworth observed in 1934, "have certain matters within our own control. Whom did we send to the

Disarmament Conference? We have been sending technical experts. . . . Surely the time has come when the people of Canada should send people who are interested in bringing about disarmament, and not technical men who are trying to do the very best they can along professional lines, military lines."[146] The charge that the presence of General McNaughton and Colonel Crerar as technical advisers to the Canadian Delegation at the World Disarmament Conference tended to undermine the Government's efforts in the cause of peace was made in an article in the Toronto periodical, *Saturday Night*.[147] It came, in due course, before General McNaughton, who wrote in some agitation to Sir George Perley, the leader of the delegation:

> In the last paragraph of his article, Mr. Grant suggests that I represent a military opinion different in some unstated respect from the policy of the Government of Canada, which I have sought to impose on our delegation. Nothing is further from the fact. I am happy in the thought that I have been in harmony with the policy expressed by our leaders and never more so than during the time I had the privilege of serving under you at Geneva and in the technical sphere where my advice has been sought, I can confidently say, both for myself and Colonel Crerar and the other officers associated with me, that we have been able to carry out our instructions with real faith in their correctness.[148]

Sir George Perley advised against a public repudiation of the charge. Had it been attempted, it would not have been believed.

V

The range and variety of the anti-militarist assault made it difficult for the victims to mount any effective counter-attack. They were moreover handicapped by the intense public suspicion attaching at that time to even the most ordinary military duties; so novel a venture as that of public relations, unless carried out with extraordinary tact and circumspection, was certain to bring the military establishment more than ever into general disfavour. An example of the counter-productivity of proselytizing was provided by an ill-advised excursion into film-making by a committee of the Department of National Defence in 1934–35. The film was called "Lest We Forget." It was immediately denounced as dishonest and misleading propaganda. Its real title, Escott Reid declared in an article devoted to an attack upon it, should have been " 'Lest we forget our simple faith in the simple war-time fables'. It is, of course, very important from the point of view of the Department of National Defence that we should not lose our faith in these fables, for if we did, we might not be so likely to swallow similar fables in the next war, and recruiting would be that much more difficult."[149] When it came to propaganda about the nature of war, the professional film-makers were much more effective than the soldiers. How can one measure the impact on the public mind of "All Quiet on the Western Front"? Parents were urged to take their children; the writer, as a child, went on his own, and sees today, as if it were yesterday, the corpseless arms left hanging on the barbed wire, the shell-shocked, blinded, screaming boy cut down in No Man's Land, the expression on the face of the amputee as he looks for the first time at where his leg had been.

The military, then, could not do much to improve its tarnished image; but it did what it could. At one level, the editor of the *Canadian Defence Quarterly* tried in the columns at his disposal to demonstrate the fallacies of Leaguers and disarmers. George Drew's "Salesman of Death" article was replied to, and its propositions firmly rejected: "Would not an effort to further international co-operation . . . be a more natural, profitable and dignified course for Canada to adopt in the sphere of world affairs, than to advocate a prohibition which, under existing conditions, has already been found to be almost impossible of attainment, and which, from a country such as Canada, might even savour of impertinence, because, after all, we have no private armament industry and the industrial and financial repercussions of prohibition, or even of control, would not affect us?"[150] The operation and administration by the Department of National Defence of relief camps for the nation's unemployed might well have been expected to help demonstrate the usefulness of the military at a time of national crisis. But, as events were to prove, the Army's part in relieving unemployment raised more problems of public relations than it solved.*

In one area of public relations, the military establishment proved to be unusually inept. This was its dealings with the "attentive public," that handful of intellectuals and interested citizens prepared to take a serious and intelligent interest in matters of defence policy. Their aspirations were not considered legitimate, and their few attempts to reach a closer rapport with the military were coldly rebuffed. In January 1935, Professor A. R. M. Lower wrote to the Deputy Minister of the Department of National Defence, explaining that he was undertaking a study of the defence of the Pacific Coast for the Winnipeg Branch of the Canadian Institute of International Affairs, and desired information for that purpose. "Matters which occur to me on which there might be information of the type I mention," he added, "are the capacity of the dockyards on the coast, data in respect to the feasibility of mining the northern

*See below, pp. 128–36, 139–41.

and southern approaches to Vancouver Island, etc. I particularly emphasize that I ask only for information which a member of the general public might have, though at the same time I might state that my study is for circulation among a small group of prominent citizens only and not for the general public."[151] This letter was passed on to the Chief of the Naval Staff, who drafted the following reply:

> . . . it is very difficult to give you any information on this subject without quoting from secret and confidential documents. I wish to assure you, however, that the defence of Canada's Pacific Coast is the subject of constant study in this Department. Our plans and policy are based on the small permanent forces which Canada maintains, but can be expanded as the forces available are increased.
>
> Our dockyards are fully capable of fulfilling the needs of our present Navy and of developing their resources as money becomes available.
>
> I very much regret that I am unable to give your Institute the information you request.[152]

This did not go very far, but to the Chief of the General Staff, to whom the draft was shown for his comment, it seemed to go too far: "In my view," General McNaughton minuted on Commodore Nelles' draft, "the only answer should be a regret that information of the character asked for can not be furnished."[153] A reply to this effect was sent to the inquiring professor. It cannot be supposed his sympathies or those of the distinguished group on whose behalf he was writing were enlisted by this procedure.*

One important section of the attentive public was afforded more

*Two years later, the Canadian Institute of International Affairs held a round-table conference on Canadian defence problems at Hamilton, Ontario. Col. Maurice Pope and Col. Kenneth Stuart were instructed by the Minister of National Defence to attend and "explain the Department's (or perhaps more correctly the Government's) policy. I was assailed," General Pope has recalled, "from every quarter. . . . Apparently, in the minds of my inquisitors, the soldiery were composed of evilly disposed persons. Why were we recommending increased provision for defence now that the day of collective security had dawned? To what extent were we under the Chief of the Imperial General Staff in London? What precisely was our policy? To my mind replies were not hard to come by but my hearers, to say the least, were quite unreceptive. . . . In the forefront of the attack was Professor A. R. M. Lower. . . .

"After I had spoken of the improvements we were making to our West Coast defences I was dumbfounded to hear Professor Frank Scott of McGill University gravely observe to the conference that Canada had made its position less secure than it had been formerly by installing a battery or two in the vicinity of Esquimalt and Vancouver! I listened in amazement to the views expressed that day. It was only too clear that the General Staff in Ottawa and this group of idealistic theorists, some of whom seemed to reflect a belief that the day when war could be considered an instrument of policy had long since passed, were living in quite different worlds. . . ." *Soldiers and Politicians* (Toronto, 1962), pp. 133–4.

favourable treatment. This was the membership of the Conference of Defence Associations, composed of officers of the non-permanent active militia representing specialized military associations such as the Canadian Infantry Association, the Canadian Artillery Association, the Canadian Cavalry Association, and the like. The origins of the Conference of Defence Associations were described by one of its leading members, George Drew, at its second annual meeting in Ottawa in 1933:

> . . . the Conference of last year actually grew out of discussions which have been taking place for some years, when the question of bringing senior officers of the different branches of the Service together for the purpose of discussing their common problems and making certain recommendations to National Defence Headquarters was contemplated. A year ago last Spring, a meeting was called here for the purpose of considering the organization of this Conference, and at that time, three officers, Colonel Hope, Colonel Beament and myself, were appointed as a committee to consider the form such a meeting should take. Following on that, an invitation was extended to the different Militia Associations to meet at a Conference here last November, and in the invitation extended to the different Associations, it was suggested that the time had come seriously to consider the necessity for a general reorganization of the Canadian Militia, so that it might fulfill the functions it is supposed to perform. . . .[154]

The object of the Conference, so the minutes of its first meeting record, was "to consider problems of National Defence, to co-ordinate the activities of the present Service Associations in matters of common interest to all services, to make such recommendations to the Government of Canada as may appear expedient, and, generally, to promote the welfare of the Defence Forces of Canada as a whole."[155] It became the custom for the Prime Minister, the Minister of National Defence, and the Chief of the General Staff, to address the Conference's annual meeting; and, because of the secrecy of its proceedings, and because its members all held the King's Commission, the addresses given on such occasions were as informative and frank as any pronouncement on defence policy in the country. "We, in the Department," General McNaughton declared at the first meeting,

> welcome the organization of this Defence Association, because it gives us for the first time in the history of Canada an opportunity to meet the responsible officers of the several Non-Permanent organizations, and to take them completely into our confidence. Indeed, we feel that these officers have every right to full information because they are, first of all, citizens of this country, and, secondly, they have devoted a great deal of time and effort and money in the very responsible task of organizing our Non-Permanent Defence Forces. Consequently, if they are to do that work intelligently and effectively, they must know the reasons which lie behind the

maintenance of the Defence Forces of this country, and it struck me that I could not do better than give to you a brief appreciation of the situation as I see it.[156]

A year later, he remarked: "I think you will all agree with me in regarding the 18th November, last year, as an epoch-making day, because that was the first occasion in the history of this country in which representatives of the Non-Permanent Forces were taken into the absolute confidence of the General Staff. I think that our experience has fully justified the action which we took, because there has been no leakage, as far as I am aware, of that confidential and highly dangerous information to unauthorized people."[157]

By 1936, the Conference of Defence Associations, which had confined itself originally to the question of the reorganization of the non-permanent active militia, had widened the scope of its discussions. One of the problems to which it had addressed itself was that of altering the climate of public opinion so that increased military preparations would be less difficult. A Standing Educational Committee had been created for gathering information about national defence and improving the "general public understanding" of defence matters. At the Fifth Meeting of the Conference, held in Ottawa in November 1936, it presented its first report. It proposed that "one or more treatises on the origin, development, traditions and present day needs of the Canadian Militia Services" be published, together with "a treatise on national security—present-day problems"; that special articles be placed in the *Canadian Defence Quarterly*, the circulation of which should be increased; and that "prominent citizens and visitors" should be encouraged to write articles and deliver lectures on the urgent need for increased military preparations. "Your Committee," the report concluded,

has recognized the serious situation which has existed for a long time in Canada. Some sections of the country are either passively indifferent or even actively adverse to any practical development of national defence. Also while there has been little or no general education of an informative character in support of national defence measures, there has been much destructive criticism from individuals actuated by a variety of motives of uncertain or questionable character. These criticisms have been directed not only against defence services in general, and the Militia in particular, but have even extended to include cadet training in schools and the Boy Scouts. We know that some interests in the country are strongly opposed to any definitely organized support of law and order. In the full realization of the weakness of our scattered and inadequate militia forces there is all the more reason that this Association, realizing and understanding the need, should take action.[158]

The Report of its Educational Committee was enthusiastically received by the Conference. "If we might take the buttons off the foils for a moment," Colonel A. M. Thomas of the Infantry Association remarked, "we might say that we are trying to sell something and we might get right down to it and say that we are trying to sell the Canadian people the policy of defence. . . . Now, Gentlemen," he continued,

we have in the Canadian Militia sixty to eighty thousand people. We have an immense sales force. It is there waiting for us to use and I would submit that the first thing we should do is to equip all the commanding officers so that they can in turn deliver their message to their rank and file, so that your sixty to eighty thousand, or, including their wives and families, say two hundred thousand, will be imbued with the idea which we want to sell to the public. . . .[159]

"There are today people who have a definite reason for antagonism towards militia training," George Drew declared darkly. "It is part of their political faith. I think all officers realize this and feel that way about it. They might organize a campaign and do something about it in their own localities to combat that subversive opinion."[160]

Clearly the Conference was in the mood for a crusade. But the Chairman of the Educational Committee introduced a note of caution. "One of the gentlemen we consulted in Montreal," he warned, "who has had a great deal of experience in publicity, gave us as his definite opinion that the use of publicity, using our side of the question only, was risky, as there was a danger we might in the end move backward instead of forward. It is only fair to have the meeting know this."[161] Apprised in this way of the dangers of fanaticism, the officers of the non-permanent active militia dispersed to begin their task of public enlightenment. It was to prove an up-hill battle.

RELIEVING UNEMPLOYED

Canadians, it has been observed, are an unmilitary people. It is fitting that perhaps the most important assignment carried out by the Canadian military during the years between the two world wars was of an unmilitary nature.

By 1932, the Dominion had become mired in the sloughs of the Great Depression, with no manner of extrication in sight. Nearly a quarter of the labour force was without work. The breadlines lengthened in the cities, the unemployed wandered aimlessly in the streets. Of the unemployed, an estimated 70,000 were single men, destitute, homeless, and mostly young. In their ragged platoons were the prospective members of Canada's armed forces should the country become involved in war. Here, also, were the prospective members of what Marx had called the "industrial reserve army," the storm-troopers of revolution.

During the summer and early autumn of that dreadful year, the Chief of the General Staff, in the course of his administrative duties, visited various centres throughout Canada.* Everywhere he went he saw men without work. The waste and degradation of depression were bound to have stirred General McNaughton's lambent imagination into devising some constructive solution, but quite apart from that there were purely military reasons for doing something and doing it quickly. That the nation was on the verge of revolution seemed not unlikely; that it was imperilled by rioting and bloodshed seemed certain. In the event of violence it would be the duty of the permanent force to come to the aid of the civil power. Its resources for such an assignment were meagre; the assignment itself altogether nasty. What better solution, albeit a temporary solution, than to take the men out of the breadlines and put them to work? And what organization better able to do the job than the Army of which he was the senior officer?

On his return to Ottawa, McNaughton had formed in his mind the idea of setting up work camps, administered by the Department of National Defence; to which able-bodied, single, homeless, unemployed men might at their own request be admitted. There, in exchange for their labour, they would be sheltered, clothed and fed until, rehabilitated, they could find employment. He put the idea before the Minister and Deputy Minister of Labour, who seemed to be attracted by it. There the matter rested. But, about a month later, on 6 October 1932, attending the opening of a session of Parliament, McNaughton was surprised when the Prime Minister, during the course of the ceremony, leaned over to him "and whispered that the Cabinet was very much interested in his scheme and asked him if he could have a detailed proposal in the Prime Minister's office by 9.30 a.m. the next day."[162]

On the afternoon of 6 October, McNaughton summoned a meeting of representatives of the Army's Engineer and Service and Transport Directorates, and outlined to them what the Prime Minister wanted.

*The following account of the origins of the unemployment relief camp system operated by the Department of National Defence is based on that given in G. M. LeFresne, " 'The Royal Twenty-Centers': The Department of National Defence and Federal Unemployment Relief, 1932–1936" (Royal Military College, M.A. History thesis, 1962), which in turn is based upon interviews by its author with Gen. McNaughton and Maj.-Gen. G. R. Turner (the latter the officer most closely concerned with the scheme next to McNaughton himself).

The Department of National Defence was to put 2,000 civilians to work immediately, at a cost per man *per diem* of not more than $1.00. Out of that sum were to be provided not only his food, clothing, shelter and a share of whatever overhead was required for the job but, in addition, an allowance of 20 cents a day for spending money. What projects could usefully and expediently be undertaken by such a labour force? McNaughton thought it could start by repairing the walls of the citadels at Quebec and Halifax, and by clearing airfields along the route of the proposed Trans-Canada airway. A preliminary check with the district Engineer's office at the two cities, and with the Controller of Civil Aviation, disclosed that work might be begun on these projects almost immediately. Armed with this information, Major G. R. Turner (the officer representing the Directorate of Engineer Services) set to work on a memorandum, dictating a final draft to his secretary at 5.30 a.m. on 7 October. At 8.30 a.m. he gave it to McNaughton to examine; McNaughton approved the draft, and at precisely 9.30 a.m. the memorandum was laid on the Prime Minister's desk.

The Cabinet went over the memorandum with care, and then summoned McNaughton for questioning. He was asked whether the proposed St. Lawrence seaway might not be a more appropriate project for the scheme: he replied that the Seaway was essentially a job for heavy machinery, while his idea was to select projects on which a great deal of manual labour would be required, so setting as many men to work as possible. The Cabinet appeared satisfied that McNaughton was on the right track, and decided to implement the scheme immediately. The Chief of the General Staff was instructed to proceed with his plans at once, and assured that the necessary legislation would follow in due course. An order-in-council of 8 October 1932 (P.C. 2248) authorized the Department of National Defence to put roughly 2,000 men to work on the construction of intermediate landing fields, on repairs to old fortifications at Halifax and Quebec City, and on the building of air stations at Trenton and Rockcliffe. Within a month the men were on the jobs.

So hasty an improvisation inevitably ran into legal and bureaucratic difficulties. The Civil Service Commission contended that the civilian foremen and other supervisory personnel hired by the Department of National Defence for the administration of the camps ought to be hired through its elaborate procedures involving, among other things, competitive examinations; officials administering the Workmen's Compensation Act argued that men in the camps were federal government employees and so entitled, in the event of injury on the job, to the high scale of allowances provided for other federal employees; the Treasury claimed that the camp inmates were civil servants and that therefore, under the terms of the Salary Deductions Act, 1932, 10 per cent of their "wages" was to go to the Government—leaving the men with 18 cents a day instead of twenty cents. Twice in the early weeks of the scheme all expenditures on it were held up for one or other or all of these reasons. Had these interruptions been sustained, it is likely that the whole scheme would have perforce been abandoned. In January 1933, however, the Department of Justice ruled that the unemployment relief camps constituted a special and emergency project exempt from the provisions of other federal legislation, and could be carried on under the authority of orders-in-council and by such regulations as might be decided upon by the responsible officers of the Department of National Defence.

McNaughton now had the green light, and threw all his great energies and administrative abilities into the perfection and expansion of the scheme. In February 1933 he reported:

> . . . the health of the men has been excellent. On the army ration a steady increase in weight and physique has been observed; the morale is good; the works reports show excellent progress in the execution of the projects, and it can confidently be claimed that the experiment, as a whole, embracing projects from the Atlantic to the Pacific, has been a success and that it has indicated a line on which the whole problem of the single, homeless man can be solved at a cost to the country of approximately one dollar per man per diem, which is very materially less than the value at the current rates of the work which can be executed.[163]

On April 15 he wrote:

> . . . I think we can now say that the experimental phase, which commenced last November, has been successfully passed through; that the many sources of trouble inseparable from a novel enterprise have been eliminated. We feel that now we can go to 'quantity production' and at the moment, thanks to authority given by His Excellency in Council on the 31st March last, we are increasing three-fold the numbers cared for, and so soon as we are within measurable distance of completing these quotas I am assured that authority for additional numbers will be forthcoming.[164]

And, on 26 June, he sent a further optimistic appraisal to the Minister of Trade and Commerce:

> . . . the work has been steadily expanded until at the present time some 80 individual projects are in hand and others are under consideration; these are distributed throughout Canada in every Province, except P.E.I. . . . The projects vary in size from a few individuals to large camps of upwards of 1500 men, the strength depending on the useful work available; one

project at Lac Seul to care for some 3,000 men to relieve the situation in Winnipeg is now under arrangement. . . .

The total strength on the 15th June 1933 was 8,034; provision has been made for 14,142, and this establishment is being increased at the rate of approximately 200 men a month. . . .

As a consequence of the experience gained since October last a simple but effective system of administration has been evolved through the adoption and use of the existing administrative organization of the Department of National Defence, and this I think without the impairment of any essential normal function of the Department. . . .

As regards cost— . . . With the capital charges for accommodation, materials of construction, tools and equipment, etc., distributed and wholly written off in a 12-month period, the figures for total expenditure per man day of relief is $1.01. Against this the average value of useful work done by the men has been 89 cents per man day of relief. . . .

Judging by the many favourable articles in the daily and technical press and the little adverse comment which has been made, I think I can claim that the traditional effectiveness and elasticity of the military system of administration has been smoothly adapted to a great civil purpose, and this without the setting up of any militaristic procedure objectionable to the minds of our general public always sensitive on these matters.

As a result of our experience to date I think I can also say that we now do not anticipate any insuperable difficulty in carrying out our projects to any magnitude that the Government may indicate.[165]

It seemed too good to be true. It was. McNaughton, isolated from public protest, taking an inventor's pride in the merits of his scheme, never quite understood to what extent the unemployment relief camps were becoming a symbol of everything that was hated about the Bennett regime.

II

Three main lines of protest soon appeared. Labour unions, though not opposed, at least in the early stages, to the principle of the work camps, became concerned lest the work done by their inmates deprive their own rank and file of employment. They accordingly insisted that projects selected for unemployment relief should involve only the roughest kind of labour, and when the men in the camps were encouraged to undertake jobs involving the skills and aptitudes of artisans, the unions promptly protested. Here was a sizable apple of discord. For it was an article of faith with McNaughton, once it became apparent that the work camps were to be as durable a feature of Canadian life as the Great Depression itself, that their inmates should not be compelled to waste themselves in crude and primitive tasks. In selecting projects,

McNaughton wrote to the Deputy Minister of Labour, "I am aware that if the idea gets abroad that with relief labour we are carrying out the ordinary work of the country we lay ourselves open to the charge of unfair exploitation of people in need." But, at the same time, he was no less urgently impressed with "the desirability that men be given an opportunity to work at their own trades so that their efficiency and earning capacity shall not deteriorate." Between these discriminants (as he called them) it was not easy to navigate. So long as it cost no more than $1.00 per day per man, he had felt free to put the men in the camps on to any type of work that seemed advisable. Men were clearing ground and grading for the proposed Trans-Canada Airway, planting trees, making roads, putting through telephone lines, all so far without public protest. The opening of a quarry to get stone for a new building at the Royal Military College had provoked complaints from the Trades and Labor Congress, and a manufacturer had objected to brick-making activity at Rockcliffe Air Station. "If the objection to this work," McNaughton concluded,

> which does not differ in principle from what we are doing at a score of other places, is sustained, then the possibility of much useful work falls to the ground and I must set about redistributing some thousands of men to work of a more "primitive" character. I think this would be most unfortunate both from the point of view of the remaining value we can leave to Canada in the form of badly needed facilities . . . but more importantly for the reason that if we are confined to "primitive" work we cannot give the men . . . a chance. . . . It seems to me that the time has now come to settle definitely once and for all the question of principle involved.[166]

The question of principle was discussed by McNaughton and the Minister of National Defence on 3 October 1933. The Chief of the General Staff warned of the "grave difficulty" in making provision for the men in the camps if the building projects had to be abandoned. "If we gave way to ill informed clamour on any project it would only be followed by trouble on others until the whole of our system was broken down." He dwelt upon the importance of the camp system as a safeguard against subversion:

> By taking the men out of conditions of misery in the Cities and giving them a reasonable standard of living and comfort . . . we were removing the active elements on which the "Red" agitators could play. . . . If we had not taken this preventative work and did not continue . . . it was only a matter of time until we had to resort to arms to maintain order. . . . No doubt the "Red" organizations fully recognized the purpose of our work and it was for this reason primarily that they were trying to break it up and force us to send the men back into the Cities where in the intolerable con-

ditions there obtaining they would soon be susceptible to their disruptive propaganda. . . .[167]

McNaughton's arguments prevailed. The men in the camps continued to be directed to the most productive tasks he could find for them. The Government was left to deal, as best it could, with the steadily mounting barrage of protest at the camps' usurpation of potential opportunities directed by both organized labour and would-be capitalists.

By 1934 their protests had become so incessant and intense that the Prime Minister felt the time had come for the unemployment relief camps to abandon the more sophisticated projects in which McNaughton had engaged them. On 29 May he spoke in this vein to McNaughton over the telephone. McNaughton stood his ground. "I said," he wrote afterwards,

> I was well aware of the difficulties which had been created; that I had not undertaken any more building than was absolutely necessary for the purpose in view; that for the whole of Canada only about 2.5% of the man-days of labour available was devoted to this class of work.
>
> The Prime Minister asked what was being done at Petawawa and I said that at the moment our principal effort was being devoted to the planting of trees and clearing and he indicated he thought this was valuable work.
>
> The Prime Minister then went on to repeat the criticism which he had heard about the men in our camps being required to work on building construction on other than a prevailing wage basis.
>
> I said again that this category of work had been restricted to very small proportions but he said that nevertheless there was enough of it being done to cause complaint and it would have to be terminated. I asked if I could give him an appreciation of the situation and after consideration if I could recommend a course of action to be followed and I asked how much time I could have. He answered that he would go into the matter on Thursday which was the first day he had free.
>
> On returning to N.D.H.Q. I saw . . . the Minister and reported the substance of my conversation with the Prime Minister. . . . In my conversation with the Minister I again emphasized that the reason we were anxious to continue the relief projects was primarily as an alternative to the use of force in the suppression of disorders in the larger centres; that I was convinced that if we had not organized our projects before now there would certainly have been considerable bloodshed; that I thought the situation was not safe yet and that on the result of discussions with the officers of the Department of Labour and others closely informed it was evident that we would probably have to care for upwards of 50,000 men during the coming winter. I again emphasized that our building operations to which the most exception had been taken were very small relatively and restricted to work which was incidental to the projects; that on the initiative of the Minister of Labour we had evolved a system by which the greater part of this work could be given to skilled tradesmen with dependents in need of relief and

residents of the vicinity; that this system had worked well; that in the draft Order now before Privy Council we had proposed to expand as far as possible and had included a sum of $422,000 for the purpose. . . .

I said it was quite impracticable to break up our projects without causing a most serious reaction. That we would certainly require to re-establish them unless the Government were prepared to accept as an alternative the employment of considerable numbers of troops.

After hearing my review of the situation the Minister instructed that no orders to close projects should be issued without reference to him.[168]

Three weeks later McNaughton repeated his defence of the camp system as it had come to operate, this time in a letter to the Prime Minister's secretary. "The most important feature of our work," he commented on a report on unemployment relief he had had prepared and was enclosing for the Prime Minister's attention,

is, of course, not reflected either in the financial figures or in the number of man days relief afforded. Projects have been directed to the breaking up of the congestion of single homeless men in the principal centres of population and if these had not been dispersed it is hardly conceivable that we would have escaped without having recourse to the military forces to suppress disorder. I cannot emphasize too strongly that this situation continues and that, so far, the improvement in employment conditions has had little effect on the class of men with whom we are primarily concerned, i.e., those who are single and homeless.[169]

But Bennett remained perturbed. A crucial series of by-elections faced his party in September, and a general election could not be much longer delayed. Meanwhile the relief camps had become a political issue. Opposed by the C.C.F. party from its (and their) inception, they were now presented by the Liberal opposition to a practically convinced public as a symptom of the Bennett Government's inability to devise any fundamental solutions to the problems of unemployment. The Prime Minister was almost ready to close down the camps altogether, and might well have taken the decision but for the fervent defence of the system by its creator. McNaughton and Bennett thrashed the matter out at a meeting on 18 July. Each repeated his arguments, McNaughton that to abandon the camps would plunge the country into chaos and quite possibly revolution, Bennett that to continue them was becoming increasingly difficult in view of public hostility. Then McNaughton spoke of the grave situation that would result if his troops were required to be used in aid of the civil power. The Prime Minister asked him if he really took so serious a view of the consequences of closure. McNaughton replied that "I fully believed that the situation this Winter would be very serious indeed unless our remedial measures were continued. . . ."[170] McNaughton kept his camps; Bennett lost his by-elections.

III

Another feature of the camp system bringing wide-spread criticism upon its administration was the amount which from the beginning it had been decided to pay the inmates. These became known, wryly among themselves, angrily among outsiders, as "the Royal Twenty-Centers." The sum of twenty cents a day for eight hours of a man's labour, often back-breaking labour, was not exactly princely even by the standards of the Great Depression; so long as it was paid, the charge that the camp system exploited slave labour was bound to be made, and made to stick. That the charge was unfair did not in the least detract from its being widely accepted as true. It was unfair in that no one was compelled (save by the whip of hunger) to enter the camps and that, once in, no one was compelled to remain. It was unfair, also, in that the twenty cents a day was not intended by the authorities as a wage in any sense, only as an allowance. Though the distinction between a wage and an allowance was eventually made to the satisfaction of the Department of Justice, the public at large remained unconvinced. If the men were being paid wages, then the federal government was violating its own minimum wage legislation; if they were paid an allowance, why was it only paid for days spent on the job?

By 1934 the criticism could no longer be brushed aside by scholastic definitions. On 29 May the Prime Minister called McNaughton on the telephone and told him "that due to the action of the Ontario Government in placing their camps on a wage basis of 25 cents an hour the Federal camps had been placed in a most invidious position and that it might be necessary, in view of the public opinion in favour of a wage basis, to close them up. . . . The Prime Minister mentioned the figure of $37,000,000 as the cost of the Ontario camps and said it was quite impossible for us to adapt our system to theirs."[171] Bennett, as noted above, was dissuaded from closing the camps on the grounds that to do so might bring on widespread rioting in the cities requiring the use of armed troops. But there remained the increasingly difficult task of defending the twenty-cent allowance against criticism by no means all of which was ill-natured or ill-informed. "The great weakness of the present system," H. J. Barber, M.P. for Chilliwack, B.C., wrote in October 1934,

> lies in the fact that it does not give these men, particularly the young men, a chance to become self-supporting and an opportunity to assume the responsibility of citizenship. Men enter these camps, not to work, for they well know that those in charge have no authority to compel them to work, but to receive at the expense of the Country shelter, food and clothing which they claim they are entitled to as long as they conduct themselves properly. They accept this for a time, then move on, roaming the country, returning to the camps when in need of food and clothing. This life undoubtedly tends to destroy the self respect and lower the morale of the men. . . . The time has arrived when these men should be placed on a wage. Allow me to suggest a wage of say $2.00 per day, with a deduction of say 60 cents per day to cover the cost of feeding. . . ."[171]

To these observations McNaughton added his own. "The scheme of Unemployment Relief instituted by the Department of National Defence," he wrote,

> never aimed at making the men self-supporting in the sense advocated by Mr. Barber. Its purpose was to meet an emergency situation and to care for many thousands until they could be re-absorbed in industry, not to set up a wholly new and socialistic substitute for the ordinary methods of organization of the economic life of the country. The aim has been and is to build up morale through work; to proceed by persuasion and not by compulsion, and to do everything possible to facilitate the flow back of men to industry as soon as they are mentally and physically fit and positions are available. . . .
>
> The task assigned to this Department is to care for the greatest number of single homeless men possible under the emergency conditions existing; to give them work with a view to re-establishing their morale and efficiency; to choose this work carefully so that by reason of doing it no others will be deprived of opportunities for remunerative employment otherwise available; to turn these men back to industry restored physically and morally and well able to earn their own living. Our task is not to centralize a large section of industry in our own hands in a permanent system either on a wage basis or any other.[172]

Replies in this sense were sent to the many correspondents critical of the "no wages" policy; but they carried less and less conviction as the depression dragged more and more men to the depths.

IV

A third criticism of the camps was that, being run by the Department of National Defence, the life lived by their inmates was the military life. "This camp," declared the *Rifle Range Worker* (a broadsheet circulated among the members of the camp at Long Branch, Ont.) on 1 May 1933, " is part of the general campaign of the Bennett Government to militarize the unemployed youth and to prepare them for cannon fodder in the next war." Such extreme comment could be dismissed for the communist propaganda which in fact it was. But from other, more responsible, sources there came many expressions of disquiet. "Are these men engaged only to work at the camps," inquired the Secretary of the Montreal Trades and Labour Council on its behalf, "or are they subject to military training certain number of hours each day? . . . Is the intention of the Government to use these men as soldiers in case of emergency? You will understand, Mr. Minister, that the workers of the country are alarmed by the sending of single men to the different military camps."[174] "We do not think," declared J. S. Woodsworth in the House of Commons on 27 June 1935, "unemployed men should be put under the control of the National Defence department. Why should they? The officers over them may be kindly men, but they are not accustomed to the problems which these young men face. Army discipline should not apply in these camps; the training and discipline of army officers does not particularly qualify them to deal with this class of men."[175]

In numerous letters and statements, McNaughton and his colleagues sought to dispel the pervasive impression that military discipline, often of the harshest kind, prevailed in the camps. "The men are not subject to any military training of any kind whatsoever," he pointed out in a draft reply to the Montreal Trades and Labor Council. "The standing instructions are that 'No military discipline or training will be instituted; the status of the personnel will remain civilian in all respects'. . . . It is neither the intention nor would it be either advantageous or practicable to make use of the personnel on unemployment relief projects as soldiers. . . . There is no ulterior military purpose and all concerned will be happy to see a restoration of trade conditions which will bring about termination. . . ."[176] To Percy W. Bengough, who had written on behalf of the Trades and Labor Council of Vancouver to state that "the military discipline is in many cases severe and unreasonable," McNaughton replied: "The facts are that from the commencement of this phase of relief the policy has been that the personnel engaged on the relief projects should remain as civilians and be treated in a manner similar to that obtaining in ordinary camps such as those established by contractors for construction purposes . . . and unlike the relief camps in the United States there is absolutely no military discipline exercised whatever. . . ."[177]

These explanations did not overstate the facts; they could, indeed, truthfully have ventured further. From the inception of the camps, as McNaughton had written, those concerned with their operation had gone out of their way to avoid any appearance of military control. "It is not considered advisable," wrote the commander of Military District No. 6 only a fortnight after the scheme had been put in hand, "that these unemployment camps should in any way be considered as military. It is anticipated that anything indicative of military control would be resented and probably lead to trouble."[178] This viewpoint of the field expressed exactly the attitude at headquarters. In their administration of the camps, the officers concerned took care to see that no one in military uniform was present. Those in charge of the various projects, as already noted, were civilian foremen; the centres of administration were also manned by civilians. Officers from National Defence Headquarters inspecting the camps and the projects always wore civilian clothes. When camps or projects were located on or near military establishments, officers and N.C.O.'s connected with unemployment relief were instructed not to appear in uniform before their civilian charges. The civilian nature of the enterprise was zealously propagated and measures to ensure its non-military appearance were meticulously observed.

Yet so long as the camps were administered by the Department of National Defence, the public steadfastly refused to allow that appearances were in fact reality. Since their administration by the Army worked so strongly against their public acceptance, it may be wondered why the Government did not transfer it to some other Department, such as the Department of Labour. The official explanation for administering the camps through the Department of National Defence was that it was the only Department whose existing organization enabled it to do the job.[179] That was true enough. Yet it might have been possible for the Government to use the facilities of the Army, with its Engineer Branch, its Ordnance Branch, its Administrative Branch, its Contracts Branch, its Financial Accounting Service, while retaining the more obviously civilian direction of the Department of Labour to ensure greater public acceptance of its contribution. To some extent this was done. Enquiries and criticism of unemployment relief were generally answered by the Chief of the General Staff but sent out over the signature of the Minister or Deputy Minister of Labour. But the real reason for the domination of unemployment relief activities by the military was McNaughton's interest in them. The camps had been his brain-child; he had become almost their sole defender against their many detractors. To have relinquished protective custody might have brought about their abolition. Abolition he adamantly opposed. He believed the good they did immeasurably overshadowed any harm. He was acutely apprehensive lest discharge of their occupants create a revolutionary situation in which his small permanent force army would be disastrously exposed. He even thought that by its administration of relief the Canadian military might regain that place in public esteem it had not enjoyed since the days of Ypres and Vimy Ridge. "Right from the very beginning of my experience at National Defence Headquarters," General McNaughton informed the Conference of Defence Associations in 1934,

> I found it was impossible to get representatives of other Departments and members of governments, both federal and provincial, to come to us on our ground. They would not come and discuss defence matters. We could not get them interested in it. We felt at the time if we were ever going to make any progress we must go to them. We had to find some means by which we could go to them on their ground. Now this Unemployment Relief Scheme has worked out very well indeed. . . . We are on the happiest relations with the Dominion Government and with the Provincial Governments, and also with the other Departments of the Federal Service."[180]

If the speaker believed these remarks, when uttered, to be an accurate depiction of the real state of affairs, he sorely deceived himself; a year later they bore no resemblance to reality at all. The Prime Minister, though also prone to self-deception, was not that much deceived. He decided, early in 1935, that the Chief of the General Staff had become a political liability, and would have to go before the General Election. McNaughton accordingly was removed from the post, to become President of the National Research Council.*

*Two versions of this episode, neither of which can be documented, have reached me from reliable sources. In one, that given in the text, the Prime Minister wanted to get McNaughton out of the limelight for his own political advantage. In the other, the Prime Minister is said to have been motivated by a desire to install his Chief of the General Staff in a less vulnerable post before a new Administration, catering to public feeling, retired him from public life. Which, if either, version is correct I do not know. Mackenzie King's comment on appointing McNaughton as Commander, 1st Canadian Army Division, in October 1939 is consistent with both: "No better evidence could be given of our disinterested action than in giving this command to one who comes more particularly from that particular group"—"the school of MacBrien, of Bennett, and Herridge." Quoted in J. W. Pickersgill, *The Mackenzie King Record*, Vol. I, *1939–1944* (Toronto, 1960), p. 38.

V

The final year of McNaughton's tenure as Chief of the General Staff was largely taken up by the revolutionary situation created by massive unemployment in British Columbia. In that province the depression had struck earliest and hardest. Its basic industries—lumbering, mining, fishing—crippled, much of its labour force was thrown out of work. The province's own unemployed were soon joined by the jobless from other parts of Canada drifting westward to escape a more severe winter. To deal with the crisis, the provincial government set up its own relief camps; no fewer than 237 such camps, located for the most part in the more remote regions, took care of nearly 20,000 men—about a third of the total relief camp population of the country. The financial and administrative resources of British Columbia proved unequal to the task; on 1 June 1933, by agreement between the governments at Victoria and Ottawa, the camps passed from provincial jurisdiction to that of the Department of National Defence.[181]

By February 1934, the unemployment situation in Vancouver had become critical. To the already unmanageable number of the jobless congregating in the city were being added daily strikers from outside. Agitators in the relief camps were calling with some success upon their inmates to leave the camps and join the strikers at Vancouver. Believing a general strike to be imminent, the provincial Attorney-General, Gordon Sloan, telegraphed the Prime Minister at Ottawa on 24 February demanding that the federal government take immediate steps to remove the men from the camps. Bennett replied, after consultation with McNaughton, that "the constitutional duty of maintaining law and order in British Columbia rests with your Government and we rely upon your effectively discharging your responsibilities. If you state you are unable to discharge your constitutional obligations and seek federal assistance it will be furnished when requested as by law provided."[182] This was the opening round of what became a protracted wrangle between the provincial and the federal authorities over which of the two governments was primarily responsible for relieving the unrest. Underlying what on the surface appeared to be a Dominion-provincial wrangle that did nothing to ease the plight of the jobless and which the country could ill afford was the political rivalry of the British Columbia premier, T. D. Pattullo, and the Canadian Prime Minister. Duff Pattullo was the head of a Liberal government. He was, moreover, firmly persuaded that the whole approach of the Conservative government at Ottawa to the problems created by the depression was fundamentally unsound, and that nothing was more ill-conceived than the relief camps. Not relief but public works were needed. But if Pattullo was determined to discredit the camp system, McNaughton was determined to defend it. It was McNaughton who, sometimes in consultation with Cabinet ministers, sometimes not, prepared most of the replies sent over the Prime Minister's name to the British Columbia authorities. The correspondence between them is as irate as any in Canadian political life.

The crisis of February and March 1934 passed without the rioting and bloodshed that the British Columbia Government believed to be imminent. While it was McNaughton's policy not to readmit to his camps men known to be agitators or incorrigible offenders, he decided to deal leniently with most of the deserters. These were eventually prevailed upon to leave Vancouver and return to the camps. "It is particularly satisfactory to note," McNaughton wrote for the Prime Minister's information on 9 March, "that due to the firm yet conciliatory stand taken by the District Officer Commanding, he has been able to pass the critical situation with the discharge of only 44 men from our camps out of a present strength of 5,548 in the area under his administration."[183] A few days later General Ashton cabled: "All quiet on Western front." So it remained, more or less, for the rest of the year.

By December, Premier Pattullo had once more became acutely apprehensive. The wise course, he advised the Prime Minister at Ottawa, would be to create a public tribunal to investigate the grievances connected with the camps.[184] Pattullo's message was referred to the Department of National Defence, where it awaited McNaughton's attention. By the time McNaughton returned to the capital, the pressures on the Prime Minister to accede to the demand for an investigation had intensified. A Christmas Day message, requesting the appointment of an independent commission of inquiry, was sent by all members of Parliament and all members of the Provincial Legislature from the greater Vancouver area. Bennett, who already doubted whether it was politically feasible to continue the camps, was shaken by this new outburst of criticism, and disposed to give in to it. But McNaughton insisted that he hold firm. Telegrams signed by Bennett, but drafted by McNaughton, were sent to Pattullo and the protesting parliamentarians. "No investigation is necessary," Bennett's message to Pattullo (which the Minister of National Defence read to the House of Commons on 21 January 1935) observed, "for the press and citizens have been invited to visit these camps ever since they have been established, and of one hundred and thirty applications which have been made for reinstatement in the camps, one hundred and twenty three have been reinstated, which indicates the sympathetic disposition of the officers in charge to the problem with which they are dealing."[185] When Pattullo, in reply, pressed his case on the grounds that only public investigation would dispel public suspicions, Bennett, again employing McNaughton's draft, suggested that Pattullo visit the camps himself: "Duty of correctly informing public of British Columbia rests with you directly and I suggest that importance which you have indicated attaches to this matter warrants you or your Ministers taking time to visit some of our camps so that your opinions may have the force of personal knowledge. . . ."[186] A further exchange of telegrams only served to dig each side deeper into its entrenched position.[187]

McNaughton remained confident that his position would be vindicated not only by abstract justice but by practical results. "I am glad that the situation in Vancouver is clearing up," he wrote on 10 January 1935, to his District Officer Commanding in Victoria. "I hope that we have heard the last of this kind of trouble. . . ."[188] But General Ashton, from his closer vantage point, had doubts about the wisdom of the government's policy, particularly its stubborn refusal to take an initiative in putting its own case before the public. He wondered whether some sort of public relations campaign had not become necessary, and expressed his misgivings, together with his suggestions, in a letter to the Secretary of Militia Services, Department of National Defence, on 5 January:

> In conversation with leading citizens in Vancouver and elsewhere . . . it is found that the actual conditions in the camps are not fully understood by the public and that the feeling does exist that many of the men refused readmission for organizing have been hardly dealt with by foremen and that these men have no court of appeal. No public statement has been made by the officials of this Department answering in any way the charges made by the men in Vancouver with the result that the public have heard only one side of the story and there is a definite feeling that the Department should take steps to place their side before the public as soon as possible.
>
> As action to this end is a matter of Government policy and should be very carefully considered, the question of the best method of meeting this situation is submitted for your decision and instructions. The main points which it is desirable to place before the public in order to gain more general support are as follows:
>
> (i) Beyond the general administration by the officials of the Department of National Defence, there is no semblance of military training or military

discipline in the camps; even in Point Grey, composed almost entirely of Non-Permanent Active Militia Men, no drill or military procedure is followed.
(ii) There are now few charges of poor feeding. . . .
(iii) The "Blacklist"— . . . Practically all men who are not definitely listed as organizers or agitators or who have proved themselves incorrigible on several occasions, are being readmitted. The public should realize that the Department cannot be expected to reinstate men whose avowed purpose is to continue agitating and creating trouble until the camp system is abolished. . . .
(v) The public are now aware of the true nature of the anti-relief camp movement:—
(a) That the Relief Camp Workers' Union is fundamentally a communist body or at least controlled by them, is directed and holds its meetings at 52½ Cordova St. in a hall which is hung with Red flags, the walls covered with Communistic devices.
(b) That their definite programme is not so much the alleviation of camp conditions but is definitely the breaking up of the camp system. . . .

No attempt has been made by any newspaper to seek an interview or an expression of opinion from this Headquarters on the situation. It is not considered at all advisable for the D.O.C. to write a letter to the newspapers and open up a controversy. His position would probably only strengthen the arguments in connection with military control and militarism. I have considered the question of suggesting that the editors of all Vancouver papers be given an interview together but I hesitate about asking for such an opportunity. The question arises as to whether the leaders of welfare organizations and other leading citizens should be invited to a conference with the D.O.C. Again I hesitate to put the D.O.C. in the position of asking for such a conference.

It has been suggested that now that the situation in Vancouver is clearing up and the men returning to camps, a statement, covering the above points, emanating from Ottawa, might have the desired effect if it were widely circulated in our local papers. It certainly appears to me advisable that some action to restore public confidence in the camp system is needed. . . .[189]

This *cri de cœur* brought no response whatever from Headquarters. About two months later Ashton tried again to impress upon Ottawa the importance of stating its case in a way which would convince the public that the facts of life in the relief camps were not as it was disposed to believe. "The newspaper clippings which we are forwarding to you," he wrote to McNaughton on 16 March, "indicate the constant attacks against the camp relief system which are being fed to the public constantly. . . . It is seldom, if ever, that anything besides adverse criticism appears in the press." He added that he had himself attempted to counteract this hostile propaganda by speaking about the camps to the Rotary Club in Victoria. "One of the newspapers definitely misquoted me but has promised to correct their statements. This," he had to concede, "has not yet been published."[190] The subject came up again in a long-distance telephone conversation on March 20. "General Ashton," according to McNaughton's account,

inquired as to the advisability of him making a public statement through one of the larger clubs in Vancouver so that the general public might be informed just what the Department had to contend with from communist organizations. . . . I told General Ashton that this was not a matter for him; that in anything he might have to say he should not talk about the communistic actions in the camps for the purpose of breaking up the camp system, but continue to stress the object of the Department in maintaining these camps and the conditions under which they were being operated. Our responsibilities were clear, and at this stage we were concerned with the men only so long as they were in our camps; that if they left they became a provincial responsibility unless and until such time as the Province called for assistance under the Militia Act; that, in consequence, any statement in respect to the situation likely to be created by men leaving our camps was a matter for the Premier of the Province. . . .[191]

Meanwhile, the chances of serious disorders which in January had seemed to be abating had by March become very much greater. "Every indication," Ashton had written on 16 March,

is to the effect that a wide-spread disturbance which it is hoped will affect every camp in the Province is shortly due. New tactics have been adopted in that the date of this demonstration is being kept absolutely secret. . . .

It is also reported that new tactics will be put into effect: (*a*) that the men will be more violent in their demeanour; (*b*) that actual sabotage, possibly including the burning of camps, will be put into effect; (*c*) that, in order to paralyze police action in aid of our camp staffs and to make their demonstration more widely felt, men of the more distant camps will not proceed to Vancouver as formerly, but to the smaller towns where they will congregate, demand food and housing and bring pressure to bear on the Government and public opinion. . . .

The strain on our group staffs and camp staffs is beginning to tell, many are getting thoroughly discouraged and a number of resignations, particularly in the case of camp foremen, are being received. One can hardly blame them as they are up against militancy all the time and are now subjected to every possible annoyance by the direct instructions of the Union. . . .

I do not want you to feel that we are unduly depressed by these conditions, but the strain on everyone is rather severe. I merely want you to know as clearly as possible the exact situation.[192]

Five days later the inevitable telegram arrived from Pattullo. This time the correspondence was conducted with Sir George Perley, who was acting as Prime Minister in the absence of Bennett through illness; but McNaughton continued to supply the drafts for most of the federal government's replies. Pattullo's message, dated 25 March, revived the demand for the appointment of a commission of investigation of the relief camps, and raised a fresh demand for their abolition.

Surely your Government must be apprised of fact that something better will have to be offered as solution of problem. Men are becoming inflamed through increasing agitation and I am fearful that there may be riots, bloodshed and loss of property. With so many things necessary and desirable to be done it is incomprehensible that your Government will not make provision so that these men can be put to work upon a basis of reasonable wages. I have tried in all my correspondence to use temperate language but the situation is getting so serious that I must convey to you in the strongest possible terms that some form of permanent solution must be found to meet this problem. . . .[193]

The next morning a meeting was held in Ottawa at the home of Sir George Perley to consider what, if any, reply ought to be sent to Pattullo. Those taking part were Perley, the Minister of National Defence, the Minister of Labour, the Deputy Minister of Labour (W. M. Dickson), the Chief Private Secretary to the Prime Minister (R. K. Finlayson), and General McNaughton. "It was decided," the latter's account of the meeting recorded,

that the reply should re-affirm the position which had been taken by the Prime Minister in respect to disturbances and possible disturbances on previous occasions and in particular
(a) that the requests for a Citizens' Committee of investigation of the camps under the Department of National Defence should be refused;
(b) that the Premier of British Columbia should be pressed himself to visit the camps and to make a public statement on the conditions;
(c) that he should be told that the Dominion Government were in no doubt, as a result of their own investigations, that these conditions were fair and reasonable under the circumstances;
(d) that he should be reminded that responsibility for the maintenance of law and order rested in the first instance on the Province. . . .[194]

McNaughton, together with Dickson and Finlayson, drafted a telegram according to these instructions, which was sent to Pattullo on 26 March. Not surprisingly it failed to mollify him. "Neither your telegram nor several telegrams from Prime Minister," Pattullo cabled back the next day, "indicate understanding situation here. . . . We are not responsible for conduct of camps and responsibility of informing public thereon rests with your Government."[195] Perley answered acidly: "You are the head of the responsible Government of your Province and surely you are not ready to admit that an investigation and report by your Government would not satisfy public opinion."[196] Pattullo's patience was now almost exhausted. "Have received your telegram of today with amazement," he telegraphed on 27 March.

Your Government's lack of appreciation this situation incomprehensible. Some of my Ministers have visited camps and report condition of camps good but that is not the point. Men have differences with foremen and are discharged from camp. Many of those discharged have been taken back but considerable numbers who are agitators have been blacklisted for good. These excite large number others. Men feel they have a grievance and for this reason and dangers involved and system as a whole public at large feels very strongly and it is to allay this sentiment that I have repeatedly recommended special committee. Our Government has never been authorized by your Government to hear complaints of occupants camps nor do I think were such investigation authorized it would satisfy public opinion. If your Government is under impression that every Ukase issued by your Government is accepted by public generally, your Government is labouring under grave delusion. Your Government is facing adverse public opinion under a system which is generally and I think properly condemned. It seems almost useless to continue this correspondence in light of your wires but officers in your service know seriousness conditions and if there is riot, bloodshed and destruction property responsibility will rest upon your Government.[197]

McNaughton's draft reply, sent to Pattullo by Perley the next day, was brief and uncompromising: "Note that you are satisfied that conditions of camps as such is good and I trust you have so informed the public of British Columbia. With respect to last sentence your telegram I again remind you that responsibility for maintenance law and order in British Columbia rests with your Government."[198]

The stage was now set for a showdown, which the strikers were not long in providing. At about the same time as Perley's cable was sent off to Pattullo, McNaughton learned from Ashton over the telephone that a general evacuation of the relief camps had been planned, probably for 4 April. Ashton reported that he had himself seen the Premier, who "was very much upset over the possibility of a serious disturbance and was still pressing for a committee of investigation." He also reported that Pattullo had gone so far as to ask the Governor General, Lord Bessborough, then touring the Province, for his opinion about what should be done: "His Excellency had taken the stand that it was more his duty to receive advice than to give it"—a stand incidentally not in keeping with Bagehot's conception of the duties of the Crown. The Premier and his Attorney-General had moreover tried to bring pressure on Ashton himself: "They asked me," he told McNaughton, "to express my opinion on this question of an inquiry, which I did not give them;

also tried to urge me to back them up in their stand; this also I naturally refused."[199] It may be, however, that these tactics were not wholly unsuccessful, for Ashton added to his account of their confrontation: "As far as I am personally concerned, I should not object to an inquiry if the Government thought one advisable. There have of course been minor mistakes made by our untrained foremen and occasionally by the superintendents but I feel I have nothing to fear in regard to the general administration which has followed the regulations laid down by Ottawa as closely as possible. . . ."[200]

The Government now lost its nerve. Late on 28 March, the Cabinet, in the absence of the Prime Minister and without McNaughton in attendance, decided to appoint a Royal Commission to investigate conditions in the camps administered by the Department of National Defence. The Commission, consisting of the Honourable W. A. Macdonald, Chairman, Charles T. McHattie, and the Reverend E. D. Braden, was authorized by order-in-council (P.C. 861) on 1 April. But the Government's surrender on the principle of inspection of the camps did not forestall the general strike of their inmates. That occurred, as anticipated, on 4 April. It may have been, as General Ashton reported to McNaughton, that most of the men had left the camp under compulsion from a militant minority.[201] But, for whatever reason, the Unemployment Relief system had broken down, and stood on the verge of disintegration. The Commission met as the strikers streamed into Vancouver. Its first witness was General Ashton. "As usual," he related despondently, "I noted in two of the newspaper reports that statements of mine were incorrectly reported."[202]

It was at this juncture that there arrived on the scene the Commissioner of the R.C.M.P., General MacBrien. His appraisal differed considerably from that of General Ashton. He recommended that the men on strike be allowed to return to the camps without fear of punishment or dismissal. Ashton, who met with MacBrien at McNaughton's suggestion to discuss the situation, disapproved of this course. The camp staffs, he pointed out, had been sorely abused by the antics of some of the militants; he was afraid that if these were allowed to return, the staffs would quit on the spot. MacBrien evidently allowed Ashton to understand that it might not be altogether a bad thing if they did quit. The camp system, he said, had lasted too long, and it was time to replace it with something else—"work with wages on construction."[203]

MacBrien's diagnosis, and even more his remedy, introduced a new and vexing factor into McNaughton's calculations. MacBrien, of course, had every right to come to Vancouver to size up the situation for himself: his own men were more likely than McNaughton's to become embroiled in any rioting, at least in its early stages. At the same time, neither his temperament nor his previous career—he had been senior to McNaughton in the army for many years—made his advice very welcome. Should MacBrien come to the conclusion that McNaughton's policies were ill-advised, he would not hesitate to interfere. If that was McNaughton's fear, it was soon realized. MacBrien placed his views directly before the Minister of National Defence by telephone and telegram.[204] McNaughton was greatly disturbed at this intervention.

I told General Ashton that a telegram, in code, was going to him now asking him to warn MacBrien of the very serious consequences that may result if he runs counter to expressed Government policy; that this telegram would ask him, General Ashton, to show General MacBrien telegrams from Sir George Perley to Premier Pattullo, copies of which he had and which gave our present policy. I also told General Ashton that a Cabinet meeting was called for 3 p.m. to-day and that at that time the Government will decide if there was to be any change in policy or not, and that as soon as this was decided I would communicate with him.

I said that I was very anxious that MacBrien should not weaken our position by giving out a lot of half-baked ideas; that I was particularly upset that he had started this and expressed opinions without having had the courtesy or the good sense to obtain information on the situation from General Ashton himself. . . .[205]

The crucial meeting of the Cabinet took place on 19 April, two hours after this conversation. MacBrien might be on the spot in Vancouver; but McNaughton had the ineluctable advantage of being on the spot where policy, in the last analysis, was decided, and where he could continue to exert his almost mesmeric influence on the members of Bennett's government. The meeting was held at the home of the Acting Prime Minister; in addition to Perley, seven other ministers attended: Stirling, Stewart, Weir, Rhodes, Hanson, Cahan, Dupré. The only other person present was McNaughton himself. Most of the meeting was taken up by a lengthy presentation by Perley, based on a memorandum prepared by McNaughton, in which the continuation of the camp system, and, more immediately, the exclusion from the camps of known agitators, were strenuously defended. The conclusion of McNaughton's memorandum read as follows:

Abolition of the camps and a programme of work and wages has been suggested by citizens and by General MacBrien. Obviously anything of this nature done in British Columbia must redound throughout Canada and it is not a matter of 20,000 or so single homeless men now in the camps but of many times that number who would clamour for like treatment.

> To employ even 30,000 men on a work and wage basis would cost about $50,000,000 per annum for labour and materials and, in consequence, any such proposal seems outside the realm of practical policy.
>
> There remains the present policy if it can be made effective, and it can be provided a firm hand is taken and maintained through the current local difficulties in Vancouver.
>
> As a first step the communist and the agitator must be curbed so that men of good-will shall have an opportunity to benefit by the care which is extended to them.[206]

As between a prospective expenditure of $50,000,000 per annum and allowing McNaughton a firm hand against communists in Vancouver, the Cabinet did not hesitate. The existing policy was reaffirmed.

As soon as the Cabinet meeting was over, McNaughton telephoned Ashton in Victoria:

> *C.G.S.*: Anything new?
>
> *D.O.C.*: Nothing new. . . . Spoke to MacBrien; he rather resented message and went up in the air and said that he gave advice when he thought it was right. Always his principle and always would be.
>
> *C.G.S.*: I have another message. Will you inform MacBrien that the substance of his telephone conversation with the Minister of National Defence last night together with his telegram were put before the Government today and our policy was reaffirmed in every particular. . . . The substance of the whole thing is that we carry on as we have been doing, there is no change in our policy.
>
> *D.O.C.*: It would be as well to give it to me in a full wire. I will see MacBrien in the morning, he is coming to Victoria . . . I will meet him at the boat . . . and give him the wire to read.
>
> *C.G.S.*: Tell him the Government is very upset with him.
>
> *D.O.C.*: He spoke as if he didn't give a damn.
>
> *C.G.S.*: He is in for serious trouble.[207]

Victory over MacBrien was easier to come by than victory in Vancouver. On 23 April, for the first time in the strike, serious rioting broke out. A radio address a few days later by the Mayor of the city, interpreting the disorders as part of "a deliberate attempt . . . to commence a proletariat revolution . . . under the auspices of communistic leadership," markedly turned public feeling against the strikers. In these circumstances the military, on McNaughton's orders, made every effort to take the strikers back into the camps, waiving the medical examination ordinarily required and taking a lenient and liberal view of the past record of applicants for re-admission. The policy succeeded. On 20 May General Ashton reported to McNaughton that "the situation is breaking and that if we keep firm over the next thirty-six hours or so it would be all over. . . ."[208] So it proved.

There remained a hard core of dissatisfied strikers and their sympathizers who, on 1 June, voted to begin what they called "a march on Ottawa" to present their demands in person to the Government, hopefully picking up recruits on their way across the Dominion. On 3 June about 900 strikers set out on their journey, jumping aboard east-bound freight trains and hitch-hiking. By the time the "marchers" reached Regina on 14 June, their ranks had grown to over 1,300. The federal Government, in order to forestall their further progress eastward, offered to pay the expenses of a delegation which could present the strikers' demands to the government at Ottawa. A delegation of eight representatives accordingly met with members of the Cabinet, including the Prime Minister, on 22 June. It was led by one Arthur H. Evans, an avowed communist agitator. The delegation demanded the abolition of the camps; the government spokesmen refused. It was not exactly a tranquil confrontation; Evans boasted afterwards that he had called the Prime Minister a "liar," while Bennett called him a "thief."[209] The delegation rejected the government's offer to set up a special camp near Regina in which the marchers could be cared for while arrangements for returning them to their camps were made, and returned to the waiting rank and file uttering inflammatory remarks about streets flowing with blood.[210]

The Government decided to handle the situation by a combination of moderation and firmness. A camp for any of the strikers desiring to enter it was set up at Lumsden, Sask., from which free transportation to camp or home would be provided; at the same time Bennett announced in the House of Commons that he had given orders to the R.C.M.P. not to allow the marchers further illegal rides on trains, and that if they proceeded eastwards by this form of transportation they would be stopped by force. "The government . . . believes as firmly as it is possible to believe," he added, "that the present movement of these marchers upon Ottawa in defiance of the law is in reality an organized effort on the part of the various communist organizations throughout Canada to effect the overthrow of constituted authority. . . ."[211] Many of the marchers had by this time had enough, and prepared to enter the government's camp; but those who tried to leave the march were violently prevented from doing so by Evans's followers, and the camp, where preparations for feeding and clothing 1,000 men had been made, was closed on July 12 when less than fifty men showed up.

On 1 July—the day after McNaughton's term as Chief of the General Staff expired—a Dominion Day meeting of strikers in Regina was forcibly broken up by raiding R.C.M.P. and local police; a policeman was killed in the ensuing fighting, two of the R.C.M.P. were very seriously injured, and there were in all about fifty other casualties, some wounded by bullets. Most of the strikers abandoned the march after this episode, and were returned to the destination of their choice at federal government expense. August saw a brief revival of the movement, and this time about 400 men actually arrived at Ottawa, camping in the vicinity of Dow's Lake for a fortnight before a shortage of funds and faith caused them to disperse.

The Liberal party promised during the general election campaign of 1935 to end the relief camps if elected. On taking office, the Mackenzie King government decided to keep them going during the winter, but transferred their administration to the Department of Labour. By the fall of 1936, the last camp was closed down, never to re-open. Whether the Unemployment Relief scheme really helped to combat the Great Depression, or whether it delayed recovery, must remain in dispute. But it unquestionably contributed to the meagre defence plant at the disposal of the Dominion when war came in 1939. Barracks at Calgary and Kingston, buildings for the Arsenal at Valcartier, the R.C.A.F. station at Trenton, airfields across the country, were the result: not much, perhaps, but something—"useful material foundations," the Army Historian has described them, "for a future re-armament programme."[212]

The Navy and the Nation

JELLICOE'S MISSION AND ITS ENEMIES

In the summer of 1918, the British Admiralty sought to reassert as the foundation of postwar naval policy the doctrine of dominion contributions to an Imperial Grand Fleet. That doctrine, propounded before the Great War, had proved unacceptable to Laurier and his Liberals, who had blocked its provisional and temporary acceptance by the Borden Government; in 1918 it proved unacceptable to Borden himself. "Upon examination," he wrote retrospectively, "I reached the unhesitating conclusion that it could not be accepted, as it did not sufficiently recognize the status of the Dominions. It seemed obvious that the acceptance of such a proposal would offend the newly awaked sense of nationhood which pervaded the people of Canada."[1] On 2 August, Borden and those Ministers with him overseas (Rowell, Mewburn, and Ballantyne) "decided we could not accept Admiralty's suggestions," and on 7 August their decision was conveyed by Borden to the First Lord. The Admiralty then proposed that Viscount Jellicoe of Scapa, just resigned from the post of First Sea Lord, should undertake a mission to Canada, as to the other self-governing dominions, so that, after surveying the scene at close quarters, he could offer advice to their governments on their postwar naval policies. Borden agreed. He consulted the other dominion premiers and secured their approval (with the exception of the premier of Newfoundland, who preferred to deal bilaterally) of the following memorandum:

The Dominion Ministers, having considered the Admiralty Memorandum of May 17th, 1918, on the Naval Defence of the British Empire, which was circulated to the Imperial War Conference, 1918, submit the following conclusions and observations:

1. The proposals set forth in the Admiralty Memorandum for a single navy at all times under a central naval authority are not practicable.

2. Purely from the standpoint of naval strategy, the reasons thus put forward for the establishment of a single navy for the Empire under a central navy authority, are strong but not unanswerable. The experience gained in this war has shown that in time of war a Dominion navy (e.g., that of Australia), can operate with the highest efficiency as part of a united navy under one direction and command established after the outbreak of war.

3. It is thoroughly recognized that the character of construction, armament and equipment, and the methods and principles of training, administration and organization, should proceed along the same lines in all the navies of the Empire. This policy has already been followed in those Dominions which have established naval forces.

4. For this purpose the Dominions would welcome visits from a highly qualified representative of the Admiralty who, by reason of his ability and experience, would be thoroughly competent to advise the naval authorities of the Dominions in such matters.

5. As naval forces come to be developed upon a considerable scale by the Dominions it may be necessary hereafter to consider the establishment for war purposes of some supreme naval authority upon which each of the Dominions would be adequately represented.[2]

The Jellicoe Mission was publicly announced in December 1918; in February 1919 it set out on the dreadnought battle-cruiser *New Zealand* for the Pacific dominions *via* India on what was to be a world cruise lasting almost a year. The Mission did not arrive in Canada until November 1919, which gave the Canadian authorities plenty of time to consider what they might wish to do.

Canada had entered the war with a two-ocean navy, but with only one vessel for each ocean, the cruiser *Niobe* on the Atlantic Coast, the cruiser *Rainbow* on the Pacific. To this complement had been added in 1914 two submarines purchased (by the Premier of British Columbia) from the United States; two other submarines were acquired as a gift from the United Kingdom in June 1919. About 60 trawlers and 100 drifters completed the Canadian fleet at the war's end, but of these only nine were in commission by the end of 1919, in various states of operational readiness; their crews were carried on the books of either *Niobe* or *Rainbow*. The project of rebuilding the postwar navy could thus start pretty much from scratch.

For some time before the arrival of the Jellicoe Mission, the future of the Canadian naval establishment was canvassed both by ministers and (much more intensively) by the naval staff. In April 1919, Sir

Robert Borden, then in Paris for the Peace Conference, had written on the subject to Lord Milner:

During the past six months I have given some personal consideration to Canada's share in the maintenance of an adequate naval force for the Empire. In the past we have had difficulty upon the question of the locality and cost of construction. It was thought that the ships should be constructed in Canada so as to develop ship-building at various points in our Dominion. This involved a great increase in cost and delay as well. As the shipbuilding yards in Canada will be fully occupied for some time to come, [*] this question does not seem to arise under present conditions. On the other hand Great Britain possesses a much larger fleet than she should presumably require to maintain in time of peace. It might be possible for the Canadian Government to arrange that Canada should take over a fleet unit consisting, let us say, of a battleship, certain large and small cruisers, with the necessary quota of destroyers and submarines. This would serve two important purposes: first, it would be a relief *pro tanto* to the necessary effort of Great Britain in maintaining adequate naval strength, and secondly, it would appeal to the pride of the Canadian people and increase their sense of responsibility.

Within a considerable period the ships in question would become obsolete and then the duty would devolve upon Canada of supplying their place with up-to-date ships of like relative power.

I am putting this forward purely as a tentative proposal and without consultation with my colleagues, except those now in Paris who are disposed to give it their approval. . . .[3]

Meanwhile, the small naval staff at Ottawa—consisting for all practical purposes of the Deputy Minister of the Naval Service, the Director of the Naval Service, and the Assistant to the Director—were undertaking a more meticulous examination of Canada's future naval requirements. A Naval Committee, composed of the three aforementioned officials, was formed in February 1919, to "discuss and make recommendations to the Minister on (1) general policy, (2) general organization, (3) reports to Council, (4) new regulations, (5) any matters referred to the Committee by the Minister." It was to meet no less than once a week, and its members were to be joined, as the occasion demanded, by appropriate technical officers.† It held its first meeting

*This prognostication, like many others of the time, was to prove excessively optimistic.

†At its 13th meeting, on 28 May, the Deputy Minister expressed the view that its membership should be enlarged by bringing in other naval officers. The Director dissented strongly. Their admission would mean that the Committee would become bogged down in detail, whereas he thought it should be "confined principally to matters of general interest to the Department and to questions of policy." This view prevailed (Naval Records, N.S. 1078-1-1). The Naval

on the morning of 6 March. At the second meeting, a week later, the three officials looked to the future:

> Discussion on the probable development of the Canadian Navy during the next two years took place, and the opinion appeared to be that the present service should be reduced as far as possible to the minimum with a view to making a fresh start after the report from Lord Jellicoe had been presented.
>
> It was agreed that it was desirable to continue the training of boys and obtain as many as possible as a nucleus for a new service, the present services being very deficient of the right type of men for petty officers, this having been one of the difficulties in running the Patrol Service during the War. . . . The young officers from the College now with the Grand Fleet would also provide a good nucleus for the future. It was felt, however, that no great activity could be expected for several years, but that the problem of providing a modern base on each Coast would probably have to be faced very soon.[4]

Work was begun soon afterwards by the naval planners on a systematic programme of development. They produced a lengthy memorandum entitled "Proposals for Canadian Naval Expansion," being, in the words of its authors, "an attempt to formulate the principles leading to a decision on any recommendations put forward by the Admiralty."[5] Four methods of Canadian contribution were identified: provision of docking and repair bases for imperial ships; provision, in addition to the foregoing, of local defence forces; the further addition of "a small service such as is contemplated in the Fleet Unit scheme"; finally, and most ambitiously, provision and upkeep of "a fleet complete in all its different types of ships, with the necessary repairing and shipbuilding bases." The planners assumed that the second of these represented the minimum commitment of a future Canadian policy.

They had next to determine the size and composition of their prospective navy. A calculation of a minimum fleet requirement was based upon an estimate of "the probable scale of attack on Canadian coasts." This, they noted, had been the method of the Committee of Imperial Defence in 1911, and its prediction that Halifax could be attacked by "one or two cruisers" and Esquimalt (or, rather, Prince Rupert) by "one or two unarmoured cruisers" had been vindicated by the experience of the War. "A reasonable scale of defence against this force would be one of 50% greater strength, that is to say, three cruisers"; this force,

---

Committee did not survive the upheaval caused by the formation of a Department of National Defence in 1922, though it lingered long afterwards in its organization charts.

together with provision for docking and repair facilities for imperial ships, might therefore be taken as a minimum Canadian naval effort. The maximum effort was arrived at "by a different process of reasoning," namely, a computation of the value of all Canadian trade, allocating 3½ per cent of this amount to the upkeep of a Canadian navy—the navy estimates for the United Kingdom in 1913–14 being a similar percentage of total British foreign trade. The sum yielded by this ingenious calculation was no less than $39,500,000; this, the planners conceded, "would provide Canada with a fleet of some size." The proper policy, they concluded, "appears to be to establish a small service (Alternative 3) but to keep in mind the possible eventual construction of a complete fleet (Alternative 4)." Permanency in policy was essential: "By this is meant that a certain sized Naval service should be aimed at in say 15 or 20 years, the whole scheme being sealed by a special Act of Parliament. The effect of such a policy would greatly tend to economy in the prevention of hurried and ill-considered annual programmes, and it would give stability to the whole service. . . . It is not too much to say that a navy founded on the above principle, even though of very small size, would be far more efficient than a numerically larger navy constructed on some haphazard principle." The types of vessels required for the future Canadian navy would be P.C. boats (a type of craft useful in anti-submarine and escort duty, small, fast and highly manoeuvrable), destroyers, cruisers, submarines, and parent ships for the submarines. Battleships were rejected for the time being, partly because there were insufficient senior Canadian officers to take command of them, partly because they could not be built in Canada. The vessels were to be scheduled for construction in two seven years' shipbuilding programmes, as shown in Table I. Thus, by 1934, the completed Canadian fleet was to comprise seven cruisers, twelve destroyers, six submarines, eighteen PC boats, and three parent ships, with a proposed

TABLE I

FIRST SEVEN YEARS' PROGRAMME

	PC Boats	Destroyers	Cruisers	Submarines	Parent Ships
1920–21	6	–	–	–	1
1921–22	–	–	1	–	–
1922–23	4	1	–	–	–
1923–24	–	–	1	–	–
1924–25	4	1	–	–	–
1925–26	–	–	1	–	–
1926–27	4	1	–	–	–
Total	18	3	3	–	1

SECOND SEVEN YEARS' PROGRAMME

	PC Boats	Destroyers	Cruisers	Submarines	Parent Ships
1927–28	–	–	1	–	–
1928–29	–	3	–	–	1
1929–30	–	–	1	–	–
1930–31	–	–	–	6	1
1931–32	–	–	1	–	–
1932–33	–	6	–	–	–
1933–34	–	–	1	–	–
Total	–	9	4	6	2

complement of 8,500 officers and men. The total estimated cost of the entire shipbuilding programme was placed at $57,740,000. "On the completion of this programme," the planners noted hopefully, "it would be for the Government to decide whether the time had arrived to extend the scheme by including battleships in the new programme of construction." Alas for such brave hopes! If the government of that day had had its way, the naval estimates for 1934 would have amounted to $422,000—scarcely enough to buy a new PC boat let alone a battleship, and in fact, as the Chief of the Naval Staff at the time afterwards recalled, "not enough to pay for disbandment."*

This memorandum was the second of thirty-seven so-called "Occasional Papers" prepared by the Naval Staff in 1919 and 1920. They dealt, in considerable detail, with nearly every aspect of Canadian naval requirements; most were ready for the arrival of the Jellicoe Mission in November 1919, and it is "almost certain" (in the words of the Navy's Official Historian) that they were given to Jellicoe by the Director of the Naval Service, Vice-Admiral Sir Charles Kingsmill, who became a member of Jellicoe's staff for the duration of his Canadian tour. "Occasional Paper No. 2" was discussed at a meeting of the Naval Committee on 9 July; it was considered "a good basis for future development."[6]

The Jellicoe Mission landed at Esquimalt on 8 November, and began to make its way overland to Ottawa. The journey took more than a fortnight, and was punctuated by a succession of public engagements and banquets. The host at many of these occasions was the local branch of the Navy League of Canada. In his after-dinner speeches Jellicoe unfailingly stressed the need for maintaining and augmenting the sea-power of the Empire. "To my mind," he declared at Victoria on the day of his arrival, "the British Navy should not be kept short

*See below, chapter VII, pp. 274 ff.

of Overseas squadrons. . . . We must see to it that our Overseas Naval forces are never again permitted to be as they were prior to the War."[7] At Calgary (where R. B. Bennett presided), he told his Navy League audience: "There is a feeling abroad that the Millennium is in sight, and that there will be no more wars. . . . I cannot help thinking that these people will want to be sure that they are absolutely secure under a League of Nations before they will consent to cutting down expenditure for Naval Defence."[8]

These, and others like them, were provocative statements. By the time the Mission reached Ottawa, on 27 November, it had become an object of national attention, and its central figure an object of nation controversy. His most pungent critic, Henri Bourassa, ridiculed the notion that the Jellicoe Mission was only an advisory mission:

Si l'on veut saisir tous les objectifs, occultes ou avoués, des vastes projets dont lord Jellicoe est le promoteur, il ne suffit pas de lire ses discours d'avant-scène ni même son rapport publié et ceux à venir. Il faut d'abord se rendre bien compte de la situation réelle de l'amiral et du rôle *principale* que lui est confié. Ici comme en Australie, on a présenté lord Jellicoe comme un "aviseur" bénévole des gouvernements coloniaux; on nous a prévenus, avec trop d'insistance pour ne pas éveiller les soupçons, que cet homme éminent se gardera bien de "dicter" une ligne de conduite aux "nation-soeurs" ou mème de leur "préparer" une politique. Fort bien ; mais tout cela n'empêche que lord Jellicoe est l'un des fonctionnaires supérieurs de L'Amirauté anglaise, du commerce anglais, de la finance anglaise. . . .[9]

Immediately on his arrival at Ottawa, Jellicoe had the first of several meetings with the Canadian Prime Minister. "We discussed the possible extent of our co-operation in naval defence," Borden wrote in his *Memoirs* with characteristic reticence, "and I acquainted him with the difficulties arising from the unfortunate stringencies of our financial affairs."[10] It was not too strongly put. After his meeting with Jellicoe, Borden discussed the Admiral's proposals with the Cabinet. "There are several members of Council," he noted in his diary, "who do not want the Government to assume responsibility for the question of Naval defence at present because of the excessive cost."[11]

AEMILIUS JARVIS AND HIS FRIENDS

One group in Canadian life at this time did not regard the cost of sea-power as excessive. This was the Navy League. In 1919 that unusual lobby had attained, if not the height of its influence, at any rate the peak of its activities. These were prodigious. Throughout the Dominion

169 branches, in addition to the practical work of training boys in seamanship and attending to the welfare of sailors, kept up an incessant drumfire of propaganda. A monthly Navy League journal, *The Sailor*, had a paid circulation of 52,000; a variety of pamphlets were as widely distributed; while any action of the government in maritime affairs was the signal for a fusillade of resolutions, approving or condemning—usually condemning. The purpose of the propaganda was to develop, direct and sustain "the sea-conscious spirit." The Navy League pamphlet *From Sea to Sea* described how this was to be done:

> The map of the Dominion shows at a glance the extreme difficulty of spreading a Sea-Conscious Spirit amongst Canadians. This difficulty must be overcome; and those who are inspired with the importance of the task, must continue to shoulder the burden. . . .
>
> As a Merchant Navy is the first step to sea power in any nation, so is the seed-sowing of fundamental national ideals in the schools, the first step to national progress. There is no medium for national propaganda comparable to the school child. The Department of Education of nearly all the Provinces have, through the endeavours of the Navy League, incorporated Naval History as a definite part of their instruction. [*] The need for Sea-Conscious Spirit in the Government was felt when the Naval Estimates were placed before the House of Commons this year. Irrespective of party, members were, as a whole, apathetic to formulating a Canadian Naval Programme. Without an informed constituency in the country, inspired by the Members and friends of the Navy League, it would have been almost impossible to have laid the foundation of a Defensive Naval Policy. The League, accepting its public responsibility, stimulated such a pressure of public opinion upon Members of the House of Commons that they quickly sensed the National Spirit in the matter, and passed the Naval estimates. . . .[12]

Members of the House of Commons might have doubted whether the Navy League's intervention was as decisive as it claimed, even though

*They had indeed prescribed a League publication for use in schools, William Wood's *Flag and Fleet*, an anthology of patriotic, even jingoistic, prose and verse of which the following is a typical selection:

> I heard Polonius declaim
> About the new, the golden age,
> When Force would be the mark of shame,
> And men would curb their murderous rage.
> "Beat out your swords to pruning-hooks",
> He shouted to the folk,
> But I—I read my history books,
> And marvelled as he spoke.
> For it was glorious England,
> The mother of the Free,
> Who loosed that foolish tongue, but sent
> Her Admirals to sea.

In 1938 the writer, at the age of twelve, was presented with a copy of *Flag and Fleet*—as a prize for proficiency in Scripture.

it spent (according to a Cabinet minister) "half its revenue on messages." But at least it had the revenue to spend. Much of it came from small individual subscriptions, some from the contributions of men of great wealth. The Dominion Government, contrary to popular suspicion, gave it nothing.* But the Farmer Government in Ontario donated $50,000 to the Navy League in 1920.

Behind most voluntary movements attempting by peaceful persuasion and outside party politics to influence the policies of governments, is to be found a solitary individual without whose messianic zeal and tireless energy the movement would be powerless, if it could exist at all. The Round Table had Lionel Curtis; the League of Nations Society, Gilbert Murray. The Navy League of Canada had Æmilius Jarvis. Too little is known of this remarkable personality. Born near Toronto in 1860, by profession a financier and industrialist, his overriding interest since going to sea for two years at the age of sixteen was all things salt and nautical. He styled himself, and was everywhere addressed, as Commodore Jarvis; but he took this rank not from the Navy but from the Royal Canadian Yacht Club of Toronto, of which he was (need it be said?) a leading light. In August 1914 he set up, on his own initiative and in his own office, a recruiting station for the Navy; it was widely supposed that through this effort alone the Government had been able, at the outset of war, to man the cruisers *Niobe* and *Rainbow*. In any event, here was the beginning of a curious non-governmental influence upon naval policy, made possible by Æmilius Jarvis's indefatigable zeal and enterprise, and by the Government's being sufficiently imaginative to take advantage of them. In 1915 the Department of the Naval Service enlisted him as its agent in purchasing two ships of American registry and in getting them out of the United States and around its neutrality act;† one became the *Hochelaga*, the other *Stadacona*, the R.C.N.'s flagship in 1919. A year later, when the Royal Navy required officers and mechanics for a motor boat patrol, Æmilius Jarvis organized and paid for a School of Nautical Instruction which duly furnished the necessary recruits. Perhaps his most important wartime mission was his purchase, on special assignment from the Admiralty,

*In 1919 its Dominion President had written to the Minister of the Naval Service: "I note that you state that whenever possible assistance has been given to our Brigades by the Department. . . . Let me assure you what has been done has been much appreciated. Aside, however, from the kind offices of securing us rifles, we are unaware of any assistance, that has rendered the expenditure of funds. . . ." Æmilius Jarvis to C. C. Ballantyne, 19 Nov. 1919. Naval Records (N.S. 1080–206–III).

†Canadian yachtsmen carried out a similar mission in 1940. See Gilbert Tucker, *The Naval Service of Canada* (Ottawa, 1952), pp. 24–5.

of six ships for use as submarine decoys—the famous Q-boats—a mission for which the "Lords Commissioners of the Admiralty . . . thrice thanked him in writing,"[13] and earned him the valued commendation, before a Toronto audience, of Admiral Viscount Jellicoe.*

By 1919, therefore, Æmilius Jarvis had acquired a unique position of influence upon the naval establishments of two countries. Naturally he attempted to use it to further the aims of the Navy League of which, in that year, he became President. No less naturally, both League and President were accused of being the agents of the Admiralty, and of seeking to impose upon a reluctant Dominion the doctrine of the Imperial Grand Fleet. The Navy League, wrote Henri Bourassa, had been established in Canada.

> à la faveur de l'excitation "patriotique" et mercantile causée par la guerre. Amorcée à grands renforts de réclames et de puffisme, on lui a donné comme objectif ostensible la promotion des intérêts maritimes du Canada. En réalité, c'est une machine impérialiste destinée à pistonner les projets de l'Amirauté anglaise. On commence à le voir. Au moment d l'arrivée de Lord Jellicoe, une deputation de la Ligue s'est transportée à Ottawa, avec son président, le commodore Jarvis, de Toronto, a fin de faire connaître aux ministres les résultats du travail préliminaire de la Ligue. Ces messieurs ont modestement émis la prétention baroque d'être . . . — *the unofficial arm* — du gouvernement en tout ce qui touche "aux questions maritimes et navales", c'est-à-dire à la marine merchande et à la flotte de guerre. L'un des délégués a parlé du recrutment fait par la Ligue pour le service naval de l'Etat. On peut être assuré que cette machine va marcher fidèlement sur les traces de la *Navy League* d'Angleterre. . . .[14]

This assessment, in so far as it attributed real as distinct from potential power to Æmilius Jarvis and his friends, was incorrect. While even a detached observer (and Bourassa observed the scene in no spirit of detachment), noting the White Ensign flying above the Jarvis Building in Toronto where the Commodore made his headquarters and whither the Director of the Naval Service repaired on his visits, might pardonably conclude that the Navy League had the Navy in its pocket, the fact was otherwise. Naval persons had been glad enough to use Æmilius Jarvis during the war; but with the advent of the Armistice his zeal for its cause became something of an irritant. In Admiral Kingsmill's professional estimation, the Boys Brigades of the Navy League were

*". . . here I want to say that the Admiralty has great reason to be grateful to Canada for placing some of the brains which Canada did place at the Admiralty's disposal. Toronto itself has reason to be proud of the share which Toronto's representative took in that business. I won't name him because he is far too modest to like it." Admiral Viscount Jellicoe, 8 Dec. 1919. *Proceedings of the Canadian Club, Toronto, for the Year 1919–1920* (Toronto, 1921), pp. 140–1.

something less than the highly strategic weapon which they were sometimes made to appear in the League's more extravagant propaganda. As early as May 1918, Jarvis had begun to jar: a request that a Navy schooner be turned over to the League was turned down by Kingsmill, who observed in a memorandum to the Minister: "I consider it would be a great pity to let Mr. Jarvis's wish to train boys on Lake Ontario interfere. . . . After all the outing they could get on the *Pinta* is more or less of a picnic and boys of the age of those in the Navy League are not, in other training establishments, sent to sea in schooners."[15] A fortnight later he appended a more far-reaching indictment: "I may say that as the Navy League is formed more or less with the idea of criticizing the actions of the Admiralty, &c., the Department cannot take any action for or against it."[16] Two years later his attitude was unchanged. It would be difficult, he wrote to his Deputy Minister, to "convince Mr. Jarvis that everything is not all wrong. . . ."[17]

Nor had the League any stout ally among the Cabinet. C. C. Ballantyne, as the Minister of the Naval Service, was the recipient of most of Æmilius Jarvis's many insistent representations; these did not dispose him more kindly to his cause. Like Kingsmill, Ballantyne was inclined to discount the importance to the nation's defence of the kind of training that the League laid on for the youth, and was reluctant to turn over naval ships and stores for the purpose. When the Navy League proposed in 1919 that the Canadian Government should acquire a former German battleship to be manned by Boys Brigades, Ballantyne was understandably exasperated. "While I fully recognize the good work being done by the Navy League," he wrote his colleague the Minister of Agriculture (who, asked by the League for victuals at less than cost or no cost at all, had turned to Ballantyne to ascertain the official attitude),

> in the way of exercising these lads and giving them some knowledge of sea conditions, I do not feel that the Department should undertake the large expense of equipping a battleship for the use of the brigade. The exercises being given to these boys are partly of an educational nature and very largely in the way of recreation and exercise, and while they are undoubtedly of great benefit to the lads there does not seem to be any very good reason for the Department . . . maintaining a large warship. . . .[18]

When Jarvis wrote to Ballantyne to say that a Navy League delegation, led by himself, proposed to come to Ottawa "to meet you and lay several matters . . . before you," Ballantyne begged off: "Admiral Jellicoe will be here," he wrote in reply, "and my time will be fully occupied with conferences with him in reference to Naval matters."[19]

The Prime Minister, however, was not able to escape. On 28 November, Jarvis presented a memorandum to Borden and to his Minister of Finance, Sir Henry Drayton, which began with the following declaration:

> The Navy League of Canada is in favour of a naval policy for Canada which will have regard to the needs of the whole British Empire and in deciding upon such policy political exigencies shall be disregarded and the opinion of the most eminent naval strategists shall be alone considered . . .

Borden and Drayton tactfully assured their visitors that "there is no doubt that a policy which will develop the sea-power of the nation is essential." But one understands how Borden must have felt when he told Arthur Meighen, after the Navy League delegates had departed, of his "very great desire to retire from political life."[20]

Æmilius Jarvis was not easily discouraged. At Kingston, Ontario, on 10 August 1920, he told a meeting of his supporters: "As you know full well, to keep up the spirit of the Navy League since the war has been a difficult task, but I am glad to be able to assure you that we are every day getting new and more important men to see the subject from our viewpoint, namely, Canada must have a career on the sea."[21] But his assurance was based on wishful thinking. The Navy League and its imperialist outlook stirred less and less response. Even Æmilius Jarvis began to realize that a new outlook was required. In June 1921, he set out a new declaration of principles in a paper called "The Significance of a Navy League in Canada"; in it are revealed clearly enough the League's belated efforts to ally itself with the rising tide of liberal nationalism in Canada:

> The strength of the Navy League lies in its nation-wide appeal, to every province, to every person, to every class and to every creed. It is also its weakness.
>
> It is its strength because of the strong concerted influence it can bring to bear coast to coast, on the solution of our problems of National and Imperial Unity.
>
> It is its weakness because, embracing all classes and all creeds, it contains within itself the germs of speedy dissolution, unless bound together by wise and efficient National Administration.
>
> Gradually as the patriotic fervour which surrounded the League's establishment subsides, there is emerging a two-fold conception of its real significance, and which is overshadowing the war time activities which marked its beginning, and which was the original conception of its founder.
>
> The *first* is that the Navy League is the outward and visible sign of Canada's Conscious Nationhood. The war was the furnace in which our Nationhood was fused and welded for all time in the sight of the other nations of the world, which brings out the *second* significance. It means that Canadian Nationality and Imperial Unity desire to express themselves

positively. . . . The Navy League comes to Canadians not as a mere society charged with the welfare of sailors, but as an aggressive League of Nation builder. . . .

We wish to have in the Navy League the very heart of the loyalty of the people. We must stand on guard against the attacks of sedition mongers of every kind and description, so that it should be made a dangerous thing for a man to be known as a disloyal citizen. Membership in the Navy League should proclaim to the world that the member has taken his or her stand on the side of right, liberty and justice, which things have been made possible to the world by the British traditions of the Sea.

The Navy League is passing through a crisis. In this we are but a reflection of the country at large. The special enthusiasm of the war is gone, and exhaustion has come in its stead. The sense of individual responsibility to one's country, which flares up into a consuming passion in times of crisis, grows cold without a crisis to stimulate it. We forget that steady and consistent regard for our citizenship responsibilities during times of peace would to a large extent prevent those devastating crises with their loss of manhood and national energy. . . .[22]

This outpouring was as confused as it was revealing. It was also as unrealistic. To declare, as Jarvis had declared, that the Navy League's strength lay in its "Nation-wide appeal, to every province" ignored the fact that in the Province of Quebec both League and Navy were anathema. The League might ignore it; no politician could. The Navy itself had a better grasp upon this crucial issue than did the Navy League. In a paper called "Some Notes on the Naval Service of Canada" prepared by the Naval Secretary, J. A. E. Woodhouse, on the eve of his retirement from the Service in 1927, the problem of Quebec is clearly recognized:

Quebec Province (with a solid block of 60 seats in the present Liberal Government) is very definitely opposed to Naval expansion. . . . An incident in 1923 throws an interesting sidelight on the French Canadian point of view. A Half Company of the R.C.N.V.R. formed of French speaking Canadians had been established in Quebec City with about 30 newly enrolled members. The *Patriot* visited Quebec, and invited the Half Company on board. They all came and were entertained. Before they went ashore it was thought good to let them hear a small speech on naval matters, concluding with a few words exhorting the men to be faithful in their drills so that should their country need them in time of war they would be ready to take their places side by side with the men of the R.C.N. The mention of the word "war" was sufficient, and the next day two officers and three men were all that remained of the Half Company. . . .[23]

In its present mood, the Naval Secretary concluded, Canada would never support a policy of naval expansion. Friends of the Navy ought therefore to undertake to change the mood. But it was essential to proceed with care. "The Navy's friends in Canada are as dangerous as her opponents.

Her friends can do incalculable harm by confusion of thought or speech. It is necessary to coordinate thought and speech by discouraging ideas of contributions to the Imperial Navy or of immediate and large naval expansion."[24] This was sound advice. A pity that it had not been available and accepted earlier.

BALLANTYNE REBUKED

Sir Robert Borden believed that the Admiralty had renounced once and for all the doctrine of the Imperial Grand Fleet and its expectations of Dominion contributions to the Royal Navy. He was not as unsympathetically disposed towards Jellicoe's Mission as were several members of his Cabinet, who dreaded the expense to which its recommendations might lead, and shared Bourassa's conviction that the Jellicoe Mission was a manifestation of a new but no less sinister imperialism. Ballantyne alone was enthusiastic. Jellicoe shrewdly perceived the divided state of mind in which his hosts greeted him at Ottawa. "Sir Robert Borden, pressed hard by Mr. Ballantyne, is in favour of an immediate start being made," he wrote to the First Lord soon after his arrival in the capital.

> On the other hand, some Ministers wish to postpone matters either for political or for financial reasons. Mr. Ballantyne, who is very much in earnest, is concerned that unless the matter is settled now, before I leave Canada, nothing will be done for several years. He tells me distinctly that unless a serious start is made now, he intends to wipe out completely the present Canadian Naval Service, as being a pure waste of money. He is right.[25]

Jellicoe's proposals for a postwar Canadian naval establishment were presented to the Cabinet on 22 December 1919. The Cabinet discussed them on 30 December. A day or two earlier, Borden had settled down to read the report: like much bedside reading, once picked up it was all too easily laid down. "Evidently this report is going to stretch out to a great length," he wrote in his diary late in the night of 28 December, "the first chapter does not present anything new."[26] Novelties came later.

Jellicoe's Report consisted of three volumes. Volume I was distributed to all members of Parliament; Volumes II and III, on the initiative of their author, were kept secret.* The Report recommended four levels

*On 5 July 1920, the Prime Minister of South Africa requested the Prime Minister of Canada to make available to him the two secret volumes of the Jellicoe Report. "Without these volumes," Smuts wrote, "it is very difficult to follow out details which though not important to the general public, are really essential to the proper understanding of the scheme which is recommended to

of naval strength, each tailored to the kind of policy the Dominion Government might decide upon. Plans 1 and 2 assumed that Canada would wish to provide only for its own defence; Plans 3 and 4 that it would wish, in addition, to make some contribution to imperial defence. Annual upkeep for each of the four forces was estimated respectively at £1,000,000, £2,000,000, £3,500,000 and £5,000,000. The Report further recommended the creation of a Navy Board similar to the Board of Admiralty, the creation of a separate ministerial portfolio dealing exclusively with naval affairs, various methods of recruiting and training officers and ratings, and much more besides.

After considerable discussion, the Cabinet settled upon a modified version of the most modest of the four Jellicoe proposals, Plan 1, with the intention of providing the Canadian navy with eight submarines, four destroyers, eight P-boats, and four trawler minesweepers. The adoption of even this tiny establishment was made contingent upon an appropriate offer of ships from the United Kingdom. In March 1920 such an offer was forthcoming, and the Cabinet recommended its acceptance. It had also been decided, however (such being the divided state of Canadian opinion), to secure the views of the party caucus before coming to a final solution. On 20 March 1920 the Minister of the Naval Service placed the proposal before a gathering of his parliamentary colleagues. What happened then, and afterwards, is best described by the words of the participants. One of these was Sir George Foster, the Minister of Trade and Commerce; he wrote to Borden (then on holiday) to tell the Prime Minister what had transpired:

> Ballantyne went in with his modified $5m. per year programme sure of success, and gave a good explanation & sat down beaming for results. Well, the Caucus knocked it sky-high—only two or three favourable & these moderately so. The agreement was that he should present it, argue for it, & Ministers should say nothing—let the Caucus have its head. So

---

you." Arthur Meighen, to whom this request passed following Borden's retirement, inquired through his High Commissioner at London whether the British authorities objected to his making the report available to the South African Government, and on 7 September received from Sir George Perley the following reply: "Colonial Office state that Lords Commissioners Admiralty consider it undesirable that unpublished volumes Lord Jellicoe's Reports on naval defence should be exchanged between different Dominions, as there might in that case be a certain danger of misconception, which will not be incurred when reports are discussed in presence of representatives of all Dominions at next Imperial Conference." Meighen accordingly cabled to Smuts: ". . . without commenting on soundness Admiralty position I am unless they alter it regretfully unable as you will realize to send the papers." Arthur Meighen to J. C. Smuts, 10 Sept. 1920. Meighen Papers. The episode offers an interesting commentary upon the evolution of the principle of Commonwealth consultation.

the Caucus had its head & made a thorough job. But two or three of our Ministers broke faith, and told members he [sic] did not want it & Sir Henry [Drayton, Minister of Finance] even clapped applause when some Member hit it hard or when Bob Greene declared everlasting war on it. Poor 'B' came out wilted & discouraged & mad—and said nothing. Next day the wires were hot over orders said to have been given by Minister to demobilize the whole force (naval), scrap the old *Rainbow* & *Niobe*, & demobilize the College. Then the mouse was in the soup sure. The Navy league spent half its revenue on messages, Hfx. & Esq. were up in arms & the rest of the Ministers were asking "who did it?".

B. was in Montreal when all this rumpus broke out. When he came back, having fought off the reporters during the interval, we found out the facts—that 'B' had sent such orders to dismiss most of the officials & had sent Kingsmill his letter of dismissal with the idea of scrapping the old if he could not get the new. Well, we had a talk over it, and ended with a compromise. (a) To give the Minister a free hand to reorganise by notice of discontinuance of present staff. (b) Accept two destroyers and one cruiser from G.B. to replace the *Rainbow* & *Niobe* for training and protection purposes. (c) Keep up the College. (d) Defer Permanent Navy policy for the present. This I took to Caucus . . . and in less than half an hour got their unanimous consent. . . .[27]

Ballantyne's own version of these events, set out in a letter to his Prime Minister, is as follows:

I was personally much disappointed, because I considered, and so did the majority of the Members of the Government, that it is time that Canada adopted a permanent policy, and more particularly, when Great Britain made such a generous offer of ships and the maintenance and upkeep was not more than $4,500,000 per annum. If the matter had been handled differently before Caucus I am sure it would have carried. Owing to some of the Ministers desiring delay it was decided that I would be the only one to speak and I was not permitted to say it was the policy of the Government; and, rightly or wrongly, Caucus got the opinion before being called together that the Government did not wish to proceed with the $4,500,000 expenditure and therefore turned it down. I am however satisfied under the circumstances that the present policy, all things considered, possibly is the wisest to adopt. It certainly has met with the unanimous approval of all members of the Union Party, and the public generally, and also has this distinct advantage that it is a disappointment to our friends the Enemy [i.e., the Liberal Opposition]. . . .

Our Naval Service will now be small but energetic, and absolutely efficient. On every hand the new policy of the Government is receiving entire approval. . . .[28]

The Navy thus acquired consisted of two destroyers—*Patrician* and *Patriot*—and a cruiser. The cruiser originally offered to Canada by the Admiralty was the *Glasgow*, a veteran of the battles of Coronal and the Falkland Islands. When the Minister told his new Director of the Naval

Service, Captain Walter Hose, that he was soon to be the proud possessor of the *Glasgow*, Hose (in his own words)

> dug my heels in and told him that was dreadful. *Glasgow* was a coal-burner and obsolete, and she would raise all the ridicule that *Niobe* and *Rainbow* had, and that we *must* have a modern oil-burner.
>
> He [Ballantyne] said: "But Hose, she has already been accepted." I stuck to it that it must be changed so he said, "Well, you had better go over to London and see what you can do. . . ."
>
> When, through Sir George Perley, Canadian High Commissioner in London, the Admiralty were informed that Canada wanted a more modern ship than the *Glasgow*, they were by no means prepared to part with one. I had learnt that all oil-burning cruisers were in active commission except *Aurora* which was in reserve—so I plumped for *Aurora*, but after much pressing for weeks, I got no change.
>
> Eventually I drafted a letter from the High Commissioner to the Secretary of State for the Colonies to the effect that the Canadian Government was most anxious to be of assistance to the Royal Navy. That the repair and supply establishments in our dockyards were available to R.N. ships on the American stations, and that the Canadian Government regretted that in the event of Canada's cruiser being a coal-burner while the R.N. ships were oil-burning, her repair and supply establishments could not be of the same value to the R.N. . . .
>
> Very shortly after that Sir George informed me that the Admiralty had agreed to hand over the *Aurora* to us. . . .[29]

The three ships—a "small but modern squadron," as the then Director of the Naval Service many years afterwards proudly described them—came sailing into Halifax Harbour shortly before Christmas Day, 1920. "The Governor-General was there," Admiral Hose recalled, "the Minister of the Naval Service was there, and I was there. . . . Too bad that our pride, in the event, should prove short lived."[30]

II

The acquisition of *Patrician*, *Patriot*, and *Aurora* was frankly conceded by the Borden Government to be a temporary measure. "In view of Canada's heavy financial commitments," the Minister of the Naval Service explained in the House of Commons on 25 March 1920, "and of the fact that Great Britain has not as yet decided on her permanent naval policy, and of the approaching Imperial Conference at which the question of naval defence of the Empire will come up for discussion between the Home Government and the Overseas Dominions, it has been decided to defer in the meantime action in regard to the adoption of a permanent naval policy for Canada."[31] As preparation for the

Imperial Conference discussions, the Admiralty sent out to each of the dominions a detailed memorandum. It endorsed the principle of dominion navies "as the system most likely to commend itself to the Dominions," and defined their strategic role as "the control of communications in seas distant from the United Kingdom, and the protection of their own coastal trade and bases." In time of war, however, the Admiralty considered that the dominion navies should be under its own central direction. "The principle which emphasizes the importance of a sound strategical distribution will be fully met if the Dominions agree that, subject to their decision to co-operate in a war, their ships and squadrons shall be available for service in any part of the world and to the general plan of campaign being directed by one central authority." Recommendations were offered as to the types of ships the dominions might most usefully provide. Grouping together Australia, New Zealand, and Canada, it proposed that these three dominions should provide their respective navies with light cruisers, and further "urged that the Australian, Canadian and New Zealand Governments should consider the possibility of gradually building up powerful submarine forces, containing a proportion of minelayers." Aircraft carriers were not recommended, not, at least, "at present."[32]

The recipient of this document, which arrived in Ottawa early in March 1921, was not Sir Robert Borden but Arthur Meighen, who had replaced Borden as Prime Minister in July of the preceding year, retaining Ballantyne as Minister of the Naval Service. Excepting the Minister, no member of Meighen's Administration shared the Admiralty's enthusiasm for embarking upon an ambitious scheme of naval development. Public opinion was apathetic or hostile; time was short and money tight; the Government's mind was on other matters where it was made up at all. "As yet the Government at Ottawa is unorganized," *The Times*' Canadian correspondent, Sir John Willison, wrote to his London editor in December 1920. "It does not know what its position is on many questions and I suspect is not eager for an Imperial Conference this year."[33] Willison specifically advised the new Prime Minister to avoid commitments on the naval issue. "At the moment," he wrote candidly to Meighen, "you are not in a political position to give anything. There is nothing your opponents want so much as a cry against you in Quebec, and out of any naval agreement to which you may consent, a cry will be made, with or without justification. As you know, I believe we should take a greater share in the defence of the Empire, but there are times when it is wise to act and times when action is unwise."[34] This was, in fact, preaching to the converted. Even Ballantyne had come to accept that, for the time being, a "Big Navy" policy for Canada was out of the question. "I am thoroughly in accord with your view-point," he wrote to Meighen on 29 April, "that there should be no increase whatsoever in Canada's Naval expenditure, either now or in the immediate future."[35] On the eve of his departure for the Imperial Conference at London, Meighen was firmly committed to the strategy of "no commitments." "He will oppose any scheme," an Ottawa news-paperman wrote privately after an interview with the Prime Minister,

> that might involve Canada in any large naval expenditure. He will take the ground . . . that, quite apart from the Dominion's finances prohibiting her from launching upon a big naval programme, that it is not the part of wisdom to enter into an armament competition with the United States, holding in support of this that whatever naval preparations are made by the Americans are directed solely against Japan. One wonders, however, how he will reconcile this view with any possible defensive alliance (if such be possible) that may be entered into with Japan.[36]

The necessary reconciliation was achieved by Meighen's successful advocacy at the Imperial Conference of non-renewal of the Anglo-Japanese Alliance. Naval commitments, so far as Canada was concerned, were limited to closer co-operation between the Admiralty and Naval Headquarters at Ottawa in the training and posting of personnel. "I arranged with the Admiralty at that time," Ballantyne later recalled,

> that they would take in the British Navy, each year, six or eight of our Naval College graduates for training purposes. It was also agreed that we would have our small Canadian Naval Unit trained with the North Atlantic Fleet, and work in the closest harmony and co-operation with the Imperial Navy. It was recognised that overseas Dominion Naval Units would not be of much service by themselves, but worked in closest co-operation with the Imperial Fleet and interchanging officers from time to time, they would be really efficient and part of the Imperial Navy.[37]

This arrangement, if it was to be of value to either Service, required that Canada provide a Navy of greater moment than the tiny squadron with which it was then equipped. But on this point the Conference was silent, or almost so. Its only published reference to naval co-operation was the following resolution:

> That, while recognizing the necessity of co-operation among the various portions of the Empire to provide such Naval Defence as may prove to be essential for security, and while holding that equality with the naval strength of any other Power is a minimum standard for that purpose, this Conference is of opinion that the method and expense of such co-operation are matters for the final determination of the several Parliaments concerned, and that any recommendations thereon should be deferred until after the coming Conference on Disarmament.[38]

And so the shaping of a permanent naval policy for Canada, held off until the Imperial Conference of 1921, was postponed further until the results of the Washington Conference of 1921–22 became known. But by the time the work of the naval powers at Washington had been completed, a new Government had come to power at Ottawa, with its own ideas about what Canada's defence forces should consist of, and about what these should do.

THE "FIVE-TRAWLER NAVY"

Mackenzie King, on becoming Prime Minister on 29 December 1921, was no stranger to the naval debate which with the exception of the war years had agitated the Dominion since 1909. He had taken a leading part in the campaign to justify Laurier's Naval Service Bill to the Canadian public, and while he strongly endorsed its opposition to the policy of Dominion contribution to the Imperial Grand Fleet,* he was less keen about its corollary feature, that of building up a Canadian fleet. With the needs and aspirations of the postwar navy, as with those of the land and air forces of the Dominion, Mackenzie King was distinctly out of sympathy. In part this reflected a genuine strategic assessment of Canada's position in the postwar world, in part the spirit of the time, in part that which was politically expedient. (Liberals and Progressives might unite in a common detestation of what both denounced as militarism, if they could not see eye to eye on freight rates and the tariff.) But there was more to it than that. Defence policy was from the outset distasteful to Mackenzie King, and for reasons as much personal as political. He had a marked aversion to the military life and the military mind whose workings he failed to understand and whose virtues he ignored. Unlike his immediate predecessors, Borden and Meighen, Mackenzie King could not feel at home in the company of serving officers. Whether or not the malaise he invariably experienced when in the presence of the military† had anything to do with his having never

*"If the Prime Minister had wished to sever the tie which binds us to Britain he could not have done it a surer way . . . than to have started to give the money of the people of this country to another part of the Empire for the construction of Dreadnoughts." Speech of Mackenzie King at Hamilton, Ontario, 1 April 1910.

†Many years later Mackenzie King wrote in his diary, on being told he was expected to speak to the troops in Britain as their wartime Prime Minister: "I felt what was like a dart pass through my bowels. It made me quite sick and faint . . . I cannot talk their jargon of war." Quoted in J. W. Pickersgill, *The Mackenzie King Record*, vol. I, *1939–1944* (Toronto, 1960), pp. 259–60.

served in the armed forces (he had spent most of the war years as an industrial consultant in the United States), it is certain that no prime minister could have been more eager to find excuses for curtailing expenditure upon defence. Nor were excuses hard to come by.

The most compelling was that provided by the apparent success of the Washington Conference in limiting the tonnages of capital ships among the principal naval powers. What was Canada that she should arm when the United Kingdom (which, at Washington, was in any case understood to include the dominions), the United States, Japan, France and Italy, all had pledged restraint? "We are in this position in regard to the question of a Navy," declared the Minister of the Naval Service soon after the results at Washington became known. "Every country in the world to-day is endeavouring to reduce its armament."[39] And so the estimates for the Royal Canadian Navy were cut, arbitrarily and, in the Minister's words, "at the stroke of a pen," from $2,500,000 to $1,500,000.

How this drastically diminished sum might be expended the Government was glad enough to leave to the Service to decide. The naval authorities duly produced the following memorandum for their Minister:

> In accordance with your instructions, the Naval Committee have considered what reductions can be made in the navy estimates.
>
> The estimates had already been reduced to the utmost limits prior to submission to you; particular items cannot be any more reduced and [the Navy] still continue to function efficiently. It is necessary therefore to cut out certain whole services in order to make reductions.
>
> *College.* The first item for extinction is considered to be the Royal Naval College; whilst this is a most efficient educational establishment, the navy derives comparatively little benefit from it, and it is not essential to the navy.
>
> A saving could thus be effected of $100,000 this year, and $150,000 next.
>
> *Esquimalt Dockyard.* Various small services performed at this establishment in Esquimalt: such as the supply base, supply organisation, etc., could be dispensed with as not being absolutely essential for the maintenance of the navy at the present time, and, consequently, the whole establishment could be closed and reduced to caretakers with the exception of a very small supply base.
>
> There would be a saving here of $50,000.
>
> *Halifax Dockyard.* A few small items can be dropped from the estimate effecting a saving of $25,000.
>
> There are no further reductions which can be made in maintaining the present Canadian Squadron. Any further reduction could only be effected by a decrease in number of seagoing ships or training establishments. The existing number is considered the least with which an efficient navy can be maintained and a fewer number would not justify the expense of maintenance.

In speaking of an efficient Navy, the Committee does not mean so much a numerically efficient Navy for War purposes as an internally efficient Navy, that is to say one in which discipline, esprit de corps, training and morale generally are such as will permit the Service to function.

If a further reduction in expenditure is considered necessary, the Naval Committee is of opinion that all ships should be paid off and the navy reorganised on an entirely new basis, that is to say, by the formation of a naval reserve force. The ships with a small permanent force would be used for training purposes exclusively. It is estimated that such a naval reserve could be maintained for $1,500,000.[40]

The Minister examined this document on 1 March. Its final paragraph pleased him greatly, and it became forthwith government policy. On 12 May he announced the Government's decision in the House of Commons, and gave the following account of how it had been arrived at:

When the Government came into office I discussed the question of the naval service a great deal with the officials of the Department. The *Aurora* is a small cruiser. There are two destroyers and two submarines. These make up the fleet. I had in my mind . . . the idea that other naval plans could be outlined and carried into operation, which would be far more effective in the way of placing Canada in a position to have an effective service than the training that can take place on these five ships. I suggested to the officers that we could divide these ships, send one or two of them to the Pacific coast and keep one of them on the Atlantic coast. I had an idea that the *Aurora* could be used on the Atlantic, and this shows my absolute unacquaintance with the naval service and what a navy is supposed to do. I had the idea that we could take two destroyers to the Pacific coast, and keep the *Aurora* on the Atlantic, and continue our training, and possibly train on the Pacific coast as well, and perhaps perform our obligations in reference to the protection of the seal fisheries at Behring Sea with the use of the destroyers. This, the officer told me, was absolutely out of the question; if we separated those ships and sent two of the destroyers to the Pacific coast, those destroyers would not do at all for the purposes of training by themselves and would be wholly unsuitable for the pelagic sealing protection. He also informed me that the *Aurora*, by itself, would not supply the training that was expected to be had by the young men in the navy. I then gave up my idea of using the ships for that purpose. We discussed the question of maintaining, say, two of them on the Atlantic coast. This presented obstacles in the way of cost for the benefit received; and as a final solution of the matter, I asked the officers of the department to prepare me a scheme which could at once give training to the men both on land and on sea, that would be more in keeping with the protection of our coasts than it would be in harmony with high-sea fighting. . . .

. . . The proposal that I have to lay before the House, and for which estimates are asked, is that we discontinue in commission the ships that we now have; that we continue the protection and care of the wharves and docks at Halifax and Esquimalt; that we provide a reserve force composed of officers and men, officers who are now in the Navy; . . . that we create on the Pacific coast at Esquimalt an establishment with one small ship and two trawlers of about 450 tons; that we establish there a portion of our naval force for training in the protection of our shores, protection of our harbours, mine-sweeping, mine-laying; that at Halifax in the east we have the same services. . . .[41]

Opponents of capital punishment would find it useful to have the victims' account of their execution. The Navy's version of these events has been recorded by the then Naval Secretary, J. A. E. Woodhouse:

The Liberal Government on gaining power . . . cut a million dollars from the naval vote . . . The ultimatum as given to the Director of the Naval Service was that $1,500,000 was all that would be allowed for the R.C.N. and that he must do what he could with it.

He reviewed the situation somewhat as follows:

(*a*) *Aurora* could be maintained on $1,500,000. *Patriot, Patrician*, two submarines, the R.C.N. Cadet College and the Youths' training establishment would have to go.

(*b*) *or*

Patriot and *Patrician* could be maintained in full commission, four mine-sweepers could be commissioned. A reserve force of 1,500 officers and men could be organized. R.C.N. Barracks with gun-drill shed and torpedo lecture room could be maintained at Halifax and Esquimalt as training centres for reserve men. Halifax and Esquimalt dockyards could be maintained as repair and storing bases.

The Dockyard at Halifax could not be maintained, and the Dockyard at Esquimalt would have to remain closed.

The deciding considerations were:

(*a*) If a Dominion is to spend money on the Navy, its people must be convinced that a Navy is necessary.

(*b*) In Canada a large majority of the people live far from the sea and do not visualize the necessity for safe sea communications.

(*c*) The first necessity therefore is to educate the people.

(*d*) The most effective method of educating the people is to bring the Navy to their doors, into the lives of families and their friends.

(*e*) A small Navy is of no value as an educative measure as its personnel live in the neighbourhood of the naval bases; but a reserve force distributed across Canada would bring the Navy home to a great number of inland people; would be the only means of doing so within the appropriation available; would form a useful field of recruiting for the R.C.N.; would give the Director of the Naval Service opportunity to visit the Reserve Centres throughout the country and address Chambers of Commerce, Rotarian Clubs, etc., on the elements of Naval Defence; would provide in the Reserve Centres a subject for articles in the press; would be the first step in the conversion of Quebec . . .

With the above considerations in mind the Director of the Naval Service recommended and the Government accepted the second alternative. . . .[42]

The wisdom of this choice was to be vindicated in later years, when the wartime R.C.N.V.R. recruited most of its ratings from the prairies and other regions of Canada far removed from the sea and maritime traditions. Outwardly Commodore Hose was optimistic. "We have had to go through an anxious time as regards the Canadian Navy," he wrote to a British colleague in August 1922, "but although I very much deplore the arbitrary cut of $1,000,000 in our appropriation, still I have by no means lost hope as regards the future, and I hope within the next couple of years to have an efficient reserve of at least 1,500 men organized and trained by the nucleus of the permanent force, and I still believe that from that we shall expand into a seagoing Service again. . . ."[43] Brave words from an old sea-dog. Inwardly it rankled, as well it might.*

The new naval policy was calmly, even gratefully, accepted by the Canadian public. The voices raised in protest were both scattered and ioslated. In Parliament Arthur Meighen scoffed at the Government's "five-trawler navy,"[44] and wrote to an indignant Haligonian: "Our members in the House are not as numerous as they should be, but we are making every effort in our power to bring home to the minds of the Canadian people the utterly indefensible conduct to which the Government is committing this country. The money being voted is paltry, and for the purpose for which it is being voted will be as good as wasted. If we cannot pay our way on a reasonable basis in the matter of defence, it would be more honourable on our part to step out of the Empire. . . ."[45] From Æmilius Jarvis came the inevitable protest of the Navy League: "We view your proposal to reduce the amount apportioned for Canadian Naval Defence to a minimum that makes the provision an absurdity from the standpoint of efficiency, with the gravest concern."[46] But the ultimate rebuke came from the Admiralty itself: "The Admiralty must frankly confess to their great disappointment at Canada's decision to abolish her seagoing squadron and to confine her naval endeavours to such secondary forms of co-operation as can be left to a force maintained on a reserve basis; for reasons already pointed out, these can be of no real assistance in the naval defence of the Empire."[47]

*Years later, he confessed to having been "heartsick at having to lay up *Aurora*—and at decision that only possible future of navy in Canada was to take it into the country (R.C.N.V.R.), so put money on R.C.N.V.R.—not in ships afloat—and so had to offer civvy street to officers of R.C.N. Only a few stayed on knowing that it was the reserve or nothing. . . ." Interview of Admiral Hose by the Naval Historian, 3 Dec. 1955. Navy Records.

DOWNING STREET DOMINATED

The Imperial Conference of 1923 offered Mackenzie King the opportunity, if it did not impose on him the obligation, of justifying his "five trawler navy" to the British Government; for the British Government had had rather larger plans in mind. Not that the Admiralty had any right to complain as it did complain. Dominion naval policy, the Imperial Conference of 1921 had recognized, was for dominion governments to decide; Jellicoe himself had written that if the Dominion of Canada was unwilling to put a self-respecting fleet to sea, better to have no fleet at all. That counsel Mackenzie King had accepted, in spirit if not to the letter. All the same, what had been done fell so far short of what was expected that when British and Canadian leaders next met face to face there were bound to be recrimination on the one hand, justification on the other. "There is apparently very formidable trouble in store for the next Imperial Conference," the new High Commissioner for Canada in London wrote to his Prime Minister in March 1923; and, a few days later: "I am sure . . . there will be trouble, for I am told that Australia has been very 'ugly' of late and most determined to have an arrangement come to by which the Navy will be contributed to by all Dominions."[48] The First Lord of the Admiralty sought to allay any suspicions of this kind. "You will receive soon, I hope," L. S. Amery wrote to Mackenzie King in July.

> the Admiralty memoranda and suggestions on Naval Co-operation. . . . You know my own views on Imperial Co-operation well enough, but you will find the whole Admiralty Staff here as definite as myself in not merely accepting as a second-best, but positively as the best policy, that under which each unit in the Empire develops its own strength directly under the control of its own Parliament and on its own lines. The conception of a centralised Navy run by the Admiralty, and subscribed to by the Dominions, is now completely extinct. The one idea is to give every encouragement to the younger navies to become really efficient and adequate to play their part in the common task.[49]

Mackenzie King replied:

> I am particularly pleased to have the assurance of your letter that, as respects naval co-operation, the conception of a centralised navy is regarded by the Admiralty staff as something of the past. So far as I have been able to gauge the effects of the War upon Canadian sentiment, it is that centralization, as regards all matters of Imperial policy, is something to be critically viewed, and that the hope of the future lies rather in the recognition of an effective co-operation between self-governing and self-controlling units than in any merging or blending of control.[50]

Soon after Amery's letter, a new batch of Admiralty papers arrived in Ottawa. The basic document, "Empire Naval Policy and Co-operation, 1923," indicated that any hope that the Admiralty had discarded its ambitions of influencing Dominion policies to its own advantage was, to say the least, premature. It sketched, for the benefit of dominion Governments and India, the four phases by means of which their respective navies should be developed:

> In the First Phase provision should be made and responsibility assumed for Local Defence Services. At the same time preparations should be made for the next phase by beginning the training of personnel for a sea-going force. Canada and South Africa are in the First Phase.
>
> In the Second Phase the first definite steps are taken in the creation of a force for work on the High Seas, as opposed to a local defence force. This phase involves the obtaining of one or more sea-going ships, and in the first instance it may be necessary, for financial and other reasons, to obtain both the ships themselves and a portion, at any rate, of the personnel from the Royal Navy. Throughout this phase the necessary training, repair and fuelling facilities should gradually be built up in preparation for the next phase. This Second Phase has been reached by New Zealand.
>
> The Third Phase is reached when a Dominion is in a position to provide and man a seagoing squadron of its own, and to take over the full control in peace of the station in which its shores are included. That station will be the normal home station of its Squadron, but interchange and co-operation with British units on other stations should be arranged. Australia is the only Dominion which is now in the Third Phase.
>
> In the Fourth and final Phase the Dominions should be capable, in addition to the Squadrons for service on their own home stations, to provide, whether in the shape of additional cruiser squadrons or of capital ship units, a substantial part of the general scheme of naval defence and, more particularly, of the Main Fleet.[51]

Other memoranda made detailed recommendations suitable to each Dominion. The Canadian Government was provided with Admiralty estimates concerning the obsolescence of existing R.C.N. vessels (those laid up as well as the five trawlers); recommendations for the types of ships which might be suitably acquired (including details of displacement, speed, endurance, fuel, and armament); a provisional building programme; a suggested disposition of vessels in the event of war between the British Empire and Japan; and numerous other proposals with regard to personnel, stores, communications and similar operational matters. But perhaps the most controversial feature of all this documentation was the suggestion in the preface to the general memorandum, "Empire Naval Policy and Co-operation, 1923" that that particular memorandum should be published:

As it is desirable that the peoples of the British Empire, on whom the burden of naval effort falls, may understand the principles on which Dominion co-operation is being sought, it will be suggested at the Imperial Conference that this Paper *only* should, subject to the concurrence of the Dominion representatives, be issued to the press. . . .

There could no longer be any doubt in Mackenzie King's mind, if there had been any doubt beforehand, that he was in for a fight.

To prepare for the impending struggle, he first cast about for help. He badly needed a senior adviser in whom he could repose his confidence; within his own Department, External Affairs, there was no one whom he felt to be both competent and trustworthy. He thought at once of O. D. Skelton, then Dean of Arts at Queen's University. On 30 January 1922, Skelton had spoken to the Canadian Club of Toronto on the subject of "Canada and Foreign Policy," in which he delivered a withering attack upon the project of imperial control.[52] Mackenzie King was greatly impressed by Skelton on that occasion. "He certainly has the knowledge," he wrote in his diary after listening to his address, "& the right point of view."[53] He was therefore elated when Skelton accepted his invitation to come to Ottawa to prepare for the forthcoming Conference and to join the delegation in London.

Mackenzie King turned to Skelton for the reason that policy makers usually turn to intellectuals, not so much for advice as for endorsement. But there was some difference in outlook between them. King's was that of the Canadian politician; Skelton's, that of the Canadian nationalist. Laurier's naval policy Skelton had described, not long before the beginning of his new career in the Department of External Affairs, as "a timely and moderate measure, a middle ground on which reasonable men could unite, and yet not a neutral and colourless compromise but a logical development of Canada's course since half a century."[54] With that description Mackenzie King would not himself have quarrelled; but neither would he have gone, nor did he by his action go, so far as to agree with Skelton's personal view of Canadian naval policy in 1923: "I am convinced that while striving for international reconciliation we must meanwhile maintain defence forces; I should like to see a decent Canadian Navy, perhaps beginning with shore defences, and air development."[55] But then Skelton did not have the responsibility of elected office. He was an adviser; and (as a distinguished authority pointed out years later) "advisers may move on to new advice."* Skelton and King made a strong team.

*The words are those of President John F. Kennedy, in a television interview of 18 December 1962.

One of Skelton's first tasks was to address himself to the Admiralty memoranda. His reaction was characteristically vigorous:

These proposals make it clear that while the Admiralty has perforce abandoned the concept of a single Empire fleet supported by Dominion contributions, it expects to attain the same end by a somewhat more circuitous route. Each Dominion is to have its own Naval Force, but the Admiralty is to be a central controlling authority, outlining policy, and fitting the various local units into a mosaic. To work out this policy it will be necessary to develop a common Empire public opinion, and if need be, force the hand of the Dominion Governments; hence the Memorandum, the first, doubtless of a series in the years to come.

It is a question for serious consideration whether the Canadian Government is prepared to sanction this policy of appeal from the British people to the people of Canada. Granted that the Memorandum is moderately phrased, and that many of its positions would be recognised as sound and all at least arguable, the question remains whether a precedent for such action should be set. It may be considered that it is no more the function of the British Admiralty to advise the people of Canada directly as to the policy they should adopt in naval affairs than it is the function of the British War Office to advise them as to fiscal policy. Such action is bound to stir up party contention and to force any government not in agreement with the policy outlined to issue a counter statement.

The specific Admiralty proposals for Canada are that she should endeavour to pass now from Phase I (local defence) to Phase II (the first steps in the creation of a sea-going force), by the building in the next twelve years of three fast light cruisers, $10,000,000 each, a squadron oiler and auxiliary patrol vessels, at a total cost of $31,000,000 or $2,500,000 a year for construction; construct oil tanker and maintain 110,000 tons of oil fuel as a war reserve ($320,000 a year for 8 years); no submarines; no estimate given of maintenance cost. The proposals are frankly based on the possibility of war in the Pacific with Japan. . . .

Skelton then set down some anticipated objections to the existing naval policy of the Dominion, together with suggestions (reproduced below in italics) for refuting those objections:

The criticisms of the Canadian Government's present naval policy which have been voiced or may be expected are as follows:

1. "The present policy is a sheer waste of money; it leads to nothing; why train men for a navy that does not exist?" (Meighen in debate on naval estimates, 1923).

The policy is a transitional one. . . . Meanwhile, training of personnel is the best course.

2. The policy is unworthy of the Dominion. . . .

The question what is worthy of the Dominion depends on the situation, the duty or danger that is to be met. . . .

3. The policy ignores Pacific danger.

There is no such danger.

4. The Canadian Prime Minister was responsible for the situation that had arisen; Meighen had led in demanding the abrogation of the Anglo-Japanese Treaty.
Later events justified his stand. In any case he was simply reflecting the United States' attitude. . . .

5. Canada is taking shelter ignominiously under the wing of the Monroe Doctrine.
The Monroe Doctrine, or rather the settled policy of the United States which is thus denoted, is a solid and outstanding fact; it would be ostrich-like to ignore it. Not the Monroe Doctrine, but community of interest is our safeguard in this respect.

6. Canada is sponging on Australia and Great Britain for defence.
Canada is not contributing in any appreciable measure to the sum of risks in which the British Empire may be involved; she is practically immune, or may easily be made so, from any permanent and crippling attack by an overseas power.

7. It is the duty of the Canadian Government to give a lead and to arouse her people to a recognition of the inadequate part they are playing.
(*a*) *It is not admitted that it is inadequate . . .*
(*b*) *The people are war-weary; they are barely recovering from a serious and prolonged business depression; they could not now be brought to support any very substantial action except by a raging tearing propaganda, which would do more to arouse international antipathies than to solve them.*
(*c*) *The party and parliamentary situation makes any such proposal not practical politics. The leader of a party resting largely on the support of Quebec and looking to the support of the prairies cannot launch such a campaign, unless convinced of an overwhelming and pressing need . . . The Opposition is not raising the question either . . .*[56]

In another memorandum, Skelton canvassed the issue of naval policy in these terms:

It is urged that a common naval policy for the Empire should be agreed upon; that each Dominion should undertake definite and substantial responsibilities, whether in the maintenance of seagoing squadrons of light cruisers and submarines, in the construction of naval bases, or in the provision of oil fuel reserves; and that the burden of constructing the new naval base of Singapore, the key to the Western Pacific, should be shared by Australia and New Zealand and possibly by other Dominions and Colonies. . . .

Reasons which may be advanced for immediate joint action:

1. The Empire is one and the sea is one: defence must be mobile, united and adequate.

2. This common interest and common obligation have repeatedly been recognised, in resolutions of Imperial Conferences, in resolutions of the Canadian Parliament of 1909, and of other Dominion parliaments, and in the common action taken in the Great War. . . .

3. The fact that the Washington Conference set standards for the British Empire as a whole makes it necessary hereafter to consider the activities and strength of all the different parts of the Empire conjointly.

4. The defeat of Germany and the agreement reached by the Washington Conference have not removed, though they have lessened, the danger of war; the direction of the danger has been changed. . . .

5. It was the insistence of Canada, as interpreted by Mr. Meighen, which led to the denunciation of the Anglo-Japanese Alliance. . . . Therefore Canada should now face the situation created by the repeal of that treaty and the removal of the check upon Japan.

Reasons which may be advanced against immediate substantial joint naval action:

1. . . . the danger of a world war less imminent.

2. Best assurance of peace lies in the continuance of constructive efforts toward international understanding along League of Nations, Washington Conference and Rush-Bagot lines. Any new step in armament may break the slowly-forming bonds of amity. . . . The question might be considered in Canada whether on governmental or private initiative, something could not be done by interchange of visits, tours of representative Japanese business men, educationalists, pressmen, etc., towards creating a friendly feeling.

3. No imminent danger of war between Japan and the British Empire. . . .

4. While Canada has not at present any very substantial naval force, it does not follow, as is frequently charged, that she is "sponging" on Great Britain or Australia for her defence. . . .

5. It was not Canada but the United States that brought the Anglo-Japanese Treaty to an end. . . .

6. With the heavy burden of taxation resting upon the people, the depression of trade, the drift of population to the United States, the war-weariness and the hope of advance by other paths, the Canadian people could not be persuaded to sanction a new and ambitious plan of naval armament except by a lurid and sensational appeal, a cry of immediate danger; such a campaign might well do more to bring on the danger it sought to avert, and incidentally lessen the country's unity and effectiveness in other directions.[57]

Armed with these arguments, Mackenzie King set out for London, their author in his entourage. He was further fortified by additional, and unsolicited, advice. "It is quite obvious," warned a spokesman for the radical West, "that Australasian and British imperialistic propagandists . . . are striving to stampede us into a participation in big naval expenditures (& so commit us to Imperial Wars, *irrevocably*), so as, primarily, to secure Australia and New Zealand in the 'mandated' territories which they have acquired in the Pacific up to the equator thus bringing them into direct and dangerous contact with Japan. . . . They cannot be trusted."[58] Raoul Dandurand, Government Leader in the Senate and Minister without Portfolio, spoke for Quebec:

On the eve of your departure for London, you will be interested in reading anew the description made by Sir Wilfrid Laurier himself of the assaults which you will have to face.

"He had a marked aversion to the military life . . ." (p. 168).
Mackenzie King at Camberley, 1926. (P.A.C.)

". . . 'not in accordance with the best military traditions . . .'" (p. 105).
Pathé News visits Camp Borden, 1921. (D.N.D.)

". . . 'crowds will still turn out to "see the soldiers"' . . ." (p. 105).
On the reviewing stand (1932): McNaughton, Herbert Bruce (Lt.-Gov. of Ontario), Maj.-Gen. T. V. Anderson (D.O.C., M.D. No. 2).

"Æmilius Jarvis . . ."

". . . and his friends" (p. 158).
(D.N.D.)

"The Navy consisted of two destroyers and a cruiser" (p. 164).
H.M.C.S. *Aurora*, *Patrician*, and *Patriot* at Esquimalt, 1921. (D.N.D.)

"No . . . better vessels of their class" (p. 272).
H.M.C.S. *Skeena* launched at Clydeside, 1930 (McNaughton, centre, in bowler hat).

"'Officers undergo training for limited periods'. . ." (p. 205).
First Provisional Pilot Officers' Course, Camp Borden, 1923 (P.P.O. G. R. Slemon on far right). (D.N.D.)

"It was in fact a shoe-string operation . . ." (p. 205).
R.C.A.F. repair depot, Winnipeg, 1924. (D.N.D.)

". . . his response to 'An Empire of the Air' was enthusiastic . . ." (p. 221).

". . . admiringly referred to as a soldier's soldier . . ." (p. 237).
MacBrien as Chief of Staff, 1923.

". . . Walter Hose was the sailor's sailor" (p. 237).
The Director of the Naval Service, 1923. (D.N.D.)

". . . always three laps ahead of his committees" (p. 258).
McNaughton in Defence Council, 1929. *L* to *R*: Brig.-Gen. Caldwell (Q.M.G.), Maj.-Ge[n.] Bell (A.G.), Maj.-Gen. McNaughton (C.G.S.), Air Commodore Gordon (Director, R.C.A.F.) Commodore Hose (C.N.S.), Desbarats (Deputy Minister), Ralston (Minister).

". . . the Navy had sympathetic friends . . ." (p. 259).
Desbarats and Ralston in the Minister's office. (D.N.D.)

These London people are after cannon fodder and Canadian money for their own ends, not for ours, and they strive to put it all over the gullible colonials.

They constantly speak of the defence of the Empire. Nobody to-day thinks of [attacking] and is in a position to attack the Empire. What the world needs today is peace all round and to talk of armaments is to create and maintain a war spirit.[59]

The Conference met for its opening session at No. 10, Downing Street, on the morning of 1 October 1923. Mackenzie King, arriving in London on 29 September, lost no time in entering into informal conversations with key British ministers before the Conference began. On 1 October he talked with the First Lord of the Admiralty, L. S. Amery, and, as he subsequently informed J. W. Dafoe (the editor of the *Manitoba Free Press* whom he had invited to accompany the delegation to ensure sympathetic reporting of the proceedings and who quickly became "an unofficial member of the board of strategy"[60]), he had

told him of his emphatic objection to publication in Canada of memorandum prepared by Admiralty urging increased expenditures on Canadian navy. Said it was an obvious attempt to influence Canadian opinion over heads government and Canadian govt. resented this. This procedure must stop.

Amery seemed quite taken aback by King's declaration.

King also told Amery that in present state of public opinion about expenditures in Canada no additional outlay on navy was possible and that he need not expect he would consent to commitments suggested by admiralty, to extent of ten cent piece. Told Amery it would be useless for him to make promises which he could not fulfill upon his return and that conditions forbade anything in the nature of a policy naval expansion.[61]

The First Lord could be under no illusions as to the Canadian position after this initial confrontation; but Amery was already noted for tenacity of purpose, and he did not easily abandon his objectives. The strategy of conversion on which he settled, however, was to prove unfortunate. He invited the dominion prime ministers on board a warship to review the Fleet at Spithead. "It was an inspection," he was later to recall, "under realistic conditions, a grey day and a gale blowing. . . . A gleam of sunlight on the long lines of ships of war, as *Princess Margaret* ran down between them, added to the impressive sense of power. Standing on the bridge with the Prime Ministers I could not help saying to Mackenzie King: 'That is why you are Prime Minister of Canada and not, at best, one of the Senators for the American State of Ontario.' "[62] Neither this remark, nor the sea-sickness to which the Prime Minister of Canada almost immediately succumbed, were well suited to the purpose of making a Big Navy man out of Mackenzie King.

Meanwhile, the Imperial Conference had been meeting almost daily.

By 17 October, after statements on foreign policy from most of the participants, and a general review of imperial defence to which the dominion premiers responded, the First Lord of the Admiralty at last introduced the all-important subject of naval defence, to which the Conference had inevitably gravitated. He began, as Skelton had anticipated, by proclaiming the principle of the indivisibility of sea power:

> Our Empire is an oceanic commonwealth. . . . The object of the naval forces of the Empire is to keep open these vital communications. . . . There is only one way . . . and that is by the capacity of the Navy to destroy or neutralize the enemy forces of any Power that attempts to disturb our Peace. . . . If we have a Fleet strong enough to do this, the whole Empire is safe; if not, then the whole Empire is doomed. . . . Sea warfare cannot be sub-divided or localized. The main reliance of each and all of us must be a Fleet capable of offensive action at any point where danger threatens. I feel bound to lay stress upon this because the opposite doctrine is so often openly or tacitly asserted. . . .

As foreshadowed in the Admiralty memoranda, the First Lord did not draw from this doctrine the corollary principle of the need for an Imperial Grand Fleet. "On that issue," he observed candidly,

> there has been in the past a certain standing division of opinion between the Dominions and the Admiralty. In past years the Admiralty has tended to the assertion of the view that a unitary navy, under direct Admiralty control, and a contribution either of men or money or ships from the Dominions, would give the greatest efficiency, and, though more than fourteen years ago—in 1909—it accepted the Dominions' point of view, it still recurred to the expression of its own contention that the other system was the best. Well, we have clearly come to the point of view now that, not merely as a matter of political expediency but from the point of view of the efficiency and strength of the future, the naval security of a world-wide Empire must be based on naval strength at home in each part of the Empire. . . .[63]

But if the security of the Empire was now to be protected by dominion fleets rather than an Imperial Grand Fleet, it was essential that the dominions each became naval powers in their own right, and that co-operation among them and with the Admiralty be continuous and intimate. "What we must aim at," the First Lord concluded,

> is the building up in each part of the Empire of a naval spirit, a naval tradition, a navy, small it may be, but rooted in the life of each of the Nations of the Empire. What applies to the navy itself applies to all that is auxiliary to it, to the provision of munitions, to everything that makes naval strength. . . . In the long run, and looking to the future, you cannot defend a world-wide Empire against contingencies, which may be equally world-wide, from one small island in the North Sea. . . . It is essential that

the Dominion Navies, as they grow, should be national in spirit, national in organization, but not local. No navy can attain real efficiency that is simply tied down to local waters. They must be sea-going navies. We also feel that the more complete the political and administrative independence of those Navies, the more essential it is that in their organization, in their training, and in their types of design, they should endeavour so to work by a progressive policy that in the hour of danger they can work together as one.[64]

What Amery actually said on this occasion is not, perhaps, as significant as what his Canadian listeners understood him to say. The speech as recorded by Dafoe is considerably more revealing:

Amery spoke at length on matter naval defence. Empire must control sea routes or cease to exist. Navy must be mobile able to go wherever Empire interests attacked. Mere accident that before war navy was massed in home waters because it happened menace was there; in future Empire might be saved by navy in distant sea. Made long technical defence capital ships. Safe from torpedo by device of the "bulge"; from air craft by nets. Severely criticized Admiral Scott for his opposition to capital ships—called him a slap-dash critic. Natural route navy for protection Empire was Mediterranean, Red Sea, Indian Seas, Singapore, Malacca Straits; strategic centre of this was Mediterranean. Defended Singapore scheme; not new; dated from 1912; merely enlargement to meet existing conditions, especially added size ships due to bulge. No objection to it by Japan. U.S. should not object especially as they had themselves no naval base in those waters. Re admiralty and dominion navies said opposition of Admiralty to scheme of 1909 and its continued expression of disagreement had been a mistake. Admiralty had changed its viewpoint and now accepted unreservedly principle Dominion navies; wanted this known for information of those in Dominions who had fought Dominion navies because they thought Admiralty wished opposition to be offered. Then went on to urge that these national navies should be merged into general defence scheme. Quoted alleged statistics as to present per capita outlay Empire Defence; Great Britain 25 shillings annually; Australia 8; Canada and South Africa 1s. Said Singapore scheme could not affect world naval situation before 1931 . . .[65]

Mackenzie King, as Prime Minister of the senior Dominion, spoke immediately after the First Lord concluded his remarks. "I congratulate Mr. Amery," he began, "on the manner in which he has presented these problems, which are perhaps the most important of all the problems we have to consider." The speech which he then proceeded to deliver is as significant as any ever given by the Canadian statesman in the course of a long and historic career. (Its crucial passages are given in Document 2, pp. 329–31, below.)

After Mackenzie King's lengthy exposition of the principle of dominion autonomy in defence policy, it could not have seemed to Amery and his British and Australian and New Zealand colleagues that the Conference could do much to promote the projects close to their hearts. But, having nothing to lose, the First Lord arranged a further meeting with the Canadian Prime Minister. In the course of their discussion, Amery attempted "to induce King to begin at once on a modest naval programme. King replied that he could not do so, nor could he commit the Government to any naval or military expenditure, especially in view of the hostility in Canada against any increased demands for defence. He said he was willing to present the need for Canada's doing more towards her own defence, but the present was certainly not the time to raise the question."[66] An exchange of letters, initiated by Amery, left things as they were:

Perhaps it may be convenient to you to have a short note, for your personal use, of the general purport of our conversation the other day. Please correct me if it does not correspond with your recollection of it.

I understood from you that while you concurred generally in the character of the suggestions laid before you in the Admiralty Paper with regard to the building up of a Canadian unit over a period of years, as in conformity both with Sir W. Laurier's resolutions quoted at the beginning of the Memorandum, and with your own previous declaration in your House of Commons [on 16 May 1922] . . ., you considered that the present political position precluded you from actually announcing any such scheme and that you would not be in a position to do so until you had had more time to educate public opinion and had also more effective Parliamentary backing. Consequently that the only thing you could do at this moment was to consider such moderate programme of expansion in personnel and other arrangements as would make it possible for you to initiate a larger policy when in a position to do so.

With regard to the question of the possibility of your taking over, on favourable financial terms, a cruiser if we laid her down now, you made it clear that while you might find yourself in a position to do so by the time the cruiser was actually built, you could not enter into any discussion or give any undertaking in respect of the matter at the present time.[67]

Mackenzie King replied:

I have your letter of October 27th. . . . From a reading of the second paragraph, it might be gathered that I had laid stress upon an existing political situation rather than upon public sentiment with respect to naval expenditure, as I believe it to exist at the present moment in Canada. It would, however, be erroneous to suppose that the country would at present countenance any increase in naval expenditure. Subject to this interpretation, I do not see anything to suggest in the way of change. . . .

With respect to the last paragraph of your letter, I should, I think, make it clear that, in the event of the Government deciding to add one or more cruisers to our Naval Service, it is quite possible that it may be deemed advisable to have any such vessels constructed in the Dominion. I mention this lest it might be assumed by the Admiralty that contracts for the construction of ships of this class, or orders for the same, would as a matter of course be placed in the United Kingdom.[68]

There remained the resolutions on naval defence. Amery and Stanley Bruce (the Prime Minister of Australia and Amery's principal ally among the dominion premiers) tried their hand at a draft which, they hoped, would be acceptable to Mackenzie King while expressing the Conference's support for such projects as the Singapore base and the naval defence of the Suez Canal. But King would not accept it. He told them that Canada would not be bound by any defence policies set out in resolutions of an Imperial Conference, for (as he wrote in his diary), "to attempt to commit us by resolution in any way was simply to make impossible any subsequent approval by parliament of anything the Conference had done in this direction."[69] The resolutions as finally published in a form acceptable to him,[70] with their weighty silences, their careful preservation of dominion autonomy, and their explicit repudiation of a single defence policy for the Empire, are sufficient evidence that what Smuts observed to Mackenzie King at the conclusion of the Conference—"You ought to be satisfied. Canada has had her way in everything."[71]—was not an exaggerated tribute.

The proposal to publish the Admiralty's memorandum on "Empire Naval Policy and Co-operation" might have best been forgotten considering Mackenzie King's unfavourable reception of it at the Imperial Conference. That was far from what happened. In December 1923, the Colonial Secretary wrote to King to say that he had been instructed by the First Lord to ascertain whether the Canadian Government had any objection to publication. King replied by cable: "Colleagues unanimous of view that First Lord of Admiralty should be informed that Canadian Government would very strongly object to publication of memorandum in question. Am writing."[72] The promised letter was drafted with meticulous care, in at least three versions (one of which was the work of J. S. Ewart, the constitutional lawyer noted for the extreme nationalism of such books as *The Kingdom of Canada* and *The Independence Papers*). However, a change of government in the United Kingdom, by which the Labour party came to power and Lord Chelmsford replaced Amery at the Admiralty, relieved the Canadian Prime Minister of having to decide which, if any, of the drafts should be sent. When, less than a year later, the Conservatives regained their majority at Westminster, no more was heard from them of publishing the memorandum. Amery's retrospective comment on the affair is not without insight: ". . . when it was suggested that the Admiralty memorandum . . . should be published MacKenzie [*sic*] King strongly objected, on the ground that this would involve an interference in the domestic policy of the Dominions. His real reason, I had no doubt, was that he feared that the publication of the memorandum might meet with too favourable a reception in Canada, and force him to do something, whereas he was firmly determined to do nothing."[73]

V

The Early Years of the R.C.A.F.

AIR POWER AT THE ARMISTICE

In November 1918 Canada had no air force. But she had airmen. Many thousands of Canadians enlisted in the Royal Flying Corps and the Royal Naval Air Service; the official figure of nearly 23,000 is far short of those who actually served. A thousand Canadian officers were killed in aerial action. Ten of twenty-seven leading "aces" (officially, pilots with five or more enemy planes shot down) were Canadians, including the renowned Major W. A. "Billy" Bishop who alone destroyed seventy-two German aircraft in combat. So substantial was the Canadian contribution to Allied air power, and so distinguished the record of Canadian airmen, that there were in process of formation as the Great War ended two identifiably Canadian air units. One of these was organized, at the suggestion of the Admiralty, by the Department of the Naval Service in June 1918, for coastal patrol and escort duty. A Royal Canadian Naval Air Service was authorized by the Canadian Government in September 1918, and training of recruits begun both in the United Kingdom and in the United States; but it was disbanded on 5 December 1918 "for the time being"—though "for the time being" proved to be a generation.[1]

The other embryo Canadian air force emerged in the United Kingdom where, during the last few months of war, thought was being given to the organization of distinctively Canadian squadrons within the Royal Air Force (the R.A.F. had been created in April 1918 out of the merger of the R.F.C. and the R.N.A.S.). After lengthy negotiations between British and Canadian authorities, agreement upon a distinctively Canadian component within the R.A.F. was reached.

Again the Armistice intervened, but it was decided none the less to proceed with the creation of two squadrons composed of Canadian pilots and observers who had served in the British air services, together with Canadian personnel as their ground crews. The squadrons came officially into being on 20 November, and were based at Upper Heyford, in Oxfordshire. Early in 1919 the first distinctively Canadian military aviation command—No. 1 Canadian Wing—was established to administer the two squadrons. At the Overseas Military Headquarters, in London, the assumption was that this unit would be relocated, more or less intact, to Canada, where it would serve as the nucleus of Canada's postwar air force. But it soon became apparent that there was no assurance that there would be any Canadian postwar air force. On 15 February 1919, the Ministry of Overseas Military Forces was informed by the Department of Militia and Defence at Ottawa: "authority not yet obtained for maintenance of Air Force in Canada after war, and in absence of such authority the squadrons . . . will be demobilized on their return."[2] The Ministry of Overseas Forces protested strenuously:

> Most strongly urge that matters of Canadian post bellum Air Force be considered seriously by Government without delay, so that trained Canadian personnel in the two Canadian squadrons, and in the Royal Air Force, may be drawn upon for future Canadian Air Force and aeronautic development before they are demobilized and scattered through Canada.
>
> Considered most desirable Canadian Air Force have its natural place in Canadian post bellum Military Forces as indicated conclusively by experiences of war.
>
> In view of great developments flying and flying machines in war, and in all countries after war, Canada surely should take definite stand now to have Air Force which would enable it to keep pace with rest of the world and particularly other Dominions in all matters relative to flying.[3]

But the Government thought otherwise. Canada's postwar air establishment would have to start from scratch. The two squadrons were accordingly ordered to return to the Dominion; and, upon their return, they were disbanded.

Canada's airmen had more things working for them as a permanent postwar force than did the two established Services. The Royal Canadian Navy, as we have seen, was handicapped by its inconspicuous part in the total war effort, by the high capital costs of creating a sea-going fleet, by the threat to Canadian autonomy seemingly posed by strategic doctrines favoured by the Admiralty, and, above all, by the divisive effects of naval policy upon public opinion. The Army's future was placed in doubt by the determination of most of those who served to turn their backs upon the ordeal from which they had just emerged and to have as little to do as possible with military life in future. But for those who fought in, and survived, the war in the air, aviation opened up glittering prospects of a new and exciting career. Far more than the other professions of arms, military aviation seemed clearly adaptable to peacetime service. Exploring, prospecting, fire-fighting, transporting goods and passengers—these were only the most obvious uses to which a nation's air power might be put when out of combat. And where, if not in Canada—with, on the one hand, its large reserves of trained and proven personnel and, on the other, its immense distances and unexploited natural resources—had aviation a more certain role in the peaceful development of an awakening nation? All this was undeniable. And yet the part to be played in this development by military aviation was contentious. Did the country require an air force, as opposed to an air service, at all? Many thought it did not.

CREATION OF THE AIR BOARD

Early in 1919, the Borden Government decided to create an Air Board. The Board should formulate aviation policy in its broadest aspects; the policy formulated, the Board should then be charged with its administration. An Act of Parliament was to bring the Board into being. The proposed legislation was carefully scrutinized by interested parties, of which the Navy was most interested.

A memorandum by the Naval Director of Stores, J. A. Wilson, dated 2 April 1919, may be the earliest reference in the official files to the proposed Air Board; its author, who later became Secretary of the Board, played an important part in drafting the Air Board bill. Extracts from his memorandum follow:

> . . . There can be little doubt that within a very few years, the commercial side of aeronautics will make great progress. Under the Peace conditions which may probably be counted on during the next decade and probably for much longer such activities will form the major portion of the duties with which the proposed Air Board will have to deal.
>
> The importance of encouraging an active Air Development on Civil lines to the Government is great apart from the actual services which it will perform, as the greater this development, the larger will be the reserve, both of men and material, which may be called on for purposes of defence in time of emergency.
>
> The upkeep of large Air Force establishments for purely Naval and

Military duties in time of Peace will be expensive and a constant object of criticism. It should therefore be advantageous to the country generally to encourage and assist the Civil development of aeronautics in every way, and to so guide and regulate its organization and any aircraft industry which may develop in Canada, so that it may form a reservoir on which to draw in any emergency. . . .

The Constitution of the proposed Board has been accordingly drafted with the importance of civil and commercial services as well as those of the Naval & Military sides in view. The latter phases of its operations will be well represented on the Board as only Naval & Military Officers had had large experience in flying operations so that at least two members will be drawn from the present services and will have had great experience in this line. These Officers will have most important duties to perform, and on them will fall the oversight of all active operations. These two officers might well be chosen from Canadian Officers at present in the Imperial Air Forces and should have good records, not merely as fighting pilots with big scores to their credit, but rather on account of their record for administrative capacity and varied experience in operations on a large scale. . . .

On the Civil Member will depend largely the success of the Board and its operations. He will preside in the Minister's absence and in addition to the Departmental duties and finance of the Board he will be responsible for all inter-Departmental relations which it is expected may be considerable. He should, therefore, have an intimate knowledge of Government organization and control and be familiar with conditions throughout the Government service.

The technical member of the Board should be chosen, not so much for his specialist knowledge in any one line, and need not necessarily have been connected with actual flying operations to any extent. What is most desirable in this Member is wide scientific and engineering knowledge on the broadest lines possible, as his duties must necessarily cover a great range of technical subjects. . . .

Provision has been made in the draft for the appointment of three other members of the Board in case the work increases unexpectedly or if for any reason it may be found necessary or advisable to appoint further members. . . .

The position of the Board and whether it should form part of an existing Department or be formed as a separate new body has been carefully considered. Under the present draft both courses are open as the Minister and Deputy Minister of one of the present Departments could be appointed Chairman and Deputy Chairman respectively and the Board could be completed by the addition of the flying and technical members. In this case either the Naval or Militia Departments would be the logical choice.

From many points of view it would appear preferable to form a separate organization. The new nature of the problems to be dealt with, their wide scope and range, and the large civil development to be anticipated, would appear to justify this view without considering the many duties now performed by the Deputy Heads of these Departments and the danger of the new body becoming ineffective through the pressure of other duties on the principal member.

The Deputy Chairman, as principal executive member of the Board, should be able to devote his whole attention to its work if possible. A separate Board will be able to devote its entire time and attention to the problems to be solved, and will give, in practice, a more efficient organization. Its views will be more independent and it will be better able to decide questions arising on their merits. . . .[4]

The original draft of the Air Board bill assigned to the proposed Board not only the authority to formulate and administer policy in relation to civil aviation but virtually supreme power in relation to military aviation. One of the clauses of the draft listed among the duties of the Board that of advising its chairman "on all questions relating to the Air Defence of Canada"; another, that of maintaining "liaison with the Naval and Military Authorities in matters pertaining to the defence of Canada" and of co-operating "with the Air Staffs of the United Kingdom and self-governing Dominions as necessary for the Air Defence of the Empire." To the Assistant Director of the Naval Staff, R. M. Stephens, who was observing the emergence of the draft bill with close attention, these clauses appeared altogether too permissive. "It is too early at the present time," he wrote on 4 April to his naval chief, "to say just where the Air Service will come in, in connection with Canadian defence, and to have both this Department and the Militia Department bound by Act of Parliament might have a very unfortunate effect." He therefore recommended that the draft be rewritten so that the duties of the Air Board would be defined not by its originating legislation but by the Government of the day. "In general," he concluded, "I consider that in setting up an Air Board it is very necessary not to put into their hands powers which the Naval and Militia Departments may later on require for themselves when the bent of aeronautical matters is clearer. . . . the drafting of the Bill requires most careful consideration."[5] In a lengthier memorandum of the same date, Stephens elaborated his position:

As the question of a future Canadian Air Service has entered the field of practical politics by the proposed Bill to establish an Air Board, the following remarks are offered on the matter:—

In aeronautical matters, it appears to me to be necessary to take very long views at the present time so as not to be circumscribed by existing conditions, as it is quite impossible to say what developments may not take place in the future. There is all the more reason, therefore, for taking care that aeronautics are started on right lines in Canada, and that things are not done too hastily.

The question which we, as a Department, are most concerned with is that of the future control over aeronautics insofar as they are concerned with Naval Defence. This question is vital and is evidently so considered in Great Britain as one Minister has been appointed to both War and Air Ministries, no doubt that the matter of defence shall not be lost sight of at this critical moment. [*]

In approaching this matter, it is very necessary to get rid of the "war" idea from one's mind—a matter which is not too easily accomplished as hitherto aeronautics have been almost exclusively a war business.

This Department has the same interest in aerial matters as in maritime matters, in which special arrangements are often made for warships.

With regard to shipping, great difficulties are frequently overcome in Parliamentary Acts by stating that the Act or part of the Act does not apply to H.M. ships. Something of the sort seems desirable in aeronautical matters, though in view of the probable large Government ownership of aircraft it may be necessary to limit the exemptions to those employed on Naval or Military work. The importance of this one matter may be realized when we consider that a Naval Aircraft might be patrolling (in peacetime) on some definite mission and yet might be excluded from ascending or descending because those particular heights were reserved by aerial regulations for particular classes of machines. That would be a hindrance to Government work and a gain to no one.

Then there is the all important question of a separate air force—by that, I mean a warlike force only. This question is one which will continue to be debated for many years to come and authorities will certainly differ on it. My personal opinion is that the aim should be to develop an Aerial Civil Department which would be responsible for all aeronautical matters other than those of defence. The Naval and Militia Departments each to have their own Air Services to suit their own needs which are totally different. The Aerial Department to be the source of design and supply for all Government aircraft and aerial research. The same Department to be responsible for the training of all pilots in flying, the Naval and Militia Departments to be responsible for the additional technical training required by their pilots. The Naval and Militia Departments to own and control their own aerodromes.

The foregoing are merely suggestions for discussion, but if the Air Board Bill goes through as proposed, then such discussion is precluded as all power and authority is handed over to the Air Board. I certainly think that the Militia Department should be consulted as to the terms of the Bill.[6]

A few days later, the draft Air Board bill was discussed at a meeting of the Naval Committee, at which (according to its minutes) "the A/Director Naval Service expressed the opinion that the powers granted

*This is not how the move to bring the two ministries under a single minister appeared to senior Royal Air Force officers. "The small importance attached by the Government to the R.A.F. and aviation in general," the then Chief of the Air Staff wrote afterwards, "was shown by the fact that [Winston Churchill] was given the combined portfolios of War and Air. This in itself was a mistake in every way . . . the combination of the two posts under one head connoted the surbordination of the Air Ministry to the War Office." Sir Frederick Sykes, *From Many Angles* (London, 1942), p. 266.

under the proposed Bill were too broad, that the Naval interests in Aeronautics were not sufficiently protected, and that the whole initiative and control over this subject would pass under the present Act to the Air Board without leaving any powers to the Naval Service in this matter."[7] The Naval Committee decided to bring the matter before the Naval and Military Committee—that predecessor of the present-day Chiefs of Staff Committee where matters of common concern were discussed and recommendations jointly made by senior officers of the two services. For once the Navy and the Army were in full agreement. "The C.G.S. is of opinion," General Sir Willoughby Gwatkin minuted for the benefit of the military secretary of the Naval and Military Committee on 10 April, "that in the Bill too little regard is paid to Naval and Military requirements, and he has ventured so to inform the Minister of Militia and Defence."[8]

Meanwhile the indefatigable Stephens was mounting in still more memoranda a barrage of additional objections to the draft bill. "The Bill as drafted does not make clear whether it is intended to establish a new Aerial Department of the Government or merely to establish an Air Board . . ."; " . . . if an Air Board is established at the present time, it should be limited to action in an advisory capacity . . ."; "The proposed composition of the Board is objectionable from a naval point of view, [as] there is no provision that any member of the Board should be a naval officer"; "With regard to paragraph 3—duties of the Air Board—there is much here which at the present time appears undesirable (from the naval point of view) to put forward in legislation. In general the proposed duties go far beyond what has been hitherto done in any other country"; "The proposed Bill provides no guarantee that the Board will be competent in any way to advise on the question of Air Defence of Canada."[9] In these objections, the Director of the Naval Service, Admiral Sir Charles Kingsmill, concurred. He also expressed his concurrence in yet another of Stephens' memoranda on the issue:

The proposed Air Board Bill came up for consideration by the Naval Committee on the 9th April, and the Naval members of that Committee expressed the utmost alarm over its provisions.

The principal objection taken to the Bill was that there were no safeguards to guarantee the interests of the Navy. Aerial policy in Canada is a case in which it seems wise to make haste slowly at the present time. There are very few persons in the Dominion at the moment, competent to evolve a policy for the Dominion. At the same time, it seems both wise and necessary to take preliminary measures to establish an Aerial Authority. The proposal of an Air Board is one which commends itself as a proper beginning.

Once the idea of aerial navigation takes a hold on the Canadian people, there is a great danger of everyone being carried off their feet and being hastened into measures which are unsound in principle. It is not easy to say exactly what steps should be taken with regard to Aerial policy, but one thing is clear: that is, that one must get away from the war idea and give due consideration to private and commercial developments.

It is, therefore, desirable to aim at the establishment of a Civil Aerial Department which should have the general direction and control of Aeronautical matters, in much the same way as the Marine Department has control of nautical matters. There is, however, in nautical affairs a very clearly defined line between men-of-war and all other vessels whether Government-owned or privately owned. There is no valid reason for departing from this principle when dealing with aerial matters. It would seem to be an advantage that the Air Board or Aerial Department should be responsible for the design and construction of all aircraft, and also for aerial research, care being taken that the Naval requirements are put forward by the presence of Naval or Naval Air Officers in that Department. . . .

It seems clear, therefore, that some steps must be taken to provide for Naval control over the equipment they will use, either an absolute control, or modified control such as is in force in Great Britain where men and machines are raised by the Air Ministry, and control of them transferred to the Admiralty for operational purposes, the administration still remaining in the hands of the Air Ministry. The advantages of this system are not altogether apparent.

In addition to any other steps that are taken in regard to the Bill, it is considered that a clause should be inserted declaring that no existing powers of the Navy are interfered with in any way by this Act.[10]

The Naval and Military Committee delegated the task of preparing an acceptable revision of the draft bill to its two joint Secretaries, Stephens for the Navy, Gwatkin for the Army. A new version, "which it is probable the Naval and Military Committee will adopt generally at its next meeting," was ready by 24 April. "I have no doubt," Stephens wrote, "that it represents the mind of the Committee in general. . . . This revised draft is based on the Air Navigation Act 1919, which is merely a temporary Act in order to tide over the interval until the definite policy is adopted by the Imperial authorities. It appears a reasonable policy for this Government to adopt. The proposal avoids the question of Aerial Defence as it practically limits action to the regulation of aerial navigation."[11] In a more formal communication, the two secretaries explained to the Committee what they had intended to accomplish in their revision: "In view of the present state of aerial development in Canada, secretaries consider it wise to avoid placing all power in the hands of the Air Board thus reserving any necessary powers to the Navy and Militia which they may require at a later date but which at present cannot be exactly formulated. In consequence all reference to Aerial Defence was eliminated from the Bill. The drastic proposals regarding complete control of all aeronautical matters by the Air Board was also modified to preserve an opening for any future requirements on the part of the Navy."[12] At the 78th meeting of the Naval and Military Committee, held on 28 April, the revised draft was approved without dissent. The following day, Bill No. 80, "to authorize the appointment of an Air Board for the control of aeronautics," received its first reading in the House of Commons. A. K. MacLean, substituting for the absent Minister of the Naval Service, explained the bill's main features in these terms:

The Bill proposes the establishment of an Air Board to consist of not less than five and not more than seven members to be appointed by the Governor in Council. It is intended that the Chairman shall be a minister of the Crown and that the Department of Militia and the Department of Naval Service shall each be represented on the Board, by one member. The duties of the Air Board will be:

(*a*) To supervise all matters connected with aeronautics;

(*b*) to study the development of aeronautics in Canada and in other countries, and to undertake such technical research as may be requisite for the development of aeronautics; and to co-operate with other institutions in carrying out such research;

(*c*) to construct and maintain all Government aerodromes and air stations, including all plant, machinery and buildings necessary for their efficient equipment and upkeep;

(*d*) to control and manage all aircraft and equipment necessary for the conduct of any of His Majesty's services;

(*e*) to operate such services as the Governor in Council may approve;

(*f*) to prescribe aerial routes;

(*g*) to co-operate with other officers of His Majesty and to assist in the carrying out of any services under their jurisdiction which may require aerial work of any nature, and to collaborate with the officers employed in existing air services of His Majesty in such extension of their present work as the development of aeronautics may require;

(*h*) to take such action as may be necessary to secure by International Regulation or otherwise, the rights of His Majesty in respect of His Government in Canada in International Air Routes;

(*i*) to co-operate with the officers of the Departments of Militia and Defence and of the Naval Service on all questions relating to the air defence of Canada;

(*j*) to co-operate with the air staffs or authorities of other Governments or countries for any purposes pertaining to air services;

(*k*) to investigate, examine and report on all proposals for the institution of commercial air services within or partly within Canada, or the limits of the territorial waters of Canada;

(*l*) to consider, draft and prepare for approval by the Governor in Council such regulations as may be considered necessary for the control or operation of aeronautics in Canada or within the limits of the territorial waters of Canada; and, (*m*) to perform such other duties as the Governor in Council may from time to time impose.[13]

A brief discussion of the bill took place on the occasion of its second reading, on 5 May. A. K. MacLean emphasized that the legislation was provisional only, and would doubtless be modified in the light of experience. "I have no doubt that in the working of it during the coming year weaknesses will develop but experience will enable us to pass legislation which will be more satisfactory."[14]

The rump Borden Government (the Prime Minister and four key members of his Cabinet were at this time attending the Paris Peace Conference) moved anything but energetically to set up the Air Board for which legislation provided. In June 1919, when the Board was still unconstituted, the Acting Director of the Royal Canadian Naval Air Service attempted to enlist the support of the Aero Club of Canada. "The next move," Major C. MacLauren wrote,

> and a very urgent one, is to push the formation of the Air Board. At present, as in the past, the Government has had no recognised authority to advise it on the question of Aeronautics. The tendency has been for anyone interested in the question, whether commercially or otherwise, to tender advice. The results need no elaboration.
>
> The appointing of a capable and independent Air Board, along the lines as previously suggested, I consider is most important. The Aero Club of Canada, being a highly representative body, should be in a position to bring considerable pressure to bear on the Government to force action. . . .[15]

On 23 June, the Government finally constituted the Air Board of Canada, although on a temporary basis. The Chairman was A. L. Sifton, Minister of Customs and Inland Revenue; the Minister of the Naval Service and the Minister of Militia and Defence were also members representing their respective Departments. The Vice-Chairman, who was intended to be the Board's chief executive officer, was O. M. Biggar, an experienced public servant and formerly assistant Judge-Advocate General. The remaining three members were Dr. R. M. Coulter, Deputy Postmaster-General; J. A. Wilson, Assistant Deputy Minister of the Naval Service; and E. S. Busby, Chief Inspector of the Customs. The composition of the Board was thus such as to ensure from the outset that it would be inadequately equipped to deal energetically with its various mandates; all its members, however competent, had other and more urgent duties to perform. This weakness was candidly acknowledged by its Chairman, in a memorandum prepared after nine months' rather unsatisfactory operation. "If, like the board of directors of a commercial company, the Board's chief duty was to deal with questions of policy and finance, this [preoccupation of its members with their regular duties] would not be so serious a difficulty, but financial oversight, and all that that entails, is necessarily a matter for the Cabinet, and the function of the Board must, in order to be useful, be rather in the nature of an administrative conference. If it does not perform this function, there is none which it can advantageously perform."[16] The composition of the Board was unsatisfactory to some, among these Arthur Meighen. "I notice Council has put through an order establishing an Air Board," he wrote to C. C. Ballantyne early in July 1919. "I could not have been present when this was done, and must express my surprise that such Departments as the Customs and the Post Office have representatives on this Board while this Department [Interior] which has taken the first steps to actually utilize Air Craft and, further, has charge of Forest Control, and Survey Work, is not represented. What explanation could be given is hard for me to imagine. . . ."[17] Ballantyne returned a mollifying reply. ". . . I really had very little to do with this," he explained. "I was simply asked by the Prime Minister to act, which I agreed to do. I quite agree with you that your Department should have some representation on this Board. . . ."[18] In consequence, the Deputy Minister of Meighen's Department was authorized to attend its meetings, though not as a full member. For the first few months of its existence the Board's activities were desultory, giving some the impression that they were being hidden from the public view: ". . . a general air of mystery has surrounded the doings of Canada's premier air authorities," commented the *Victoria Colonist* on 8 October 1919. "From the very meagre details released to date, it is almost impossible to form any definite opinion of the trend of events aeronautical in Canada." But nothing was being hidden, for there was nothing to hide.

In March 1920, the Board's Chairman, A. L. Sifton, prepared a memorandum in which he suggested certain changes in its composition for the future. "The most satisfactory constitution for the Board," he wrote,

> would appear to be to have represented on it the two interests which it is designed to serve, namely, civil aviation and military aviation. The statute indeed has the representation of the latter definitely in contemplation, and if a senior staff officer of the Naval Service, a senior staff officer of the Militia, and a senior officer representing the Canadian Air Force were members of the Board, the development of military air strength along lines which would ensure the essential co-operation between the air forces and the sea and land forces would be very efficiently secured. The interests of civil aviation would be equally promoted by the placing on the Board of the

heads of the two branches into which the civil work under the Board has been divided, namely, the head of the Flying Operations Branch, who is responsible for all civil Government flying, and the head of the Certificate branch, who is responsible for the regulation of civil flying by members of the public. The remaining member of the Board should be a civilian Vice-Chairman, who would be responsible for the administration of the Department generally with particular reference to finances. . . .

The suggested organization has the further advantage that it removes the possible ground of criticism that, although charged with the control of military and civil aviation, the Air Board as now constituted has upon it neither a soldier nor an airman.[19]

A reorganization of the Board along the lines suggested by its Chairman was carried out the following month. The Minister of Militia and Defence, Hugh Guthrie, replaced Sifton as Chairman. O. M. Biggar remained as Vice-Chairman and principal executive officer. The other members resigned, and were replaced by Major-General Sir Willoughby Gwatkin, the former Chief of the General Staff who some weeks earlier had been appointed Inspector-General of the newly formed Canadian Air Force; Captain Walter Hose, representing the Naval Service; Lieutenant-Colonel R. Leckie, Superintendent of Flying Operations; Lieutenant-Colonel J. S. Scott, Superintendent of the Certificates Branch; and Dr. E. Deville, the Surveyor General, representing the Department of the Interior, "The new Board," wrote one of its new appointees soon afterwards, ". . . comprises a naval, military and air force representative, together with heads of branches. It is expected that members of the new Board will take a much more active interest in the affairs of the Board than did the last and that they will devote a very considerable part of their time to matters pertaining to the air."[20]

GETTING OFF THE GROUND

An urgent issue before the Air Board in its early and provisional form was to decide how a military aviation force for the Dominion ought to be developed. Advice was received very soon after the Armistice from the Air Ministry, at that time engaged in its own struggle to have the Royal Air Force survive as an independent service; advice from that quarter, needless to say, was that Canada should create an air force of its own, separate and distinct from either army or navy. This was set out in an Air Ministry memorandum of 26 April 1919—a covering letter emphasized that its points "carry with them the fullest consideration of the Air Staff"—which further addressed itself to both the civil and military aspects of postwar aviation in the Dominion. In regard to the former, it affirmed that "in the particular case of Canada with its vast distances and unlimited possibilities for expansion, it is not too much to urge that failure to establish . . . a central form of control at the earliest possible moment, and before rash steps have been taken by any particular body without proper technical advisers would be a matter of very deep regret in the years to come." That this advice might appropriately be tendered in relation to any new government undertaking in no way detracted from its soundness. In regard to military aviation, the Air Ministry advised: "It is unlikely that Canada will need to provide a large force in time of peace, but none the less as the wars of the future will be largely wars of the air, and, as in consequence the first blow struck will be almost coincident with the declaration of war, some form of national aerial defence will undoubtedly be necessary. . . ."[21] Through the murk of the official prose there gleamed perceptibly the visionary genius of Sir Hugh Trenchard.*

The Air Board was favourably impressed by these views. The Naval Service was not. The Navy had by no means abandoned the hope that it might again develop its own air arm, and had retained an Acting Director of the disbanded Royal Canadian Naval Air Service on the staff at Naval Headquarters. A meeting of the Naval Committee on 27 March 1919 had rejected out of hand the "proposals of the Militia Department that the whole matter of aeronautics come under the Minister of Militia. . . . The Committee was agreed," its minutes record, "that some action to institute a suitable Government organization for dealing with aeronautics generally was urgently required, but that in addition the Naval Air Service should be maintained as an integral part of the Department's activities, with close co-operation with any other organization that might be formed." By 1920, though disappointed by its failure to obtain any substantial funds for an air force of its own, the Navy had not altered its views as to the need for such a force, as the following paper (probably the work of the Acting Director of the R.C.N.A.S., Major MacLauren) makes clear:

> The acceptance by the Government of any one of Lord Jellicoe's proposals will involve the establishment of an air force. It may, therefore, soon be necessary to decide whether a separate air force should be created, or whether the Navy should have its own air force.
>
> There is probably no question before the services at the present time, regarding which it is more important that a correct decision should be made.

*Who was even then reflecting upon what was to become the famous "Trenchard Memorandum." See Andrew Boyle, *Trenchard* (London, 1962), p. 351.

It is the more important because any error made in the beginning would probably not show itself to any serious extent for some years. . . .

There is one fundamental difference between the Air Force and the other two services. The Navy is always on the sea and the Army is always on the land, that is, they are operating in their own particular elements, but the Air Force is only occasionally in its element—the air.

In war time, as soon as an airman alights on land, he becomes dependent on the military for almost everything. . . . The argument is equally applicable to an airman alighting on board a ship. . . .

Air Officers are naturally reluctant to press arguments of this nature to their logical conclusion, because it then becomes evident that the total size of a nation's Air Forces is dependent upon the requirements of the Army and Navy, and therefore their existence is largely in the hands of these two Services. A force such as the Royal Air Force is in effect primarily employed in raising and training personnel, and designing and producing machines, to hand over to the Army and Navy to use. . . .

In Canada particularly the time seems inopportune to establish an independent air force. Such a force would require a separate organization at Headquarters and other divisional points and its own establishments involving no little expense. It would be difficult to justify this expenditure in view of the fact that an independent air force would have practically no scope for its activities except in case of war with the United States and such a war is not in contemplation at the present time. In any other war aerial activity would be limited to co-operation with army or navy. Insofar as the Navy is concerned . . . not only is a naval air force desirable, [it is] also necessary. . . .[22]

Holding these views, the Navy was naturally distraught on learning that the Air Board had reported favourably on the project to create a separate Canadian air force. Insult was added to injury when it developed that the Air Board's first steps in that direction were taken without proper consultation with the naval authorities. "In the report of the 6th meeting of the Air Board held on the 28th November," the Assistant Director of the Naval Service, R. M. Stephens, wrote in evident indignation to his chief,

it appears that the Board instructed the Vice Chairman to prepare a recommendation to Council for the formation of an Air Force. No proposals have been put before the Department to this end. . . .

The formation of a Canadian Air Force is of great importance to this Department, and the representative of the Department, namely the Minister, was not present at the meeting. It is submitted that his attention should be drawn to the fact that no proposals have been put before the Department and it is very desirable that they should be, before final action is taken by the Air Board.[23]

Arrangements were made that, should the Minister find it impossible to attend future meetings of the Air Board, a member of the Naval Staff should attend on his behalf; Commander Stephens was proposed for the job; nothing was likely to escape his watchful eye.

He did not like the way things were going. Early in 1920 he appealed to the Deputy Minister of Justice for an opinion as to whether "the Air Board Act covers the establishment of an Air Force, by which I mean a Military Service corresponding to the Army and Navy."[24] "I would answer," came the reply, "in the negative."[25] But that was scant consolation. The Air Board clearly regarded itself competent to lay down policy in military, as in civil, aviation; and with its ministerial representation, what it wanted to do it did. "The question of the constitution of a Canadian Air Force," its first annual report observes,

> was an early subject of consideration by the Air Board, and on December 22 [1919] there was adopted, for submission to Privy Council, a memorandum covering the general lines of the organization proposed. A final decision on this subject was, however, postponed until the general policy with regard to Canada's future sea, land and air forces was determined, and it has consequently not been possible to take any further steps in this direction. The very large number of ex-officers and airmen of the Royal Air Force in Canada are expected enthusiastically to support the proposals if it is found possible to adopt them.[26]

The memorandum of 22 December was incorporated in an Order in Council (P.C. 395) on 18 February 1920. It is the first public statement of military aviation policy in Canada (see Document 3, pp. 332–4, below).

II

The new Air Board, with its changed personnel, took over from the old on 19 April 1920, and in a matter of days the Canadian Air Force was born. On 23 April authority was granted by order-in-council (P.C. 876) for the Board to employ a tiny staff of three officers and three other ranks for a period of six months, for the purpose of supervising and completing the organization of the Canadian Air Force Association, to prepare the way for the creation of squadrons and units, to draft regulations for pay, discipline and other service matters, and to perform "such other duties as the organization of the Canadian Air Force may involve."[27] Major-General Sir Willoughby Gwatkin, formerly Chief of the General Staff, was appointed Inspector-General of the C.A.F., with the rank of air vice-marshal. The staff was duly assembled, and took up quarters in the Air Board's offices at 529 Sussex Street on 17 May.

The formation of the headquarters was accompanied by a public appeal to former Canadian members of the R.A.F. to enlist in the new

Canadian Air Force. By June some 1,000 officers and 500 cadets and airmen had already applied; on the strength of this enthusiastic response, the Air Board recommended that a complement of 1,340 officers and 3,905 airmen be commissioned and enlisted without pay, while in the meantime an advance party of no more than sixty officers and airmen should be sent to Camp Borden, where it was proposed to locate the training centre for the C.A.F. These recommendations were approved by order-in-council (P.C. 1426) on 30 June. On the same day, the Minister of Militia and Defence explained his Government's policy:

> . . . We have in Canada about twelve thousand of the most highly trained military air men, of whom we know, that are to be found in the world. It is not proposed to begin by providing for anything like that number. A paper establishment has been authorized up to 5,000 men including all ranks. The proposal is, briefly, to recruit, as far as possible, the trained air men that are to be found in Canada to-day for the purpose of retaining their interest in, and sympathy with the work in case it may develop for commercial, scientific or other purposes as well as for military operations. . . . All we need is to give a limited training to a limited number of air men in Canada to keep their hands and their eyes in. We propose doing this by means of provincial associations. In each province of the Dominion the Lieutenant Governor has undertaken to form a provincial association and to enlist as many air men as he can in the service. We propose to give these men a limited training each year, taking them to one of our training stations . . . to give them one month's flying amounting to, I think, two hours a day per man. The cost of flying is considerable, I understand it is about $6 an hour per man, so it is only proposed to give each man one month's training of two hours' flying per day, and for the present year we propose to limit that to about seventeen hundred men. The objects to be attained by the Air Board are not by any means all military. . . .[28]

This modest proposal did not command the acceptance of the official opposition. Henri Béland expressed scepticism of the alleged commercial and scientific applications of aviation in Canada, and his determination not to vote any money for military purposes. "The war is over," he declared, "and the Government should put a stop to these expenditures."[29] His leader agreed. "To enter this year," Mackenzie King remarked, "before the work of demobilization is completed, upon an air service for military purposes is the height of absurdity. . . . We can well afford to dispense with the military end of it this year, [and] I think that we should reduce the total vote for air services by $800,000."[30] The proposed Air Board appropriation to the Provincial Air Force Associations was accordingly brought to a division in the House of Commons, and carried by a vote of 46 to 26.

Had it been necessary for the Canadian Government to pay for the essential equipment for even this limited programme of training, the new C.A.F. would never have got off the ground. Its creation was made possible only by the gift of equipment from the United Kingdom. The matériel thus furnished to the Dominion, partly in return for equipment given by Canada to the British flying services during the Great War but mostly as an outright donation, included 114 aircraft and, in addition (as the Vice-Chairman of the Air Board explained in July 1920), "complete material to equip four squadrons, about 300 vehicles, mostly motor vehicles, and nine air ships, 32 Bessoneau hangers, certain other hangers and photographic and other kinds of equipment. . . . Without this," O. M. Biggar added, "we would not be in anything like the position we are. Canadian finances are not in a strong state now and if we had not been supplied with this gift we would have had great difficulty in securing the necessary equipment to do the training."[31] The total value of the equipment thus received was placed officially at between $5 and $6 millions; but, as the C.A.F.'s senior operational officer, Air Commodore K. C. Tylee pointed out, "these values were disposal board values, and if we had to replace the equipment to-day it would cost us at least fifty per cent more."[32]

Its acquisition had been by no means automatic. The Air Ministry had begun disposing of surplus equipment early in 1920, not in any random fashion but as part of a deliberate policy to encourage the development of air power throughout the self-governing dominions and colonies. A considerable scramble developed among the prospective claimants, from which it was by no means clear that Canada, notwithstanding its great contribution to the war in the air, would emerge with the lion's share. Already in February 1920 the Air Board's Director of Air Services urged from Argyle House "the necessity of a definite Canadian Air Board representative being on hand at the Air Ministry to pick out the best of the material available. Newfoundland and India, I believe, are asking for lighter-than-air craft and consequently if we are in on the ground floor the best of the material will come to us and not go to other Colonies. . . ."[33] A fortnight later, Colonel Glen's appraisal sounded a note of urgency: "As regards lighter-than-air craft," he wrote to O. M. Biggar,

> the situation, as far as we are concerned, is becoming more unfavourable. Following Canada's lead in the asking for equipment comes Australia, South Africa, New Zealand, etc., and it has been a constant fight to retain the equipment we asked for, owing to the fact that Air Ministry officials tend towards encouraging Empire development and not individual colonies in their Lighter-than-Air development. However, I have managed to retain

12 Airships and 6 Kite Balloons, although I am afraid Hangers will have to be cut down to some extent. . . .[34]

And to Colonel R. Leckie, Director of Flying Operations under the Air Board, he wrote the following day:

At the moment the total number of Sheds available for a gift to all the Colonies is represented in the following: 3 Portable Sheds; 2 Steel Sheds.

In an interview with General Maitland on Wednesday the question of this allocation was thrashed out. I stated that in view of the fact that Canada had paved the way in respect to enquiring after and accepting Lighter-than-Air craft, the fact that as regards troops in the field we were foremost in numbers and also in regard to the personnel of the Royal Air Force during the war the greatest percentage were Canadians, that we were entitled to the first choice of material available. General Maitland agreed with me on this point but stated that in view of the fact that they must cover Empire developments and distribute material without prejudice, so as to encourage each Colony as much as possible in their efforts towards an Air Service, he thought it advisable to allot the material as fairly as possible, still bearing in mind that we were the first Colony to make representations towards acquiring this material and that our war effort, both as to Troops and Personnel in the Air Force, entitled us to the greatest consideration as to the allocation of material. He has practically promised me the Steel Shed lying at the contractors works in the Midlands and one Portable Shed. This leaves one Steel Shed at Malta, for either South Africa or Australia, and two Portable Sheds surplus to go to the colony as their choice indicates. . . .[35]

As is so often the case, the enthusiasm of those in the field was not fully shared by those at the desk. "I note . . . remarks regarding portable and steel sheds for airships," the Director of Flying Operations replied, "The question of operations for airships in Canada is still very indefinite. Our estimates have not been approved and indications point to the fact that they will not be sufficiently large to allow of considerable operations in lighter-than-air craft this year at least. In the meantime, however, you may proceed in collecting whatever you can get in the way of sheds."[36] This dampening response was not very helpful; still less so were the exasperating postponements of decisions on scarce items of equipment to which the Canadian officers overseas had managed to lay claim. "I am afraid there has been considerable delay on this side," Colonel Leckie wrote apologetically to the Canadian Air Force Liaison Officer in London on 24 March 1920,

in making decisions in matters which you must consider, from your point of view, as vitally important. I wish to inform you, however, that this delay has not occurred at the Air Board but rather on account of the complexity of the Departmental situation here. I am very keenly alive to your difficulties in England and am hastening decisions on all these matters as soon as possible but I have found in the Civil Service that one can move only as fast as other Departments will let one and that is sometimes not very fast. . . .[37]

And on 9 April:

. . . the question of shipping of lighter-than-air and transport to Canada is still held up owing to the fact that the Order-in-Council authorising this has not been approved although it has been recommended by the Air Board for at least three weeks. Now every effort is being made to hasten the decision and while I do not think there is any doubt but that decision when made will be favourable the above is quoted to give you some idea of the difficulties we have in getting ahead. . . .[38]

In view of these difficulties, the charge that such air equipment as Canada eventually received was being pressed upon a reluctant recipient by an over-anxious donor appears wildly inaccurate. Nevertheless, this was the charge that was laid at the Canadian Government's doorstep by opposition members of Parliament. "The acceptance of a gift may entail very heavy responsibilities on the donee [*sic*]," observed A. R. McMaster on 30 June. "I am very much afraid that the Government has accepted these airships without, so far as I know, taking the Canadian people into its confidence, and now it finds itself at this late hour of the session obliged to come before the House to meet very heavy obligations indeed. It was a splendid thing to have the young manhood of Canada so distinguish themselves in the air at the front, but it would be a sad thing if, in order to keep these young men in the condition of skill which they attained at the front, we should be obliged to incur expenses which the country is really unable to bear."[39] Ernest Lapointe perceived a sinister connection between the imperial gift and the approaching Imperial Conference—". . . we may be placed in a delicate position to refuse concurrence in plans which will be submitted to the conference by the statesmen of the United Kingdom"—while the Leader of the Opposition disclosed his suspicion that "the British Government has adopted the policy of getting rid of its surplus war material by presenting it to some of the Overseas Dominions in order to reduce the cost of maintenance."[40] It was not the last time that Mackenzie King was to look a gift-horse from the United Kingdom intently in the mouth.*

*As when, on 10 January 1944, the Canadian High Commissioner in London was "plunged . . . into despondency" by the reaction of his Prime Minister to an Admiralty offer to Canada of two cruisers and two destroyers. "The telegrams revealed suspicion," Mr. Vincent Massey wrote in his diary, "that there were still some strings attaching to the gift and they also interpreted the transaction not as a gift at all but an effort to relieve the Admiralty of the embarrassment of manning the new vessels . . . thoroughly mean-spirited. . . ." Quoted in Vincent Massey, *What's Past is Prologue* (Toronto, 1963), p. 390.

III

On 3 July 1920, Air Commodore K. C. Tylee, one of three officers charged under the Air Board with bringing the new Canadian Air Force into being, addressed a meeting of the delegates of Provincial Executive Committees of the Canadian Air Force Association at Winnipeg, to explain to them the kind of Service he and his colleagues were attempting to create. "The only excuse for the formation and the existence of a Canadian Air Force," he declared,

> is its use in time of war. We have got to train people so that after ten or fifteen years we will have available, in the event of war, a complete flying corps. This flying corps must be complete in all details with its own ground units, supply units, communications units, as well as war units and training units. We will work out, as soon as possible, a paper war organization, and the aim will be to train individuals so that they can be allotted to the various niches in this organization to make it complete. When this is completed, we can, in the event of a national emergency, immediately complete the actual formation of a self-contained air force.
>
> I would like to point out here a difference in principle that we wish to emphasize between the present militia idea and our air force idea. In the militia a man is a soldier for two weeks in the year and a civilian for the other fifty. Our idea is that everybody who joins the Air Force will be an Air Force man twelve months of the year, will be on duty one month every two years, and will be on leave the rest of the time. We do not want a man to come into the Air Force unless he realizes that by doing so he pledges himself, in the event of war, to immediately go to war or to undertake the duties which he is ordered to undertake that day. We don't want him, in other words, if he is not prepared to go into his particularly located place of our wartime organization on the day of mobilization. . . .[41]

This warning was no deterrent to recruitment. By the end of 1921—after the first full year of operations—1,281 officers and 1,350 airmen had applied for training, of whom 505 officers and 1,166 airmen had received training. The total strength of the permanent Air Force—"that is to say" (defined the Report of the Air Board), "the number of officers and airmen who, being on duty or under training, are on the pay roll"—was 54 officers and 239 airmen. The Report thus described the C.A.F. and its activities:

> It is (as it should be) a separate service—separate, that is to say, from the naval and military services—and it is autonomous. It is capable of expansion in case of emergency, but at other times its functions are almost exclusively instructional. It consists of Headquarters, at Ottawa, and of what is, in

effect, a School of Aviation, at Borden Camp. There is no permanent establishment; there are no embodied units; and service formations (thirteen squadrons) exist only on paper. . . .

Borden serves not only as a training centre, but also as a place of storage for aircraft and aircraft material. The British Government erected hutments, workshops, hangers, etc. for the detachment of the Royal Air Force which, during the war, was stationed there. These, left standing when the Royal Air Force withdrew, are utilized, and they afford ample accommodation.

Officers and airmen undergo training for limited periods once every two years; and special facilities are provided for those who make civil aviation their profession.

Training is conducted, as far as possible, on the system which obtains in the Royal Air Force. Both for officers and for airmen there are courses "short" and "long": the former continue for twenty-eight days, the latter for three months. Officers are instructed in flying, also in "ground duties," which includes navigation, photography, wireless telegraphy, armament, rigging, repair of engines, and so forth. Airmen, classified by trades, are trained as mechanics.

During the year, the Canadian Air Force co-operated, for training purposes, with the other services. Two aeroplanes from Borden "spotted" for the batteries of artillery which carried out their annual practices at Petawawa; in co-operation with the cavalry there encamped, they participated in various tactical exercises; also, on several occasions, cavalry and artillery officers were taken up and given lessons in "observing" from the air. Fifty-six flights were made. Average duration of flight, one hour; total distance flown, about 4,200 miles.

A machine from the Air Station at High River, Alta., rendered assistance during artillery practice at Sarcee Camp; but it did not more than make one flight—a flight of, approximately, 375 miles, covered in five hours. . . .[42]

These were modest enough beginnings, but clearly not much of the $800,000 allotted to military aviation could have been wasted. It was in fact a shoe-string operation, and the shoe-string very quickly began to fray. Within the first year of its inception, the Canadian Air Force was subjected to criticism by those in a position to know something of its weaknesses from first-hand experience.

Of such critics, none were more qualified than the officers entrusted with the task of creating a flying corps which would be of some use to the country in the event of war. This they quickly realized was beyond their power with the meagre resources at their disposal. On 2 February 1921, Air Commodore Tylee wrote a frank and discouraging appraisal to the Inspector-General:

From experience gained in the last few weeks, I am forced to the conclusion that without a change of policy in the Canadian Air Force, my original programme for the next fiscal year cannot be carried out, and that, therefore, the estimates for next year should be revised before going to the Government.

I am fully convinced that under the present regulations, sufficient competent mechanics and officer instructors cannot be maintained to do the work outlined. Incompetent mechanics or incompetent officer instructors will surely cause accidents involving death. A very few such accidents will make it impossible for the Provincial Secretaries to obtain pupils, and everything will automatically come to a standstill, resulting in waste of public funds and the destruction of the Canadian Air Force.

I consider that this destruction of the Canadian Air Force would be a great misfortune to Canada. It can, in my opinion, only be prevented by changing the existing regulations, to allow for the employment at full pay of a small cadre of competent mechanics and officer instructors for a period—subject to discharge for cause—of not less than two years, and to allow for the employment in winter months, if necessary, of commercially employed mechanics and officers. The various provincial executive committees of the Canadian Air Force agree with me strongly in these views. . . .[43]

Sir Willoughby Gwatkin passed this communication on to the Vice-Chairman of the Air Board, who in turn forwarded it to the Minister, Hugh Guthrie. Guthrie had meanwhile received a no less well-informed critique from two prominent civilians, Lt.-Colonel R. W. Leonard and Lloyd Harris, both members of the Executive Committee of the Air Force Association of Ontario. They wrote, in part:

Present Plan of Organization. Apparently at the commencement, it was deemed advisable to have two distinct branches of the Air Board, one for military training and the other for civil training for commercial flying. This, we think, has resulted in overlapping and in handicapping the military section. As we understand it, the difficulties imposed on the Canadian Air Force operating the military branch renders it almost impossible to secure the services of a type of man necessary for this work because of the lack of permanency, as men are recruited for this branch for a short period only and also the rates of pay for such men on such work are much less than those paid in the civil operations branch.

Recruiting for the military branch has been done through the Provincial Executive Committees and the Provincial Committees have sent men to Camp Borden from different provinces, who when they arrived at Camp Borden were found totally unqualified for the work they were expected to do. This has resulted in the work being carried on under great difficulties and another result has been the introduction of an element of danger in the operations which should be avoided. It is extremely difficult to secure in Canada qualified men for the ground work which consists of the mechanical work to be done on the machines and which should be efficiently performed, otherwise casualties will occur for which there should be no need. From the reports we have had from those we met at Camp Borden, we find that this condition is exceedingly dangerous. . . .

Our suggestion as to changes in the present form of organization would be, in order to avoid overlapping, to bring the two branches together with one central authority and direction. . . .

Training and Qualifications Necessary. During the war, we were only trying to recruit our young men and training them to fly and to shoot which did not involve any special knowledge of the mechanical problems of the flying machines. Canadians were very quick to adapt themselves to this new work and made their records because of their resourcefulness and adaptability. This was all that was necessary from them in war-time but in our peace development, the problem is much larger. . . .

In Canada we have never previous to the war manufactured an article as delicate and as fine as the aeroplane motor and the aeroplane. The type of construction with the fine limits in the mechanical parts and the precision required in its manufacture and the necessity of the most careful tests of all materials used, requires a class of mechanics which at the present time does not exist in Canada.

Practical pilots for commercial flying should not only be properly qualified for flying but they should also have the thorough mechanical and technical knowledge and training in aerial navigation, taking latitude and longitude, wood-craft, etc. . . .

We doubt if we can develop a staff of men who would be suitable for this profession under the present system and plan of organization. In the report of the Committee submitted to Council dated February 18th, 1920, it was laid down as a principle that "Casual and superficial training must be rigidly avoided". As now organized and under present plan of operations, we cannot see that the training men are receiving can be other than casual and superficial.

It is our desire to make any suggestions which will be of a constructive nature and after reviewing the whole situation, we have thought that the best results can be obtained and men efficiently trained for this very special profession, by the establishment of a training college which would provide facilities for thorough education in all branches required to efficiently train our Canadians for this particular work. . . .[44]

A copy of this letter was sent by its authors to the Prime Minister, who considered it with some care. On 7 February Meighen wrote to Lloyd Harris: "The principle which Colonel Leonard and yourself impress upon us in your letter to the Hon. Mr. Guthrie is well worthy of immediate consideration. The extent to which we can go along the lines you suggest is of course limited by our means. It looks to me as if expenditures in this line soon get very big."[45] Harris wrote immediately in reply to point out that "the object which Colonel Leonard and myself have had . . . was to enable the Government to economize on this branch of the service and at the same time to make it more efficient. The appropriation for the Air Board at the last session was $2,250,000 and I understand that a request is to be made for $5,000,000 for the next year. We think that under the plans suggested that $1,000,000 should be ample to carry it through."[46]

The Government was content to reduce the estimates without reforming the organization. The Air Board vote for 1921–22, placed before the House of Commons by the Minister on 23 May 1921, was $1,625,000, of which $825,000 was for the Canadian Air Force. "Owing to the small amount of our grant," the Provincial Air Force Association secretaries were instructed by an Air Board officer, "it will be necessary to curtail expenses in every possible way. . . . It will be very difficult to carry on and make any showing with the grant this year, and everybody working in conjunction with the Canadian Air Force will have to use every means in their power in an endeavour to save money."[47] The axe did not fall without protest. On 9 June, the Officer Commanding at Camp Borden wrote as follows to the Secretary of the Air Board:

With reference to draft of Provisional Establishment for this Station . . . whereby the establishment is cut down to that for a Squadron, I desire to place on record that in my opinion such establishment is an impossible one in regard to its paucity and is absolutely detrimental to the interests of the Canadian Air Force.

Outside of Air Headquarters, Ottawa, which it may be observed is theoretical and not practical in its functions, this Station is self contained and although it may be reduced to a squadron there still remain the various Departments and Units necessary for the proper carrying on of a station.

Up to the present date there apparently has been no definite policy formed in regard to the Canadian Air Force and it is now understood that the Air Board have almost finally decided to build up this force on a non-permanent basis, that is, without the necessary nucleus of a permanent staff to train and instruct officers and airmen who report from time to time; this, I contend, is absolute false economy and will simply result in, sooner or later, the Canadian Air Force dying an unnatural death.

There should be a definite policy whereby there is a permanent force established as in the case of the Royal Air Force in England, the Australian Air Force, or for that matter, any force at all, e.g., the Army, or the Navy, or else the Canadian Air Force should be disbanded. . . .[48]

To this appeal the Government, then readying itself for a general election, turned more or less a deaf ear. The Prime Minister's views were fairly stated in a letter written a few days before his defeat at the polls. "You ask for my views," Meighen wrote to an official of the Aero Club of Regina,

as to the measure of financial and other support which should be accorded by the Government of Canada to (1) Aviation generally and (2) The maintenance of the nucleus of a Canadian Air Force. I think that under present conditions the measure of support and assistance is the measure we are adopting. You will recall that last session the opposition voted unanimously, including the Farmers, for reduction by a very large figure of our vote for defence. Nevertheless, the Government adhered to its position, and still adheres to it, although being attacked throughout the entire country by both wings of the Opposition for spending too much on defence. Whether we should increase or whether we should diminish still depends in no considerable degree on the results of the present disarmament Conference. We shall, of course, have to continue to encourage civil aviation for commercial and governmental purposes to as full an extent as the finances of the country will justify. We would like to do more of this kind of work at the present time but cannot under the circumstances.[49]

Throughout 1921, the Inspector-General of the Canadian Air Force had been in correspondence with Royal Air Force authorities and others to secure for his Force symbols appropriate to its status. As the result of his efforts, approval was given for the design of the C.A.F. ensign, with its now familiar roundel on a light blue ground. Plans were made for a ceremonial hoisting at Camp Borden, a ceremony which Gwatkin understandably wished to make, as he wrote, "as pompous as possible." The date of the ceremony was fixed at 30 November 1921—a week before the general election. No minister of the Crown considered it politically expedient to put in an appearance, and military authorities from the other Services invited to attend for some reason declined the invitation. So it was a family affair.[50]

IV

"The new Government," wrote the Inspector-General of the Canadian Air Force to Sir Hugh Trenchard on 14 December 1921, "are pledged to rigid economy; and what their attitude towards the C.A.F. will be I do not know."[51] He doubtless could have guessed. Early in 1922 the military and civil officials of the Air Board were advised of the Government's decision to reorganize the Air Services and, following their reorganization, to reduce radically expenditures upon them. In keeping with advice tendered to the preceding administration by authorities within and without the Service, the Liberal Government proposed to merge the Civil Operations Branch with the Canadian Air Force, to do away with the Air Board, and to bring the conduct of all government aviation, civil and military, under the direction of a single Air Force officer responsible to the newly created position of Chief of Staff, Department of National Defence, who, in turn, was responsible to the Minister of the new Department. "The old system of three directorates," stated the Report of the Air Board for 1922,

> each responsible to the Board for one function of its duties, thus:—

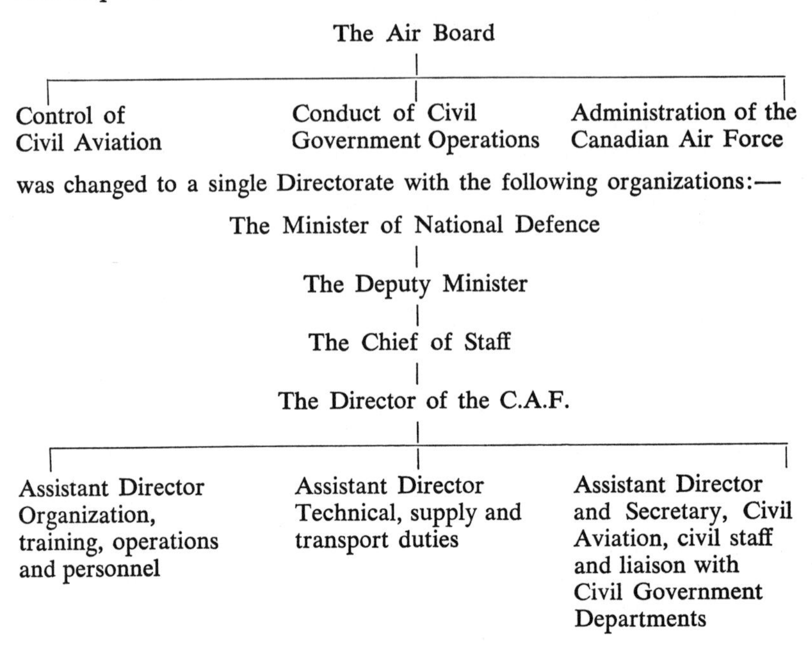

Accompanying this reorganization, which indeed had been designed to make it possible, was a drastic reduction of expenditure. A total of $1,000,000 was allotted by the Government for both civil and military operations, $625,000 less than the sum voted by the preceding Parliament. At meetings of the Air Board during the spring of 1922, its members anxiously discussed the consequences of the proposed reductions. On 13 March, its minutes relate,

> the Officer Commanding the C.A.F. reported he had made arrangements to reduce the C.A.F. establishment from 391, the present strength, to 171. This would allow only for the training of officers. Training of mechanics would have to cease for the time being. . . .

On 17 March:

> Further discussion took place on the Estimates for the coming year. The Director of Flying Operations pointed out his difficulty in making arrangements with his staff under the present uncertainty. In any case if he were not granted more than $445,000, he would have to make considerable

reductions. Halifax would be left in charge of a care and maintenance party; the operations for the Indian Department in Manitoba and Northern Ontario would be cancelled; and the Forest Survey work based on Cochrane also. He desired if possible to maintain all stations where any capital expenditures had been made and carry out the work as outlined for the Government departments as far as funds permitted.

The Inspector General explained the circumstances under which the revised estimates had been forwarded. The Secretary stated he thought the vote would probably be "one million dollars for Air Services" as he had advised the Finance Department, in reply to an enquiry from them, that without further knowledge of the plan of reorganization it was impossible to give any details as to how the money would be allocated. All employees should recognise that until re-organization was completed their positions were uncertain.

And on 22 March:

The question of reorganization was again discussed with special reference to the reduction of staff which must follow the reduction of the estimates. The Inspector General said that he had notified the Minister that, on or shortly after April 1st, a very considerable reduction would be made in the strength of the C.A.F. . . .

"When we begin to apply the axe," Gwatkin had warned, "there may be protests. But it cannot be helped: the situation must be faced."[52]

The decision to merge civil and military flying operations was taken by the Government in the face of advice from the Air Force to keep them separate. In a memorandum to the Chief of the General Staff, Gwatkin had made his personal opposition to the proposal very clear: "When I took over as I.G.", he wrote, "I thought how good a thing it would be for the C.A.F. to carry out all flying operations. Since then I have gained experience, and I have changed my mind."[53] He added: "If it has been decided, definitely, that the C.A.F. is to assume control, then I advise that the change be gradual; that civil operations remain for a while somewhat as they are." In another memorandum he had written:

If the Minister has given definite instructions that, directly the new Act is passed, the C.A.F. is to take over all civil flying operations, there is nothing more to be said; otherwise, it might be well for you to hasten slowly. I suggest that, as a first step towards the end you have in view, the C.A.F., already established at Borden, should assume charge of the Air Station at Halifax and Vancouver; and that the others should remain under civil control temporarily—i.e., until the weather clears and visibility is good.[54]

This advice, at least, was accepted. The Report of the Air Board for 1922 records: "As the operation season had opened and all Stations were busily engaged on the execution of the programme of flying for other Government Departments, it was decided not to disturb this work by adding the task of reorganization. This was therefore postponed till the end of the flying season in the fall. The changes necessary to bring them into the new scheme were made gradually and as far as possible without disturbing the work of the Stations."[55]

On 12 May, the Minister of Militia and Defence put before the House of Commons the Government's proposed expenditure of $1,000,000 for civil and military aviation during 1922–23. He was both proud of and candid about what had been done. "We cannot promise much extension of the work [of government flying on civil operations]," Graham admitted cheerfully, "with the estimate where it is." When the Leader of the Opposition observed: "The minister has been pretty frank. The only object he has in mind is to keep the defence estimates down, and thereby be able to show that the Government has kept its pledge," Graham responded: "If the other men do the same thing it will be all right."[56] He conceded that the reduction would make necessary a curtailment of training: "We will be doing less flying. . . . At the present time there is little or no training being done at Camp Borden . . . work is being cut in every particular, [otherwise] we could not make this reduction. . . ."[57] That was what the country wanted, and Members of Parliament knew it; opposition criticism, with one exception, was not that the savings were harmful but that they were illusory, the cost of air services being borne elsewhere. The exception was the Conservatives' defence critic (later, their Defence Minister), D. M. Sutherland. "As far as I can understand from the minister's explanation," he said,

> the Air Force, as a defensive force, is practically going to cease to exist; the civil aviation is going to be continued if some arrangement can be made with the provinces to employ these people, who will be under the Department of National Defence, purely as a civil force, and the services of those men who attained such wonderful experience and training during the war will be dispensed with. . . . So far as I can gather, the only body of, I will not say men, but of anything savouring of military training in this country, which body is going to be maintained and for which the estimate has been kept up, is that of the Boy Scout movement in Canada. . . .[58]

It turned out to be not quite so bad as that. "By exercising the greatest economy," the Report of the Air Board for 1922 records, "it has been possible to maintain all the Air Stations established in the country, although the work at some of them has had to be reduced."[59] Training of officers and airmen at Camp Borden ceased throughout the year, a scheme for cadet training at Canadian universities had to be dropped, and many requests from other government departments for assistance had to be turned down. The total number of flying hours put in by such of the Air Force as survived was less than 1,000, as compared with an average of roughly 1,600 hours during each of the two previous years. The wonder was that, with the available funds, it was possible to do as much. But those who had made the Air Force their career were naturally perplexed and resentful. "The present system will never be satisfactory in the Permanent Force, either in peace or war," wrote the officer in charge of training at Camp Borden to the Director of the C.A.F. early in 1923.

At the present time there is no organization in the C.A.F. capable of specializing in the practical operation of aircraft. It would appear that the main idea of the C.A.F. is to keep a few machines and pilots in the air to do fire patrol and aerial survey. Much attention has been paid to this, but the practical training of the Air Force has been much neglected in the past.

In my opinion the efficiency of any part of the Air Force should be judged by its striking power and its ability to turn out in case of national emergency Flying Officers who are capable of performing any or all of the duties performed by aircraft in war. This, of course, could not be done with our present organization, and my object in writing is to ask if consideration can be given to the organization of a School of Aeronautics in this camp, to instruct all Officers in the practical uses of aircraft.

As a further observation, I would like to point out that if a number of bombing machines were required, or machines fitted with machine guns, to settle some disorder, it would be practically impossible to provide them from this Station, owing to the fact that there is no Officer here who understands the installation of bomb racks and bombs, or machine guns; in other words, we are practically a civilian organization. . . .

I do not want it to appear that I am desirous of carrying this to the extreme, but it seems to me very advisable that we have at least a very small striking force ready in this country. Our condition might be compared to that of the Artillery if they were without shells or sights for their guns. . . .[60]

To this outburst, the Commanding Officer replied sharply, although not unsympathetically:

The question of intensive Air Force training rests entirely with the Government. Our appropriation at the present time is barely sufficient to carry the overhead of the Force, and allows only for very limited training of permanent personnel, and no training for non-permanent. Instructions have been issued by higher authority that the work performed for other government departments is to be continued. By undertaking this work, it uses up any surplus funds which would otherwise be available for the purchase of strictly Air Force equipment and in training Air Force personnel along the lines suggested. . . .[61]

V

Not even the most economy-minded of governments could for long remain indifferent to the deterioration of the equipment of the Canadian Air Force, and the consequent mounting danger of injury or death to its personnel. This problem was the subject of a memorandum to the Inspector-General by the Director of the Technical and Stores sections. "The question of the airworthiness of the flying equipment at present in possession of the Air Board," he wrote on 30 May 1922,

is one requiring very serious attention. I have on one or two previous occasions reported that in my opinion this war material should be disposed with as soon as possible. There are many factors that make it essential that efforts should be made to equip the Air Board with new machines. In the first place the machines that we have were all built during the latter part of the war when good quality timber was very scarce, with the consequence that the machines were built from second grade material.

Five or six years have now elapsed since those machines were built, and during this time a certain amount of deterioration is bound to have taken place.

In most cases the machines have been given very close attention by the Station Superintendents, but in most cases the Station Superintendents are not trained engineers and they are liable to overlook defects. . . .

Is is not possible for something to be done to replace this equipment in order that our present clean record of no accidents due to defective equipment can be maintained? This question is altogether apart from the question of the increased efficiency of the work that can be carried out with machines of a more modern design.[62]

This memorandum was passed on by Gwatkin to the Chief of the General Staff. "Every word . . . in it is true," Gwatkin wrote to General MacBrien, "and I hope you will persuade the Minister to include in Supplementary Estimates a sum of $200,000—sufficient for the purchase of twelve machines of British make, suitable for use in time of war. I regard this as a matter of urgent importance."[63] MacBrien replied: "I shall take this matter up with the Minister, but do not think there should be need to ask for the full sum of $200,000. When the reorganization is carried out according to the estimates prepared by Lt.-Colonel Gordon, there should be a large saving, approximately $150,000, and this sum would be available towards meeting the cost of new equipment."[64] Gwatkin thought this unrealistic. "Please bear in mind," he wrote, "that out of the $150,000 you hope to have, you will have to pay for construction, as well as for material required for the upkeep of aircraft already on charge. The balance (if any) would not go far towards purchasing what both Gordon and Stedman consider necessary, namely, (1) Six Avro machines (single seaters) for use at High River, replacing D.H. 4 machines, which latter are now in rather poor condition; and (2) seven supermarine flying boats (with amphibian landing gear), replacing American flying boats. . . ."[65] The Chief of the General Staff then had a further discussion with the Minister. He was not, he reported to Gwatkin, "prepared to make any recommendation for a supplementary estimate this year, but would be willing when the Estimates for 1923–24 are prepared, to make an addition of the amount necessary to obtain the requisite aeroplanes and flying boats."[66] "I do not see," he wrote a day or so later, "how we can do anything more."

On 15 November 1922, the Chairman of the Air Board concurred in the following text of a draft submission to the Governor General in Council:

> The undersigned has the honour to report that the operations conducted during the past three years by the Air Board, in connection with Forestry, surveying, customs and other branches of the Government Service, have only been possible through the utilization of the gift material received from the Imperial Government after the Armistice. This gift did not include any seaplanes suitable for use in Canada. It was therefore necessary to purchase a number of flying boats, also of war type, in the United States, from surplus war material. After three years' constant use and exposure in the open, many of both classes of machines have deteriorated and cannot be depended on for successful operation.
>
> To continue purchasing obsolescent types is inadvisable, as modern machines can perform the work much more efficiently, and can give much better results and greater assistance to the other Departments of the Government in whose Service they are employed. The purchase of new machines is essential, if flying is to continue on a sound basis in Canada.
>
> It is therefore submitted that authority be given to call for tenders for new aircraft and spare parts, of a value not exceeding $250,000, and to accept the most satisfactory tenders received. This will provide a portion of the much needed equipment. The aircraft to be delivered during the months of April and May, 1923, and to be paid for from the appropriation of the next financial year. The present appropriation is only sufficient to cover the operations of the Canadian Air Force, so the above mentioned sum will have to be added to the annual appropriation for next year. . . .[67]

This submission was presented to the Cabinet, and there approved, with the result that in the vote for 1923–24 provision was made for the purchase of nine new flying boats. These were on hand by 1 April 1924, when the new King's Regulations and Orders for what had become the Royal Canadian Air Force went into effect.

The organization of the R.C.A.F. closely followed that of the Army. Provision was made for a permanent and a non-permanent active air force.

The strength of the former, in 1924, was 68 officers and 307 airmen, divided among six units—the Vancouver, High River, Winnipeg, Camp Borden, Ottawa, and Dartmouth Air Stations. The first units of the non-permanent force were not recruited until 1932. The director of the force was made responsible for Civil Aviation and Civil Government Air Operations, as well as for military training. By 1927 the civilian duties of the R.C.A.F. had so increased as to cause the Government to embark upon a further re-organization, by separating civil and military aviation. The R.C.A.F. now became the military branch of the air services, under, as before, its own director responsible to the Chief of the General Staff. Civil Government Air Operations were placed under a separate director. A third division, Controller of Civil Aviation, was formed, as was a fourth, an aeronautical Engineering Division. All four were placed within the Department of National Defence.

These moves seemed to open the way for increased military training for R.C.A.F. personnel, the lack of which had been continuously lamented by its commanders. "As the reorganized R.C.A.F. will be purely Air Force in character and functions," the Director observed in a memorandum to the Chief of the General Staff in August 1927, "it naturally follows that its policy and equipment will be considerably altered to what it was whilst undertaking civil operations." Aircraft acquired in future should be "strictly Air Force or Service types," rather than those designed primarily for civil aviation duty. The Vickers machines for which provision had been made in the 1927–28 estimates—"one Varuna, one Vedette, one Velos and one Vanessa aircraft with engines and spares"—would be, in his estimation, "orphans" in a purely military air force. "It is therefore proposed that we abandon the idea of ordering these orphan aircraft, and devote funds for them to purchase machines with a strictly military value. . . ."[68] This proposal was duly approved. In 1928 the Department of National Defence purchased from the United Kingdom four Siskin and four Atlas aircraft. These machines, noted the *Ottawa Citizen* on 16 March 1929, "are used in training permanent force officers on war type aircraft, teaching them aerobatics, bombing, gunnery, and the other manoeuvres which go to make first-class fighting pilots who can be called upon to act as instructors at a moment's notice should an emergency arise."

These modest improvements in the country's military aviation did not go unremarked or uncriticized. The decision to keep civil government air operations under the Department of National Defence seemed particularly to exercise pacifists in the House of Commons. J. S. Woodsworth accused the Government of attempting to build up a para-military formation in the guise of civil dress. "There is always present in the minds of those who are directing this force," he declared, "that one of these days the force may have to be transformed . . . the very character and build of the aircraft [are] such that they could be readily converted. The whole idea of possible war is kept to the forefront."[69] This the Minister of National Defence denied. "The build of the civilian aircraft," Ralston claimed, "is exactly what is required for civilian work. There is no special adaptability."[70] Later in the debate he affirmed that the Siskin army pursuit planes were the only exclusively military equipment in possession of the R.C.A.F., and that it was not intended to buy any more. As for the retention of civil aviation within the Department of National Defence, that was entirely an economy measure: "If we placed civil aviation under another Department, we would be doubling our overhead. Then the Department of the Interior would want an air force, as would also the Post Office Department and the Department of the Railways, each with its own organization, and we would be trebling or quadrupling the overhead . . . , and would not have uniformity of training."[71]

AIR AND THE EMPIRE

Air force policy, while not so crucial as naval policy, was an important subject under discussion at the Imperial Conference of 1923. The Air Staff in London, as the Admiralty had done, provided each dominion with the benefit of its views as to what might be its most effective contribution to imperial defence. The paper sent out to Canada in October 1923 contained, among others, the following observations:

> While it is of course realized that the requirements of each Dominion are entirely for settlement by the Dominion itself, and must depend largely on factors on which the Air Staff are necessarily only imperfectly informed, it is hoped that the suggestions now named may be helpful in the discussion of the particular case of Canada in the light of the principles formulated in the Air Staff Memorandum on "The Development of Dominion Air Forces" (C.I.D. Paper 206–C).
>
> 1. The Canadian Air Force at present consists of three flights of flying boats, one flight of day bombers and reconnaissance aircraft, one experimental flight and the nucleus of a flying training school and aircraft depot. The force is at present in process of reorganization.
>
> With the exception of the Training School at Camp Borden, the units mentioned above are almost entirely employed on duties for the Civil Government Departments.
>
> 2. If, in considering the organization of the National Defence, the possi-

bility of war with the United States is considered to be sufficiently remote as to obviate preparations for the present, it is suggested that the air requirements of the Canadian Defence service will assume moderate proportions.

Moreover, as the Dominion Government are aware, the actual cost of the air forces will be even lower than might be expected from the size, since a very substantial return will be derived from their employment on such work as forest, fire and survey patrol, for which they have already been extensively used in Canada.

3. The functions which the Canadian Air Force should be ready to perform, apart from such peace time work, are as follows:—
(*a*) Co-operation with the military forces;
(*b*) Reconnaissance of the Pacific Coast to locate hostile vessels or convoys approaching from the West;
(*c*) Attack of ships which may approach the Pacific Coast with the object of bombarding towns or landing troops;
(*d*) Reconnaissance from Naval vessels.

Following paragraphs detailing the type of aircraft thought best adapted for the performance of these functions, the Air Staff paper proposed the following units as "a foundation for the future organization of the Canadian Air Force":

2 Army Co-operation Squadrons
1 long distance Reconnaissance and Bombing Squadron;
1 Fighter Squadron;
1 Squadron of Flying Boats, Float-planes or Amphibians;
1 Flight suitable for embarking in light cruisers.

"Upon this foundation," the Air Staff paper concluded, "could be built in the future such air forces as the Dominion Government may consider necessary in the light of further discussion."[72]

Mackenzie King was in no mood to deal with these proposals on their merits. He was interested not in defence but in deflection. And the Air Ministry was deflected along with the Admiralty and the War Office. Its spokesman, the Secretary of State for Air, put its case as persuasively as he knew how. Forewarned, no doubt, by the Canadian Prime Minister's hostile reception of the Admiralty's suggestions, Sir Samuel Hoare began his statement to the Conference on 19 October by declaring explicitly that the Air Ministry had no intention of encroaching upon dominion autonomy. "I have not the least desire," he said,

to attempt to press a policy of centralization upon the Dominions. All that has been in my mind in making these suggestions [in the Air Ministry's memoranda] is that the Prime Ministers may find that with their comparatively small Air Forces, as in the nature of things they will probably be, the overhead expenses for training and for technical and expert development may be so great as to make the cost almost prohibitive, and it occurred to me that with our training facilities here, both elementary, higher and Staff, we might, by means of an agreed system of co-operation, be able to help you in avoiding anyhow some of those heavy overhead charges. From our own point of view it would be extremely valuable to maintain the continuity of air training and air strategy by having a number of Dominion pilots working, being trained and doing perhaps higher courses in connection with the Royal Air Force here.

He did not attempt to conceal his view that "the greater the development of the Dominion Air Forces the better it will be for us and the easier it will be to solve our problems"—problems the most urgent of which at the moment was the discrepancy which existed between the respective strengths of the French Air Force and the R.A.F., to the disadvantage of the latter.[73]

These views seemed eminently reasonable to all those present—all, that is, except Mackenzie King, who to all those present except himself seemed the very personification of unreason.* How difficult he could be became apparent when a draft resolution on imperial air defence was circulated for approval. Before Mackenzie King got hold of it, the draft expressed the Conference's belief in

The desirability of the development of the Air Forces of the Empire upon such lines as will make it possible, by means of the regular interchange of personnel, the adoption of a common system of organization, administration and training, and the use of uniform manuals, patterns of arms, equipment and stores, for each part of the Empire to take such share as it desires in Imperial Defence with the least possible delay and the greatest efficiency.[74]

In this form the draft was placed before the Conference, meeting late in the afternoon of 6 November to examine and approve the draft resolutions submitted to it. Mackenzie King had not apparently seen the draft before. He asked that its wording be changed in a number of particulars, and his revised version, hastily typed, was then circulated around the table. It read:

The desirability of the development of the Air Forces in the several countries of the Empire upon such lines as will make it possible, by means of the adoption, as far as practicable, of a common system of organization and training and the use of uniform manuals, patterns of arms, equipment, and

*Smuts told Mackenzie King—in, King wrote, "a very good natured way"—that he was "a very terrible person"; Curzon, less good-naturedly, wrote privately that Mackenzie King was "obstinate, tiresome and stupid." Quoted in R. MacGregor Dawson, *William Lyon Mackenzie King: A Political Biography* (Toronto, 1958), pp. 476–7. Had the Irish delegation been present, it would have supported King against the others.

stores (with the exception of the type of aircraft), for each part of the Empire as it may determine to co-operate with other parts with the least possible delay and the greatest efficiency.[75]

This formulation wrought no fewer than five changes in the original. The phrase "Air Forces of the Empire" became, in Mackenzie King's version, "Air Forces of the several countries of the Empire." The proposal that these Air Forces engage in "the regular interchange of personnel," Mackenzie King deleted—a deletion which did not escape comment. "I do not know whether it is accidental," L. S. Amery observed (knowing, as he must have done, that it was anything but accidental), "but the reference to the interchange of personnel, which is a thing we have encouraged, both in Military and Naval matters, has been left out; I do not know whether it has slipped out in the re-drafting." Mackenzie King replied: "That was one of the phrases which I thought it would be better to take out. Our Government would, I think, be perfectly willing to arrange for an interchange of personnel, but I am inclined to think that the words might be misunderstood or misinterpreted if they were inserted in the Resolution, and might convey a wrong impression." A third alteration was King's inclusion of the saving phrase "as far as practicable"; a fourth, the deletion of "administration" from the Air Ministry's trio of "organization, administration and training." The fifth and final change was the insertion of the phrase "with the exception of the type of aircraft" at the conclusion of the list of items of equipment for which standardization was deemed desirable. The significance of this fifth amendment was considerable, for no recommendation of the Air Staff had been more strongly put than that the Air Forces of the Empire should fly the same aircraft; its wisdom was not apparent until much later.*

Mackenzie King's last minute alterations of the air defence resolution were not pleasing to the United Kingdom delegates; but there was

*In December 1940, a Canadian newspaperman wrote following an interview with the General Director of the Aircraft Production Branch of the Department of Munitions and Supply: "Airplane industry in a mess due in large part to the difficulties of getting into production and, in larger part, to the stupidity and stubbornness of the British manufacturers and the British authorities. . . . Looking back, . . . our aeroplane industry and the air training plan should have been based upon United States machines. We could have built up our industry easily on this basis. Instead we trusted Britain to supply the advanced trainers under the plan and have tried to get into production on British models and have experienced nothing but headaches. The best airplane factory in Canada—at Malton—has been useless because it was tooled to produce Lysanders and only got into production when Britain ruled this craft obsolete. . . . Meantime Malton cannot get into new production because the British can't agree on new models. . . ." Grant Dexter to J. W. Dafoe (no date), Dafoe Papers.

little they could do about them, short of precipitating a first-rate row which they ardently desired to avoid. "I cannot pretend that I like [Mackenzie King's draft] quite so well as the other draft," confessed Lord Salisbury who, as Lord President of the Council, presided over the Conference's deliberations on defence policy, "but, so far as I am concerned, as representing the Government, I am quite prepared to accept it, although, as Mr. Mackenzie King knows, there are one or two words which I should much prefer to be differently expressed."[76] The Conference then approved, albeit with reluctance, the draft as the Canadian Prime Minister had amended it, and it is his version that appears in its published report.[77]

Air defence and aerial communications engaged the Imperial Conference of 1926 to a greater extent than they had its predecessor in 1923. In part this emphasis was due to the frustration of the Admiralty's efforts during the years after the Armistice to enlist the support of all the dominions for a unified system of naval defence; in part to the considerable advance which had been made in aeronautical technology. Great expectations were entertained especially of lighter-than-air dirigibles and, undeterred by the disasters which had already engulfed the *R.38*, the *Dixmude*, and the *Shenandoah*, the British Government by 1926 was pressing forward the construction of two gigantic airships of this type, the *R.100* and *R.101*, which, it was hoped, would be able to carry 100 passengers and freight a distance of 4,000 miles without refuelling. A memorandum prepared for the Conference by Sir Samuel Hoare, the energetic Secretary of State for Air under whom the airship programme was proceeding, entered into considerable detail about what had been done and what remained to be done, noting particularly the implications of the airship for imperial unity: "Regular transport services of this order of speed would place the system of Imperial communications upon an entirely new basis. It would then be possible to develop very greatly, and in several spheres, an Imperial co-operation based upon frequent personal consultation." The dominion governments were asked to embark upon the construction of mooring masts (at an estimated cost of £70,000 each) and to provide meteorological facilities.[78]

In 1923, Mackenzie King had greeted all such projects with stony reserve or outright rejection; in 1926, his response to Hoare's conception of "an Empire of the air" was nothing short of enthusiastic. Indeed, even before he knew anything about it, he had resolved to co-operate with the British Government in any reasonable plan it might advance for air defence and air development. "I thought while in

England," he wrote on 25 October 1926, "we should show our willingness to co-operate in both these directions to a considerable measure, and when we returned to Canada stress this phase as part of Canada's co-operation."[79] Three days later, when Hoare had concluded his statement to the Conference on Britain's plans for imperial air communication, Mackenzie King allowed himself the uncharacteristic luxury of unqualified approval:

> Prime Minister, we have, I think, been thrilled, if I may use that word, by the survey that has been given us by the Secretary of State for Air of the Air Communication programme of the Empire. It is difficult to find words wherewith adequately to describe it; it was certainly fascinating. One would be inclined to use the word "romantic" if one did not know how practical the Secretary of State for Air is. I think I may say it is prophetic. It certainly suggests a solution of many of the problems of communication between different parts of the Empire to which hitherto distance has presented formidable barriers. . . .
>
> In regard to the specific request which the Secretary of State for Air has made . . . the Canadian Government will only too readily co-operate with the British Government in the way he has suggested, by immediately taking steps to see that mooring masts to secure the landing places for airships in Canada are erected; also that the work of meteorological organization is commenced forthwith. . . .[80]

Spokesmen for the other dominions likewise offered their Government's support. At the end of the discussion, Mackenzie King, responding to a suggestion by Hoare that an Imperial Air Conference be held in the near future, declared "that it would be a source of great pride if it could be held in the Dominion."[81] Hoare accepted the offer a few days later. "I am very glad to think," he wrote, "that Canadian co-operation will be forthcoming in this vital experiment on which we, for our part, are proposing to expend 1½ million pounds and which holds the promise of developments alike in the political, commercial and defence spheres, the importance of which to the Empire it is difficult to exaggerate."[82]

Mackenzie King was as good as his word. Notwithstanding criticism at home of his sudden departure from the hitherto sacred precepts of "no commitments" and "Parliament will decide," he held firm to his promise, and the Speech from the Throne of 26 January 1928 announced that "a site for an airship base has been purchased near Montreal [where] an airship mooring tower will be erected." The cost of the mast, together with the St. Hubert base, estimated in 1926 at £70,000, amounted at its completion to over $1,856,000.

By July 1930 all was in readiness to receive the *R.100* on its maiden trans-Atlantic voyage. The great airship reached its destination safely, though not uneventfully—a severe gust of wind damaged its fabric 200 miles east of Montreal—after a journey lasting 79 hours. One of the last official acts of Mackenzie King's second ministry—his Government had been defeated in the general election only a few days earlier—was to despatch, on 31 July, a telegram of congratulation to its captain. "The completion of this journey," he wrote afterwards, "was the consummation of our voluntary undertaking at the Imperial Conference. . . ."

But it was an ill-fated project to which Mackenzie King had precipitately pledged his country's backing. The *R.100* made its return journey safely enough. Its sister ship was not so fortunate. On 5 October, bound on its maiden voyage to India, the *R.101* crashed and burned in France, killing forty-seven of the fifty-four people (including many of the airship authorities in the United Kingdom) on board. A shaken British government cancelled the entire programme of airship development, and it was never resumed. The tower at St. Hubert stood as a monument to the tragedy until it too, like the airship once moored there, was dismantled for scrap.

VI

Chains of Command

ORIGINS OF THE DEPARTMENT OF NATIONAL DEFENCE

In Canada, as elsewhere, the proposal to combine the administration of the fighting services in a single department of government attracted favourable attention during the months immediately following the Armistice. Any measure promising economy was assured of sympathy in Ottawa; a measure promising both economy and efficiency seemed almost too good to be true. The politicians could not do other than support it. The military, which might have been expected to oppose in principle so radical a reorganization, proved to be its chief supporters. As long ago as 1907, Admiral Fisher had denied, in his characteristically expressive language, that "fighting efficiency is inalienably associated with big Estimates! The exact opposite is the real truth! Lavish naval expenditure, like human high-living, leads to the development of latent parasitical bacilli which prey on and diminish the vitality of the belligerent force whether in the human body or in the fighting ship!"[1] Or, he might have added, at defence headquarters.

The proposal that the two existing Departments of Militia and Defence and of the Naval Service be replaced by a single Department of Defence was originally put forward in 1920 by the Inspector-General of Militia, General Sir Arthur Currie. Not long before his retirement from the Army, Currie contacted both the Prime Minister and the Minister of Militia and Defence to recommend this change. To Arthur Meighen he wrote: "May I now suggest to you one or two things. 1. To group the Militia, the Air Services, and the Navy under one Department, presided over by a Minister to be known as the Minister of Defence."[2] And to Hugh Guthrie: "Since my association with the Militia Department last December, I believe much real good work has been accomplished. There were other things which we discussed, but which, as yet, have not taken definite form, that I would like to see carried through. The chief of these is the creation of a Ministry of Defence, which would include the Militia, the Air Services, and the Navy."[3]

Currie's retirement from the armed forces deprived them of the principal advocate of a unified administration. However, other senior officers in both the Navy and Army were favourable to the proposal. On 24 August 1921, the Director of the Naval Service, Captain Walter Hose, wrote to the Inspector-General of the Canadian Air Force, Sir Willoughby Gwatkin:

> . . . several press reports to the effect that the United States Naval and War Departments were to be merged into one Department of National Defence have appeared in the United States Service papers and also in the general press. . . .
>
> I quite agree with you that such an amalgamation would be a tremendous benefit here and I hope we may discuss in the Defence Committee the best steps to be taken to further such an organization. When the next Cabinet is formed would seem an opportune time. . . .[4]

Soon after the results of the general election of 1921, when it had become apparent that Mackenzie King would form the next Government (although not yet of whom that Government would consist), the military began to exert pressure in the direction of the desired reform. On 15 December, the Defence Committee (successor to the now defunct Naval and Military Committee*) expressed its unanimous opinion "that the establishment of a Department of Defence, charged with the administration of the Navy, the Militia, the Air Force and the R.C.M.P., will be conducive to efficiency as well as economy,"[5] and its members were charged with the responsibility of notifying their respective ministers of this conviction. Within the next few days, the incoming Prime Minister was in receipt of communications from three highly influential individuals connected with the military establishment, each strongly advising him to proceed with the reorganization without delay.

*The Defence Committee came into being in October 1920. Its members consisted of the Chief of the General Staff, the Director of the Naval Service, and the Inspector-General of the Canadian Air Force, the Royal Canadian Mounted Police being represented by an associate member. Its assigned functions were: "To co-ordinate effort in pursuit of a common policy and, especially, to ensure the co-operation of the forces—sea, land and air—in the event of war or other emergency. . . . It advises on questions relating to organization, administration, and combined training, preparation for defence, procedure on mobilization, and on such other questions as may be referred to it." *Report of the Air Board for the Year 1921* (Ottawa, 1922), p. 5.

The first of these came from the Deputy Minister of Militia and Defence, Major-General Sir Eugène Fiset:

> I hope you will not think I am going outside my prerogatives if I dare to place before you my views re the re-organization that I think should take place in our system of defence. I consider I am simply doing my duty as a private citizen, in view of the financial crisis that Canada is facing, in daring to express an opinion based on long experience and the extraordinary responsibilities I had to face during the last seven years.
>
> I think the time has come that a Department of National Defence, embracing the Naval Department, the Air Force, the Royal North West Mounted Police, and the Militia Department, should be formed. By such amalgamation a strong and experienced man could save between three and four million dollars a year by a thorough re-organization of the Departments above mentioned, by reducing (by amalgamation and absorption) the four different staffs now administering these different services—in reducing the Permanent Force and Permanent Staff of the Militia Department—the Staff and rank and file of the Air Force—and the Staff and ratings of the Naval Department.
>
> It so happens that the four Departments above mentioned all have a Pension Act, thus simplifying very much the question of disposing of the surplus officers and men "except naval."[*]
>
> You can easily imagine what a difference in the general administrative Staff such an amalgamation would make—One Deputy Minister for the whole—one Pay Department—one Purchasing Department—one Quartermaster General in charge of Demand and Supplies, etc. etc. The overhead charges would thus be reduced to a minimum, and the fact that the Royal North West Mounted Police will be administered by the same Ministerial Head would enable a reduction in the Permanent Force by an equal number, and enable the Government to deal with "Aid to Civil Powers in time of Emergency" with a complete force under one control. I could go on ad libitum elaborating these advantages, but I think I have said enough without encumbering you with a mass of details.
>
> You have no doubt noticed that England is taking steps to reorganise her Defence Force on the above mentioned basis; and so is South Africa; and surely the time has arrived for Canada to take similar steps.[6]

Another representation on the same subject arrived three or four days later from the Chief of the General Staff, Major-General J. H. MacBrien. It was in the form of a memorandum, entitled "On Necessity for Ministry of Defence" and was dated 19 December 1921:

> 1. In Canada, the strength of Defence Forces which are maintained in Peace, or mobilized for War, is a matter of policy to be decided by the Government. In the past, the policies of the various Governments have led to the formation of our present Defence Force, consisting of Navy, Army and Air Force, organized as separate Services.

*I.e., the Naval Service had no Pension Act—a deficiency of which its Director was acutely conscious, and which he strove mightily to remedy.

2. The object of all organization in Government Departments is to secure a maximum of economy combined with the most efficient execution of work. This involves the carrying out of the work with a minimum of friction. The fewer component parts of any organization—the less chance of friction there is.

3. Economy and Efficiency—also Economy and Safety—have to be balanced when deciding upon military policy and organization. Usually economy will be served best by centralization, rather than by distribution of responsibility. Centralization also reduces friction. Every system of Organization possesses its own characteristic inconveniences. Therefore, the present Organization of Canadian Defence Force is not without its disadvantages.

It is considered that many of these disadvantages may be removed by the organization of one Department charged with the Defence of the country.

4. In both Peace and War—in Training and Fighting—the Navy, Army and Air Force are mutually dependent on one another. This being the case, it is evident that some central Authority and Co-ordinating Body should be formed to direct the general allotment of the resources of the country between the various Services. Such a Central Authority would prevent competition for personnel and material, and eliminate overlapping and waste. This very necessary Co-ordinating Body can be supplied by the organization of the Ministry of Defence, which includes a Defence Council.

5. It is an axiom of war that before a Defence Force can defend (that is, fight), it must be trained; and before it can train, it must be organized and equipped. Nowadays, in war, it is a case of nation versus nation; not only armed forces versus armed forces. So long as war is apt to recur, it is essential that an efficient system of Organization should be adopted. This Organization should be such as to best conserve and use the resources of the country. Therefore, Organization must be the key-word of the Canadian Defence Policy.

6. The question of forming a Ministry of Defence has received much consideration since the close of the Great War. It was carefully considered and recommended by the Imperial Defence Committee, assembled at the War Office in 1919, on which I was the Canadian representative. It is again recommended by the Sir Eric Geddes Economic Committee.[*]

7. This matter has also been discussed by the Defence Committee, at a recent meeting of which it was unanimously decided to recommend to the new Government the formation of a Ministry of Defence for Canada. It is the opinion of the members of the Defence Committee that very large economies will be effected if this recommendation is accepted.[7]

The third representation was a letter from Sir Arthur Currie himself. "May I make a suggestion to you," he wrote to the new Prime Minister,

which is in accordance with a recommendation I made while I was Inspector-General? That you amalgamate the Departments of the Militia, the Canadian

*Whose reports, published as Command Papers 1581, 1582, and 1589, were known colloquially as the "Geddes Axe" Reports.

Navy and the Air Force, re-christening the Department "The Department of Defence." The name sounds well, and if the amalgamation took place I am quite sure you could effect a very large saving. For instance, the Quartermaster-General of the Militia might very well act as the Quartermaster for all three Departments, and so could the Adjutant General; while the heads of the Signal Departments, and Machine Gun Department might well undertake the supervision of all such work in the three Services. I believe that such a reorganization would be in the best interests of the Services and that it would appeal very much to the people of the country generally. . . .[8]

This advice, coming with such force and unanimity from quarters both interested and disinterested, offering alluring prospects of economy, and probably coinciding with the instincts of the incoming Administration, was immediately accepted. Mackenzie King's first official statement as Prime Minister announced the decision to amalgamate, as did the Speech from the Throne of 9 March 1922 which promised Parliament that "With the object of promoting economy and increasing efficiency, a Bill will be submitted to you, providing for a Department of Defence, in which the various branches of the defence forces of Canada will be co-ordinated under one ministerial head."[9] Co-ordination had already been foreshadowed by the allotment of the two portfolios, Militia and Defence, and the Naval Service, to a single Minister, George P. Graham.* As the impending reorganization drew nearer, shivers of trepidation began to shake the bureaucracy. "I understand that quite a number of heads at Ottawa are to fall," Sir Arthur Currie wrote to a friend a few days after the announcement in Parliament. "There is no doubt that military matters are unpopular in Canada, and I believe the authorities would be wise to confine their attention to the retention of capable staff. . . ."[10] And on 20 March, Sir George Foster wrote in his diary: ". . . Quite a flutter in militia circles re cutting down and laying off owing to amalgamation of Defence forces. It may well be done —there have been altogether too many high salaried men kept on the Rolls."

*That these portfolios were not in themselves regarded as important is evident from the fact that they were among the last to be assigned when Mackenzie King was forming his Cabinet, and in the event given to Graham, whom he would have preferred to have excluded. "King was suspicious of Graham because he was too favourable to the big interests and too closely associated with the machine gang in Ontario." R. MacGregor Dawson, *William Lyon Mackenzie King: A Political Biography* (Toronto, 1958), p. 359. However, Graham's "no-nonsense" approach and his capacity to survive in the jungle were useful qualities for the troublesome job of making one department out of two, and these Mackenzie King no doubt recognized in appointing Graham to his posts.

DRAFTING AND DISSENSION

Behind the scenes in Ottawa, there was now being waged a struggle of more enduring significance than that of those who, feeling their careers imperilled, sought in the usual ways to protect them. Its protagonists were the senior officers of the Royal Canadian Navy and, to a lesser extent, of the Canadian Air Force, who had reason to believe that, unless they stood firm against encroachment, the very identities of their respective Services were threatened by the impending reorganization—a reorganization which they nonetheless favoured in principle. Their apprehension is reflected in the diary entries of the Director of the Naval Service during the early weeks of 1922:

3 January: Many rumours are about concerning the formation of a Ministry of National Defence instead of the present Ministries of Militia and Naval Service and the Air Force under the Air Board, also that the Supply services of the different forces are to be combined. . . .

4 January: Still no news of when I can see the Minister who is out of town. Rumours of impending changes continue. In fact General MacBrien himself told me he thought the Air Force would be taken over by the Militia. He favours this change on the ground of economy, saying that if Canada had a big Air Force its own independent organization might be justified but that he did not think it was with such a small Air Force as we have. I feel rather anxious lest changes in the Administration of the Defence Forces will be suggested to the Minister by Militia Officers and that the Minister may take action without consultation with the Naval and Air Force authorities, so I arranged to go and see Sir W. Gwatkin [Inspector-General, Canadian Air Force] at his office in the afternoon to talk matters over.

It appears that Sir Willoughby is also anxious and had written to Mr. Graham stating that he hoped soon to be able to pay his respects and that he hoped the Minister would give the Air Board an opportunity to inform him on its views as to Administration.

I urged Sir W. to try and get an Air Board meeting (of which the Minister of Militia is chairman) as soon as possible.

7 January: Went to Government House skating party. Met Mr. J. A. Wilson, Sec'y. to the Air Board, up there. He tells me that Gen. Gwatkin got a reply to the letter he wrote to Mr. Graham and he (Mr. G.) promised that all interested parties would be consulted before any change was made in the Air Board Administration.

10 January: Discussed the possibilities of one National Defence Dept. with our Deputy Minister. I told him I had heard that the Minister had issued instructions to the Militia Dept. to prepare a draft scheme for amalgamating the Navy, Militia and Air Force into one Department and I was afraid that if it was left to the Militia Dept. they would be the first in the field and that we might find ourselves in the position of having to pull the only drawn up scheme to pieces unless we set to work and also prepared a scheme to present to the Minister. Mr. Desbarats agreed and it was arranged to hold a naval committee meeting tomorrow at which the matter should be discussed. I then had a talk with Stephens [Assistant Director of the Naval Service] who is in accordance with me on the general plan of formation of a Defence Department.

11 January: Had the Naval Committee meeting this morning re our proposals for a Department of Defence. Desbarats gave his views of what he expected the outcome would be—a Department dominated entirely by the Militia. Stephens also thinks that the Militia will dominate the Department in spite of any unrefutable arguments for equal representation and control which might be put forward by the Navy and Air Force. I said I thought all that enhanced the necessity for the Naval Dept. to have prepared all ready a constructive scheme, which the Minister would have to take into consideration simultaneously with any scheme prepared by the Militia, instead of our being placed in the position of mere critics of the one set of proposals laid before the Minister.

Stephens suggested that a sudden transformation from the three departments with their own distinct systems of administration, supply and conduct of operations to a single joint department would be dangerous if not impossible, and that, while agreeing that one dept. of Defence is what is required for economy and efficiency of co-operation, the three separate organizations should continue as at present, under one Minister, until a new organization should be worked out without undue rush and haste. That our proposal should stipulate for a Committee to be appointed by the Governor in Council, together with sub-committees on War Staff, Administration, Supply and Accounts, who should work out a new draft Defence Act, and the organization of one amalgamated Department. This was agreed to by the Committee and Stephens was directed to prepare a draft recommendation to the Minister.

16 January: Went to see Sir W. Gwatkin this afternoon. I told him I had suggested to our Deputy today that when he sees the Minister he should propose to him to hold a meeting consisting of the Director of the Naval Service, Chief of the General Staff and Inspector General Air Force as representing the technical side of the three services interested in the new Departmental organization, and the Deputy Minister of Navy, Militia and Vice Chairman of the Air Board, as representing the Civil administration and financial side, and that the three forces should bring with them their proposed plans in writing, also that each technical and civil chief should be called on to make a statement (brief) of their view of the situation and that there should be no argument.

Apprehension existed as well among the senior officers of the Air Force. "I am a little afraid," wrote its Inspector-General to Sir Hugh Trenchard, a few days after the election, "of an attempt being made to bring it under the Militia Council; but I am doing all I can to convince people that it should continue to be organized and administered as a third service—unified and separate."[11] Trenchard, then fighting a similar battle of his own, lent his authority to the cause of independence; a letter from him, "stating that for the proper development of the Air Force, independent control was essential,"[12] was read by Gwatkin to a meeting of the Air Board. The Air Board discussed the proposed reorganization at several of its meetings during January and February 1922. Discussion could not be as frank as that taking place in the Naval Committee owing to the presence of the Minister and representatives of the other Services; but even so, the Board placed itself on record as follows:

> It was agreed that the principle [of reorganization] was sound; that the Air Board should co-operate with the other Services to the fullest extent possible in endeavouring to secure a sound basis for the new Department; that the Air Board was willing that all services not distinctly aeronautical in their nature should be pooled; but that the Air Board as a body for the control of aeronautics in Canada should be preserved; and that any effort made to divide its aeronautical functions among other organizations should be opposed.[13]

In March the hard news of the 60 per cent reduction in the estimates for air services became known, and with it the hopes for continued autonomy died away. The Canadian Air Force now became a directorate of the General Staff; and while this was to be, and was understood to be, a temporary measure only until such time as an expansion of air power justified the resumption of independent operation, it left the Navy as the sole countervailing force against complete militia control of the armed services.

Meanwhile, the drafting of the Defence Department bill was going badly. The Minister had duly received the Navy's memorandum. He reacted coldly, even with some hostility, to its complaint that the Navy was being excluded from discussion of the reorganization and its demands for equality of status. "I am sure," Graham wrote to G. J. Desbarats, the Deputy Minister of the Naval Service,

> I have discussed the proposed amalgamation with you several times. You will also recall you gave me a memorandum on it. I have intended calling in Captain Hose, but have put it off from day to day. I have no doubt you can readily realise that I have been pretty well pressed for time. However, after having your views, the views of the Air Board, and the views of the Militia Officers, I decided that as they were at such variance, no good would be accomplished in getting these Officers together.
>
> Even in Great Britain, the question of the advisability of consolidating the Defence Forces is now under consideration, and the Government has

fully made up its mind that, with the small force in Canada, it is the part of wisdom to combine it all in one Department.

There will be a very material reduction in every branch of the service so far as the expenditure is concerned, but I hope to be able to bring it about with as little friction and with a minimum of hardship as is possible.

I shall be glad at any time to see any of you, but nothing that can be said will alter the intention of the Government to carry out the proposed consolidation.[14]

Graham's reply makes it evident that he misunderstood the nature of the Navy's objections, which were not directed to the principle of a single Department, nor even to the drastic reductions in personnel that might be necessary as a consequence of reorganization, but solely to the manner in which the reorganization and corresponding reductions were to be put into effect. In retrospect it is easy to see what hapened. The double uncertainty of impending reorganization coupled with drastic cuts in estimates for the three services had rattled everyone concerned, and resulted in anything but the right frames of mind in which to consider the problem with statesmanlike detachment. ". . . The atmosphere is at the moment rather unfavourable to free discussion," the Vice-Chairman of the Air Board wrote to Graham on 15 February, "owing to the admission of officers of the Department of Militia (doubtless for wholly sufficient reasons) to a confidence on the subject of the proposed legislation from which their opposite numbers in the other Departments concerned have been excluded. The solution of the problems involved will, I think, be found comparatively easy when they are discussed after the removal of that handicap and before the three present departments cease to retain their separate existence."[15] Graham replied:

There is a grave misconception as to the tentative Bill. Surely a Minister has a right to discuss with his Deputy Minister, matters affecting the Department. He is the only man, so far as I can ascertain, who has seen the Bill in question. It has not been discussed by Officers of the Militia, and, in framing its contents, a memorandum from every Branch interested was read and re-read.

The Bill provides for nothing but consolidating the Defence Departments with one Minister and one Deputy Minister, with a Council of National Defence. It was fully explained the other day, to which everyone seemed agreeable.

I am not a military man, but have had some experience in organization of business forces, and if I had the sympathetic interest of the various interests affected in the consolidation, I could whip the thing into shape in one hour. I have no desire to be arbitrary, because I am almost an extremist in the other direction. However, I intend to have a Bill ready for the opening of Parliament, providing for the carrying out of the Government's policy.

My only object is economy and efficiency. I am firmly convinced that with the proper system of co-operation, millions of dollars could be saved for the country.[16]

II

The Fourteenth Parliament of Canada met for the first time on 8 March 1922. True to his word, the Minister of Militia and Defence had his draft legislation ready. It was introduced for first reading (as Bill No. 15) on 23 March, and debated by a Committee of the House (as Bill No. 27) on 4 April. The resolution placed before Parliament by Graham on the latter date read as follows:

1. That it is expedient to bring in a measure to create a department of the Government of Canada to be called the Department of National Defence, over which a Minister of the Crown shall preside who shall be called the Minister of National Defence.

2. That the Minister shall be charged with all matters relating to Defence, including the Militia, the Military, Naval, Air and Police Services of Canada.

3. That there shall be a Deputy Minister of National Defence who shall be appointed by the Governor in Council, and hold office during his pleasure, and such officers may be appointed as are necessary for the carrying on of the business of the Department.

4. That the Governor in Council on the recommendation of the Minister may appoint an officer who shall, in relation to the Naval Service, exercise all the powers and duties vested in the Deputy Minister of the Naval Service by or under The Naval Service Act, and who shall have the rank and salary of a deputy head of a department, and shall be a member of the Defence Council.

5. That the Governor in Council on the recommendation of the Minister may appoint an officer to be known as Comptroller, who under the Deputy Minister of National Defence shall be charged with all financial matters pertaining to the Department of National Defence.

6. That any person whose position is abolished on the coming into force of the Act to be based upon these resolutions may, on the recommendation of the Minister, be appointed by the Governor in Council to such position in the Department and with such rank, title and salary as shall be prescribed.

7. That if any person is removed from office or an appointment in consequence of the abolition of his office or his appointment by the Act based upon these resolutions or by any order or regulation thereunder, or is retired within two years after the coming into force of the said Act, the Governor in Council may grant him a gratuity, retiring or superannuation allowance, or pension not exceeding such as he would have been entitled or eligible to receive if he had been retired under the provisions of any Act applicable to him, after adding from one to three years, as the Governor in Council may deem advisable, to his actual term of service.

8. That provision be made to vest the powers, duties and functions vested in the ministers and deputy ministers under the various Acts relating

to the Naval Service, the Militia, Militia Pensions, the Royal Military College, the Royal Canadian Mounted Police, and the Dominion Police, in the Minister of National Defence and the Deputy Minister of National Defence respectively:—provided that the powers as vested in the Deputy Minister of the Naval Service under the Naval Service Act shall be exercised by the officer appointed for that purpose aforesaid.

9. That provision shall be made to constitute a Defence Council to advise the Minister on all matters of defence, including or relating to the Militia, the Military, Naval, Air and Police Services of Canada, and on all matters referred to it by the Minister, and to perform such other duties as may be prescribed by the Governor in Council.[17]

Paragraph 4 of the bill, together with the proviso in Paragraph 8, represented the price that had to be paid for the Navy's acquiescence in the legislation as finally drafted. This feature of the bill was one of two to be criticized in debate. General Mewburn, a former Minister of Militia and Defence, remarked that it seemed to him "that the services of only one deputy minister are all that should be required. . . . From my own personal experience I think that the present deputy minister of Militia and Defence is capable of carrying on three or four important departments now that the war is over, and, I think, with due economy."[18] Another former Minister of Militia, Hugh Guthrie, raised the same objection, claiming that the proposed reorganization would not differ very substantially from that already in existence:

We have a Deputy Minister of Marine and Fisheries now, Mr. [Alex.] Johnston, a Deputy Minister of Naval Service, Mr. Desbarats, and a Deputy Minister of Militia and Defence, Sir Eugène Fiset; and the only change you propose is to take the Naval Service into the other department under the Deputy Minister of Militia and Defence, retaining the Deputy Minister of the Naval Service, Mr. Desbarats, but calling him something else. That is not a consolidation or amalgamation, to my way of thinking. I feel sure that you could drop Mr. Desbarats and carry out your scheme without him, saving the country $6,000 per annum. You would depend then for your guidance in regard to matters pertaining to the Naval Service upon an expert in that Department.

The Leader of the Opposition, Arthur Meighen, remarked: "In a word, the minister is maintaining an organization that will prevent him from accomplishing anything in the way of the object he has in mind," and inquired acutely which of the two deputies the staff of the proposed Department would be under.[19] Yet another former Cabinet member, H. H. Stevens, denounced not only the proposed position but launched a personal attack on the incumbent: "I have during the past eleven years gone to the Naval Service Department on many occasions, and whether it was through purposeful stupidity or absolute incompetence,

I do not know, but I never could get from the Deputy Minister of Naval Affairs any satisfaction at all, and he is the only civil servant of standing in Ottawa I would say that about."[20] Graham rose loyally to the defence of Desbarats, describing him as "capable and courteous," but he was obviously tried by the Opposition's criticism of the dual deputy arrangement, which he knew as well as his critics to be indefensible on purely administrative grounds. He did what he could to head them off. "I have studied this thing for the last two months," he declared, "and I want to assure the House that the practical way of effecting this amalgamation is to allow us to retain the Deputy Minister of Naval Service to look after that branch of the department for a year at least, until we get the other branches thoroughly absorbed. I would not propose this if I did not think it was absolutely necessary."[21] And again:

> My hon. friend suggested, rather sneeringly, that I should give this matter consideration. I can assure him that I have given it consideration every day for the last six weeks. . . . My judgment and the judgment of the Government, after fully considering this question of retaining the Deputy Minister of the Naval Service, is that the only satisfactory way, under the present conditions, to bring about this amalgamation, which must come about gradually and cannot be the work of a moment, is that the able deputy minister should be retained for the time being in his present position as head of the Naval Service branch.[22]

T. A. Crerar, the Leader of the Progressive party (on whose support the Mackenzie King Government relied for its continuation in office), agreed. "I believe," he said, "that latitude should be given to the minister to carry on this re-organization in the way he thinks best for the service. If there are two deputy ministers next year, or the following year, and this Parliament is asked to vote their salaries, the question then can very well come up for reconsideration."[23] (Desbarats, after some months in an acting capacity, became Deputy Minister, Department of National Defence, in 1924.)

A second criticism of Bill No. 27 was both more fundamental and far-reaching. Its intention of placing the Royal Canadian Mounted Police under the direction of the Minister of National Defence was assailed from all sides of the House. "I do object," declared the Leader of the Opposition,

> to the Mounted Police being taken out of a civilian department and made part of the military forces, and I see no reason for the step whatever. The Mounted Police from its inception has been a civilian force, and the very credit that accrues to it to-day throughout this Dominion is derived more from the fact that it is a civilian force than from any other consideration.

Make it a military force and throw around it the military atmosphere and the trappings of the militia, and you will not find the Mounted Police held in the same regard. . . .[24]

"I do feel very strongly," General Mewburn stated, "that the Mounted Police should not be interfered with. . . . We have had troubles in the past, strikes and that sort of thing, and although under the present Militia act it is within the power of a municipality to call upon the militia to turn out for the preservation of law and order, that is the very last resort that should be adopted in this country. . . . One or two members of the Mounted Police force can do more for the preservation of law and order than any number of militiamen that might be called out. . . ."[25] T. A. Crerar, for the Progressives, agreed. "It is not sound policy to include [the R.C.M.P.] with the arms that have to do with defence. I am among those who believe that the administration of civil law and the maintenance of civil order should be kept away as far as possible from that relating to the defence of the country."[26] To this criticism the Minister proved remarkably receptive. "If I were not a member of a government," Graham confessed, "and were sitting somewhere else, I might express the personal opinion that I think the secret service of Canada ought to be under the Minister of Justice."[27] Two days later, on his own initiative, Bill No. 27 was amended so as to leave the R.C.M.P. outside the jurisdiction of the Department of National Defence. It is not often that Parliament so constructively affects government legislation.

The bill received Royal Assent on 28 June, but the Act did not come into force until 1 January 1923, so as to allow time for the departments involved to make the necessary preparations.

Such was the legislative foundation of what the new Minister of National Defence hoped would become "a well organized, snappy, defence force that will be a credit to Canada without being too expensive."[28]

CHIEFS AND SUPER-CHIEFS

It would have been too much to expect that with the creation of the new Department of National Defence, the deep-seated and powerful rivalry of the Services would disappear overnight. A year or two, it could reasonably have been thought, would have to pass before harmony prevailed and the new Department functioned as it was meant to function. As it turned out, it took a decade or two, rather than a year or two.

For this prolonged disunity, personalities were more responsible than organization charts. Throughout most of the 1920's, the Department of National Defence was riven by a bitter and continuing feud between the Chief of the General Staff and the Director of the Naval Service. The first of these positions had been held since August 1920 by Major-General James Howden MacBrien, C.B., C.M.G., D.S.O. Jim MacBrien was often admiringly referred to as a soldier's soldier, and with good reason. Born at Port Perry, Ontario, in 1878, he began his military career as a militia private in the 34th Ontario Battalion at the age of nineteen. Three years later he joined the North West Mounted Police. (Four years after his retirement from the Army in 1927, he was persuaded by R. B. Bennett to become Commissioner of the Royal Canadian Mounted Police, a post at that time of depression and internal crisis as difficult to fill properly as any in the Dominion.) In 1901 he resigned from the N.W.M.P. to fight in the South African Constabulary, in which he remained until its disbandment in 1906. Returning to Canada, he was commissioned in the permanent force in 1907. The outbreak of war found him on course at the Staff College, Camberley, and, at the request of the British authorities, he was posted to the War Office where he stayed until the arrival of the 1st Canadian Contingent on Salisbury Plain. By 1916 he had risen to the rank of Brigadier-General. He was a fighting officer: twice wounded in action, six times mentioned in despatches. He is remembered by surviving fellow officers for his extraordinary aplomb and coolness under fire, and for a wry sense of humour which he retained in the gravest moments of battle. His crisp competence and his courage earned him the admiration of all ranks. But the qualities which made MacBrien so outstanding an officer in the field were not those needed for success in the frustrating environment of peacetime administration. Like most of the officers of the permanent force of the 1920's and 1930's, he had little conception of, or interest in, the workings of the bureaucracy, nor had he the tact or patience needed to get his way without alienating those who stood in his path. The imperturbable field commander became the abrupt and impulsive desk officer. The new Department required tolerance and affability, but MacBrien became increasingly impatient and choleric with the passing of the years.

His main opponent was the Director of the Naval Service. If Jim MacBrien was the soldier's soldier, Walter Hose was the sailor's sailor. He had even been born at sea (on a P. and O. liner in the Indian Ocean —his father was the Bishop of Singapore). He entered the Royal Navy's training ship *Britannia* in 1890, at the age of fifteen, passed into the

Fleet two years later, and was sent as a cadet to join the flagship of the China Squadron. For the next twenty years, the young officer cruised in every ocean on every class of ship from torpedo boats to battleship. His first command was a gunboat, his first major command (in 1909) a cruiser. He was loaned by the Admiralty in 1911 to the Canadian Naval Service; a year later he voluntarily left the Royal Navy for the Royal Canadian Navy. Commander Hose spent the first two years of the war at sea working with British and Japanese naval units in Pacific waters; in April 1917 he was posted to Naval Headquarters at Ottawa, his first shore appointment for a quarter century. After a further tour as Captain Superintendent, Halifax Dockyard, he was posted in March 1920 back to Ottawa, where he became, successively, Naval Assistant to the Minister, Assistant Director of the Naval Service, and, in January 1921, Director of the Naval Service. In the latter capacity he became the Government's chief adviser on naval matters. No one could have been more tenacious in protecting what he conceived to be the navy's interest. Quiet, even reserved, Walter Hose was intensely loyal to the Service in which he had spent his life. Encroachments upon its autonomy he would not permit. Resignation (as subsequent events were to show) was preferable to being in any way a party to surrendering naval rights and naval traditions; but the Director was not without the politician's sense of timing and knew when and how to employ this weapon of last resort.

MacBrien wanted to direct all three services within the framework of the new Department of National Defence. Hose was determined that the Navy would run itself. These diametrically opposed aims made a clash between the two officers, so evenly matched in experience and tenacity of purpose, virtually inevitable. The lines of their protracted struggle were drawn very early in the game.

II

"About the beginning of January 1923," the Director of the Naval Service wrote soon after that date, "I gathered from hearsay that the Chief of the General Staff . . . had received an appointment as Chief of the Staff of the Department of National Defence, and that Militia Orders had been promulgated giving instructions that Maj.-Gen. MacBrien was to be so addressed in future." On 17 January these rumours were officially confirmed. "I was sent for," Commodore Hose recorded,

> by the Acting Deputy Minister [G. J. Desbarats], who showed me a chart . . . of the Departmental organization, showing the line of authority from

the Minister of Defence to the Defence Council, which had been drawn up by Major Gen'l. MacBrien and brought by him to the Act'g. D.M. for concurrence. The Acting D.M. informed me that he wished me to consider it carefully and its effect on the Naval Service and to let him have my remarks. . . . I informed the Act'g. D.M. that I had no knowledge of any appointment having been made of a Chief of Staff. The Act'g. D.M. then showed me an Order in Council (P.C. 2446) authorising this and other appointments in the Department of National Defence. . . .[29]

The order-in-council, dated 24 November 1922, read as follows:

The Committee of the Privy Council have had before them a Report, dated 15th November, 1922, from the Minister of Militia and Defence, submitting that the creation of the Department of National Defence, pursuant to The National Defence Act 1922, will necessitate a certain re-adjustment on the Headquarters Staff of those appointments, the duties of which will be materially increased in the new Department.

The Minister, therefore, recommends that, upon the coming into force of The National Defence Act, 1922, Chapter 43 of the Statutes of 1922, and under and by virtue of the powers conferred by the said Act, the following appointments and regulations for and concerning the Department of National Defence be approved:—

Deputy Minister of National Defence and Vice-President of the Defence Council. Major-General Sir Eugène Fiset, Kt., C.M.G., D.S.O., and to continue to remain seconded as an officer of the Permanent Headquarters Staff from the Permanent Active Militia.

Chief of Staff, Department of National Defence and member of the Defence Council. Major-General J. H. MacBrien, C.B., C.M.G., D.S.O.

Adjutant-General, Department of National Defence. Major-General Sir E. W. B. Morrison, K.C.M.G., C.B., D.S.O.

Quartermaster General, Department of National Defence. Major-General E. C. Ashton, C.M.G.

Judge Advocate-General, Department of National Defence, and responsible to the Deputy Minister and transferred from the Branch of the Adjutant-General accordingly. Lieut.-Colonel R. J. Orde, R.C.A., and to continue to remain seconded.

Deputy Chief of the General Staff, Militia Services. Lieut.-Colonel and Brevet Colonel (Hon. Brig.-General) A. G. L. McNaughton, C.M.G., D.S.O., and to be temporary Colonel on the Staff whilst holding this appointment. This officer to continue to hold the appointment of Director of Military Training and Staff Duties, and to be paid under the provisions of the Pay and Allowance Regulations, applicable to the latter appointment.

The Vice-President of the Defence Council, the Chief of Staff, Adjutant-General, Quartermaster General and Judge Advocate-General, Department of National Defence, shall, in relation to the Canadian Militia, have the same status and perform and exercise all the powers, duties and functions which, prior to the coming into force of The National Defence Act, 1922, were had or possessed, exercised or performed by the Vice-President Militia Council, the Chief of the General Staff, Adjutant-General, Quartermaster General, and Judge Advocate-General, respectively.

The provisions of the Pay and Allowance Regulations applicable to the Vice-President Militia Council, the Chief of the General Staff, Adjutant-General, Quartermaster General and Judge Advocate-General immediately prior to the coming into force of The National Defence Act, 1922, shall be applicable to the Vice-President Department of National Defence, Chief of Staff, Adjutant-General, Quartermaster-General and Judge Advocate-General, Department of National Defence, respectively, in the same manner and to the same extent as they would be had The National Defence Act, 1922, not been passed.

Except in so far as they are inconsistent with anything herein contained, or anything contained in any other Order in Council or regulation which has been, or which may be issued hereafter concerning the Department of National Defence, the ranks, status, appointments, rates of pay and allowances of all personnel of the Royal Canadian Navy, Canadian Militia and Canadian Air Force, and all regulations and orders now in force pertaining to the Royal Canadian Navy, the Canadian Militia and the Canadian Air Force shall continue and remain in effect as if the National Defence Act, 1922, had not been passed.

The Committee concur in the foregoing and submit the same for Your Excellency's approval.

The chart prepared by General MacBrien for the future organization of the higher echelons of the Department of National Defence, and shown for the first time to Commodore Hose by G. J. Desbarats on 17 January looked like this:

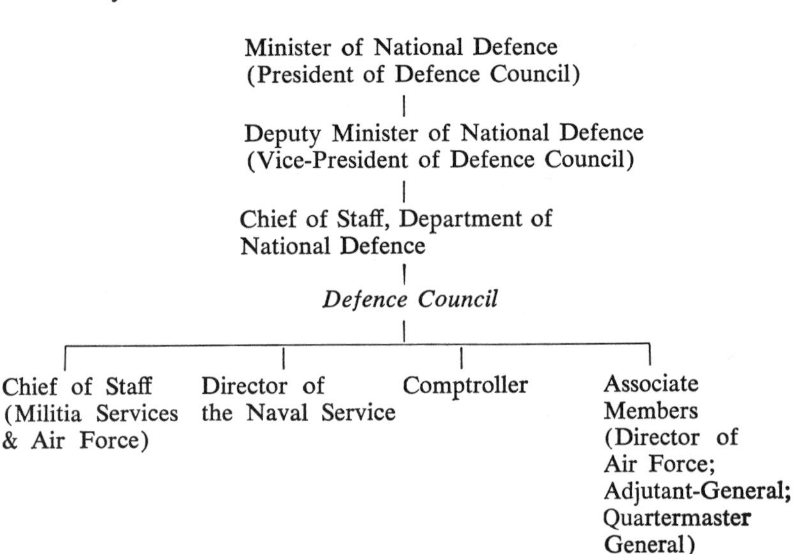

[Figure 1]

On being shown these documents, Commodore Hose recorded, "I retired to my office and very carefully considered the chart given to me by the Acting D.M. I then wrote and forwarded to the Acting D.M. a memorandum on the subject setting out my objections to the plan. After forwarding this memorandum I received a copy of P.C. 2446, and thereupon wrote and forwarded another memorandum to the Act'g. D.M. dated 19th January." The first of the two memoranda read as follows:

In accordance with your verbal request the following remarks are forwarded on the draft chart presented to you by the Chief of the General Staff showing the line of authority in the Department of National Defence.

It is first desired to impress the essentially different duties, responsibilities and organization of the Navy and the Army.

The duty of the Royal Canadian Navy is above all the defence of the maritime interests of the country in time of war or emergency.

The work of the Navy in this regard has in its broadest sense but little in common with the other national objects and activities, the defence of which redounds on the Army; it is only in certain well defined functions of Naval Defence where the actual co-operation of the two forces is of primary importance.

The strategical policy of development of Naval Forces, the training of personnel, the conditions of their life and work, the weapons used in the Navy are all specialized to such an extent that only an officer with many years of specialized training and experience is qualified to control them and the final responsibility for efficiency both in the policy and practical activities of the Navy must rest, under the Minister, with the Naval officer selected and appointed for this duty.

It is under these conditions that an officer, the Director of the Naval Service, is appointed in the terms of the Naval Service Act.

The appointment of any Officer as Chief of the Staff of the Department of National Defence would, by the title, appear necessarily to entail the following effect on the relations between the Naval and Military forces respectively.

The Director of the Naval Service is a member of the Staff of the Department of National Defence, and as a member of the Staff must be subject to a certain measure of authority from the Chief of Staff; consequently the Navy must be under such authority.

The Army is likewise under the same measure of control by the Chief of Staff.

In the event of either a Naval or Military Officer being appointed as Chief of Staff, therefore, the Army in one case and the Navy in the other comes under control, in its policies of strategy and development, even if not in detailed administration, of an Officer who is not qualified by the training or experience to give final authoritative advice to the Minister.

The power in the hands of such a Chief of Staff, even if not fully exercised, is bound to have its effect on the destiny and development of the Navy, and the rank and file of the Service cannot be expected to have any confidence in headquarters administration if finally direct and authoritative advice to the Minister on their problems lies in the hands of an officer unqualified for such a position by reason of lack of technical knowledge and personal experience.

I may be mistaken, but I gather that one argument advocated by those in favour of a Chief of Staff is that it makes a single senior officer responsible for and with authority to convene the technical heads of the Services to consult on plans for defence arrangements.

This point I cannot but maintain is academic rather than practical. Defence Councils or Committees have existed for years without the necessity for any such one person being apparent.

The technical head of each defence force should be in a position to request the other or others to confer on these points and the results of their deliberations can then be submitted to the Minister.

The argument leads to one conclusion which may be stated as an axiom to the effective development and conduct of the respective defence forces:—

There must be a clear and direct channel of communication between the Minister and *each* of his advisers, i.e., the technical head of the Navy and the technical head of the Army.

The title Chief of Staff of the Department of National Defence abrogates this principle.

It conveys to the Naval or Military Officer who holds the title, the power, and, in fact, the duty, of weighing his own views against those of the other technical heads, and of conveying to the Minister an opinion on the matter, which, besides lacking in experience of the responsibilities, life and conditions of the other service, cannot fail to be affected by the weight of his responsibility for meeting, especially with limited funds, the urgent necessities of the portion of the Defence Forces which he actively directs.

The title and position do not appear to be in the least conducive to economy or efficiency, but must convey the impression of absorption rather than amalgamation of the respective forces.

Attached [Figure 2] is an alternative Chart for the line of authority in the Department of National Defence showing the Chief of the Naval Staff

DEPARTMENT OF NATIONAL DEFENCE

Minister of National Defence

|

Deputy Minister of National Defence

|

Defence Council

President—The Minister
Vice-President—The Deputy Minister

|

Chief of Naval Staff	Chief of General Staff	Comptroller	Associate Members of Council[30]

[Figure 2]

and the Chief of the General Staff (the title commonly in use for the Chief of the Military Staff and so used in Order in Council P.C. 1252 of 20th June 1922) in charge of their respective services and each directly under the Minister and the Deputy Minister.

In this connection I would strongly recommend that the necessary legislation be put into force to change the title of the Director of the Naval Service to Chief of the Naval Staff, the former title giving the erroneous impression that the Naval Service is a directorate under the Defence Council in the same sense as the directorates of supplies, medical boards, etc.

The memorandum of 19 January read as follows:

With reference to Order in Council P.C. 2446 dated 24th November 1922, a copy of which was forwarded to me by you on the 18th instant, I have to bring before your consideration certain points in which it appears that the above quoted Order in Council does not entirely meet the requirements of the Department of National Defence, and others in which the titles conveyed on Officers are misleading as regards the scope of their jurisdiction over the individual forces included in the Department.

The primary omission in Order in Council P.C. 2446 is that in spite of the importance of the functions of the Naval Service and of the work and responsibilities of the Naval Service in connection therewith, there is no mention of any Naval Officer as an Officer of the Department of National Defence charged with any specific duties and responsibilities in connection with the administration of the Department.

The inference cannot but be that in general the administration of the whole Department, including the Navy, is placed in the hands of a body of Military Officers under the Minister and Deputy Minister of the Department.

This is a matter of fundamental importance and the omission, if permitted to stand, would be fatal to the proper conduct, administration and efficiency of the Navy.

As pointed out in my memorandum of the 17th January 1923, the title of Chief of Staff, Department of National Defence, is considered very undesirable.

If it is intended that the duties of the Chief of Staff, in relation to the Department of National Defence, should be in accordance with the natural interpretation of such a title, it undoubtedly conveys a measure of jurisdiction and control over the Director of the Naval Service, and consequently over the Navy in the manner indicated in my memorandum of the 17th instant, and would be fatal to the proper and efficient functioning of the Navy.

In view of the provision of Section 9, paragraph 2, of the Naval Service Act which charges the Director of the Naval Service "with the direction of the Naval Service", under the Minister, I feel it my duty to indicate the above points in connection with Order in Council P.C. 2446 as being of fundamental and vital importance to the proper "direction of the Naval Service".

To overcome the above noted features of Order in Council P.C. 2446, which are incompatible with the proper conduct of the Navy within the Department of National Defence it is strongly urged that the following adjustment should be made:

1. The insertion of a position to the Chief of the Naval Staff, Department of National Defence—who shall be the Director of the Naval Service.
2. The elimination of the title Chief of Staff, Department of National Defence, and substitution therefore of the Chief of the General Staff, Department of National Defence.
3. The inclusion of a paragraph directing that the duties, status, functions &c. of the Chief of the Naval Staff shall, in relation to the Naval Service of Canada, be as performed by the Director of the Naval Service under the Naval Service Act. (This paragraph to run on lines parallel to the similar provision regarding Military Officers given titles and appointments under the Department of National Defence.)

I would further call your attention to another feature of Order in Council P.C. 2446, of which I question the advisability in view of its possible relation to the Royal Canadian Navy, viz., the appointment of an officer as Adjutant General of the Department of National Defence.

Undoubtedly an Adjutant General is required for the Militia, but his duties do not necessitate any measure of control over the Navy or any of its branches, technical or civil.

It is understood that the duties of Adjutant General carry responsibility largely in connection with allocation and distribution of personnel and these duties must be carried out by Naval and Military officers respectively for their own forces. I cannot but consider it very undesirable to provide for an Adjutant General of the Department of National Defence since this would imply a certain measure of jurisdiction in Adjutant General's duties over all the services amalgamated in the Department.[31]

On 19 January, Commodore Hose had a second interview with the Acting Deputy Minister of the Department of National Defence.

I informed him that I had originally intended including a paragraph in my memorandum of the 19th to the effect that it would be impossible for me to accept, by acquiescence in the organization indicated by P.C. 2446, the responsibility for Director of the Naval Service under such conditions, but that, on further consideration, I thought it advisable in this memorandum only to indicate my conviction that such organization was fundamentally unsound. I, however, informed the Act'g. D.M. verbally that I wished to make it very clear, and that I should like the Minister to understand, that if P.C. 2446 were not cancelled or amended so that the organization was clearly based on the equality of the Naval and Military Services under the Minister, I should have, in the first place, to request to see the Prime Minister, and, if the present proposed organization were persisted in it would be my duty to tender my resignation as I felt that I held my position in trust for the Royal Canadian Navy and that I had no right whatever to accept for that Service a position of subordination to Military Control.[32]

III

"Subordination to Military Control" was indeed what it was coming to. Late in 1922, the former Deputy Minister of Militia and Defence resigned from the new Department, thereby ending the anomaly, of which complaint had been made in parliamentary debate, of two deputy ministers for a single department. But there was no intention of allowing the remaining deputy to consolidate full authority. Desbarats' title of Acting Deputy Minister was retained, despite Fiset's resignation, until 1924. Fiset himself had written to the Minister shortly before his resignation: ". . . My departure from the Militia Department will create a rather awkward situation in the civil branch of this Department. There will be no officer left in the Civil Staff of your Department who possesses any technical knowledge of the military organization of your Department. The Minister will, therefore, be compelled to consult and depend more on the advice and recommendations of his chief adviser."[33] That is exactly what happened. A few days later, Graham wrote to Mackenzie King:

> I am very anxious to be allowed to increase General MacBrien to $9,000 as proposed some months ago.
>
> He has taken over the duties of the Inspector General, with no increase in staff, which formerly cost in the neighbourhood of $20,000. I have also abolished the position of Master General of the Ordnance, and quite a bit of the work of that branch has devolved now on General MacBrien.
>
> We have had some heart to heart talks during the past month and a half, and while standing up strongly for the Militia on every point, as that is his duty as well as his life, he is doing everything possible to meet my wishes in working out little details here that are of great importance to our friends as well as to the smoothness of the running of the Department.
>
> I do not care to bring this question up again unless you are favourable, but it would help mightily in this Department if it could be done. General Fiset is going on November 1st, and it is imperative that General MacBrien be contented and satisfied, because I will have to lean on him to a far greater extent than I have hitherto.[34]

By the beginning of 1923, General MacBrien was seated firmly in the saddle, and showed no sign of wishing to dismount. On 20 January he informed the Director of the Naval Service of his intention to reorganize the Department along the lines foreshadowed in P.C. 2446, and issued a summons to a meeting in his office to discuss the matter.

(Meetings of the Defence Council had previously been held alternately in the offices of the Chief of the General Staff, the Director of the Naval Service, and the Director of the Air Force.) "This clearly indicates," Commodore Hose commented on MacBrien's communication,

> his view of the position of the Chief of Staff which gives undoubted control and authority over the Director of the Naval Service, with a controlling position of advice to the Minister in Naval as well as in Military and Air matters. I considered it quite impossible to accept for the Navy such a position in any defence committee, and, in order not to precipitate an undesirable situation, I immediately forwarded a copy of Maj. Gen'l. MacBrien's memorandum under personal cover with a private note to the Acting D.M. suggesting that perhaps it would be as well if he were to indicate to Maj. Gen'l. MacBrien that it would not be desirable to proceed any further in the matter of the defence committee until the question of the status of officers of the Department of National Defence had been settled.[35]

General MacBrien, in a note to the Acting Deputy Minister, observed that the Director of the Naval Service seemed to be experiencing "some hesitation in taking instructions" from himself as Chief of Staff; Commodore Hose promptly replied, through Desbarats, that he experienced "no hesitation whatever in *not* taking instructions from the Chief of the General Staff," and that nothing would persuade him to attend meetings of a Defence Council under the conditions that MacBrien assumed ought now to prevail.[36] This firm stand brought about a temporary détente. "Matter of Defence Committee", Desbarats minuted on 12 February 1923, "is in abeyance."

It was well for the country that no problem of national security requiring even a semblance of concerted effort by the sister services presented itself at this time, for the policy machine in its disordered state would have been wholly unable to deal with it. The extent of its disarray was disclosed by its reaction to a proposed treaty, then under consideration by the Government, to revise the Rush-Bagot Agreement of 1817. The Government had submitted a draft of the proposed treaty to the Naval Service. Commodore Hose had found it satisfactory. The General Staff, however, were not consulted, nor did the Director of the Naval Service see fit to inform it of the contents of the draft. When, in answer to a question in the Senate, the Government leader replied that the draft treaty had been submitted "to the Chief Executives of the National Defence Department," the military were understandably miffed. Colonel J. Sutherland Brown, recalling an earlier paper submitted by the naval authorities on the subject of "Naval Co-operation on the Great Lakes," was indignant to think that their advice on the draft treaty had been sought and relied upon: ". . . Not only have they no clear vision as to what military operations would mean on this Continent," he wrote to MacBrien, "they have little more vision as to the co-operation that the Naval Authorities should give on the Great Lakes, nor do they seem to have studied the question . . . in any serious way."[37] MacBrien immediately complained to the Minister. "So far this Treaty has not been seen by me or by the Directorate of Military Operations, the Branch of the Staff most directly concerned with the defence of Canada," he wrote to Graham in June 1923. "It is submitted that the military authorities should be permitted to give their opinion on the draft Treaty . . . One of the main reasons for the formation of the Department of National Defence was to obtain close cooperation in questions . . . such as this."[38] A copy of the draft treaty duly reached the Chief of Staff, who, though knowing that it had met with Commodore Hose's approval, prepared a memorandum taking exception to the terms of four of its six Articles.[39] Partly because of such sharp disagreement among the Government's defence advisers, the draft was never pressed forward to signature and ratification.

This contretemps, and others, caused the Minister of National Defence to realize, belatedly enough, that a first-rate row was in the offing unless his two senior service officers could be brought to some mutually satisfactory understanding. He turned, accordingly, to the Judge-Advocate General, of whom he requested a solution based upon the system of defence organization then in use in Australia (where defence policy had been directed through a single ministry since 1921, as it had been before 1915). "You will have to take into consideration," Graham warned his prospective Solomon,

> not the situation as it ought to be, possibly, but as it is. After several days consideration, knowing that friction exists, is being rapidly intensified, and will continue to be so until the problem is solved, I have fully made up my mind that the best way is to take as an example the Australian Defence Department. It has gone through all the difficulties which I am now encountering, but a member of that Government informs me that it is now working very smoothly. I intend to approve, as nearly as possible, of the scheme adopted by the Australians, but of course local conditions must be taken into consideration. In working out this scheme, please get in consultation with the Acting Deputy Minister, the Chief of Staff, and the Director of Naval Service, to whom a copy of this memorandum is being sent.[40]

The Judge-Advocate General's memorandum was ready by the end of the month. It reviewed the Australian system, and conceded that its application to Canada would require that "the naval and military branches (the Air Service being included with the latter) each be responsible direct to the Minister . . ."; but it noted that the precondition for the successful operation of this system, satisfied in Australia, was that "the Naval and Military Forces [be], approximately, of like magnitude." It then continued:

> As far as can be ascertained, there are only two alternative methods by which such liaison and co-ordination can be systematically and easily effected:—
>
> 1. By making the Chief of Staff responsible to the Minister for the co-ordination between the Naval, Military and Air Services in respect of defence policy, and for all service matters in which more than one service is represented or concerned. In order to effect this co-ordination, there should be a Departmental Committee, of which the Chief of Staff should be the President and of which the Director of Naval Service, the Director of the Canadian Air Force, and such other officers as may be co-opted should be members. Matters concerning defence policy and service matters in which more than one service is represented or concerned would be considered by this Committee, and the Chief of Staff would be the medium of communication between the branch of the service concerned and the Minister in such matters. In all other matters not covered by the foregoing, each branch of the Service would have direct access to the Minister.
>
> 2. The alternative to (1) would be to make the Deputy Minister responsible in place of the Chief of Staff, and to give equal status in each service so that neither one would be subservient to the other. This co-ordination would be effected by a committee composed of the heads of the services, presided over by the deputy minister, but would necessitate the abolition of the appointment of Chief of Staff and the reviving of that of Chief of the General Staff as the co-ordinating military authority, and the establishment of an appointment of Chief of the Naval Staff as the co-ordinating Naval Authority.
>
> The heads of both the Naval and Military branches agree that there must be co-ordination and liaison, and that one of the two alternatives should be followed. The Chief of Staff does not concur in the second alternative, but approves of the first. The Director of the Naval Service considers that the power of control given by the first alternative to an officer of one or the other of the individual Services is fundamentally unsound and impracticable on account of his lack of technical knowledge and experience in the other Service. The Director of the Naval Service observes that the status of the two Services must be on a parity, and that this is the case in Great Britain and Australia. The Director of the Naval Service is not prepared to concur in the first alternative, but does concur in the second.
>
> One or other of these two alternatives must be adopted. There does not appear to be any middle course which it is possible to take . . .[41]

The Judge-Advocate General did not venture to recommend which of the two devices ought to be adopted.

All this told the Minister of National Defence nothing that he did not already know, and carried the affair no closer to an acceptable solution. Meanwhile, both MacBrien and Hose were pressing for a decision. "The present organization," the latter wrote to Graham on 7 March, "is, I regret to say, one most unsuitable for the proper direction of Naval Defence and entirely at variance with the Australian system which, as you state, is the best example on which to work. . . . A solution of the problem is most urgent and I beg to request that it may be dealt with as promptly as possible."[42] Whether by flipping a coin, or yielding to the pressure of the Army, Graham determined to proceed to form the Defence Committee with the Chief of Staff as President, and the Director of the Naval Staff was so informed on 7 April. The inevitable memorandum came back two days later:

> With reference to the Minister's memo. of 26th January to the Judge Advocate General, instructing him to draw up a plan based on the Australian principle, this does not appear to have been done. . . .
>
> The inclusion of "Associate members" drawn from the Department of National Defence does not seem to be necessary as Council or Committee can always call in officers of the Department to assist them in dealing with any particular matter in hand.
>
> The inclusion of Associate members from the Department of National Defence merely tends to cause an unbalanced committee with preponderating weight of one service.
>
> It may be desirable to add members to the Committee from other Departments; these would be associate members.
>
> The procedure which has been carried out for many years here has been a Defence Committee consisting of the heads of the various services. These have all been on a parity in committee and no chairman has been necessary.
>
> Members communicated items for agenda to the Secretary and he arranged with the members for a convenient date and time of meeting.
>
> The proceedings in this manner have been conducted for many years with success and harmony. No efficiency or economy is seen in changing what has proved a most satisfactory arrangement.[40]

IV

At this juncture, George Graham, doubtless without regret and probably with considerable relief, left the Department of National Defence to devote his full time to the affairs of the Department of Railways and Canals, a portfolio he had held concurrently with National Defence since 18 January 1923. He was succeeded by E. M. Macdonald, whom Mackenzie King had brought into his Cabinet in April "as a conciliatory gesture to the Maritime Provinces."[41] Macdonald had not sought to become Minister of National Defence, nor may it be said that the post sought him. According to his own account,

Mr. King came to see me and offered me the portfolio in the Government of Minister of National Defence. He said that as Mr. [W. C.] Kennedy, who had been the original Minister of Railways, had died, he was anxious that Mr. Graham, who had had experience as Minister of Railways, should take that Department. . . . I gave some thought to the matter and told him very frankly that I had no ambition to become Minister of National Defence . . . I intimated to him I thought my long party service entitled me to become a member of the Cabinet without Portfolio. . . . He said he regretted this very much indeed, but he thought that I was entitled to the recognition for my party services and he offered me the position of a member of the Privy Council of Canada without Portfolio. . . . One step led on to the other. Mr. Graham was the Minister of National Defence and Acting Minister of Railways. The responsibilities of the two Departments were very great, and I was urged by him, the Prime Minister and all my colleagues to agree to take over the position of . . . Minister of National Defence in order that each Department of government might have a Minister responsible for the administration of it. . . .[45]

E. M. Macdonald was Minister of National Defence for the next three years. In the affairs of the tiny military establishment over which he was required to preside he had no interest and of them no knowledge: it was typical that in his memoirs he referred to *Patrician* and *Patriot* as cruisers. The Director of the Naval Service naturally enough regarded Macdonald's appointment as a golden opportunity to accomplish what he had failed to secure under his predecessor, and lost no time in putting his case to him. In a memorandum of 16 May 1923, addressed to the Minister, Commodore Hose traversed the now familiar terrain, buttressing his argument with an apposite quotation from Admiral Mahan on the causes of the collapse of the French Navy:

"The immediate reason was that, to a service of a very special character, involving special exigencies, calling for special aptitudes, and consequently calling for special knowledge of its requirements in order to deal wisely with it, were applied the theories of men wholly ignorant of those requirements—men who did not even believe that they existed.

"Entirely without experimental knowledge, or any other kind of knowledge, of the conditions of sea life, they were unable to realize the obstacles to those processes by which they would build up their Navy, and according to which they proposed to handle it . . ."

"The same results," Hose concluded, "must follow to the Canadian Navy or any other Navy that is subordinated to any measure of control by Military authorities." Nearly a year went by without action. "I earnestly beg to request," the Director of the Naval Service wrote to the Minister on 9 January 1924, "that the question of the organization of the Defence Staff may be taken up in the near future, with a view to settling the existing differences of opinion. . . . Memoranda are from time to time being received by the Naval Service from the Militia Branch which indicate that it is the opinion of the Military Officers of the Defence Staff that the Naval Service Branch should act on instructions received from them. This I cannot concur in. . . ." This was followed by the most lengthy of all the documents composed by Hose on the subject, a memorandum of 17 January 1924. At long last, some action seemed to be imminent. The Director of the Naval Service secured an interview with the Minister on 29 January in which Hose explained directly to Macdonald what he regarded as the offensive features of the various Orders in Council having to do with the organization of his Department. "I am pleased to say," he reported afterwards to Desbarats, "that the Minister was kind enough to inform me that he would take immediate steps to have these Orders in Council amended."[46] That Macdonald really meant to act is evident from the minutes of the Defence Council for 31 January: "The Honourable the Minister informed the Members of Council that it was his intention to revise the various Orders in Council relating to the Organization of the Department."

But the year passed, and nothing was done. By December Commodore Hose's patience was wearing thin. The entries in his diary relate the dispiriting course of events:

10 December: Again made enquiry if Minister would see me. Reply Minister too busy at present, several out of town people waiting to see him; said he would "see me later". Have been making frequent enquiries to see Minister for last 10 days, main subjects being my memo. to him of 26th November re increased Naval appropriation, urgency of settlement of vexed question of Departmental organization and revision of certain Orders in Council . . .

13 December: Had ¾ of an hour interview with the Minister . . . Finally informed Minister I could not any longer hold myself responsible for any unfortunate occurrence which might take place owing to the unsatisfactory state of the organization of the Dept., relative to the respective status of the Navy and the Militia, and that I must press him to get the question settled before Parliament opens. Minister informed me that he intends bringing before Cabinet on Tuesday the Colonial Office memo. putting forward Admiralty proposals for Naval Staff co-operation and that he considered that that would supply the necessary opening for re-consideration of existing Orders in Council re organization of the Department.

15 December: Saw D.M. and told him of my interview with the Minister. Also told him I was very glad Minister had promised to see Cabinet with regard to Admiralty Staff Memorandum tomorrow and that he considered that would provide an opening for revising the Department's organization. I told D.M. I had made up my mind to "take the most serious step" if definite action towards settling the question of organization were not taken before Parliament opens as I was tired of protesting and continual protest without action made me and the Naval Service look ridiculous . . .

17 December: Yesterday was to have been the day Minister was to take up Adm'y staff memo. with Cabinet. Cabinet met but Minister was absent through sickness. Rotten luck.

18 December: Saw Minister this forenoon. He told me he was bringing Adm'y Staff proposals before Cabinet this p.m. . . . Gen. MacBrien was in with Minister for some time before I went in and for some reason looked very "black" as he passed me outside.

19 December: Saw D.M. this p.m. He had no news of Cabinet meeting yesterday . . .

23 December: Saw D.M. this morning. He tells me Minister has not yet been able to bring [reorganization] before Cabinet. All Cabinet meetings lately have been taken up with the Crow's Nest Pass Agreement and Cabinet has saddled our Minister with the legal phases of that question. . . .

Early in 1925, E. M. Macdonald became seriously ill, recovering sufficiently to hold on to his portfolio but not sufficiently to dispose effectively of the mounting tension within his Department. A head-on collision of the protagonists became more and more likely, as each seized on the most trivial of problems as a pretext for a conflict over principle. The organization of the Departmental Library was one of these. Late in 1924, the Chief of Staff submitted a recommendation to the Defence Council that the Director of Military Operations and Intelligence be named President of the Library Committee, which should have as its two other member representatives from the Navy and the Air Force. This position of implied inferiority the Director of the Naval Service would not accept. When a naval officer submitted a request that the Library purchase a book appropriately called *The Sea—Its History and Romance*, the Director minuted upon it: "Recommended. W.H. 13 February 1925." This drew from General MacBrien the following communication to the Deputy Minister: "Mysterious 'W.H.', the writer of minute (2), seems to be unaware of the authorisation and formation of a Departmental Library Committee. It would be wise to bring that fact forcibly to 'W.H.' 's attention soon as well as to carefully instruct him to send such communications, properly signed, to the President of the Library Board."[47] The Deputy Minister did not take kindly to this studied insult, and replied with a memorandum to the effect that the Library might suitably be administered by himself. "As the Library is a joint one for the whole Department, and is a civilian administration, this procedure should give the best results."[48] MacBrien thereupon weighed in with everything he had:

1. Formerly the Library was divided into two sections—
(i) Minister's Library (Parliamentary and reference);
(ii) General Staff Library (Military Literature).
These have always been under the direction of the D.M.O., as President of the Library Board. If you desire to take over the Ministry section of the Library I have no objection but the General Staff Library should remain under the Chief of Staff.

2. It would be quite improper for a civilian to have control of a purely military library.

3. I have been appointed Chief of Staff of the Department of National Defence and the supervision of the Library should be part of my work. If you are to take over military duties there would appear to be no need for a Chief of Staff. As stated before, I object to the Deputy Minister of this Department taking over any of the duties which properly belong to military officers.

4. The Militia Council was formed years ago to replace the Commander-in-Chief and now the Defence Council has taken its place. The chief function of the Council is to give the Minister military advice. The chief function of the Deputy Minister is to give financial advice and he should confine himself to this and leave the purely military questions to those who are specially educated and experienced in dealing with them.

5. I note that the file has come from the Naval Service so presume that the objection was raised in that Branch.[49]

Desbarats stood his ground. "The administration of the Departmental Library," he noted in reply, "is placed under the direction of the Deputy Minister by the K.R. & O. This library, while no doubt chiefly used by the Military members of the Department, is for the use of the whole Department. The choice of the Military books would naturally be determined by the Military members who are the interested parties. It hardly seems to me that the three last paragraphs of your memorandum apply to this case."[50] But MacBrien remained adamant.

The last three paras. of my letter of the 17th ultimo apply, most definitely, to this case and to all similar ones in which the direct responsibility of the military personnel to the Minister is questioned, also to those cases where it is the expressed desire of the Deputy Minister to assume Military duties. In case you are not convinced of the necessity of experienced officers dealing with military matters and still desire to assume military duties, I request that this matter be brought before the Hon. the Minister at as early a date as possible. As the principle involved is most important and a fundamental one I desire to be present when the question is placed before the Minister for his decision.[51]

Meanwhile Commodore Hose had examined this correspondence, and wrote to the Deputy Minister to say that "I am not prepared to accept the jurisdiction of the Chief of Staff Branch, Militia Service, for the Naval Section of the Departmental Library".[52] MacBrien then wrote to the Minister:

> Now that the Director of the Naval Service has definitely stated his objections to the Library Committee as authorized by the Minister of Defence and recommends a procedure of his own, the issue is simplified.
>
> The objections of the Director of the Naval Service to the organization of the Defence Department in the first instance and to every proposal since the passing of the Defence Act makes it quite clear that it is necessary for the Government to decide whether or not the Defence Act is to be repealed or the organization of the Department completed. It is now a question of whose services and advice the Government wishes to retain. It is quite evident that the two factions cannot work together.
>
> The formation of the Defence Department was commenced on my recommendation. The Defence Act was prepared by General Fiset, the Judge Advocate General and myself and came into effect on January 1st, 1923. Reorganization proceeded satisfactorily until the departure of General Fiset and the coming to the Department of Mr. Desbarats and Commodore Hose. Since then nothing has been done. The proposal for and authorization of the Library Committee is a fair example of the way things have been blocked. The Committee was approved over two months ago, and no action has been taken since, except that the Director of the Naval Service and the Deputy Minister have raised obstacles and objections.
>
> The lack of co-operation now existing and diametrically opposite views held makes it desirable in the interests of efficiency and economy for the Government to give an early decision and make a selection of personnel which can work harmoniously together.[53]

But the breaking point had not yet been reached. Somehow the Department continued to limp along, in spite of the overbearing manner of the Chief of Staff and the passive resistance of the Naval Staff. A representative of the Air Force, on MacBrien's instructions, was duly named to the Library Committee, but Commodore Hose refused to appoint a naval representative. If *The Sea—Its History and Romance* was ever purchased by the Library, it is not on its shelves to-day.

Another clash between Hose and MacBrien occurred almost a year later. In December 1925 the Director of the Naval Service took exception to the manner in which an Army officer's title appeared in a draft of a letter from the Chief of Staff to military authorities in the United Kingdom. The Deputy Minister, in response to Commodore Hose's suggestion, revised the letter, without consulting MacBrien, before sending it over to the Department of External Affairs for transmission overseas. On hearing what had been done, MacBrien almost exploded. "This case," he wrote angrily to Macdonald on 11 December, "is a fair example of the attitude of obstruction and interference pursued by the Director of the Naval Services, aided and abetted by the Deputy Minister in matters where co-operation within the Department is involved."[54] He demanded that despatch of the letter be held up until the Minister himself decided what it should say. The Director of the Naval Service was not sent a copy of MacBrien's letter to the Minister, but in due course he came across it in the official files. The allegation it contained, he wrote at once to Macdonald, "is an accusation so serious for the head of one of the fighting services to make officially against the head of another service and is at the same time so unwarranted, that I cannot permit it to rest as it stands."[55] He demanded either a retraction or an official investigation. To MacBrien, Hose wrote a restrained letter protesting only the manner in which the recommendation to delay transmission of the contentious despatch had been made: "In a case such as that of the Memorandum in question, affecting the Naval Service under my orders, and the Militia Service and Air Force under your orders, I consider that the correct procedure is for you as head of the Militia Service and Air Force, and myself as head of the Naval Service, to sign the memorandum as a joint recommendation to the Minister." The nature and method of MacBrien's reply suggest just how strained their relations had by this time become: he returned Hose's letter to him, and across it he had written: "I am not interested in what you do or do not do or in your methods of working. . . ."[56] Indeed he had become disenchanted to the point of tendering his resignation. "It is very apparent," he wrote to the Minister in June 1926,

> that no confidence is placed in me and no value attached to my recommendations by the Government. It is now more than three years ago since my advice has been taken on any important military question affecting the Department of National Defence and its organization. Any usefulness which I may possess through long training, varied experience and an intense desire to serve my Country is practically nullified by the opposition of a Civil Servant and a junior Naval Officer who is paid the same salary as I am.
>
> Within the Department my influence and usefulness are waning as it is recognized that there are stronger influences than mine prevailing. I feel that as yet I have the confidence of the Officers of the Militia, Air Force and some of the Navy. I cherish their regard more than most things in life and desire to retire before losing it. . . .[57]

This wish, at least, was granted. By the year's end, General MacBrien was seeking other employment, preferably as far away as possible from the scene of his recent frustrations. "Anxious for service in China in any rank and appointment," he cabled to the Chief of the Imperial General Staff. "Willing sail first ship."[58]

By the end of 1926, the Department of National Defence had reached a nadir of inefficiency, confounding the hopes and expectations of those who, four years earlier, had brought it into being. It was at this juncture of its history that, about to lose its senior military member, it acquired a new Minister. James Layton Ralston replaced the ailing and ineffectual Macdonald in October. Under him, friction abated and morale dramatically improved.

The resignation of General MacBrien opened the way for the abolition of the ill-fated office of Chief of Staff, Department of National Defence. An order-in-council (P.C. 827), approved on 4 May 1927, brought about this long-sought-after reform. One further step remained to make Commodore Hose's triumph complete; it was taken by an order-in-council (P.C. 372) on 7 March 1928:

> The Committee of the Privy Council, on the recommendation of the Minister of National Defence, advise that the officer holding the position of the Director of the Naval Service of Canada, under Section 9 of the Naval Service Act, 1910 (9–10 Edward VII, Chapter 43), be appointed as Chief of the Naval Staff of Canada, his duties remaining as defined in clause 2 of section 9 of the said Act.

VI

Equality of status does not guarantee equality of function. So long as the Naval Service remained small in size and unimportant for strategy, its position as an autonomous community within the defence establishment in no way subordinate to another in any aspect of its affairs was bound to remain at the mercy of any strong-willed personality in a sister-service, whatever orders-in-council might say to the contrary. The resignation of Major-General MacBrien in 1927 brought a brief respite to the Navy, which continued under Major-General H. C. Thacker when he occupied the revived post of Chief of the General Staff, Department of National Defence, during 1927 and 1928. But it was a lull before storms.

Major-General Andrew George Latta McNaughton became chief military adviser to the Government of Canada in his forty-second year. He was born in the small Saskatchewan town of Moosomin, and was educated and practised as an engineer before the Great War. During the War he commanded an artillery brigade in France, where he was Counter Battery Officer. At the end of the war he was commanding the heavy artillery of the Canadian Corps, a brigadier-general at 31. But for the entreaties of General Currie (who had leaned heavily upon McNaughton's advice and support in battle), he would most probably have returned to his civilian profession after the Armistice, but his old commander persuaded him to stay on in the Army and take a key part in the difficult tasks of postwar reorganization and planning. McNaughton spent most of the 1920's at National Defence Headquarters as Deputy Chief of the General Staff. In 1926 he attended the first course offered at the Imperial Defence College. In 1927 he assumed command of Military District No. 11, and applied to the problem of planning the defence of the Pacific Coast an intimate knowledge of the geography of British Columbia acquired when as a young engineer before the War he had travelled among its mountains and its rivers. (A quarter century later he was to apply this expertise to the problem of what to do about the immense resources of the Columbia River system.)

"Andy" McNaughton, as he was known in Army circles and to the public at large, brought to these varying assignments a questing intelligence which refused (like that of his great contemporary Charles de Gaulle) to remain within the compound of the conventional military wisdom of the day. Before audiences from Empire Clubs, Canadian Clubs, Rotary Clubs and the like he spoke his mind on such controversial subjects as the impact of scientific technology on military strategy, the proper size and composition of a Canadian defence establishment, the need for close co-ordination of the armed forces. He was no jingo general*; but his outspokenness, joined to the force of his personality and his striking appearance, drew caustic comment from those of his countrymen always ready to tarnish any brass hat that shone too brightly. "His Most Excellent Highness Brig. General A. G. L. McNaughton, C.M.G., D.S.O.," began an editorial with heavy sarcasm,

> recently issued an edict that all combatant officers of the Canadian Army must become proficient in the French language. The explanation of this is said to be that they may study the methods of warfare of Napoleon the First and thus keep the Canadian war outfit thoroughly up-to-date. It is said that the officers have not taken kindly to the edict, as they would prefer to learn Latin in order to study the methods of Julius Caesar, but

*"When any professional soldier," McNaughton remarked on one occasion, "even mentions in public the possibility of future wars he is in danger of being labelled a firebrand and is accused of promoting war for his own professional advantage. I think those of us who had experience of the last war are the most pacific people on earth and it is just because we know something of the real misery of war that we are bending our energies to making our own defence as secure as possible. . . ." Speech to the United Services Institute of Vancouver Island, 10 May 1928. McNaughton Papers.

that the edict, coming from so great a mogul, must stand even against protest from the War Department [sic] at Ottawa. . . .[59]

That sort of criticism might be borne with equanimity. It sometimes happened, however, that McNaughton's far-ranging discussions of military affairs brought a rebuke from the Department of National Defence. "Brief amplification epitomised report of your address Canadian Club Vancouver," a telegram from Ottawa reproached him in December 1928, "seems to indicate dangerous approach to statements of policy which has always given trouble and causes newspaper enquiries. . . . Take utmost care nothing approaching policy is discussed publicly without consultation and approval."[60] But such rebukes were few and far between. For McNaughton's speeches were invariably constructive; they usually enhanced the none-too-lustrous reputation of the military*; and their author was obviously destined for the most senior position in the Canadian Army. He succeeded to it on 31 December 1928.

As Chief of the General Staff, McNaughton dominated his colleagues in the military establishment as a great oak dominates a scrub forest. There was no one to match his qualifications or to rival his reputation. He was always three laps ahead of his committees. His grasp of military matters in their widest sense was sure. He had perfect confidence in his own powers. At the same time he was ready to listen to advice whatever the rank of his adviser; he seemed to be incapable of pomposity. These qualities earned him the admiration and warm regard of the Army, in two world wars and in the years between.

Such a leader, it was obvious at once, would not be content to confine his advice to army affairs only. McNaughton quickly took it upon himself to offer his opinions and exercise his authority in the realms of aerial and naval strategy. The Navy soon discovered how insubstantial were guarantees of autonomy provided by orders-in-council.

*"There is no doubt in my mind," J. W. Dafoe (certainly no militarist), had written to McNaughton after reading the text of his speech to the Canadian Club of Montreal of 10 November 1926, "that our Department of Defence in following out the programmes noted in your address is on the right lines. In this respect the very economical policy of the Department forced by the exigencies of the country may, by obliging the Department to make a secondary use of the regular educational machinery of the country, do better work than if lavish appropriations had been available, which might have induced development in overhead and pipe-clay." (Dafoe to McNaughton, 6 Dec. 1926. McNaughton Papers.) A senior officer, having been present at one of McNaughton's speeches which had provoked ill-natured comment in the press, wrote to reassure the Minister: "His audience without exception carried away a feeling that after all the militia, apart altogether from its military role, was doing good in preparing the youth of the country for citizenship. . . ." (Letter from unidentified officer to J. L. Ralston, 14 Dec. 1928. McNaughton Papers.)

"The Naval Staff," wrote Commodore Hose within two or three years of McNaughton's appointment,

would appear to have been resting in a fool's paradise in considering that their position, prestige and responsibility in the council on defence as a whole was now on a secure foundation. The idea of military superiority in defence councils seems to die hard in some minds, and of late, while the title of a super-chief is lacking, the functions of such an office have in fact been delegated to the Military Chief, and that in a manner which is so insidious that it has rendered the position of the Naval Chief even more difficult than when the Military Officer actually held the title.[61]

In J. L. Ralston and G. J. Desbarats, Minister and Deputy Minister of National Defence, the Navy had sympathetic friends on whose support they could count.* But under their successors they were not so well off. With the defeat of the Mackenzie King Government in the general election of 1930, Ralston went into opposition, and Lieutenant-Colonel D. M. Sutherland, a politician with twenty-four years of service in the active militia, became Minister of National Defence. Desbarats, who had been Deputy Minister of the Naval Service before becoming Deputy Minister of National Defence and had remained a staunch ally of Commodore Hose throughout the interservice quarrels of the 1920's, was succeeded in 1932 by another long-time militia officer, Lieutenant-Colonel L. R. LaFlèche.†

*Ralston had begun to feud with McNaughton in 1929 or 1930, and the latter was on the point of resigning. See J. W. Pickersgill, ed., *The Mackenzie King Record*, Vol. I, *1939–1944* (Toronto, 1960), p. 359.

†LaFlèche's appointment as Deputy Minister was criticized by Toronto Conservatives on the grounds that he was French-speaking and allegedly a Liberal in politics. The Prime Minister, defending the appointment, made no reference to the allegation but maintained that "since Confederation this appointment has been held by a French-speaking Canadian." (R. B. Bennett to Joe Harris, M.P., 5 Feb. 1932. Bennett Papers.) That was not strictly correct: the position of Deputy Minister, Department of National Defence, dated from 1923, not 1867, and LaFlèche had had only one predecessor in the person of G. J. Desbarats. It was true, however, that the Deputy Minister of the Department of Militia and Defence had been traditionally a French-speaking Canadian.

Years afterwards, LaFlèche's appointment was criticized by a former officer of his Department on entirely different grounds. "For some misguided reason," Lt.-Gen. Maurice Pope has written, "it has seemed to be held that the deputy head should have military experience and carry military rank. Never has there been a greater error. The deputy minister is a civil officer, and he has a civil function. It is no part of his business to give military advice to the minister. On the contrary, he is responsible for the civil administration of the department, and for finance in all its aspects. In the thirties, by reason of quite special circumstances, he was at one time practically crowded off the scene which was unfortunate, at another he had been allowed to elevate himself to a position more or less equivalent to that of a civilian chief of staff, and strove to constitute himself the channel of communication between the military staffs and the minister. . . ." *Soldiers and Politicians* (Toronto, 1962), p. 77.

Now, more than ever, the Army had the inside track. Its already dominant position was strengthened further by the close relationship which developed between the new Prime Minister and the Chief of the General Staff. Both Bennett and McNaughton were by nature energetic, autocratic, and impulsive. Had they fallen out, it would not have been surprising,* but this was a case of like attracting like. Bennett was quick to perceive and to make use of McNaughton's potent combination of inventiveness, decisiveness, and organizational ability. The military field then offering little scope for these talents, the Prime Minister employed them in non-military affairs. Thus, it was McNaughton, rather than any civilian or committee of civilians, who took charge at Bennett's request of the arrangements for the Imperial Economic Conference which met in Ottawa during the summer of 1932. His expertise in hydroelectrical and related projects led to his membership on, and domination of, the government's interdepartmental advisory committee on the St. Lawrence Seaway. In November 1932 he assumed control of unemployment relief camps throughout the Dominion. He had become perhaps the most powerful public servant in the country.

VII

Soon after becoming Prime Minister, Bennett set out for an impending Imperial Conference. Before his departure, the Chief of the Naval Staff

> made enquiries as to whether his services would be required in connection with the delegation in order to be properly prepared on the question of co-operation in naval defence.
>
> He was informed that the Prime Minister considered that Conference to be so predominantly one on political and economic questions and would refer so little to defence matters that advisers from the Department of National Defence would not be required.
>
> It was not until almost the last minute before the Delegation left Ottawa that the Chief of the Naval Staff was informed by the Chief of the General Staff that he had received instructions to the effect that he was required. The Chief of the Naval Staff was not required.
>
> As a matter of actual fact naval questions—as was well known would be the case—were brought up for discussion† and it transpired that the Chief of the General Staff took with him the proposed naval policy worked out by the Chief of the Naval Staff, presented it in London to the Canadian

*A falling out took place during the Second World War.

†Among them the suggestion of the Admiralty that oil fuel reserves—80,000 tons at Esquimalt, 30,000 tons at Halifax—be stockpiled by the Canadian Government. The suggestion was not acted on. There were consequently no reserves by September 1939.

Prime Minister and was the official adviser delegated to discuss the points with the Admiralty—in fact carried out one of the highest functions of a Chief of the Naval Staff.[62]

At this usurpation of his duties Commodore Hose was highly indignant (the more so since McNaughton was able to attend the launching of one of the Navy's new destroyers); but, as he noted afterwards, he had been presented with "what was practically a *fait accompli* and was unable to take any preventive measures." He vowed it would be different next time. It was.

Early in 1932, the Canadian Government began taking stock of its military position in preparation for the forthcoming General Disarmament Conference to be convened at Geneva under the auspices of the League of Nations. To the Chief of the Naval Staff it appeared very much as if, once more, the Government was content to allow its senior Military Adviser to speak at Geneva on behalf of all three services. To prevent this happening, Commodore Hose sought out the Minister of National Defence on 5 January; he was told "that the matter of making appointments to the Delegation was entirely in the hands of the Department of External Affairs and that no recommendations were being sent from the Department of National Defence."[63] He then sent a memorandum to O. D. Skelton, Under Secretary of State for External Affairs:

The following is submitted in the event of the Government deciding to attach any Chiefs of Staff of the Defence Services as Advisers to the Canadian Delegation to the forthcoming Disarmament Conference.

Should the Government consider it inadvisable for any Chiefs of Staff to accompany the Delegation this memorandum has no import.

In the former event I would respectfully submit that both the Chief of the General Staff and the Chief of the Naval Staff should be appointed as Advisers, and not the Chief of the General Staff alone.

At the Conference there will be a distinct Naval question which, in many of its aspects, is independent of the problem of reduction and limitation of land and air forces. Furthermore, there is an inter-Commonwealth problem in naval matters which does not arise in the case of the other two Services.[*]

The defence policy recommended for the Dominion, explained in detail for each of the three Services, will be found in the report drawn up by the inter-departmental committee appointed to enquire into and advise on the Disarmament Conference.[†] The requirements to carry out the proposed policy will also be found.

---

*The problem in question was the allocation of naval strength among the United Kingdom and the self-governing dominions of the British Commonwealth which had agreed to accept for purposes of international disarmament negotiations a single quota in tonnage afloat.

†The inter-departmental committee had been created in January 1931; its members were General McNaughton, Commodore Hose, and O. D. Skelton.

I would point out that, in the scheme of defence indicated in the Committee's report, it is distinctly shown that it takes no account of the possibility of danger from the south.

If defence measures are considered by the Government as in any way necessary for the Dominion, therefore, they must of needs visualize the possibility of danger from overseas, danger in particular to Canadian seaborne trade and danger of un-neutral acts in Canadian territorial waters, matters in which the naval policy of the Dominion is of primary importance.

The Chief of the *Naval* Staff is solely responsible for the naval side of proposed defence policy, and has reached the conclusions indicated as the result of forty years of naval service, twenty of which have been under the Canadian Government, thereby gaining extensive experience of the various national problems which have to be taken into account, under the particular conditions obtaining in Canada, before a naval policy practicable for the Dominion can be drawn up.

Furthermore, the Chief of the Naval Staff has accompanied as adviser in naval subjects, the Canadian delegates to the Imperial Conferences of 1923 and 1926, the Three Power Naval Conference of 1927 and the London Naval Conference of 1930.

I submit, therefore, that if Chiefs of Staff are required with the Canadian Delegation at the forthcoming Conference that naval advisory duties should be carried out by the Chief of the Naval Staff and not be delegated to the Chief of the General Staff who, in the nature of things, has had no naval service or experience.

To do otherwise would not be in the interest of efficiency of the Delegation and to say this is in no way a detraction from the deep respect felt for the Chief of the General Staff in his own sphere.

On the other hand, it could not but be considered by myself and by the whole of the Naval Service as a serious reflection on the capabilities, prestige and position of the Chief of the Naval Staff.[64]

This forthright document was duly laid before the Prime Minister. On 13 January the composition of the Canadian delegation was officially announced; the published announcement stated that "Mr. L. B. Pearson of [the Department of] External Affairs and Major General A. G. L. McNaughton, Chief of the General Staff, are appointed as technical advisers to the Delegation."

Here was what appeared to be a declaration of war. Commodore Hose, on learning that he had been excluded from the delegation, went immediately to the Minister of National Defence, but Colonel Sutherland could only tell him that the whole matter was being handled by the Prime Minister—which was almost certainly true. Nevertheless, the Chief of the Naval Staff extracted from the Minister of National Defence a promise that he would see the Prime Minister and put to him the Navy's point of view. A few days went by, with no result; correspondence with Sutherland convinced Hose that his Minister was at best a tepid supporter. He accordingly sought an interview with the Prime Minister. At their meeting on 20 January, Commodore Hose repeated to Bennett the argument of his memorandum, adding that the question of the appointment of one Chief of Staff if the other was appointed was really a matter of principle; he "informed the Prime Minister of something of the difficulties the naval staff had had to pass through in the Department of National Defence." Bennett replied that "he saw his point, but that he (the C.N.S.) should see Sir George Perley, the Chief of the Delegation, and that the Prime Minister would see Sir George Perley later." And so Commodore Hose went round to Perley's office, and repeated his story. Later that evening, when Hose enquired of Perley whether a final decision had been reached, he was informed that it had been reached, and that the decision was that the Chief of the Naval Staff would not accompany the Chief of the General Staff to Geneva as technical adviser to the Canadian delegation. If after the Conference opened it was discovered that the services of a naval adviser were required, Hose would be duly sent for.

This did not meet the situation at all. As Commodore Hose wrote afterwards, "there does not appear to be any reason for requiring one Chief of Staff more than another except on the grounds that one was to do duty for the Navy as well as the Militia—in fact to be a super-Chief of Staff." That, as Hose knew perfectly well, was exactly McNaughton's conception of his duty. After so many battles on the same ground, the Chief of the Naval Staff was not prepared to surrender it now. He immediately wrote a letter to the Prime Minister, slept on it overnight, re-read it in the morning, and, at 10.30 a.m. on 21 January presented to Bennett's Private Secretary the following communication:

> I beg to submit for your consideration that, as Chief of the Naval Staff, I may be appointed as a technical adviser to the Canadian delegation attending the Disarmament Conference in the same manner as the Chief of the General Staff, and that, if approval of this submission cannot be otbained in time for me to proceed by the same steamer as the Delegation, I may be permitted to proceed to Geneva by the next available ship.
>
> In accordance with your instructions I interviewed Sir George Perley in the forenoon of the 20th instant and fully explained my reasons for asking that, as regards attendance at a general disarmament conference, there should be no discrimination between the values set on the technical advice required from the Naval and Military Chiefs of Staff and particularly my objection to a Military Officer being in any way considered as a proper adviser on any matters connected with the Naval Service.
>
> Sir George Perley, in his concluding remarks to me, said—"I understand it is your opinion then, that either both Chiefs of Staff should go or none." I replied that that was the case.

I submit that the suggestion that the immediate attendance at the Conference in its opening phases by the Military Chief is essential, but that the importance or necessity of the presence of the Naval Chief is problematical and can await the development of the situation in Geneva, is not in accordance with the purposes of the Conference or with the position of the Navy in the responsibilities of National and Imperial defence requirements.

Furthermore, such a procedure, on such an occasion, does not cover the principle involved, namely, that in matters concerning defence as a whole the Chiefs of Staff of the respective services have an equal, joint and individual, responsibility.

It is true that, in my conversation with you, Sir, yesterday morning, the proposal was made by you that Sir George Perley should cable you later if he considered my presence necessary, but I thought I had quite explained to you that it was on the matter of appointment now, and the principle involved, that I was appealing to you.

I understood that you would see Sir George Perley later in the day after I had explained to him, as the Chief Delegate who was to negotiate for the Dominion at the Conference, and that you would then make your final decision.

I submit that it is in accordance with the true interests of the National Defence and the proper responsibilities of the Naval Staff therein that I earnestly prefer this request that the Chief of Staff may be immediately appointed on the staff of the Canadian Delegation to the Disarmament Conference.[65]

The Prime Minister's reply was received by Hose later that afternoon. It read:

I have your letter of the 21st instant which I have read with care.

I repeat, that if in the opinion of the Canadian Delegation your attendance at Geneva is required, I will so advise you. At present the appointment you request will not be made.[66]

The Chief of the Naval Staff thereupon drafted a letter of resignation.

But he did not send it. It happened that during the hours that Commodore Hose was debating in his own mind whether the lack of naval representation at Geneva was an issue important enough to justify so drastic a step as his resignation as Chief of the Naval Staff, his attention was diverted elsewhere. A revolution broke out in San Salvador; two Canadian destroyers on a winter cruise in the Caribbean happened to be in the vicinity of the Republic; and the Admiralty requested that they be despatched thither to protect British lives and property. They were duly sent. In Commodore Hose's words, "it appeared to the C.N.S. that he would be exceeding the requirements of his duty to request to be relieved as such a moment," and he consequently refrained from submitting his letter of resignation. This brought two or three weeks in which to think things over; and, after reflection, it seemed to him that he could better protect the autonomy of the senior Service as its Chief. So he stayed on. Events of the following year vindicated the wisdom of his decision.*

Commodore Hose did not go to Geneva after all; the Conference never got sufficiently under way. General McNaughton returned to Canada after a sojourn in Geneva of only a few weeks, leaving as sole technical adviser to the delegation Colonel H. D. G. Crerar. By April, Crerar's principal activity in that capacity consisted, as he complained in a letter to McNaughton, in joining the leader of the Canadian delegation for "12 or 14 holes of golf" in the afternoon: "I like golf, as you know, and normally I would have no objection to such a proceeding, but I feel that I need all the time I can scrape up trying to get 'into the picture' here—and so the interruption is not really welcomed. However, I have been getting back to the office at about 4.30, and working on at 'reading up' or other matters until nearly 8, when, as a rule, Pearson and I go over to the 'Bavaria' and have a cheap but satisfying meal."[67]

VIII

Modern warfare, in General McNaughton's view, required a greater degree of centralized direction than the theory and practice of Canadian defence organization allowed. By October 1932, his ideas of how the Department of National Defence ought to be reorganized had become clear in his own mind. He set them out in the form of a draft submission to the Governor-in-Council, together with an explanatory memorandum (see Document 4, pp. 335–42, below). The central recommendation of these documents was the revival of the position of Chief of Staff, Department of National Defence. McNaughton's version of this proposal differed significantly from that recommended in 1922 by Major-General MacBrien in that it did not require that the position of Chief of Staff be occupied by the senior military officer. The most senior officer of each of the three branches of the Service was to be eligible. This concession, while great in theory, amounted to very little in practice so long as the Army, by reason of its size and influence, continued to constitute the predominant part of the defence establishment. Its acceptance by the senior officers of the smaller services would be necessarily an act of faith; for not in the foreseeable future could any of them look forward to occupying the commanding heights.

In December 1932, McNaughton made his preliminary inquiries of the Navy. There was little point in trying to convert so dedicated an

*See below, Chapter VII, pp. 272–83.

apostle of service separatism as Commodore Hose. In any case, relations between the two Chiefs had become strained as a result of the "delegation episodes" of 1930 and 1932, and Hose was due for retirement in a year or two. Accordingly McNaughton sounded out his probable successor, Captain Percy Walker Nelles. Nelles did not favour McNaughton's proposal, but he was by no means inflexibly set against it, and promised that he would "fully consider the matter" and declared himself to be "open to conviction." But in less than two years time he was as implacably opposed to McNaughton's ideas as his predecessor had ever been. The reason for his change in attitude is clear enough. During the intervening months McNaughton had recommended cuts in the estimates of the Royal Canadian Navy of such drastic dimensions that, had they been accepted, the Navy could not have continued to exist.* "Can the Royal Canadian Navy," its senior officer asked rhetorically in April 1934, "look with pride and trust to a head who, as lately as 1933, tendered to the Canadian Government the advice that the Naval Service should practically be abolished, and who, now, without reference to the Naval Staff, proposes himself as head of that service?"[68] The Navy would never forget, nor forgive, that great betrayal.

The Navy's disapproval notwithstanding, the Chief of the General Staff submitted his proposals for the reorganization of the Department of National Defence to the Minister, who was inclined to be favourably disposed towards them. The Chief of the Naval Staff (Nelles had become Acting Chief early in 1934, and formally succeeded Walter Hose on 1 July) accordingly mounted a counter-attack in the form of a number of memoranda opposing the concept of a single Chief of Staff. Some extracts from these follow:

> If the C.G.S.'s recommendation is that there should be one supreme Chief of Staff (either a Naval, Military or Air Officer), to the Department of National Defence, solely responsible to the Government for the efficiency and co-ordination of the work of all three Services, I submit that such a recommendation, aside from not being in the best interests of the Naval Service, is absolutely unconstitutional and contrary to the laws of Canada. The National Defence Act, 1922, in no way alters or amends former Section 9 (now Section 7) of the Naval Service Act. This latter section can only be altered by Parliament.
>
> I am also of the opinion that such a recommendation would not be acceptable to any Canadian Naval Officer. . . .[69]

> I agree heartily with the necessity of co-ordinating the work and policy of the three splendid services comprising the Department of National

*See below, Chapter VII, pp. 274–83.

Defence, but am convinced that you have been ill-advised that the most efficient way of co-ordination is to appoint a Service Officer as the head of all three Services.

No normal officer in the services can have sufficient knowledge of the services other than his own to efficiently administer them. If there be such a capable individual available at the moment can we guarantee his successor will be equally capable and is the Government willing to legislate for an individual? . . .

Co-ordination there must be, but it must be brought about by the civilian, the Honourable the Minister, or his Deputy, who have both knowledge of Government and of Service requirements.

The object of the Navy and the practically common object of the Army and Air Force are distinctly different. The former is to provide a defence for trade and coasts and to function immediately in an emergency. The latter is to provide the training cadre for much larger forces which will be available to function as armed forces some six months after the outbreak of war.

Canada cannot afford, nor has she the need for, a large navy. She does need a Navy sufficiently large to afford some measure of immediate protection to her trade, coasts and ports, and to enforce her neutrality. The Naval Officer heading the Canadian Navy, by the Naval Service Act, must be a Rear Admiral or a Commodore. As you stated, it is absurd to imagine a Naval Officer at the Head of the Army. I agree most emphatically, but it is no more absurd than any proposal to head the Navy by a Major General or an Air Commodore . . .

Co-ordination and co-operation there must be but it will not come under one Service Chief of Staff. Though not ideal, the present organization permits of complete co-operation in the Defence Council, or failing the use of the Defence Council, then in the Joint Staff Committee.[*] By frequent use of the Joint Staff Committee we get co-ordination and the most complete co-operation by the three heads of the Services, each expert in his own Service, sitting together, meeting frequently in discussion, the co-ordination being brought about by the Chairman, the Honourable the Minister, his Deputy, or by the Senior Officer present.

---

*The Joint Staff Committee had been authorised on 9 June 1927. It consisted of the Director of the Naval Service, the Chief of the General Staff, and the Director of the Air Force (members); the Commissioner of the R.C.M.P. (associate member); the Director of Military Operations and Intelligence (Secretary). The Chairman was the Minister of National Defence or, in the Minister's absence, the Senior Officer of the three Services. Its object and terms of reference were defined as follows: "For the purpose of co-ordinating effort in pursuit of a common policy and, especially, to ensure the co-operation of the Forces (Sea, Land and Air) in the event of war or other emergency. To that end the Joint Staff Committee will advise on questions relating to organization, administration and combined training, preparation for defence, procedure, &c., mobilization and on such other questions as may be referred to it by the Naval, Military or Air Services." It was the forerunner of the Chiefs of Staff Committee created in 1939.

For a "Military" Officer to act as a single co-ordinator would be seriously curtailing or short circuiting the prerogatives of the Honourable the Minister. In December 1932 the present C.G.S. informed me that he had no objection to my having access to the Minister but that the one Chief of Staff must have direct access to the Prime Minister. . . .

The answer to our problem is simply to have a Defence Board, an organization which is already in existence as the Defence Council, or alternatively, the Joint Staff Committee. By the *use* of our present system we get co-ordination and co-operation.[70]

In practice, matters of policy are raised in Defence Council from four main aspects, the Military and Air by the Chief of the General Staff, the Naval by the Chief of the Naval Staff, and the financial by the Deputy Minister.

The responsibility of co-ordinating what may or may not be quite opposing views rests on the Honourable the Minister. Is it now the wish of the Government that this duty be taken away from the Minister?

Any fault in the present system does not lie in the organization but in the failure to use it. The last Defence Council meeting was held on 3rd December 1930. This may be due to the fact that the Honourable the Minister has so many calls upon his time, or some other reason unknown to me. . . . Whatever the cause of the failure, the result is a complete lack of co-operation, trust and co-ordinated policy between the Services. Realizing the supreme importance of co-operation, the Naval Staff is eager and anxious to co-operate in every conceivable way with the other two Services. Mutual and trusting co-operation is absolutely essential.

The lack of trust appears to be mutual, but I should like to emphasize the fact that it is difficult for one Service to trust a sister Service which has recommended the disbandment of the former to and for the advantage of itself and that without consultation of the Service concerned. . . .

If one man is chosen to be made the Super Chief of Staff of all the Services it is inevitable that sooner or later his advice will be biassed and biassed judgement is a form of dictatorship which is intolerable. The Super Chief of Staff, brought up in one Service, must have a greater understanding of and be in greater sympathy with his own service to the detriment of the other two. This inevitable partiality has shown itself in the past and will in the future, in the preparation of estimates, in allotments for training, in operations of the forces singly or combined and in ceremonial functions. . . .

I can readily understand that some Canadian Army and possibly some Canadian Air Force Officers can see no objection to the appointment of a Supreme Chief of Staff and, in all fairness, I consider that, due to the similarity of the objects and aims of their Services, there may be few concrete objections to the proposal from their point of view. The complete dissimilarity of the object of the Navy to that of the other forces must be pointed out here. . . .[71]

These forceful representations had their desired effect. No action was taken. In November 1934, a new Minister of National Defence—Grote Stirling—was appointed to succeed Colonel Sutherland; not himself an Army officer, and with a son just entering the Naval Service,* he may fairly be presumed to have been less sympathetic to General McNaughton's project than his predecessor. Six months later, McNaughton himself resigned as Chief of the General Staff to become President of the National Research Council. No more was heard thereafter of the "super-Chief" proposal, until it was revived—and implemented—in the early 1950's in the form of the post of Chairman of the Chiefs of Staff Committee.

*M. G. Stirling, in 1963 Rear-Admiral, Director of Naval Personnel, R.C.N.

VII

Depression and Depletion

NADIR OF THE NAVY

Like the Abbé Sieyès accounting for his record during the terror of the French Revolution, a Canadian officer accounting for his record during the Great Depression might have answered with no less justifiable pride, "I survived." The depression years were in truth a struggle for survival for the three services. Of the three, the Royal Canadian Navy came closest to losing it.

Forced by lack of funds and interest to become largely a land-locked reserve establishment, the Navy after four or five years in that unhappy status had suffered a sharp decline in morale, efficiency, and general *esprit*. "I regret to say," the Director of the Naval Service wrote to the Prime Minister in May 1926, "that there is undoubtedly a growing conviction right throughout the Canadian Navy that the Government takes no interest whatsoever in it, and that the hard and efficient work done by all to make it truly Canadian and really efficient is not in the least appreciated by the Cabinet."[1] Though it violated the cardinal rule imposed on officers at Staff Colleges—"Don't bleat"—the Director's complaint was well founded. There was no interest in the Navy in the Cabinet, nor indeed in the country. At the Imperial Conference later that year, Mackenzie King stated that Canada's naval policy was to develop "the local defence of the waters in the vicinity of Canadian coasts and the approaches to our ports," and to replace officers and ratings on loan from the Royal Navy by Canadian personnel.[2] But even this programme, modest as it was, could not get very far without ships.

By 1927, the sea-going part of the Canadian Navy was literally on the point of foundering. "The plates of the boilers of *Patriot*," wrote the out-going Naval Secretary, "are in very bad condition; she could go to sea for a short cruise in Eastern Canadian waters, but even so there would be some risk. The plating of *Patrician* is in better condition than that of *Patriot*, but is not satisfactory."[3] The Cabinet of that day, with one exception, might well have accepted the loss (with no hands) of these ships at sea. Fortunately for the Navy, the exception was James Layton Ralston, who had become Minister of National Defence in October 1926. "During 8 months of office," the Naval Secretary wrote in 1927, "he has shown the greatest interest in the R.C.N.; has fought through the Cabinet the request for two destroyers, to replace *Patriot* and *Patrician*, and has the intention, during the current recess, of urging the Government to accept and give to Parliament a naval policy. It will be on a small scale, but, if approved by the Government, it will be a policy—and that is the all-important feature."[4]

Urged on, indeed, driven, by the energetic Ralston, the Government proceeded with the first expansion of the Navy since the acquisition of *Patriot*, *Patrician*, and *Aurora* in 1920. The two destroyers were paid off, and the funds which were to have been used to refit them were applied instead to the modernization of two destroyers loaned by the Admiralty. These ships, which entered Canadian service as H.M.C.S. *Champlain* and H.M.C.S. *Vancouver*, were intended to tide the Navy over until its own new destroyers became operational; they remained in Canadian commission, however, until 1936.

The decision to acquire two new destroyers was taken in the face of considerable opposition. C. C. Ballantyne, Minister of the Naval Service in the Borden and Meighen administrations, thought it a waste of money to buy new ships when, as he argued, the United Kingdom would be pleased to give ships to Canada. "If you will refer to the naval debate in '19 or '20," he wrote to the Conservative leader of the opposition, R. B. Bennett,

> you will note vigorous opposition from the Liberals—Denis of Joliette stating that Canada required no naval defence of any kind as we had the protection of the Munroe [sic] Doctrine; Duff of Lunenburg and many others made similar speeches. King himself criticized the Government for accepting these ships of war from Great Britain. Now we find the same Liberal Government accepting two destroyers from England; they are not loaned to the Government although the Government may say so. The Admiralty are only too pleased to give these destroyers to Canada.
>
> Now I come to the meat of the cocoanut. The Vickers shipyard, in this city [Montreal], is owned and controlled by Liberals that stand high in the Party and it would be a nice plum for them to make a big profit by building these destroyers here. The Admiralty having a plethora of warships of all

kinds, I know from my experience as Minister, and my interviews with the Admiralty, that they would be only too pleased to give Canada the number and type of ships she would require. Why, therefore, put the Country to the expense of building here?[5]

Important opinion within the Liberal party itself was unsure of the wisdom of the decision. "I have been cogitating over the building of those two Destroyers," Raoul Dandurand, Government leader in the Senate, wrote to Mackenzie King in November 1928.

I recognize that it is our duty to protect our country on sea as on land in the measure of the perils which may loom up. . . . We must be ready to defend our Ports and Coasts, but the moment seems quite inappropriate for Canada to launch warships when you have just signed the Kellogg Peace Treaty and just after your Geneva speech.

What are our perils? They are inexistent [sic] on the Atlantic. Must we do something presently for our protection on the Pacific? You know the situation as well as myself. It is a question of confidence.

We have so far been a happy people because we were without fear. The Ten-Year Treaty with Japan has still four years to run. The Paris Pact ensures the renewal of that Treaty.

It will seem ludicrous to announce the building of warships which will mean an increased expenditure on capital account next session and a likewise increase for the maintenance and the manning.

I simply suggest an adjournment. If we proceed now, all the effect of your recent attitude, which was acclaimed by the country, will be lost. Could you not discuss this viewpoint with Ralston?[6]

But Ralston, spurred on by the Director of the Naval Service, was no less adamant in his insistence that the ships were needed. The only issue was where they should be built. The tenders from Vickers of Canada being 50 to 60 per cent higher than those of British shipyards, the Government decided to place the order in the United Kingdom. The firm of Messrs. John I. Thorneycroft was selected for the job. *Saguenay* and *Skeena* were launched less than two years later, and were commissioned in 1931. No navy in the world had better vessels of their class.

II

With *Champlain* and *Vancouver* in commission, and *Skeena* and *Saguenay* on the stocks, the Canadian Navy, after a decade of neglect, now seemed destined for a new lease of life. For the first time in many years the Naval Staff began to think of further expansion. A memorandum presented to the incoming Bennett Government by the Chief of the Naval Staff in August 1930 "urgently submitted that steps should be taken immediately, and the necessary appropriation be included in the Naval Estimates for the coming year, for the replacement of the four Trawler Minesweepers by four modern minesweeping vessels. . . ."[7] Commodore Hose elaborated this request at one of the infrequent meetings of the Defence Council, convened by the new Government on 29 August 1930:

The most vulnerable point open to attack in Canada, the point where the most vital damage could be effected to her national existence, lies in her Overseas trade. . . . In addition to the danger of attack on the focal points of Canadian trade in the vicinity of Canadian coasts, there is a danger of Canada being drawn into a state of belligerency due to her inability to undertake the obligations of neutrality through having insufficient force at hand to prevent the perpetration of unneutral acts of belligerence in Canadian territorial waters. . . .

It is not recommended that any measures should be taken to expand the Naval Defence forces to cover the protection of distant trade routes until the essentials of national responsibility of local defence is adequately covered.

It is more important to have numbers than individual unit size and offensive power. One cruiser is more than powerful enough to deal with an armed merchant raider, but her range of visibility is limited. On the other hand, 2 or 3 destroyers would render the position decidedly dangerous for a light cruiser; each would be a match for most armed raiders; and for search purposes they would cover a large radius. . . .

The Naval force considered essential to be maintained in peace time as a defensive measure to protect the focal points of Canada's overseas trade and the requirements necessary to carry out her obligations as a neutral should comprise:

1 destroyer leader, 5 destroyers, and 4 twin screw minesweepers; this force to be provided by systematic development which will insure it being truly Canadian in personnel. It is estimated that the final maintenance cost of such a force would be between four and one-half and five million dollars annually. . . .[8]

The Navy's immediate requirements were four modern minesweepers, retention of *Champlain* and *Vancouver* until the end of 1936, and an authorized increase of personnel from 896 officers and men to 1400. The Chief of the General Staff, who was present at the meeting of the Defence Council, advised it

that the problem of the maintenance of neutrality and the naval defence of Canadian Ports had been considered from the general viewpoint of what would be required from each of the three services acting in co-operation, and that the responsible officers of the Militia and Air Services endorse fully the conclusions reached by the Chief of the Naval Staff as to the composition of the Canadian Naval Force required; it is being understood that this force covered the eventuality of danger *either* on the East *or* West Coast and not on both simultaneously. . . .[9]

Such inter-service harmony was as rare as it was desirable. But it was not to last.

The dispute between General McNaughton and senior naval officers over further proposed reorganization of the Department of National Defence has been described in the preceding chapter.* The dispute over organization was accompanied and complicated by a dispute over doctrine. The Chief of the General Staff had come to believe, with many strategists of the time, that the advent of airpower had rendered obsolete many of the traditional concepts about the role of sea-power. The Canadian Navy's tasks of defending the coasts and the focal points of trade could, McNaughton felt sure, be better accomplished with the limited funds at the services' disposal from the air than from the sea. The Air Force, accordingly, should be strengthened; the Navy, accordingly, had to suffer, if necessary to disappear.

The decision of the Bennett Government in May 1933 to slash the already mutilated allowance of the defence forces by a further $3,673,023 provided the Chief of the General Staff with an opportunity to put these strategic precepts into practice. On 1 June McNaughton had an interview with the Prime Minister. "I pointed out to him," he recorded afterward,

> that the proposals as now formulated by the Treasury Board would involve the disbandment of the Royal Canadian Navy; that the money provided in the current estimates was insufficient for the Air Force, and that the amounts for the Militia Services were the absolute minimum that could be accepted having regard to the internal situation.
>
> I told him that I was preparing a memorandum for submission to the Treasury Board this afternoon to this effect; that in the conclusion I was saying that I felt the substantial reduction in funds called for could not be whitewashed across the whole three Services, but that having regard to efficiency it would be necessary to concentrate on the absolute essentials, i.e., the Militia Forces and the Air Force. . . .[10]

The concluding portion of McNaughton's memorandum read as follows:

> The situation with which we are faced involves a very large reduction in the funds to be made available for Defence and to distribute these reductions over all the Forces would result in weakness everywhere. In consequence it is my opinion that the whole question must be reviewed and that we must narrow our purpose in defence to
>
> (a) the forces necessary for the maintenance and support of the Civil Power;
>
> (b) the creation of a minimum deterrent to seaborne attack. . . .

---

*See above, pp. 260–68.

With regard to (b), any naval force less than that recommended in August, 1930 [i.e., 1 destroyer leader, 5 destroyers, 4 twin-screw minesweepers], could not be considered adequate. Moreover it is of the nature of naval forces that they cannot be rapidly expanded to meet emergencies and, in consequence, it seems to me that little purpose is served in maintaining a small nucleus.

On the other hand Air Forces even in small numbers are a definite deterrent in narrow waters and on the high seas in the vicinity of the shore; they can be developed with considerable rapidity provided a nucleus of skilled personnel in a suitable training organization is in existence; pilots engaged in civil aviation can be quickly adapted to defence purposes; civil aircraft are not without value in defence, and any aircraft manufacturing facilities are equally available to meet military as well as civil requirements. That is, from a comparatively small current expenditure a considerable deterrent can be created in a relatively short time, and this is particularly the case in Canada where aviation plays a large part in the economic life of the country, a part which is increasing naturally at a rapid rate.

This being so it appears to me that the most important element in defence which should be retained is the nucleus Air Force. . . .[11]

The Government accepted McNaughton's advice. It was decided that of the proposed cut of $3,673,023 from the funds of the three Services, the Navy would have to bear the loss of $2,000,000. As the Navy's estimates had been previously set at $2,422,000, the sum remaining to it was so small as to mean the virtual disbanding of the Service. It was not enough, indeed, to pay off the men.

The delicate task of communicating the news of the Navy's prospective demise to the Chief of the Naval Staff was undertaken by McNaughton, who met with Commodore Hose and placed before him the recommendation of the Treasury Board that " 'the maintenance of the Ships and Establishments' of the Naval Service should be conducted on the sum of $422,000."[12] To no one's great surprise, Commodore Hose indignantly rejected the suggestion. "I regret to have to state," he wrote to the Minister, "that as 'a basis of discussion', such a proposal is entirely outside the realm of practicality for many reasons which it is unnecessary to set forth in detail, since the single fact that one-sixth of the year for which an appropriation of $2,422,000 was granted has already transpired, results in practically no funds being available for the remainder of the financial year."[13] In a further memorandum the Chief of Naval Staff sought to provide the R.C.N. with some strategic justification:

1. On the 29th August 1930 the policy which had governed the direction of the Naval Service in its plans and operations for the preceding ten years was laid before the Honourable the Minister of National Defence in Defence Council was approved at that time by the Council.

2. The Chief of the General Staff expressed himself as being in entire accord with this policy and stated that while the Militia needed many requirements for its proper development, he felt that the primary need for defence was the bringing up of the Navy to the standard suggested by the Chief of the Naval Staff and in fact that, if he had any difference of opinion, it was to the effect that instead of a total of six destroyers, we needed six destroyers on each coast.

3. I am now informed by the Chief of the General Staff that his advice to the Government differs materially from the policy approved by the Defence Council three years ago and from the same policy which was accepted by the Right Honourable the Prime Minister at the Imperial Conference of 1930.

4. In view of this change of opinion on the part of the Chief of the General Staff I feel that it is incumbent upon me to review briefly the above Naval Policy and to state the conditions which, in Naval opinion, absolutely militate against the safeness of a reliance upon military and air force defence to the exclusion of a properly effective naval force, in the event of financial conditions being such that all three services cannot be brought up to the standard requisite for a properly balanced and effective defence force.

5. First, the fortunate geographical situation of the Dominion, 6,000 miles away from any possible enemy on one side, and 3,000 miles on the other, renders the possibility of territorial attack from overseas negligible.

6. On the other hand, the attack on Canadian trade, while, thanks to the aforesaid geographical situation, in a comparatively less dangerous position to that of other countries, since the main naval forces of any overseas enemy would be occupied with more important duties; still, the volume of Canadian overseas trade, amounting to approximately $3,000,000 on the ocean every day of the year, would be sufficient to warrant attack by light enemy forces.

7. Such an attack, if not properly countered, at the focal points of trade off Canadian coasts, would paralyze Canadian industry.

8. This clearly demonstrates that from the point of view of defence of Canadian national life from enemy attack our trade and not our territory is the real object to be defended and the focal points of that maritime commerce of Canadian coasts is the truly vulnerable link in the chain of our economic and industrial life.

9. There are three factors which govern the minimum size of the Canadian Navy.

10. The first and most important is being an effective instrument to ensure the country not being drawn into any outside war.

11. This is particularly important in the possible case of the United States being embroiled with any overseas power and can only be effected by a sufficiently powerful but, at the same time, a very moderate naval force with air patrols acting in conjunction and military coast watching.

12. The second factor is in the unfortunate event of being drawn into war, and consists of the defence of the focal points of trade above mentioned.

13. The third factor is that no navy, any more than any industrial concern, can be run effectively or economically, below a certain minimum size. If reduced below this minimum the industrial output in the latter case, and the defence output in the former, are not sufficient to warrant the overhead involved.

14. In this connection, or perhaps as a fourth factor, it must be emphasized that a navy cannot be improvised at short notice. It differs very materially from the air force and the militia in this respect.

15. With reference to the neutrality patrol, this cannot be effectively carried out over territorial waters by aircraft attended by sea-going tenders and without a definite naval force.

16. There are many periods, and particularly in winter time long periods, during which air reconnaissance directed against delinquent belligerents cannot be effected; and speaking as a naval officer, especially in a submarine desiring to utilize neutral harbours for replenishment or rest before making an attack or depredations along the United States coast, no air force would be any deterrent, though it might delay the action desired by the submarine. The utilization of periods unsuited for air work would be a matter of no difficulty.

17. In the event of enemy submarines conducting depredations along the United States coast, naval opinion in that country and, what is perhaps more important, public opinion, would undoubtedly credit the enemy vessel with having made use surreptitiously of neutral harbours and, without doubt, the United States would feel that purely airplane patrol without properly effective naval forces, was insufficient to prevent such a happening and would be practically driven to establishing such a patrol on our coasts, thereby themselves infringing our neutrality with the inevitable result that we should either be embroiled with them or be treated by the United States' enemy as a belligerent.

18. With respect to the second factor, namely the defence of the focal points of our trade; a properly equipped raider would be able to operate on the focal points of our trade without being brought to book by any air force. It is impracticable at most times for air craft to examine and board any vessel in the open sea.

19. Merchant shipping would sooner or later be organized into convoys and aircraft cannot afford the necessary convoy escort.

20. Again, as a naval officer, I have to state that no air force without effective naval forces could act as any deterrent to the menace and attack of Canadian shipping at the focal points of trade.[14]

On each of these points McNaughton furnished the Minister with his own observations, mostly in disagreement:

1. Yes.

2. Yes. The C.G.S. was of the view that the minimum Naval Force which would be of use was 6 destroyers, and consequent on the difficulty and long delay in moving ships from one coast to the other, that a force of this size would be desirable on each coast.

3. No. The advice now given by the C.G.S. is based on a restricted thesis. In 1930 the defence not only of the coasts but also of the focal points of maritime trade was contemplated. With the drastic reduction in votes, and the certainty that no adequate naval force will be provided, it is necessary to relinquish the idea of defending the focal points and to concentrate whatever resources there are on the more vital problems of the creation of a deterrent

to attack, or to the violation of our territorial waters if we should be neutral in a war between the U.S.A. and a Far Eastern or European Power.

The Navy is required absolutely if we undertake defence of focal points. It is not absolutely essential for the other and more important aspect of the problem. For this the Air Force presents a much less expensive though probably not a complete solution; there may be occasional minor incidents which cannot be provided against.

4. No change of opinion by C.G.S. The C.N.S. is considering a case which has now become purely hypothetical and which is indicated to be quite outside the bounds of practical solution. The C.G.S. does not propose to tilt at windmills, but to give first place and adequate attention to what is vital, not to divert force to secondary objects clearly unattainable.

5. No territorial attack is possible without a period of warning of some months. It is on this thesis that the idea of nucleus forces capable of rapid expansion is predicated. The Naval Force cannot expand appreciably in the period likely to be available.

6. To protect this trade would involve large sea forces. The C.N.S. does not propose this, which even in 1930 was clearly beyond our resources. He wishes to defend focal points, but this also is now beyond our powers. To be practicable, we must draw the lines of defence still closer in.

7. Probably for a time, but in our case with a long open land boundary with a friendly power the danger is not vital.

8. No.

9. —

10. 1st. Very desirable but not essential.

11. The Canadian Navy is said to require trips to southern waters for training. They are liable to cause incidents there. They are strong enough to provoke trouble, but too weak to meet it when far away from the support of the Air Force.

12. 2nd. See above. We can now not expect to be able to defend the focal points. It is better to concentrate on the vital points which we can cover with the means which are indicated will be available.

13. 3rd. Agree. The Navy is now too small for efficiency. With further reduction it cannot expect to make any appreciable contribution to defence.

14. 4th. Agree. This is one reason why it is useless to keep a nucleus navy.

15. A matter of opinion. I disagree, although I would like a naval force to support the Air if sufficient funds were available. In any event the Air can provide a large measure of protection to our neutral position, and a very definite and probably sufficient deterrent to its infringement.

16. Agree. No form of defence, air, land or sea, either separately or in combination, is completely proof. The Air alone and in moderate strength is better by far than a small Air Force and an inadequate Navy.

17. I do not agree. I believe the Air can create an adequate deterrent; there will be incidents of course but not many.

18. A properly equipped raider will operate anyway in the face of any Navy we can contemplate with the resources indicated.

19. Even the larger naval forces contemplated in 1930 make no real provision for escort duty.

20. Naval tradition. A matter of opinion not borne out by post war experience in Chile, Dutch East Indies, etc., where naval forces have fallen before the lowest scales of air attack.[15]

III

The lines were now clearly drawn, and a showdown was as clearly inevitable. It was not long in coming. On the morning of Friday, 23 June 1933, Commodore Hose received a message that his presence was desired at a meeting that afternoon of the Treasury Board in the office of the Minister of Finance. In consultation with two of his officers, he decided that "I should bring this vexed question to a head and write a strong protest to the Minister."[16] He thereupon drafted the third of three memoranda defending the Navy's position. (The two preceding had dealt, respectively, with the financial and strategical aspects; this dealt with the constitutional aspect.) It read as follows:

With reference to the suggested reductions in the Estimates for National Defence and in particular those relating to the Naval Service; discussions between myself, the Deputy Minister and the Chief of the General Staff elicited a statement from the latter that he had given advice to the Government on the subject.

This advice was to the effect that in the event of sufficient funds for properly effective Naval, Military and Air Forces respectively being unavailable the Service of the least value was that of the Navy, and that sacrifices must be made in that Force first; further, that with an effective Air Force and Militia a sufficient deterrent would be provided against aggressive action on our coasts. I have already forwarded some brief remarks on the strategical aspect and do not propose to enlarge upon them at this time. I have, however, to protest most strongly against the tendering of advice by one Chief of Staff on matters of defence which affect the status of the Navy in the whole scheme of national defence.

By the provision of Order in Council P.C. 1252 of the 20th June 1922, a Defence Council was created. The duties of this council were prescribed as being:—"To advise the Minister on all matters of defence, including or relating to the Militia, the Military, Naval and Air Services of Canada, and on all matters referred to it by the Minister". The fact that the Chief of the General Staff has advised the Government and that this advice has not been made the subject of consideration by the Defence Council has the effect of nullifying the whole purpose of the above-mentioned Order in Council.

In doing this it creates an absolutely impossible position for the Chief of the Naval Staff and indicates a lack of confidence by the Government in him as a responsible officer to tender advice on national defence, even though the problem is one in which maritime security with its naval responsibilities is a vital factor.

In view of the advice which the Chief of the General Staff informed me that he had tendered to the Government it is very difficult to avoid a connection between that advice and the proposals for reduction forwarded from the Treasury Board, which are tantamount to the abolition of the Naval Service.

The present situation could have well been avoided by the proper convening of the Defence Council for the purpose for which it was created, and it is only by adherance to the principle actuating the provisions of Order in Council P.C. 1252 that any Chief of the Naval Staff is in a position to accept the responsibilities incumbent upon his position.[17]

This memorandum, Commodore Hose wrote afterwards, "was only typed in time to send it by special messenger so that it was received by the Minister in the hallway of the East Block, Parliament Buildings, as he was on his way to the Treasury Board meeting. The Minister read it there in my presence but made no comment."[18]

The crucial confrontation between the Treasury Board and the Chief of the Naval Staff took place almost immediately after Commodore Hose completed his memorandum for the Minister of National Defence. The following is his account of what transpired:

After a short wait in the anteroom of the office of the Minister of Finance, I was, rather to my surprise, called in first to appear before the Treasury Board.

The members present were Sir George Perley in the Chair, Mr. Guthrie (Minister of Justice), Dr. Manion (Minister of Railways and Canals), Mr. Duranleau (Minister of Marine and Fisheries) and Dr. Sutherland (Minister of National Defence); also Mr. Ronson, Secretary of the Treasury Board.

Sir George Perley commenced by saying that he had noticed in my memorandum that I had stated the Navy could not surrender more than $200,000, and by impressing upon me that $14,000,000 had *got* to be saved in all from the various Government Departments, and asking how it was that the Navy could not economise to a greater extent.

I informed him that our estimates had already been cut three times and that further reductions were impossible without impairing efficiency to an extent which would render it most uneconomical to run the Navy at all as overhead charges would be out of all proportion to the output of defence value. I further said that the Service was not in a state of sea-going and fighting efficiency at present and could not stand any further impairment.

He said that all departments would have to suffer in efficiency and asked me what I would do if the Prime Minister issued an edict that $600,000 *was to come off*.

I said that I regretted I should have to state that I had been told to do the impossible and that I could not possibly accept any responsibility for proper conduct of the Service.

"Do you mean", said Sir George, "that in such an event you would resign?"

I said that Sir George had put a very serious question to me and that on my own initiative at this juncture I would never resort to such an expression.

He said he understood that but that he desired to know if I should feel compelled to resign.

I then said that the only answer I could give to such a categorical question was in the affirmative, my reasons being that I was convinced that any further reductions beyond what I had carefully worked out were bound to result in such inefficiency and such demoralisation of the personnel that there was bound to be disaster; that if I continued to hold office and to draw my salary I should still be responsible for the good order and proper conduct of the service and could not evade my share, and a big share, of condemnation for accepting a situation which I had realized would result in the collapse of discipline and morale and probably danger to life.

Sir George was good enough to say that he realized I had not raised any issue of resignation.

Dr. Manion then reminded me that ten years previously I had accepted a much bigger cut than 25% and had made up my mind to buckle to and do the best possible, and asked me if it would not be a more patriotic thing to do that now rather than "say that you will quit."

Dr. Sutherland then intervened and said that was hardly putting the Commodore's attitude fairly.

Dr. Manion said that perhaps he had spoken more brusquely than he had meant and he did not intend in the least to be nasty, all he wished was to ask if I could not see my way to adopting the same attitude to-day as I did ten years before.

I informed him that the reason I could not do so was because the conditions in the Service were very different now to what they were then.

At that time (1922 really) when we were arbitrarily cut from 2½ to 1½ million dollars we had the *Aurora*, *Patriot*, *Patrician* and two submarines presented by the Admiralty. Our total complement was only 500, of which 450 were drawn from England and only 50 young Canadians.

To-day we had ships which had cost the Canadian taxpayers some seven or eight million dollars, that our complement was nearly 900 in the permanent force and that 850 of these were Canadians who had devoted their life and training to the Service.

Dr. Manion expressed himself as entirely satisfied with the answer but still wished to know why we could not "lay up the ships for a bit."

I informed him that you could not lay up ships and at the same time keep the men trained and told him, as one of many examples of the vital importance of training, how the torpedo armament of each of our new destroyers consisted of eight torpedo tubes, that each torpedo cost $12,000 and that torpedo practice with both ships meant risking nearly $200,000 unless the torpedo ratings were highly trained in the intricate work of adjusting and caring for the torpedoes.

I also mentioned the skill and practice required in manoeuvring destroyers in close order and at high speed.

Dr. Manion threw up his hands and said "I'm convinced. You've made a clear case to me. I have nothing more to say."

However, he did in the course of further remarks, say that he was a pacifist but regretted that in the present state of international affairs it appeared inevitable to have some defence.

This gave me the opportunity to expound the policy which had governed naval plans and operations for the last twelve years and governed them today, and I laid particular strength on the fact that the Naval force we desired was, under existing conditions, the most necessary guarantee against being drawn into war in the not impossible event of war between the U.S.A. and Japan. That, without an effective naval patrol to prevent the perpetration by belligerents of un-neutral acts on our Pacific Coast, Canada, and consequently the British Commonwealth, would be most certainly drawn into a war which *might* otherwise be avoided.

Finally, I stressed that our destroyers were a component part of a very limited destroyer tonnage for the whole British Commonwealth and that the parity the Commonwealth had conceded to the next greatest naval power would be less than parity unless all units were maintained in a state of seagoing and fighting efficiency.

Consequently, I contended that, if the Dominion Government was not in a position to maintain the destroyer force we possessed in a proper condition, negotiations should be entered into with the British Government regarding transfer of the ships and a certain proportion of our personnel.

Sir George Perley was pleased to say that I had made a perfectly clear case and proposed to the remainder of the Board that it was impracticable to reduce the naval appropriation beyond $200,000 and that otherwise the only course would be to negotiate with the British Government with a view to handing over our vessels to them.

The Treasury Board agreed unanimously.

I may say that in my opinion there is not the faintest chance of the Government proposing to hand over the ships and men to the Admiralty—far too big a political issue would be raised, and the outcome resolves itself into our having to effect savings of $200,000, not $2,000,000.

There was, as a matter of fact, much more cross questioning than I have indicated but the above were the most important points.

The Board thanked me for my exposition of the naval case and as I left Sir George Perley said—"Well, Commodore, you have put it all over us. Now you had better go and find that Admiral and give him a drink!"[19]

The subject of Perley's parting remark was Admiral R. A. R. Plunkett-Ernle-Erle-Drax, Commander-in-Chief of the America and West Indies Station, Royal Navy, who, fortunately for the Royal Canadian Navy, was visiting Ottawa at the time its future was in jeopardy. Commodore Hose had not hesitated to take advantage of his presence in order to fortify his case against the proposed ruinous reduction of the estimates. "Your visit and your remarks to members of the Government," Commodore Hose wrote to him afterwards, "were certainly most opportune." He added the following details about his interrogation by the

Treasury Board, in addition to those contained in the foregoing memorandum, of which he also sent the Admiral a copy:

The three dominating points in the long cross-questioning I had at the hands of the Treasury Board on Friday were:—

1. The grave question put to me by Sir George Perley as to the action I should take if arbitrary instructions were issued to take $600,000 (25%) off our appropriation. Any hedging on this would certainly have resulted in those instructions being issued.

In this connection, thank Heavens the suggested amount was as high as $600,000; if they had been more moderate and suggested $300,000, i.e., $100,000 more than what I had said I could do, I should have been in a much more difficult position.

2. The answer I was able to give to Dr. Manion as to why I was able to meet the Government in 1922 and not now.

My answer to that had to be very convincing as otherwise—and I feel sure it was in the back of their minds—one would have had the Navy accused of a political bias. (The 1922 incident was under a Liberal administration.)

3. The point concerning the Canadian Naval forces being a part of the naval strength of the British Commonwealth. A point you had stressed earlier with Sir George and had clearly impressed him with.

I should have no objection to you apprising the Admiralty confidentially of the situation if you feel that it would serve a useful purpose to render them au fait with the conditions under which we have to operate.

I am so sorry not to be able to accept your kind invitation for Wednesday but I dare not leave here as, although we have got our fish in, I cannot feel absolutely safe until he is gaffed. In other words, until we have the official communication from the Treasury Board which will not be until all Government Departments have been through the process of squeezing in order to extract a total of $14,000,000. . . . I hope and believe that I shall not have occasion to write and tell you that my optimism is ill-founded.[20]

Nor was it ill-founded. The vote for the Naval Service, as finally approved by the Treasury Board and passed by the House of Commons, was $2,222,000. Canada was to continue to have a navy after all. But it had been a close call.

IV

Though defeated by the Chief of the Naval Staff on this occasion, the Chief of the General Staff did not alter his views on the dispensability of the Naval Service under conditions of financial stringency, and on his right and duty to tender advice to the Government on strategy in its broadest aspects. In September 1934, following Hose's retirement as Chief of the Naval Staff, McNaughton impressed his ideas upon the visiting Admiral of the Fleet Sir Roger Keyes. "I told the Admiral," his memorandum of their conversation records,

that our present position was that we had two destroyers, one modern and one semi-modern, at Esquimalt, and that we did not see any possibility of reinforcing this squadron during a state of tension; that these vessels were quite inadequate to give us a naval means of meeting the problems which would be presented either in a war of defence or in the maintenance of neutrality; that there was very little likelihood in my opinion of the very large sums of money required to build up the naval service to the point where it might be useful. In this connection we had thought that we should have on the Pacific coast at least a flotilla of five or six modern destroyers together with sloops and other auxiliary vessels. On the other hand the air development in Canada was proceeding naturally and would shortly provide a very considerable air force distributed throughout the Dominion which could, over the Trans-Canada Airway, be concentrated on the Pacific Coast at short notice; that if we analysed our problems of defence on the Pacific coast, it would appear that they were all in the category of defence in "narrow waters" and on that account we felt that they could be handled by aircraft. . . .[21]

A few weeks later, he expressed similar views at a meeting of the Canadian Institute of International Affairs in Ottawa. "It was pretty well agreed," a transcript of his remarks on that occasion records,

except perhaps in certain naval circles, that the growing power of the air arm had made it impossible for the Navy to act collectively in what were termed narrow waters. . . . It was no longer possible for large naval forces to act effectively within a radius of some 400 to 500 miles of shore-based aircraft in reasonable numbers.
. . . In view of the relative wealth, resources and manpower of the United States and Japan, it was impossible for Canada to make provision for an effective measure of naval defence. On the other hand there was a possibility of turning our natural air development to good account in the way of defence, and if we concentrated our efforts to this end it seemed not unlikely that we could at least provide an effective deterrent to hostile action in our own narrow waters. We could not defend our trade routes as this task required prohibitively large naval forces. Nor could we effectively defend focal points of trade as even for this the naval forces required were clearly beyond our means. But in our narrow waters, which of necessity had to be entered by an enemy who desired to attack our territory, we had a means of defence in air action supported by minor naval forces.[22]

And in 1935, General McNaughton underlined, with evident approval, the following pasage from the "Service Notes" of the *Army, Navy & Air Force Gazette*:

. . . in the case of South Africa, a different policy of defence has evolved. . . . She discards a Navy altogether, places her ports in a state of defence and takes to the air. And is not a similar policy suitable to all the other Dominions too? . . . And would not imperial solidarity be better preserved if we once more assumed the position of being able to guard our Empire by taking that position in the air which is forever lost on the sea? . . .[23]

The view that Canada could not afford, or did not require, a Navy of its own was held as well in less exalted circles. At the Third Annual Meeting of the Conference of Defence Associations, meeting in Ottawa in November 1934, Colonel George Drew urged the delegates to deal with defence policy in its broadest aspects. "While we have been discussing the question of what artillery, cavalry and infantry units could be changed to another unit, Germany is re-arming, France has about doubled her hitting power, and the same thing applies all the world over, while we are sitting around wondering whether a certain unit will be happy in its new uniform." After advocating increased expenditure upon the Royal Canadian Air Force, Colonel Drew turned his attention to the future of the Navy.

Is the navy we have to-day any use? The answer must necessarily be "No". We have four destroyers, and it seems to me that no one can say that these destroyers would not be utterly ineffective in defending our coasts against any specific enemy. They would meet capital ships and the destroyers that we have would be utterly ineffective against them.

Then as to taking part in the general Empire naval picture, I am of opinion that they could not be used for convoy purposes.

Then, as an aid to the Customs enforcement, I am satisfied that the destroyers we have are much too big for this purpose. . . .

Well, if my criticism of the picture is correct, I am afraid that we must admit that the naval equipment we have today is nothing but a salve to our patriotism and a gesture to the British Empire. My own idea . . . is that we either have too much or too little in the way of ships. . . .

Supposing we had no ships in Canada to-day; that we had not a single man in the Canadian Navy. Does anyone suppose that we would recommend the purchase of four destroyers as the basis of our naval establishment? . . . I think a few modern aircraft of flying boats, manned by the Navy, capable of carrying torpedoes, would be infinitely more powerful than the destroyers we have to-day. . . .

I think that the Naval Service of Canada, until such time as Canada is prepared to spend real money on capital ships, would be of the best service to the Nation by making some arrangements with His Majesty's Navy for the transfer of these destroyers to the United Kingdom, and in their place we spend quite a substantial sum on the maintenance of modern, up-to-date flying boats and surface craft. . . .[24]

In Colonel Drew's audience were two senior Naval officers, present as observers only for the Navy was not formally represented in the

Conference. Lieutenant-Commander E. C. Sherwood attempted to ward off Drew's attack:

Colonel Drew has said that capital ships would be used for raiding. In the last war, there were no capital ships used for raiding, and the destroyers did do convoy work.

If you had seaplanes looking after the coast defence, how would you board a ship? I do not know whether a seaplane can do that or not, especially in bad weather. . . .

With regard to the cost of training in the present Navy, I would suggest that if you gave us more money it would be greatly improved. You must remember that it takes seven years to make a sailor against three for a soldier. . . .[25]

The second naval officer present was the Chief of the Naval Staff himself. "I do speak with great diffidence," Commodore Nelles declared, "and I only do so because I have been invited to by the Chairman." But there was nothing diffident about the forthright defence he proceeded to deliver:

As for my Navy, I may tell you that the Navy is just as well organized to-day, and its duties are just as efficiently carried out, as they ever were. There is no reorganization necessary in the Navy, it is merely the lack of money that keeps it as small as it is. . . .

Colonel Drew raised the question of destroyers not being capable of working against capital ships. I may as well tell you that there are no capital ships coming to Canada. As far as we can see it at present, if war is between Japan and England, then the attack by capital ships would be on Singapore, and possibly our West Coast by smaller craft. If between Japan and the United States, then we might get capital ships on our coasts, but we would be neutral. I put it to you, however, that destroyers are the very finest ship for defence or attack within our means. Submarines would be a very effective help, but a submarine force is a very expensive service. . . .

I agree with Colonel Drew that it would be a tremendous advantage to have many more aircraft, flying boats and convertibles, but they cannot take the place of naval craft. You can take surface craft many places in bad weather where aircraft would find it very difficult to go. Also while aircraft can sight an enemy raider very much quicker than surface craft, they cannot identify or stop them. I think the functions of the Navy and the Air Force could be co-ordinated, but they cannot be undertaken one for the other. You cannot lay or sweep for mines with aircraft. . . .

There is no doubt about it. Canada has not a sufficient naval force, but as long as we have money we can go ahead. In any event, four destroyers are at least a good start, and we must have a beginning. . . .

I speak to you not in the spirit of criticism, but rather to advise. I told you that the R.C.N.V.R. are not members [of the Conference of Defence Associations] but they do meet in conference, and I suggest, with apologies, that it would not be within their province to suggest the reorganization of the Army or the Air Force, and if such a resolution were passed I would not permit it to stand. I expect, however, that this is but an honest endeavour to improve the defence forces of this country. I do say, however, that this is not the right Association to suggest that the Navy be reorganized, and you can be perfectly sure that the Naval Staff, both in Ottawa and on the Coasts, are striving just as hard as every other Service to get one hundred per cent value for their money.

Finally, I want to say that we in the Navy look for and hope that we will get your assistance, your co-operation and your sympathy, just as much as we, on our side, try to co-operate and assist you.[26]

This intervention stilled further debate on the future of the Navy, though not the Navy's displeasure at what it held to be an unwarranted attack. "Defence Council is proper place for discussion," Commander Sherwood noted afterwards. . . . [Defence] associations can be used to disseminate Dept.'s view to lower ranks—not to be used as lever against other Services."[27]

The resignation in 1935 of General McNaughton as Chief of the General Staff removed for the time being the most influential advocate of air power at the expense of sea power; his successors were not as sure as he that the Navy had outlived its usefulness, and in any case lacked his great prestige and powers of persuasion. Estimates prepared by the Bennett Government for 1935–36 allowed the Naval Service $2,395,000; the following year it had more than double that amount at its disposal. The increasing likelihood of a general European war, and of Canada's involvement in that war, assured the Navy of an important role in the coming conflict. But the Royal Canadian Navy never forgot, and never forgave, the Army's efforts to get rid of it.

VICISSITUDES OF THE R.C.A.F.

The Royal Canadian Air Force, though it did not come quite so close to extinction as its sister Service, experienced its share of tribulations during the depression years.

Their impact made itself felt first in the estimates for civil aviation, which for 1932 were cut back $244,000 from the $2,500,000 voted for 1931. The Minister of National Defence tried to put the best face on this reduction, which he attributed mainly to the transfer of air protection services to the prairie provinces along with their natural resources; though the strength of the permanent air force would be lower by eight officers and twenty-three other ranks than that of the preceding year, no personnel were being dismissed.[28] But behind the scenes the cut had a demoralizing effect, as the following extracts from R.C.A.F. reports to the liaison officer in London make clear:

16 June 1931: . . . A feeling of uncertainty exists throughout the whole of civil aviation owing to the drastic measures of retrenchment which have taken place. We are even having difficulty in obtaining maps for operations owing to lack of funds in the Departments concerned. . . .
30 June: The air Estimates came up in the House and were passed without a hitch. The Opposition even went so far as to complain that the Air Estimates were being cut to the detriment of Aviation generally, Civil Aviation in particular. . . . We hope to get up a barrack building at Trenton this year, but at present the Government is devoting all its time to the depression and to the Western drought. . . .
19 December: . . . judging from the protests received, most of our officers are being intellectually starved to death from lack of manuals. . . .
1 February 1932: . . . The aircraft manufacturers here had a conference with the Premier the other day and presented a petition asking for orders. They stated that they had been invited to enter Canada and start work and the Government would be in a position to give them assistance. The Premier, however, comes from Missouri whenever anyone wants money. He stated that the Government's commitments were in heavy difficulties due to the reductions in revenue, and he refused to permit the Air Service to spend the money authorized by Parliament for the purchase of aircraft.
Therefore, no orders have been placed and it is doubtful if any will be; but the Department is asking for tenders for 23 Fleets, 6 Tutor 626, all without engines, and 28 inverted Gypsies.
Fleet has had the Kinner taken out and an inverted Gypsy fitted in place. . . . There was difficulty with the propeller . . .
In spite of all this, it is fully expected that the Treasury will be advised that the funds allocated for aircraft can be counted as unexpended revenue and returned. . . .[29]

Austerity was now the order of the day. Interspersed at regular intervals among the files of National Defence Headquarters for 1931–33 are the chits by which its senior members meticulously indicated the disposition of street car tickets for transportation between the Woods Building and the various ports of call on official business in the capital. Any extra expenditure, however slight the project or small the amount, came before the Chief of the General Staff for his personal consideration and decision. "I think that the O.C. [Camp Borden] has made a case for the dish washing machine, the mixing machine, and the toaster, in addition to the bread slicer," General McNaughton wrote to the Quartermaster General on 23 March 1931, "and that on its merit this proposal should be approved."[30] Less fortunate was a proposal that the men's barracks at Borden should be converted into officers' quarters. The Minister "thinks that after the 1st May [the officers] should be able to manage under canvas for six months," a General Staff officer wrote plaintively to McNaughton in January 1932, "and that, in the meantime, they must shift as they are at present. If the personnel attending training courses . . . cannot be furnished with improvised accommodation, then he says some of the courses must be cancelled. . . ."[31] A few days later he reported that "a proposal is now being put before the Minister to fix up the interior of the Men's Barrack Block and kitchen accommodation at a cost of about $6,000. . . . This seems a reasonable solution of the difficulty, but it is possible the Minister may not sanction the spending of even this amount of money just now."[32] And, on 9 February: "The Minister continues resolutely to refuse to authorize any expenditure which he thinks can be postponed. Consequently no real progress has been made regarding the fixing up of accommodation for the Air Force officers at Camp Borden. . . ."[33]

The reason for the Minister's hesitation in approving any additional expenditures was disclosed soon enough. On 17 February senior officers at the Department of National Defence learned with dismay that the Government had presented to the House of Commons drastically reduced estimates for the Army and Air Force. The money available for both military and civil aviation throughout 1932–33 was only $1,750,000, as against $5,232,000 for the preceding fiscal year. The Director of Military Operations and Intelligence cabled this distressing news to the Chief of the General Staff, then in Geneva for the Disarmament Conference: "Department officials not consulted before these reductions submitted to House. . . . Appears all C.G.A.O. activities must cease. Discharge of all but 9 of total of the 79 non-permanent air officers authorized by Minister this morning. . . . Reduction in air sub staff may be necessary. Suggest your recall to Minister but he is not inclined to be precipitate in this matter."[34] A cable the following day told General McNaughton of the "discharge of the remaining 9 Non-Permanent Air Officers plus 100 Air Force other ranks. . . . No change in the situation regarding your recall. . . ."[35] On 19 February, Colonel Matthews got off a letter to McNaughton telling him in more detail of what had happened:

. . . the Departmental Estimates as submitted to the House of Commons have taken us completely by surprise, even the D.M. apparently had no inkling as to how deeply the axe would be applied. Since then, of course, there has been much discussion of ways and means, and I cannot help feeling it is most unfortunate that you are not here to assert your influence and authority. I fear that there is great danger of much of the Signal Corps activities in connection with Civil Government Air Operations, Air Mail Routes, etc., going by the board, as a result of these economies, and that much of the work which you have put into it for a number of years past may be wasted.

I cabled you on February 17th and again on February 18th in Government code in order that you might have some idea of what was going on. Today nothing very definite has transpired and there is little that I can add to those cables which would be of value. Several times since the Estimates were brought down I have endeavoured to make my position clear to the Minister in the presence of the Deputy, and as I said before I think it is most unfortunate that you are not here at the present time. . . .

The Air Force, of course, is entirely shot to pieces, and I cannot help feeling that probably more sub-staff personnel will have to be discharged in order to keep within the limits of the estimates provided for next year.

So far nothing has happened in the press to indicate what pressure may be brought to bear by the commercial aviation interests to provide some money in a supplementary vote to continue some sort of C.G.A.O. in the N.W.T. The Minister's opinion seems to be that no supplementary vote will be authorized for any of the services. . . .[36]

The Chief of the General Staff was naturally gravely concerned at these developments and angered that the cuts had been made in his absence and without any consultation. "Feel great anxiety and concern reductions Air Force," he cabled Matthews, "which appear involve effectiveness this organization both civil military. Cable substance revised programme. Express Minister respectful request no irreparable action will be taken until I can return to present case myself."[37] Matthews cabled in reply:

Your request conveyed personally to Minister and importance emphasized. Revised air programme contemplates distribution complete vote $1,750,000 as follows: civil aviation $190,000, aeronautical engineers $15,000, Air Force including Civil Government Air Operations $1,545,000. Estimate this allotment Air Force will provide full pay and allowances 100 permanent officers and 600 airmen and 5,000 hours flying. This arrangement only possible on account of reserve stock gasoline on hand. Only bare amount left for upkeep of equipment. Division reduced flying time between Air Force and Civil Government Air Operations not yet definitely settled. $85,000 unfinished contracts Trenton allowed for; if exceeded may necessitate further reductions airmen. Plan contemplates closing of outside Air Force and Civil Government Air Operations stations to care-taking basis and concentrating all officers and men at Borden with possibly detachment Ottawa. . . .[38]

Meanwhile, the Government's sudden dismissal of the airmen had created something of a furore. On 19 February fifty of the dismissed officers and two hundred or so airmen offered their services to the Chinese Government in its struggle against Japan in Manchuria. They presented their offer in a signed memorandum to the Chinese Consul

General at Ottawa, who promised to transmit it immediately to Nanking. The memorandum stated that because of the Canadian Government's decision to reduce the air estimates so drastically for the coming fiscal year, there would be enough unemployed Canadian aviators to furnish two complete air squadrons for Chinese defence, and that in the absence of any declaration of war between China and Japan their enlistment in the Chinese service would be wholly legal. Whose idea the scheme may have been is uncertain, but it was a shrewd stroke for it publicized the plight of the dismissed airmen in a way nothing else could have done. "To the Press," commented the R.C.A.F. officer reporting the incident to the liaison officer in London, "the mere fact that the R.C.A.F. had been wrecked was an unfortunate incident, but that R.C.A.F. officers, in order to earn their bread and butter, were willing to go to China, was news. And so the R.C.A.F. got on to the Front Page, and stayed there for two weeks. . . ."[39] On the evening of the day that their offer became known, J. L. Ralston attempted to move the adjournment of the House of Commons "to discuss a definite matter of urgent public importance in connection with the dismissal of between two and three hundred officers and men of the Royal Canadian Air Force without regard to their families, their overseas service or period of enlistment, and the embarrassing situation which may arise if they are forced by the necessity of employment to accept service with another nation."[40] The Speaker ruled the attempt out of order, but a few days later Ralston delivered what an official of the Department of National Defence described as "a slashing attack on the Government" for its "absolute brutal and ruthless cut or dismissal regardless of salaries, contracts, abilities and responsibilities."[41] The Government, however, was able to show that there had been no violation of contract in the airmen's dismissal, and the Minister of National Defence, D. M. Sutherland, responded to Ralston's assault with a counter-attack no less slashing:

> In bringing this matter before the House the hon. gentleman has not had the interests of the Air Force at heart; it is simply an effort at self-glorification and an attempt to gather part of the advertising which the Chinese situation has been receiving. . . .
>
> The Government is faced undoubtedly with a very difficult situation, and every minister who has charge of a department has had to do his share in meeting it. A Minister is in this position: many people think that I, for instance, represent in the House the Department of National Defence, the navy, the army and the air force. I do not do that. I represent the people of Canada in dealing with those branches. When a question of this kind arises, the rights of the country as a whole must be borne in mind as against

those of the Defence Department, and therefore there can be no doubt as to what the decision must be. If there is a portion of the Department of National Defence the maintenance of which cannot be justified at a time when there are men, women and children having difficulty in getting enough to eat and wear, that portion must go, and when it is part of the air force that can be spared at this time, it must go. . . .[42]

In the event none of the officers or men offering their services to the Chinese Government ever went to the Far East. Five airmen who had gone previously to Shanghai on their own account were stranded there and had to be brought back at Canadian government expense. The Canadian trade commissioner in Shanghai reported to the Government that there was "absolutely no chance of employment,"[43] and this assessment, repeated in the House of Commons by the Prime Minister, discouraged any airmen who might otherwise have set out. On 1 March the R.C.A.F. liaison officer in London was informed by his colleague in Ottawa that the Chinese affair had "all blown over by now. Some of the lads will join the Mounties and most will have a pretty thin time."[44] On 17 March: "Things are just at a dead standstill awaiting the return of the C.G.S. This means we have not yet adopted a policy regarding training or any other subject; there is still no flying and everything has ceased."[45] And on 31 March:

If I could give you any news I would, but there isn't any. If our future lay in our hands, I have no doubt that we would form a policy, give the orders, and at the instant of zero we would start. Most of us here are hoping that we will be moving towards a scheme of definite military training, army co-op., naval co-op., bombing, fighting, etc.; but what can mere would-be warriors do when outside influences want us to fly the air mail?

After extended observation and inquiry of politicians, rail-roaders, busmen and the like, the general supposition which is prevalent is that our cut was due to the following:

(a) The C.N.R. is costing the country about $1.5 million in deficit per week.

(b) Even Perry's busses, who have asked for mail contracts, to be delivered at post offices along the bus routes, were told by the P.O. that its orders were to give all it could to the C.N.R. The Inter-Colonial busses offered a better service and cheaper rates—but the C.N.R. must be up-held.

(c) A commercial operator spoke to a Big Political Gun about the situation, and the B.P.G. who seemed to understand the situation replied: "Did you ever hear that the railroads are losing money?" He went on to say that the official view among the Big Political Guns of the C.N.R. and the Government was that the railways were the arteries of Canadian life, while the air mail, the Air Force and the airmen were flashy luxuries. So the air part is in hock, and the railroads are still losing money. . . .

As for us—that is, the R.C.A.F. and the C.G.A.O.—the long practice the junior staff have had in twiddling thumbs has made us expert in the art. Some of us are even trying it on our toes.[46]

The account of these events conveyed by the Canadian liaison officer in London to the Air Ministry was, understandably enough, more optimistic. "There is no reason why this curtailment should entail the wiping out of either the Royal Canadian Air Force, or the almost certain extension of the Aircraft Industry," Squadron Leader T. A. Lawrence wrote to the Chief of the Air Staff of the Royal Air Force on 29 March 1932. "The Permanent Service will, I feel, weather the storm, and the Aircraft Industry in Canada supplies practically all the demands of commercial aviation and should find the latter an outlet for the time being. The status of the Non-Permanent R.C.A.F. Officers was always a more or less precarious one, and these officers were originally taken on, on the understanding that their services might be dispensed with at the pleasure of the Government, at any time."[47] This was putting the best face on the matter. But that is what liaison officers are for.

The Chief of the General Staff returned from Geneva in March 1932, too late to do anything to cause the Government to change its mind about the Estimates for 1932–33. The next battle was to be over the Estimates for 1933–34. It began in December 1932, on a gloomy enough note. "The Honourable the Minister instructed me this morning in respect of Draft Estimates for the coming fiscal year," the Deputy Minister of the Department of National Defence, Colonel LaFlèche wrote to McNaughton on 19 December. "There is nothing of particular moment in respect of Militia Services, but the Minister desires that a very appreciable reduction, say about $1,000,000, be made in proposed estimates for Air Services."[48] McNaughton, however, had other ideas; and was evidently successful in making them prevail. He reported to LaFlèche on 1 December:

The Air Force Estimates were further discussed this afternoon by the Hon. the Minister, the S.A.O. [Senior Air Officer] and myself, and in accordance with his decision the following action is being taken:
I. The cost of flying for other Government Departments including the proposals for new Air Route developments in connection with the Atlantic Services is being separated from the Votes for our own Services. The cost of the Radio Beacon at St. Hubert, approximately $23,000, will be included in this Section.
II. The total for the Air Force and Civil Aviation has been fixed by the Hon. the Minister at $2,250,000, i.e., an increase of $500,000 over the votes of 1932–33.[49]

That was a promising start. The problem was now to keep the figure at the higher level, and this could not be done. On 6 February 1933, General McNaughton reported to the Minister:

> The estimates to cover the real and proper requirements of the Air Force and Civil Aviation for 1933–34 amounted to $2,387,000 which is an increase of $637,000 over the funds provided last year.
>
> In accordance with instructions these estimates were in the course of revision downwards in an endeavour to create a balanced programme at a figure not exceeding $1,750,000, the amount provided last year; before the figures for this were available, a further reduction of $150,000 was notified.
>
> The situation now is that $1,600,000 has been included in the Main Estimates to cover the R.C.A.F. and Civil Aviation. The estimates for Civil Aviation submitted in the amount of $224,600 have now been reviewed . . . and reduced to approximately $100,400. The amount provided for Civil Aviation last year was $195,000, and assuming that the estimates of the current year can be reduced to this figure the amount available for the R.C.A.F. would be $1,405,000, which compares with $1,555,000 provided for the current year, or a net decrease of $150,000. It was only possible to carry on the Service with the funds provided last year, i.e., $1,555,000, on account of the reserves of equipment, gas and oil and other supplies available from the previous year; these reserves are now substantially exhausted.
>
> The estimates for the R.C.A.F. submitted provide for a small increase in the Permanent Air Force working establishment; the additional training required to maintain the efficiency of the Service; a limited purchase of stores and equipment necessary to maintain and operate the aircraft on hand, and to purchase a few additional aircraft urgently required for training; for the further construction at Trenton to make it possible to vacate Borden and to consolidate the training establishment at Trenton; certain expenditures on the development of the aerodrome at Winnipeg, and preliminary expenses in connection with the organization of the non-Permanent Air Force; also the additional expenses to cover the cost of flying operations to be undertaken by other Government Departments.
>
> After reviewing the situation with S.A.O., it has been agreed to recommend that the following savings should be effected:
> [Details follow, with a total savings of $445,000]
>
> The above represent the very maximum reductions from the draft estimates as submitted which can be recommended, and if these figures are accepted it will be necessary to have a Supplementary Vote for $175,000.
>
> If this is approved, it will not be necessary to discharge any officers, airmen or civilians presently on strength; the entry of young officers will be restricted from 10 to 4, and of airmen from 47 to 34, which numbers are below requirements for replacement of wastage.
>
> All barrack and aerodrome construction, other than what can be effected in relief of unemployment, will be abandoned, and the amount available for Engineer Service will be restricted to below the bare essentials of maintenance.

The purchase of aircraft will be limited to 2 to meet an urgent training requirement.

A small amount has been retained to cover the preliminary organization expenses of the Non-Permanent Active Air Force but no provision has been included for their flying training.

A limited course for Civil Pilots in Air Navigation and Instrument Flying has been retained but the personnel will receive no pay or allowance or transportation expenses.

The result will be that at the best the standard of flying and of technical equipment will be maintained but no progress can be expected. To do this the present small reserves of stores and equipment must be used up.

In the foregoing no mention has been made of flying operations for other Government Departments the cost of which last year was met from funds provided in the estimates of the several Departments concerned. The approved programme required an expenditure for the R.C.A.F. to meet out of pocket costs only of $137,000, and a special supplementary appropriation for this purpose will be required. It is recommended that authority be given to proceed to the preparation of detailed estimates on the basis of Supplementaries as follows:

R.C.A.F.	$175,000
C.G.A.O.	$137,000
Total	$312,000[50]

A fortnight later, the Senior Air Officer, in a memorandum for the Minister, added his own plea for an additional appropriation:

We beg to draw to your attention the fact that owing to the reduced Air Force estimates for the last two years, there are presently no aircraft available which are fit to operate on patrol duties on the Pacific.

We have 5 Vancouvers requiring overhaul, reengineering and modification which could be made available for this service at an approximate cost of $20,000 each, including fitting of wireless, bomb racks and machine gun mountings (for which the craft have been designed) and the provision of a limited supply of ammunition none of which is presently available in Canada.

As regards engines, 3 Wasp engines additional to the stock on hand will be required; estimated cost $25,000, making a total cost of $175,000. . . .

It is recommended accordingly that a sum of $175,000 be made available to meet this urgent and immediate requirement.[51]

But neither the Minister nor the Government was in any mood to furnish funds for Supplementary Estimates, however urgently the Services required them. They decided, instead, to cut a further $14,000,000 from the Budget for 1933–34, in what was optimistically described as "controllable expenditure." How this cut was to be borne by the armed forces had yet to be determined; in the meanwhile, they were to spend as little as possible. An order-in-council (P.C. 612, 31 March 1933) provided that "a direction be issued to all Officers of the Public Service to the effect that, pending receipt of official notification of the application of such reductions, no expenditure shall be made or commitment incurred, whether chargeable to an item in the estimates or a continuing statutory authority, unless it be strictly unavoidable to meet immediate needs." This augured ill for the R.C.A.F.'s proposed supplementaries. General McNaughton discussed these with the Prime Minister by telephone on 18 April. "I advised him," he wrote later, "that the two supplementaries that we were putting forward were absolutely essential; that the Vote as it stood represented 97% fixed charges, and that there was no possibility of a properly balanced training programme or of the carrying out of any of the important flying for other Government departments unless the supplementaries in question were approved."[52] But Bennett was unmoved. Instead of the $137,000 requested for Civil Government Air Operations, the Government allowed $97,000; instead of the $175,000 requested by the R.C.A.F., it allowed nothing at all. The latter refusal drew an anguished memorandum from the Senior Air Officer. "The effect on the Royal Canadian Air Force of the non-approval of the Supplementary Estimate for $175,000 which was requested to provide funds essential for the maintenance of the Force," it declared, "is viewed with concern."

2. The drastic reduction of the Force in March 1932, in consequence of the reduction of the votes for "Aviation" from $5,442,000 to $1,750,000 disorganized the Force and necessitated a complete reorganization, but this could not be made really effective on account of shortage of funds, so the Force marked time for the fiscal year except in respect of such air operations for civil government departments as were made possible by the Departments concerned providing the necessary funds.

3. The further reduction in 1933–34 Main Estimates from $1,750,000 to $1,600,000 has all come off the Air Force primary allotment, and in consequence the Force at present has 97% of its appropriation committed to fixed charges. The remaining 3% is barely sufficient for expenses incidental to administration, leaving no funds for essential matters which, if not provided for, will further cripple the Force to such an extent that recovery will take years.

These "essential matters" were then listed and discussed in order of priority: appointment to commissions in the permanent force of at least five previously trained officers of the non-permanent force; enlistment of thirty-four airmen to make good a deficiency that existed in essential technical trades; commencement of a flying training course;

enlistment and training of twenty apprentices; flying training of existing personnel; organization of Non-Permanent squadrons; naval and army co-operation and aeronautical development; advanced training of twenty civil pilots and eight civil air engineers; purchase of two modern training aircraft for service trials. The memorandum concluded with some figures to illustrate the effect of the "drastic reduction" upon the operations of the R.C.A.F.:

Service flying in fiscal year 1931–32 (exclusive of civil government operations)	23,245 hours
Service flying in 1932–33 (This amount was possible under the reduced appropriation by depletion of stocks of supplies and equipment)	6,868 hours
Service Flying provided for in Main Estimates 1933–34	1,200 hours
Service flying that would have been provided for by the Supplementary Estimate for $175,000	5,670 hours.[53]

Instead of assistance, the R.C.A.F. received only a suggestion for further economy. This took the form of the letter of 30 May 1933 from the Secretary of the Treasury Board to the Minister of National Defence, enclosing the Board's scheme of "proposed reductions in controllable expenditure, which have been suggested as a basis of discussion," to a total amount of $13,432,287. Of this sum, the Aviation estimate was to provide $100,000, made up as follows: 5 per cent of the cost of personnel, $5,000; 10 per cent of the balance (i.e., 10 per cent of cost of personnel less $5,000), $30,000; and an arbitrarily assessed "further reduction" of $65,000. That the Treasury Board's suggested cut was no more than $100,000 had been due, of course, to McNaughton's own counsel that the Navy was the most dispensable of the fighting Services and should therefore bear the brunt of financial sacrifice.* But McNaughton was apparently determined to fight on all fronts: his reply to the Treasury Board's request for his opinion as to the effect of the proposed reductions upon the efficiency of the R.C.A.F. was strongly pessimistic:

1. 5% cost of personnel ($5,000) . . . cannot be done without impairing the Service as the Air Force has already been reduced by the reduction of

*See above, pp. 277–9.

the vote in 1932–33 below the minimum necessary for an efficient Air Force organization.

2. 10% of balance of vote ($30,000) . . . can only be effected by further reduction of personnel to the extent of 3 officers, 8 airmen and 3 civilians. . . .

3. Further reduction ($65,000) . . . would have to be spread throughout the Service, reducing all units still further below efficient working strength, and would affect the carrying out of work from various units for Civil Government departments. . . .

The situation has been carefully reviewed with the purpose of effecting every economy consistent with the maintenance of the minimum strength and efficiency required; and having regard to all factors, it is recommended that an *additional* amount of $175,000 should be provided for the current year.[54]

But McNaughton did not get an additional $175,000 for his beloved air force. He was not even allowed to absorb the $100,000 cut suggested by the Treasury Board. By the time Government laid down its hatchet, a total of $195,000 had been chopped from the aviation vote of $1,600,000. The $1,405,000 available for both military and civil air operations in the fiscal year 1933–34 was the lowest in the history of the air force since the earliest days of the Air Board.

Though it had not been threatened, as its sister Service had been, with virtual extinction, the R.C.A.F. in the event suffered even more than the R.C.N. as the result of the curtailment of its funds to one-quarter of what they had been two years earlier. Under the circumstances the best it could do was to wait for better days. Military flying ceased, government flying all but ceased. In October 1933, the Assistant Senior Air Officer, Group Captain G. O. Johnson, addressed himself to the future of the Force in a memorandum prepared for (and minuted upon by) the Chief of the General Staff:

1. During the past and current fiscal years, the limited appropriations provided for the Royal Canadian Air Force have so restricted activities that little progress has been made in manning, training and equipping the Force for its proper function as an arm of the Defence Forces of Canada.

2. The policy has been to restrict activities in order to retain the maximum number of trained personnel so that they will be available, when conditions improve, to form the nuclei of the permanent units and formations which are necessary for the air defence of this country.

3. The Royal Canadian Air Force and the Department are frequently criticized in the Press for not having any Air Force squadrons equipped and trained for service, but the situation cannot be appreciably improved on the appropriation of $1,405,000 which is the sum available for the current year.

4. Complete elimination of Civil Government operations would release some personnel for employment in Service units, but such a course would be

detrimental to the public interest, and would deprive the Force of a very practical field for the flying training of personnel.

5. Before estimates for 1934–35 can be prepared, an indication of policy is necessary, the courses of action being:—

(*a*) A considerable increase in appropriations to provide for the manning, equipping and training of essential service units as outlined in para. 6 below.

(*b*) Continuation of the present policy of curtailing activities to retain personnel on appropriations insufficient to provide for (a). This has been the policy for the past two years and the morale of the Force has suffered considerably thereby. Furthermore, it has broken the continuity of personnel intake, which will affect the Force for many years.

(*c*) Reduction and re-organization of the Force to a basis proportionate to the current appropriation. This would necessitate elimination of all Civil Government operations and the closing of the Winnipeg and Ottawa units.

6. I recommend that policy (*a*) be adopted and that 1934–35 estimates should provide for the following as a minimum:

1 Flying Boat squadron located for the present at Vancouver, pending development of a station on Vancouver Island suitably located, to be the base of a coastal reconnaissance squadron.

> [*Minute by General McNaughton*: Machines available being modified and proposal will include re-equipping with Wright engines. Concur.]

. . .

1 Flying Boat squadron to be located at Dartmouth; the station to be reconstructed on a basis suitable for permanent occupation. . . .

> [*Minute by General McNaughton*: Concur. The use of Dartmouth will mean bringing machines and Permanent body to Ottawa each year.]

1 Fighter Squadron consisting of a Headquarters and two flights to be located at St. Hubert. . . .

> [*Minute by General McNaughton*: Not at present. 1 Flight presently at St. Hubert for Air Mail to remain there as it seems unlikely that during next year we will be able to hand over this work. The Flight of fighters at Trenton should remain.]

1 Army Co-operation Squadron consisting of a Headquarters and two flights to be located at Ottawa . . .

> [*Minute by General McNaughton*: For next year A.C. Flight to remain at Trenton]

1 Bomber Flight to be located at Winnipeg, and to be the nucleus of a Bomber Squadron. The R.C.A.F. has no Bomber unit at the present time, and a start should be made in this regard. . . .

> [*Minute by General McNaughton*: Arranged for next year should remain as a detachment for operations with strength dictated by the work in sight]

1 Training Group located at Trenton. . . .

> [*Minute by General McNaughton*: We should plan to shift from Borden to Trenton]

1 Test and Development Flight located at Ottawa.

> [*Minute by General McNaughton*: As at present][55]

The extent of the disarray into which the R.C.A.F. had fallen as the result of the policy of parsimony of the past two or three years was indicated further in a memorandum by Group Captain Johnson on "Service Aircraft in the R.C.A.F.," prepared for McNaughton in March 1934. "There is only one modern Service aeroplane in Canada," the Group Captain reported. "It is a Hawker Audax, the property of the Royal Air Force, on loan to the R.C.A.F. for one year for winter trials." The minimum aircraft requirements for peacetime he summarized as follows:

	First line	*Second line*	*Total*
Fighter aircraft	12	–	12
Army co-op. aircraft	12	18	30
Bombers	12	6	18
Flying boats	10	–	10
	46	24	70

Against these requirements the R.C.A.F. could muster the following:

	First line	*Second line*	*Total*
Fighter aircraft	–	9	9
Army co-op. aircraft	–	5	5
Bombers	–	–	–
Flying boats	–	5	5
	–	19	19

Nor did numbers (or lack of numbers) alone tell the story. The "second-line" aircraft available might more accurately be described as third- or fourth-line. The nine fighter aircraft were the elderly Siskins, which the R.A.F. had introduced in 1924 and had altogether discarded by 1932. Of the nine, only one had any armament; two were two-seaters used for instruction; one was badly damaged; and the remaining five had no service equipment of any kind and needed modifications at an estimated cost of $3,000 each to bring them up to the level of second-line aircraft. The Army co-operation aircraft were Avro Atlases, described by Group Captain Johnson as "moderately satisfactory as second line aircraft" but requiring a great deal of maintenance as the result of their wooden construction. The five flying boats consisted of civil government Vancouvers converted by more powerful engines and service equipment into "satisfactory" second-line aircraft suitable for medium-range coastal reconnaissance and instruction, but powerless to defend themselves against carrier-borne fighters.[56]

That in its drive for economy the government had become uneconomical, at least so far as the air force was concerned, was recognized by the Minister of National Defence in the House of Commons on 16 March 1934, when he presented the R.C.A.F. estimates for 1934–35 to the amount of $1,805,000, an increase of $400,000 over the preceding year. Asked to account for the increase, the Minister replied:

I think most hon. members will agree that the air force estimates have been reduced most drastically during the last three or four years since I have been head of the Department. Two years ago we had to let out quite a large number of the personnel to make the vote possible. Since then the vote was reduced again and everyone concerned was of the opinion that it would be a very false move to let out further personnel. Consequently there was not really enough money in the last vote to get the full benefit of the air force as we had it. We had too much personnel for the amount of money—that is, to allow them to fly. As a matter of fact, they were grounded too much, as the expression is, and it must be realized that, granted that we are to have an air force, we must have more money for them to operate. There will be some new planes purchased, and everything that goes with them in the way of apparatus and equipment to assist in the training.[57]

This statement marked the turning of the tide. Never again were the fortunes of the nation's air power at such a low ebb. But the tide came in slowly. In May 1934, the Senior Air Officer, Group Captain G. M. Croil, reported to the Chief of the General Staff that "at the present time the R.C.A.F. is not in a position to put even one completely equipped service Flight into the field in the event of a national emergency, and although this may be a serious admission to make, it must be accepted as an actual statement of fact."[58] A year later, the Chief of the General Staff, soon to resign the post, argued in one of his last memoranda for the strengthening of the country's air defences. If war came, General McNaughton reasoned, there would be time enough for the Army to expand to the dimensions of an Expeditionary Force; but for the Air Force there would be no breathing spell.

The outbreak of hostilities under present conditions would to-day, possibly, and tomorrow, probably, be signalized by an immediate attack by air. Indeed, such an attack might be made before a formal declaration of war had been made. It is conceivable that attempted air attack from an aircraft carrier might not be kept secret, but direct attack (by trans-oceanic flight) could easily be kept secret as the destination of aircraft cannot be gauged as can that of a Naval or Military Force. Therefore, there would not be time for any Canadian Air Force to expand in sufficient time to meet an attack. . . .

The R.C.A.F. lacked sufficient equipment and manpower adequately to perform even one of its three functions of co-operating with the navy, co-operating with the army, and defending the coasts and home territory. Its personnel, McNaughton recommended, should accordingly be raised from 1,157 officers and men to 2,329 officers and men. "I fully appreciate," he concluded,

the responsibility I have assumed in not requesting greater provision for the Land Forces at this time, and I do so primarily because I believe that the most urgent requirement is to lay the basis of the Air Force organization which is essential to our defence on the Pacific Coast in the particular contingency which I regard as the most probable, namely, the defence of our neutrality in a war in which the U.S.A. might be engaged with a Trans-Pacific Power. It seems that in this event we would be friendly to the U.S.A. and that our liabilities would be restricted to the enforcement, against the Japanese, of the Rules of Neutrality prescribed by the Treaty of 1872 and also by the Hague. Failure to do so will result in the occupation by the United States of the coast of British Columbia and of our islands in the Pacific, following the precedent established in the Great War when the Allied Powers took possession of parts of Greece, and also in consequence of the fact that it will be vital to the safety of the great cities on the Pacific Coast of the United States that no enemy submarines and aircraft bases be established within effective radius of action.

The requirements for Forces sufficient to discharge our obligations for the maintenance of our neutrality in the West are neither extensive nor very costly, and it seems to me that by their absence we are taking a risk to our future wholly disproportionate to the interests we have at stake.[59]

These arguments commended themselves to the Bennett Government, with the result that part of its legacy to the new Administration which took office in October 1935 was a $4,302,900 vote for the Royal Canadian Air Force.

MALNUTRITION IN THE MILITIA

The militia under Meighen had not fared very well; that it would fare worse under Mackenzie King became plain enough during the course of the election campaign of 1921. Returning from the hustings in the Maritimes, the future Prime Minister of Canada alighted from his train at Levis, Quebec, for a few minutes' walk before continuing the trip back to Ottawa. Strolling on the jetty, he was astonished to observe quantities of shells and other munitions of war being unloaded from a freighter into boxcars. Perhaps more delighted than astonished, for a splendid roorback was now his for the taking. He wrote at once to the Prime Minister—and also to the Press, wherein the Prime Minister first read it—demanding answers to a number of questions the formulation of which was designed to impress their reader with the notion that there existed some heinous conspiracy for the conversion of Canada, without the consent of Canadians, into a vast munitions dump to serve the sinister purposes of imperialism.*

It is clear, both from the tone of Mackenzie King's letter to Meighen and from its inordinate length—inordinate even for its author—that King thought he was on to a good thing. It is clear, also, that its publication six weeks before the general election both nettled and alarmed its recipient. Meighen lost no time in replying publicly to his rival's letter which, he declared, "has not yet reached me, its publication being evidently deemed more important to you than its communication to myself," and promised an immediate and explicit disclosure of the facts in the case so as to remove "from the public mind the wholly erroneous impression which your letter is designed to convey."[60] He turned to the Chief of the General Staff for the explanation, which was soon forthcoming. No ammunition or war equipment of any kind, Major-General MacBrien stated, was purchased by Canada since the end of the war. The ammunition which Mackenzie King had seen in the course of his perambulation on the Levis jetty was the equivalent of that in the possession of the Canadian Corps at the time of the Armistice, and was being returned to Canada by agreement between the two Governments. In receipt of this reassuring information, Meighen made it available to Mackenzie King (and the Canadian public) in a crushing rejoinder.[61] But King, not Meighen, had correctly judged the temper of the times; and King, not Meighen, was Prime Minister at the end of the year. He never was persuaded that the facts were as Meighen had stated them. A year later he wrote to his newly appointed High Commissioner in London:

> Nothing will convince me that behind the shiploads of munitions which have come to this country since the War there are not payments chargeable to Canada which there has been every effort to conceal. I would like to have had the power to go into this whole matter under Royal Commission, but it would involve the Commission conducting part of its inquiry in Britain and interrogating officers of the British Government which would probably have been strongly resented had it been attempted, and I thought it wise therefore not to press the matter further. . . . My impression is that it will be found that we have been charged on the books of the Treasury for the munitions thus supplied; that this charge has been made against a credit which should stand in Canada's name. In all probability, on every shipment profits have been realized. . . .[62]

---

*Most of Mackenzie King's letter to Meighen—and of Meighen's reply—is given in Roger Graham, *Arthur Meighen*, vol. II, *And Fortune Fled, 1920–1927* (Toronto, 1963), pp. 122–26.

No such discovery was ever made, for the sufficient reason that there was no infamy to discover. If the "Levis episode" had any infamous aspect, it was other than its creator thought. So far from the Dominion's arsenals bulging with ammunition, the truth was that even after the recovery of the Canadian Corps' stockpile Canadian reserves were dangerously low. As a memorandum from the Militia Department pointed out in 1921, "When all ammunition and shipments are received from England, the reserve in Canada will be 500 rounds per gun which constitutes one day's supply. . . . It would be unwise to give this statement to the public as it would show how weak our position really is."[63]

On coming to power in December 1921, the Liberal Government inherited from the preceding Meighen Administration a militia vote of $11,016,939. One of its first acts was to reduce the militia estimates for 1922–23 to $9,797,406. It did not prove possible to meet its military obligations with this reduced sum, and there was accordingly a certain manipulation of departmental funds which did not, however, escape the watchful eye of the Opposition. "I happened to learn the other night from a Militia officer in this city," wrote the former Minister of the Naval Service, C. C. Ballantyne, to Arthur Meighen from Montreal on 26 December 1922,

> that the Government are spending some $300,000 more on the militia than the estimates voted by Parliament last session. It appears that the Government found that they could not maintain even the skeleton of the Militia with their altogether too small vote, which they were forced by their own members to reduce last session below what they really wanted to go. To get around this, they got a vote through in the Public Works Department (I do not know under what heading) but probably "Rent of Public Buildings, etc.", and therefore they are having vouchered such items as Ordnance Stores, Rent of Drill Halls, etc., sent to the Public Works Department, and paid by the latter and which are really Militia estimates. I understand that the Deputy Minister of Public Works has been making serious objections to some of these payments, but he has been over-ruled, and made to pay out of P.W. vote $300,000 for Militia. . . .[64]

"This is very interesting," Meighen replied, "and altogether likely it is true. It is on a par with other manipulations to hoodwink the public and to pretend to be doing something. I am preparing a list of questions designed to bring out the facts."[65] The questions were duly asked, but the facts remained obscure.

For the next three years, the militia estimates continued to fall. For 1923–24, they dropped slightly from $9,797,406 to $9,668,671. "Owing to continued shortage of money," a résumé of defence activities prepared by the Army's Historical Section in 1927 noted, "the militia training this year [1923] was confined to officers, N.C.O.s and specialists. About 38,000 trained for averages of about 8 or 9 days. The peace establishment (not strength) of existing Militia calls for about 130,000 all ranks. Militia activities being curtailed in every direction."[66] The summary provided by the same source for the year's activities in 1924 was even more dispiriting:

Consequent on drastic necessity for economy the rates of pay for the Permanent Force had to be reduced and many men took their discharge. This involved serious reduction in efficiency of units, especially the technical services.

About 30,000 Active Militia trained. Officers, N.C.O.'s and specialists trained chiefly at Camp Schools for 16 days; of the remainder, in most units a bare minimum necessary to maintain unit organizations trained for nine days at local headquarters. Owing to financial stringency, Non-Permanent Artillery carried out no firing practice. . . .[67]

The Prime Minister would have been happy to have been able to dispense with all militia activity. In February 1924, Mackenzie King wrote to the Minister of National Defence, E. M. Macdonald, to remind him

of the suggestion I made at our meeting of the Cabinet to-day that you consider the advisability of transferring either temporarily or permanently to the Municipalities in which they may be located many of the armouries and drill halls which have been erected in different parts of our country. Were it proposed either to sell or lease these buildings as community halls to be used for such public purposes as the Municipalities concerned might desire, very considerable economies could, I believe, be effected, and at the same time a course of action which would commend itself very strongly to the public. It is not exactly turning spears into pruning hooks and swords into plough-shares, but it would be something along the same order. . . .

I believe if you could announce that at least one hundred armouries or drill halls in Canada had been converted at this time into Community Halls to serve primarily Community ends, you would be taking a course which would be to the credit of the Government from one end of Canada to the other. . . . A transition from military to community purposes is much in accord with the spirit of our time.[68]

For 1925, the expenditure on the Militia was $8,819,743. This sum, the Army's Historical Section noted two years later, "compares with $10,998,162 in last complete year before the war (year ending 31 March 1914). In addition to this reduction regard must be had to the diminution in the purchasing power of the dollar. It may safely be said that $8,819,743 does not represent more than $5,000,000 at pre-war values." Training of the N.P.A.M. was on the same restricted scale as during the preceding year, although a special supplementary vote "made it possible for detachments of about 35% of battery strength to resume artillery practice at central camps. Reserves of ammunition have been steadily decreasing and now much below minimum required for the several types of guns."[69]

II

With the appointment of J. L. Ralston as Minister of National Defence in October 1926, the military establishment acquired for the first time since the Armistice a powerful and persuasive spokesman in the Cabinet. During his regime, the National Defence estimates climbed steadily, from roughly $12,500,000 in 1925–26 to roughly $21,000,000 in 1929–30. In the era of the Kellogg-Briand Pact, this was a remarkable achievement. The lion's share of the increase went to the Air Force and the Navy; the militia, permanent force and reserve, had to make do with about $11,000,000 annually. But it was the militia's quota which most provoked the handful of dedicated anti-militarists in the House of Commons to their spirited if futile assault upon the Department's estimates. Their attack was usually touched off by the vote for "Cadet Services," not only because it came before the House earlier than the other National Defence items (the Votes being presented in alphabetical order), but also because the military training of the nation's youth was most deeply offensive to their sensibilities. "To my mind," Agnes Macphail declared in more than one of her yearly protests against it, "cadet training is the most vicious part of our national defence scheme." When the estimates placed before them in April 1927 disclosed that the Department desired to increase the Vote for "Cadet Services" from $400,000 to $500,000, the members of the little group could hardly contain their indignation. Agnes Macphail moved that the Vote be reduced by $499,999: "I have never attacked a permanent army"—she did not mean it literally but her zeal was such that no one would have doubted her if she had—"but I do object to imposing on our boys our own ideas instead of letting them think for themselves. . . . Fear is one cause of war and fear can be largely eliminated by early training. Military training in the schools thrives on fear and produces it . . . creates a bombastic military spirit of toy soldierism. . . . I wish the people would say to the Department of National Defence and the government: take your hands off the schoolboys of Canada. . . ."[70] To which E. J. Garland, Progressive Member for Bow River, Alberta, added: "I have watched children, including my own, long enough to realize that there is no instinct in them to quarrel, no desire to kill one another. . . . What changes them is enrolling them into this sort of cadet training where they drill in stiff military attitudes and the Prussian spirit is developed in them. The little child becomes imbued with the war slogans, military jargon, the dreadful spirit of war that poisons life for him, and that some day he spews up in gasping death upon the battlefield. . . ."[71]

A Minister of National Defence confronted with these kinds of argument who was tactless in manner and unskilled in debate might have found himself in difficulty. But Ralston neither ridiculed nor ignored his opponents. "I have listened for two days," he declared in reply to them on 11 April,

> to the enunciation of principles to which I believe every hon. member of this House can subscribe, in relation to the horrors of war and the desire for peace. . . . The people of this country do not quite realize exactly what is the duty which has been imposed upon your humble servant in filling this portfolio. I am presiding over the Department of National Defence, not over a department which has to do with the propagation of the principle of the abolition of war, and I do resent the remarks made by the hon. member for Winnipeg North Centre [J. S. Woodsworth] when he said we have professional militarists whose job it is in this thing, men who are at it in season and out of season, trying in every way to use their influence to perpetuate war.[*] . . . I have yet to meet a professional militarist. . . . I believe at least ninety-nine per cent of the men in the Department of National Defence and in the militia generally throughout Canada would be delighted if the time came when this country could do without its defence forces and disband them entirely. I want to say further that so far as I am concerned this portfolio of national defence is in the hands of my leader and of His Excellency the Governor General, because I do not propose to be here any longer than is absolutely necessary, in my humble judgment, to see that we have at least some form of defence such as that which is regarded as necessary having regard to conditions in the world. . . .
> . . . I believe sincerely that when I come to Parliament . . . and . . . I ask this House to be good enough to grant to His Majesty a sufficient sum of money to provide one permanent force soldier for every 3,000 inhabitants of the Dominion of Canada; when I ask that they grant a sufficient sum of money to provide for the training for about nine days of one citizen out of every 300 in this country, it seems to me after all that the charge of being busily arming can be hardly sustained. It seems to me that I have been about as modest in my requests as I can be, and notwithstanding the opinions which have been very freely expressed around this chamber by those who, if they were asked, would not sincerely pretend to be military experts. . . . I do prefer to take, as I should, the opinions of those who advise me in connection with this matter, and they advise me that this is the minimum which any self-respecting and self-reliant country in our position should expect to provide for its defence services. . . .

---

*See above, p. 118.

Now I come back to the cadet vote. . . . I do want to suggest that the word "militarism" has been pretty badly man-handled in this country for some time now. Militarism means the man or the country who puts the social and economic and commercial side of life second, and the military side first, and I have yet to find very much of that spirit in the Dominion of Canada. I think it is because of the free and, I think, improper use of that word, that some of us have got very far on the wrong track. I have seen the cadet corps. . . . I do not think there is anything rough or Prussian . . . about them. It seems to me it is pretty good training for any citizen, but any parent is at liberty to differ with me and say to the cadet instructor: I do not want my boy to take up that training. When we have that situation, where it is optional with the parent, optional with the school, and optional with the province, and when the physical training accounts for pretty nearly three-fifths of this vote, I submit that the criticisms which have been offered have not perhaps the foundation which they might appear to have had when hon. members first addressed this House.

I just want to say, in conclusion, in connection with this whole matter, that I am trying without offending the feelings of anybody to make the department as efficient as possible in a small and modest way, and I do commend this vote personally to hon. members for their support.[72]

With what was perhaps an ideal defence of departmental estimates, even their most bitter opponents did not find it easy to quarrel further. "I feel sorry," J. S. Woodsworth conceded, "that we have in the present Minister of National Defence a gentleman whom I think we all very highly respect. It makes it perhaps a little more difficult to speak against his estimates. . . ."[73] And, the following year, Agnes Macphail added her own tribute: "I entreat the Prime Minister," she said on 23 May 1928, "to transfer his Minister of National Defence to a department where his great ability and driving force will be of greater benefit to Canada."[74]

Without Ralston as their spokesman, the military would have fared far worse. Yet even with Ralston they had not fared very well. A few weeks after the defeat of the Liberal Government, the General Staff prepared a survey for their new Minister of the state of army equipment:

The deficiency in ammunition in Canada is a question which cannot but cause grave concern to those whose interest or responsibility have brought them into the present situation. . . .

The present deficit in gun ammunition is undeniably serious. What is more serious still is the fact that there is little or no sign that we have reached the climax. The present situation is the result of successive post-war years of stinted economy. At the termination of the war, Canada found herself the owner of the equipment of the Canadian Corps. This heritage, insofar as ammunition was concerned, amounted to the sum of approximately four million dollars. Field Army ammunition to this value was brought to Canada from Great Britain and, together with stock of Coastal Defence ammunition then on hand, became the capital upon which we have since existed. . . .

If the tide does not turn soon, training must, of necessity, be curtailed. The greater the delay in facing this problem, the greater the sum required to rectify the situation. It would be difficult to predict what effect a further curtailment of training would have upon a militia whose treatment since the war has been far from generous. On the contrary, it is not difficult to anticipate the reply of Parliament to a demand for an increase in expenditure out of all proportion to previous estimates. . . .[75]

A General Staff review of the military situation, prepared early in 1931 disclosed "(i) a complete absence of such modern arms as tanks and armoured cars; (ii) a very serious lack in Artillery and Engineer units, such as medium, heavy and anti-aircraft batteries; . . . (iii) an obvious shortage in units and formations of services such as mobile workshops." The outlook was gloomy. "Short of a decision to allot a very much greater proportion of the national revenue to the requirements of direct defence, it is evident that not only will it be impossible to make further progress . . . , but that year by year the defensive capabilities of the present Militia Organization must diminish. Apart from the obvious deficiencies in organization, the fighting power of existing units is steadily deteriorating, through increasing obsolescence in the arms, ammunition and equipment now available."[76]

III

The nation was by this time in the grip of the Great Depression. So far from fresh funds for the forces being available, the service estimates were slashed across the board. The non-permanent active militia, for the shoe-string operations of which $2,324,000 had been made available during the fiscal year 1930–31, was cut back to $1,606,000 for 1931–32. To get along on that amount, all N.P.A.M. training at camp was done away with; there was just enough to allow city regiments to train for four or five days at their own local armouries, providing they did so without pay. Some anxiety was expressed lest this economy measure prove too much for the N.P.A.M. to bear and the whole militia reserve system crumple under its weight. A. E. Ross, the Conservative member for Kingston who was in close touch with militia opinion, referred to "the feeling that the infantry does not count now, that it must be all artillery. . . . There is a feeling throughout Canada that perhaps the present chief staff officer is just a little strong willed in regard to the course to be followed."[77] Another Government back-bencher, W. W.

Kennedy of Winnipeg South Centre, criticized the decision to abolish camp training. "In September or October each non-permanent unit commences training. They go to the armouries one or two nights a week, for two hours a night. The officers, the non-commissioned officers and the men attend. These men are paid nothing and expect nothing; they give their time to the militia and to their country. What recompense do they receive? Drilling together and getting to know each other, there is built up a spirit of camaraderie which means something to young people. When summer comes these young men look forward to the opportunity of getting an outing of one or two weeks, and that is a great incentive."[78] The Attorney-General of Ontario, William H. Price, writing privately to the Prime Minister, thought that the decision to suspend camp training was in the circumstances the right one, but expressed his apprehension about the morale of the militia.

> They have been carrying on more or less effectively on account of the fact that the pay which is granted to the officers and often to the non-commissioned officers and the privates, is turned back to regimental funds for the purpose of carrying on the units. This means, practically, that all these men perform their services, do their drilling and all the other things at no personal cost to the State except the general upkeep.
>
> In view of the fact that this winter may bring on very bad conditions and that the Militia should be strong, not only in body but in spirit, might it not be wise to include something in your Supplementary Estimates that would make them feel that their services were appreciated? We have 95% of the Militia of Canada at our back. We have seventeen Conservative soldier members sitting in the Legislative Assembly of Ontario, four of whom are in the Government. Neither the Liberals nor the Progressives have any. May it not be that at this time we would be unwise to estrange such outstanding support? From a national standpoint and from a party standpoint some further consideration might be given to it.[79]

These were powerful arguments from a powerful source. Doubtless they played their part in causing the government to provide the N.P.A.M. with an additional million dollars, bringing the available funds for 1931–32 to $2,600,000. Even so, the reserve militia had no more than about $15 to spend on each man of its authorized strength.

Militia life under such conditions was hard and it was earnest. The Canadian Scottish Regiment's experience was typical. "Am having a bit of difficulty with the Department at Ottawa," one of its officers wrote privately in September 1932. "They refuse to take over our Courtenay [B.C.] drill hall, and as a matter of fact refuse to consider any other obligation even though it is only $20 a month. The Agricultural Society there refuse to come down in their price, so I am between the devil and the sea. We cannot afford to eliminate 'C' Company and cannot afford to carry on with the rent." In the event the officers paid the rent themselves.[80] What they got for it was another matter. "I find that it is nearly impossible for us to carry on with our Parades owing to the condition of the . . . building," another officer wrote to its owners in January 1933. "Windows broken from the outside, doors broken off hinges and the front doors being opened allowing children to play there, leaving it in a filthy condition which necessitates our cleaning it up before using it on drill nights."[81] There being no heat, one of the officers gave his lectures on "Tactics and Section-leading" in the dining room of his own home. Trainees were introduced to short-wave radio, but "at no expense to the public"—a phrase, the Regiment's historian records, "so common in the 1930's that it was frequently referred to as the motto of N.D.H.Q."[82]

To keep the regimental spirit alive throughout the years of malnutrition of the military required devotion and frequently sacrifice of the time and money of the citizen-soldiers.

> There was no pay for any of the Camerons of this era. All pay earned was contributed to the regimental funds in order to provide for a full-time regimental clerk. . . . Instead of individual pay, the [men] received street-car tickets, coffee and sandwiches. . . . Each [officer] had to provide himself with regular khaki and Sam Browne for normal parades and activities as well as full dress kit. . . . A hand-me-down deal [existed] by means of which a man could outfit himself for about one hundred dollars. . . . Those who kept the unit together did so at great personal cost in time and money, and . . . in the face of much public jeering at "Saturday soldiering." . . .[83]

> . . . I was a Captain commanding the Supply Details. We had a Horse Transport Company. We had harness. The troops were trained to take the harness apart, put it back together, and hang it up in the Quartermaster's Stores. That is about as far as it went. We never did have a horse. We never did have a waggon.
>
> We had a Mechanical Transport unit. . . . They had no equipment whatsoever—absolutely none. From 1926 until the outbreak of war we never had one item of mechanical transport issued to us. Not a motorcycle, not a van, not a truck. . . .
>
> Training was possible only by using our own imaginations and ingenuity. . . . I heard . . . about 1933 or '34 . . . that the Post Office had decided to write off two vans. . . . I went down and begged them, and got them. A firm in town had a big, solid-tired flat-top, which I got from them. . . . We had a couple of motor-cycles which we purchased out of our own funds, and in order to train our motorcyclists we produced a device with rollers which were held in place by a heavy steel and timber form which sat on the floor. . . . We taught motorcyclists without going anywhere. . . .

We got no pay. We waived our pay into the regimental fund—every cent of it. . . . When we attested a private soldier, he signed a waiver of pay along with his attestation card, or he wasn't accepted. . . . We used the money to buy equipment, to look after our weekend exercises, and to assist the sergeants and the other ranks to have some comforts in their common quarters. . . .
. . . I got the Army printing done on the Board of Education presses operated by the apprentices that came in for training. I got my annual exercises printed in the same way. There was no money for things of that kind. We bought our own typewriter for the Orderly Room and we coaxed someone to come in and type. Really my Orderly Room was at home. . . .[84]

I used to pay out of my pocket about seven hundred dollars a year to keep a little company of thirty men going, and to hire the horses on Saturday afternoon to mount my men and take them out to ride. . . . I don't know why we did it. . . . It became our hobby. . . . During the period of worst unemployment in the early 1930's, in many cases I had to provide carfare to get my company out to parades. . . . I even bought a set of corsets for my Sergeant-Major's wife so she could go to a regimental dance. I had a good Sergeant-Major. . . .[85]

In and around Cobourg [Ontario] military training was in higher repute than in most parts of Canada. The best type of young men joined the local batteries or the Cobourg company of the Midland Regiment. . . . Our meagre week at summer camp was our nearest approach to field training. . . . We drew pay for our days at camp but in the batteries to which I belonged this was all put into the unit pool to buy equipment that the government did not provide. The total ammunition allowed to a battery in the week at camp for its practice shooting was ten shells. So generous was Canada to its citizens who were trying to make ready to defend her. It can be imagined with what grave responsibility I called the fire orders for the battery when my shell was to be fired. Of course we only used one shell for each set of fire orders. So we trained to meet the German army.[86]

It is evident from this last account that the allegation of A. E. Ross, quoted above, that "it must be all artillery," was not wholly justified. Artillery, because of the scarcity and cost of ammunition, was in fact as neglected as any branch of the service. George Drew, one of the leaders of the Canadian Artillery Association, wrote to the Prime Minister in May 1931:

to let you know what the situation is at the present time so far as the Artillery is concerned.

Following the interview which General Dodds and I had with you in Ottawa, I obtained reports from the various units throughout Canada. They have all been doing their best to maintain the interest of the men in local training by every device possible, but in spite of every effort I am informed that the situation has become most discouraging; that it is practically impossible to get enough men out to make the local training worthwhile because of the doubt which the men have that there would be any subsequent training. I have asked the various battery commanders to express their opinion regarding this, and the invariable answer is that the trained men feel that with no camp training and with no possibility of moving our guns in any local camp that they are wasting their own time as well as public money by carrying out the purely routine training which is possible with Artillery confined to Armoury training. . . .

In almost every case, grave concern is expressed by the battery commanders over the possibility of re-establishing any sort of an effective organization for some years, if at least a modified training camp is not held this year. . . .[87]

He wrote again at the end of 1931, this time to the Minister of National Defence:

Since the withdrawal of harness from practically all the militia batteries, the guns have become completely immobile. No adapters have been issued, which makes it impossible to move them with trucks which could be obtained locally, nor would authority be granted even if we had the equipment in any of the larger centres, because the guns are not equipped with the rubber tires which are necessary to make it reasonably safe to move the field pieces over hard roads. As a result, all we can do is train the gunners on guns which almost assume the role of garrison pieces, and train the other specialists independently. It is true that very valuable preliminary training can be carried out before going to camp, but it is not very effective in teaching a gunner his real job, which is that every member of the battery takes his part in directing the shell fire of the battery at a given target. . . .[88]

The plight of the artillery is the more remarkable in view of the almost fanatical insistence by the then Chief of the General Staff upon the importance of artillery in modern warfare. There is no doubt that General McNaughton was greatly concerned at the shortage of ammunition and the lack of artillery training, but he was, at first at least, disposed to be optimistic. "I am afraid our military training will be somewhat restricted this year, but we are hoping that the cuts are temporary only and that our Votes will be restored just as soon as the financial situation improves a bit."[89] So he wrote privately in April 1931. Two months later the Minister of National Defence informed the House of Commons that the vote for artillery stores had been cut by $232,000, that the production of small arms ammunition was to be reduced by one million rounds for the year, and that consequently the Dominion Arsenal at Quebec would be placed in the custody of caretakers.[90]

IV

Nothing that the Government did to curtail defence expenditure ran more directly counter to General McNaughton's recommendations than its decision to slow down the production of ammunition. So far from accepting this as a necessary economy, the Chief of the General Staff had since his appointment pressed vigorously for the expansion of the Dominion's munitions production capacity. In 1929 this consisted of two government arsenals, one in Quebec City, one in Lindsay, Ontario. The Dominion Arsenal in Quebec had been in continuous operation since its construction in the early 1880's,* and had become sadly obsolete. Already in 1919 it had been described in a General Staff memorandum as "far from satisfactory. The site being in the middle of the City is precluded from expansion. The buildings are out of date and insanitary; congestion is evident and a good deal of the plant and machinery is worn out and obsolete notwithstanding that every effort has been made to maintain efficiency."[91] The valiant efforts of the Director to keep the plant in working order over the next ten years† could not overcome the fundamental inadequacy of the Dominion Arsenal to meet even the greatly restricted needs of the militia for training purposes, so that about $250,000 had to be spent annually in the United Kingdom to purchase ammunition and to make repairs. The Dominion Arsenal at Lindsay, constructed in 1916, was more modern than the Quebec plant, but it was equipped to produce small arms ammunition only; it had been closed down in 1919.

General McNaughton, on becoming Chief of the General Staff in 1929, attached the utmost importance to the attainment of self-sufficiency in both guns and ammunition, for which an entirely new Dominion Arsenal would be required. Over the next year he addressed a series of imploring memoranda to his Minister on the subject. One of these, dated 12 May 1930, noted the

> ever increasing repair bill for guns, etc. For example, last year certain 18 pdrs. had to be sent to England for straightening, a simple process which we could not handle on account of lack of presses. . . .
>
> Our deficit on establishment of ammunition is now nearly $5,000,000 in value and increasing. Until a proper arsenal is available it will not be possible

*". . . A manufactory of cartridges is to be established shortly at Quebec, which will render the Dominion independent of England for its supply of ammunition; this I consider a move in the right direction . . . Whenever the time of action may arrive it is *essential* that the Canadian shall not find himself with a weapon inferior to that of his enemy, or disaster will result. . . ." *Annual Report on the State of the Militia for 1880*, by the General Officer Commanding (Ottawa, 1881), p. xiv.

†"In spite of very unfavourable circumstances, Colonel [Count H. R. V.] de Bury had maintained the whole establishment of the Quebec Arsenal in perfect order and had perfected it unceasingly, even making extensions when the budget made it possible. In the course of 1924, several additions were made to the machinery and a small workshop was built. . . . A power house was established in 1925. . . . That year the Arsenal built two special Brinell testing machines for .303 cartridge cases and in 1926 the annealing furnace of the rolling mill was rebuilt. . . ." *The Dominion Arsenal at Quebec, 1880–1945* (Quebec City, 1947), p. 58.

to develop the nucleus of trained specialists who could act as instructors, etc., for the mobilization of Canadian munition industries in emergencies.

If we had not had the nucleus in 1914 for shell production, the business would have gone elsewhere, probably to the United States, and Canada would have been denied hundreds of millions of dollars of external trade . . .[92]

But the Government remained unmoved by his arguments. Twelve years later, when the country was at war and the production of munitions not yet all it should have been, General McNaughton told Mackenzie King that "when Ralston was previously Minister of Defence . . . McNaughton . . . had his resignation written out and would have handed it in, had the election not come in 1930 and changed the situation."[93] The principal difference between McNaughton and Ralston at this time was that the Chief of the General Staff thought the construction of a new Dominion Arsenal essential, while the Minister of National Defence did not.

But the Bennett Government did little more to advance the project. Depression compelled further postponement. The military continued to put up the arguments: Treasury Board continued to knock them down. Meanwhile the military continued to plan. An Arsenal Committee of the General Staff picked out a site, at Valcartier Camp, Quebec (the site originally selected at Little River, Quebec, was abandoned because of the higher cost of construction), drew up designs, and sent an ordnance officer to the United Kingdom to learn something of the art at the Royal Arsenal, Woolwich, the Royal Small Arms Factory, Enfield, and the Royal Gun Powder Factory, Waltham. It concluded that what was required was a munitions complex capable of producing ammunition for both small arms and cannon, automatic rifles, machine guns, and cannon; its total cost was estimated at around $35,000,000. At the outbreak of war, the amount which had been spent on munitions plant was more like one-hundredth of this sum; between 1939 and 1944, nearly ten times that again. "Had Canadian governments accepted the recommendations of their military advisers," the Official Historian of the Canadian Army has written, "which three successive administrations felt themselves unable to entertain, the Canadian land forces in the Second World War could have been armed with modern weapons from the outset. As it was, they made do for many months with the equipment of 1918."[94]

V

1932 brought more bad news for the militia. "The N.P.A.M. vote on which we are now basing our estimates," an official of the Department of National Defence wrote to the Chief of the General Staff in February, "is $1,837,400." (It had been $2,600,000.) "It is difficult for us to see on what basis the reductions to the estimates were made, as no opinions were secured by those concerned before the reduced figures were returned to us."[95] But next year was worse still. On 30 May 1933 the Treasury Board sent out its fateful letter proposing, "as a basis for discussion," reductions in the estimates of all the armed services. The militia estimates, by ruthless pruning, had already been brought down to $8,273,484 (from which the permanent force was to receive $4,910,034 and the N.P.A.M. $1,994,000)—a low point for the century—but the Treasury Board's suggested reductions would have cut this to $7,066,474. There was no consolation in the fact that the air force would suffer even more, for General McNaughton, who was responsible for the nation's strength in the air as for its strength on the land, had already formed the opinion that the R.C.A.F. was vital, if anything was vital. He accordingly sought to protect the air arm from further debilitation, along with the permanent force and non-permanent active militia, if necessary by sacrificing the nation's strength at sea. (The arguments deployed by McNaughton on behalf of the R.C.A.F. at the expense of the R.C.N. have already been examined [see above, pp. 277–9, 284–8]; his detailed recommendations for the Militia Services appear in Document 5, pp. 343–5, below.)

In 1932 the British Government revoked its Ten-Year Rule—the supposition, until then governing its defence planning, that no major war in which the United Kingdom might be involved would occur for a decade. Plans for re-armament got under way in 1933; by 1934 rearmament itself had begun. In November 1934, R. B. Bennett told the Conference of Defence Associations, meeting at Ottawa, that discussions which he had had with British ministers earlier that year showed them to be desperately anxious about the deteriorating international situation. "The Foreign Office had definite information to the effect that Germany was re-arming apace."[96] In December, Sir Maurice Hankey, representing the Committee of Imperial Defence, visited Ottawa and discussed with Bennett and General McNaughton Britain's defence plans. He asked McNaughton how far he ought to go in disclosing these "to Canadian political leaders outside of the Government"; McNaughton, after discussing the matter with the Prime Minister, "advised him to be 'discreet' for fear of leakage to unreliable persons."[97]

The increased tempo of military activity abroad had little effect upon the military affairs of the Dominion. The Prime Minister remained indifferent to the dilapidated condition of the country's defence forces, and took no interest in the activities of the Department of National

Defence with the exception of its unemployment relief camps and the construction of new barracks in and about his home town of Calgary. In this latter project his interest was intense, even obsessive. As he told General McNaughton on 18 July,

> he was most anxious that this should be a creditable work; that he looked to the Defence Department to see that the work was placed in hand expeditiously and that it was carried out in the best style and taste. . . . The Prime Minister laid emphasis on the fact that the building should be fire-proof or as nearly fire-proof as possible. . . . He asked about partitions. . . . The Prime Minister said that particular care should be taken with the basements and that he would like to see them and the outside walls well up by the winter months. He said that he favoured central heating and mentioned that gas was available for heating but he intimated that there might be pressure brought to bear to use coal. . . . The Prime Minister then mentioned that the Bennett-White Construction Company and the Carter-Halls Company were two reliable contractors who could be trusted to execute any plans properly and he intimated that he thought that contracts for separate buildings should be let locally as soon as the plans were ready. He impressed upon me that he was most anxious that we should proceed to the full extent of the $1,200,000 presently available and this could, if necessary, be increased to $1,300,000 if really required. . . .[98]

Such a show of interest, and such a sum of money, might well be thought misplaced. Certainly McNaughton thought them so. As his term of office drew to a close, his patience became exhausted. On 5 April 1935, he took the unusual, indeed unprecedented, step of writing to the Prime Minister a personal letter protesting the disrepair into which the Canadian armed forces had been allowed, through lack of funds, to fall:

> You will recall that on several occasions you have impressed on me my responsibility for bringing to your attention any matters which, in my judgment, appear to prejudice the proper discharge of the duties of the Department of National Defence.
>
> Naturally I have been reluctant to make use of any special means of informing you so long as there was reasonable assurance that full and adequate information was reaching you through the medium of Privy Council and, in point of fact, I have never yet formally availed myself of the opportunity which you invited to have matters of serious import brought directly to your attention.
>
> In your absence [through illness], the Estimates for the Land and Air Forces, which I am responsible for putting forward and which were prepared on a minimum basis, have received scant consideration. They were arbitrarily reduced by very large amounts without any opportunity whatever being given, as is customary before Treasury Board, for explanation as to the needs of the situation and I am impressed from many private conversations I have had with Ministers that they are quite unaware both of the serious deficiencies which exist and of the vital need for correcting the situation.

I am now informed by the Minister of National Defence that the modest Estimates which we had proposed to raise in the Supplementaries will not be entertained and, in addition, that certain works urgently needed which we had put forward under the proposed Public Works Construction Act for 1935–36 have been struck out, again without any opportunity being given for explanation.

Under the circumstances, I have thought it necessary to review the situation in a secret report which I understand it is the intention of the Minister of National Defence to circulate to Members of the Government. . . .

As Chief of the General Staff I am a Staff Officer and as such it is my duty to ensure that full information on any matter of vital importance to the defence of Canada reaches you as the head of the Government for your consideration and decision. Once that decision is given, whether it be acceptance in whole or in part or not at all of the advice I have tendered, you may rest assured that, loyally, I and those associated with me, will do the very best we can with it and that we will seek with every means within our powers to have it accepted and implemented by those under our authority. It is from this point of view that in the past, despite preparations for Defence which I know to be inadequate, I have sought to hide and make little of our deficiencies.

In my recent contacts with officers of our Non-Permanent forces throughout the country I have observed an increasing realization of our lack of proper preparation and it is now only a question of a short time until these matters are generally known by the public of this country. I apprehend, that at the first breath of danger, real or imagined, this question will become a public issue of the first magnitude. I deplore this for many reasons not least of which is the inevitable waste which will ensue if our preparations are thrown off an orderly basis of development at reasonable and economic rate.

The paper which I send you outlines the position in language which I have studied to make moderate . . .[99]

McNaughton's paper was entitled "The Defence of Canada." In it he reviewed the changing background of Canadian defence policy since the Great War, and furnished illustrations of existing deficiences in equipment and aummunition:

As regards reserves of equipment and ammunition, the matter is shortly disposed of. Except as regards rifles and rifle ammunition, partial stocks of which were inherited from the Great War—there are none.

As regards equipment, the situation is almost equally serious, and to exemplify it I select a few items from the long lists of deficiences on file at NDHQ:

(i) There is not a single modern anti-aircraft gun of any sort in Canada.

(ii) The stocks of field gun ammunition on hand represent 90 minutes' fire at normal rates for the field guns inherited from the Great War and which are now obsolescent.

(iii) The coast defence armament is obsolete and, in some cases, defective in that a number of the major guns are not expected to be able to fire more

than a dozen rounds. To keep some defence value in these guns, which are situated on the Pacific Coast, we have not dared for some years to indulge in any practice firing.
(iv) About the only article of which stocks are held is harness, and this is practically useless. . . .
(v) There are only 25 aircraft of service type in Canada, all of which are obsolescent for training purposes. . . .
(vi) Not one service air bomb is held in Canada.
The situation as generally outlined above with respect to equipment and ammunition is one that can be viewed only with the gravest concern. And with the rapidly deteriorating international situation the position is becoming more and more disquieting . . .[100]

McNaughton' memorandum was circulated among members of the Cabinet on 28 May. On the following day he appeared before the Cabinet. It was his last act as Chief of the General Staff. Whether he impressed his audience is not known; it had at any rate reason to feel depressed. McNaughton's memorandum was not the only grim news to have come its way that week. From Geneva, a few days earlier, the Canadian Advisory Officer had reported a discussion at the League of Nations. Anthony Eden had told him that Mussolini was "engineering for war."[101]

DOCUMENTS

DOCUMENT 1

Extracts from "Defence Scheme No. 1," 12 April 1921. (Army Records)

DEFENCE OF CANADA—GENERALLY

Section I. Problems to be met by the Empire

The Imperial General Staff is of the opinion that the possible eventualities, which the Empire must be prepared to meet, fall roughly under two main headings:

(a) A struggle for the existence of the Empire such as that from which we have only recently emerged.

(b) Minor crises which may be only local in character but which may synchronize or spread until a situation develops straining the resources of the Empire very greatly without enabling us to take the extreme methods which would be justified by a great national emergency.

These latter cases would probably call for the employment of the full authorised Forces of the Crown in the various parts of the Empire, namely, Regular Army and Permanent Forces; territorial forces and militia forces, to be kept up to strength by voluntary enlistment, but would not call for national service in the case of other parts of the Empire or Levee en Masse in the case of Canada.

The major eventuality is a plain straightforward issue, but it is considered by the Imperial General Staff that it could scarcely arise without the inclusion of one of the great civilized powers in the enemy's ranks. Although there are indications that we may be faced by a hostile Russo-German combination and signs of danger from other centres are not absent, the British Cabinet has come to the conclusion that a war similar to that which has just been concluded is not likely to recur during the next 5 or 10 years.

The Imperial General Staff held at the same time that such an eventuality cannot be lost sight of entirely, and though neither the locality nor the chief actors can at present be foretold, it will be wise to take such general measures as will enhance the value of the Land Forces of the Empire as a whole, without prohibitive expenditure, such as (a) the co-ordination of military thought throughout the Empire, including measures for ensuring the close co-operation of Staffs, which was so marked a feature of the recent struggle, (b) the standardization of establishments and equipment, (c) the drawing up of schemes in each part of the Empire for the distribution of man power as between the three Services and the industries necessary to maintain armies in the field with a view to obtaining the maximum value for the available manpower. From this it will be possible to assess for different parts of the Empire the relative proportion of effort to be devoted to each of the three Services, which will best suit the requirements of the Empire as a whole, (d) the extension in Peace time and the expansion in War of industries intimately connected with the supply of warlike material in order that Indian and Dominion Forces may be, so far as possible, self-supporting, (e) the distribution of responsibility for the collection of intelligence and arrangements for co-ordinating the results.

The above are matters which will be discussed at the approaching Imperial Conference.

The Defence of Canada, therefore, falls under two categories:—

(a) Direct Defence, i.e., the immediate defence of our country against invasion by hostile forces;

(b) Indirect Defence, by which we send an Expeditionary Force to bring the hostile country or countries to action in their own country or countries, or in any case, in territory beyond the confines of the Dominion of Canada.

Section 2. Three Defence Schemes Necessary

For a struggle for the existence of the Empire, it would appear that four cases may occur:—

1. A European Combination
2. The United States
3. Japan
4. A combination of the above.

Only (2) and (4) of the above and possibly in a lesser extent (3) would put Canada in immediate danger of invasion and call for the Levee en Masse. It is necessary, therefore, to draw up three different Defence Schemes:—

1. For the Defence of Canada against the United States.
2. For the Defence of Canada against Japan.
3. For the Organization and the Despatch of an Expeditionary Force to help the Empire in case of a European Combination or a Minor Crisis . . .

Section 3. General Strategical Situation of Canada

. . . *The first thing apparent then in the defence of Canada is that we lack depth.*

Depth can only be gained by Offensive Action. To carry out an Offensive Action against the United States, with our population in a ratio of 1 to 12 and the United States' Regular Army of 175,000 Enlisted Men, and with between two and four millions of men who were lately embodied for service, is a difficult and on the surface an almost hopeless task, but on further study, it would be found out that it is not as hopeless as it appears on the surface and that Canada has a good many advantages in her favour.

To carry out an Offensive Action against the United States means, first of all, Quicker Mobilization; secondly, the immediate despatch of Flying Columns on the declaration of War; thirdly, the despatch of our Formations at Peace Strength to be followed rapidly by drafts filling them to War Establishment; fourth, a speedy mobilization of our Reserve Units by General Recruitment and by putting in force the Levee en Masse, as soon as Proclamation is made; fifth the completion of the organization of our Formations by the inclusion of Reserve Units; sixth, the despatch of Reserve Units to certain garrisons or certain strategical points; seventh, the early formation of Depots.

Time is of the essence of everything of our mobilization and of our early operations. To keep up this offensive and to continue the successful defence of Canada, will require the timely arrival of reinforcements from the Empire and particularly from the United Kingdom and the full use of the man power and resources of the Empire in other theatres of operation, namely, the Atlantic Seaboard of the United States; the Southern Seaboard, i.e., the Gulf of Mexico, Florida and Mexico; the Pacific Coast.

In order to carry out this Offensive, well chosen lines of Offence should be decided upon, these to produce the greatest results, firstly, to increase our Depth; secondly, to increase our resources by the occupation of hostile territory; thirdly, to increase the moral [*sic*] of our population with a corresponding decrease of moral of the enemy; fourthly, to cover the organization and mobilization of our man power and to prevent the destruction of our resources and lateral communications; fifthly, to gain time until the arrival of help from the various parts of the Empire, as soon as the man power and the resources of the Empire are mobilized and transported to their various spheres of action.

SEA POWER

Sea Power is another of the most important factors in the Defence of Canada. To keep open for periods, at least, the seas for the transport of Britannic and Imperial troops to the various Theatres and for the protection of our Atlantic and Pacific Coasts, to prevent our flanks from being turned, to prevent our Ports of Disembarkation for help from the Empire being occupied or destroyed.

Control of the Great Lakes

Another important strategical feature in the Defence of Canada is the control of the Great Lakes. On all, except Lake Ontario, the Americans have a preponderance of shipping and they have in the States bordering the Great Lakes a Naval Militia of considerable size, which could be made use of to arm and man United States' Mercantile Great Lakes boats.

Timely arrival of British ships of suitable size in Lake Ontario and the proper protection of the Welland Canal, might ultimately give us control of Lake Erie.

Many Canadians, including many navigating officers, are serving in the United States' Great Lakes Mercantile Marine. Further information concerning this question will have to be gathered and action taken to put their service into use at the appointed hour.

WINTER CAMPAIGN

A winter campaign, for obvious reasons, by a large force, is not feasible, but the subject should not be lost sight of, as we might be forced into a winter campaign and in any case mobilization might have to take place during the winter and tactical raiding would be feasible.

POLITICAL QUESTIONS

1. Statesmen decide on the Time, Circumstances and the Locality of War and leave it to the Soldier to make the best of them. It is hoped that our Statesmen will act in such a manner to give us as many advantages as possible in case war becomes inevitable between the British Empire and the United States of America. Members of Parliament and Members of the Senate are drawn from various sources of life, most of them with no War Service and very many of them with no militia connection and no knowledge of the vast machinery required for War and of the terrible disadvantage of loss of the initiative at the commencement of a campaign. It is your duty then to do what you can within your sphere of action to see that such political personages are enlightened on questions of Defence.

2. French Canadians (all Roman Catholics) form nearly one third of the population of Canada. They took little interest in the Great World War. There may have been "Vatican" influence, but it would appear that the main reason for lack of interest was lack of proper political control and leadership from Ottawa. The Roman Catholic Church in Canada is suspicious of the Militia. It has no reason to be so. It has everything to gain and nothing to lose by supporting the Militia. If the United States ever conquered Canada, the dual language would be done away with at once and the Roman Catholic Church would have much less power and influence by one hundred fold.

3. Americans in Canada. Many in British Columbia. Well over 50% in Alberta. Over 50% in Saskatchewan. Many others holding important positions, especially in manufactures and transportation, in other parts of the country.

4. Census, 1921. Commanders should obtain information from the Census, 1921, as soon as the Census Report is compiled, as it will give the latest information of foreign population and of man power of the various Commands and Districts.

5. Provincial Jealousies. Friendly rivalries between the East and the West and between the various Provinces may help to stimulate matters, but every care should be taken to prevent Provincial or Parochial matters interfering with broad questions. There is a tendency for Provincial politicians to interfere with proper organization and there will probably be the same tendency to prevent the proper distribution of troops in time of war. This tendency may only be eliminated by education.

. . .

Section 9: Allies or Possible Allies of Great Britain

Japan. Japan is still an Ally of Great Britain. The question of the renewal of the Japanese Treaty comes up this year. Whatever Japan's attitude may be at any other time, there is not much doubt, in case of war between the British Empire and the United States, that Japan would take immediate military action against the American Republics, in which case it would make matters much more favourable to us, especially at the beginning of the campaign, if we would find that Japan would carry out her traditional policy of delivering their Declaration of War and a Military Operation at the same time . . .

France. France has always taken a friendly interest in the United States.

She came to her help during the Revolutionary War and for years the American Army organization and tactics were based on the French system. France has seen more in the last two years of the modern "Yank". She is dissatisfied with American action, with the low rate of exchange of the franc in the United States, with the attitude of the United States towards the League of Nations. It would appear then that the United States would get no support either actively or sympathetically from France.

Mexico. It has a turbulent and unruly population estimated from 12 to 15 millions. For over 100 years it has been a pin-prick on the American Southern Flank. The Mexicans have not shown themselves, generally speaking, opposed to British interests. In case of war with the United States it is not unlikely that Mexico would cause trouble on the Southern Frontier, causing a goodly force of United States' troops to be concentrated towards Mexico. If Mexico became an active participant in a War against the United States, it would be an area of operation for Britannic or British Empire troops against the Southern States, having for its object the capture of Galveston and New Orleans, and blocking the Mississippi River.

The South American Republics. Many of whom are not hostile to British interests and might decide to support the British Empire. Many of these Republics possess Navies of a useful size which would be a tremendous factor in operations against the Panama Canal.

Section 10: The Strategic Importance of Newfoundland, Alaska and West Indies.

Alaska. The Alaskan Coast presents harbours to be used as submarine bases of operation against the British Columbian Coast. A sufficient force of regular troops might be kept on the Southern Alaskan Coast to capture Prince Rupert by a *coup de main*, immediately after the declaration of war.

Newfoundland. . . . enters largely into the Defence of Canada. American occupation of the Island would have far reaching results. It would be on the flank of the sea routes between Great Britain and Canada and it would be a menace to all our shipping and a base for naval operations against Nova Scotia, the Gulf of the St. Lawrence, and the St. Lawrence River generally. Newfoundland would appear to be a rendezvous and a probable base of operations for the British Grand Fleet.

West Indies. The West Indies are admirably situated as bases for naval operations against the Southern States and particularly against the Panama Canal. They are situated on the flank of the Panama Canal route and if, by any chance, the United States' fleet or any great portion of it was in the Pacific at the outbreak of war the use of the Panama Canal for concentration on the Atlantic Coast might be denied absolutely to them.

. . .

CHAPTER TWO: PROBABLE ACTION OF THE UNITED STATES

Main Objectives. The main objective of the United States force would undoubtedly be Montreal and on to Ottawa. The next important objective of the United States would be the occupation of the Ontario Peninsula, including the cities of Hamilton and Toronto. The other objectives at which the American Land Forces would be moved against would be Quebec, Winnipeg, the Island of Vancouver and South Western British Columbia, i.e., the area including Vancouver and New Westminster.

The grain growing Provinces of Manitoba, Saskatchewan, and Alberta which now have a large percentage of Americans, are especially attractive to the United States, and there is just a possibility that they might make the conquest of these Provinces the ultimate objective of their campaign....

First attempt Invasion of Canada—Mode of:

It is considered that the first attempt of the invasion of Canada would take place as mentioned above by the use of Flying Columns, to carry out a great strategical stroke to catch us unawares before the Canadian Militia was mobilized. If this was not successful, it is considered that there would be a period elapsing of possibly a couple of weeks before a determined effort would be made to advance on Canada by Divisions of all Arms.

Organization of Our Flying Columns for Immediate Action

This emphasizes the fact that our Flying Columns must be organized for immediate action: that our Divisions must get underway with units at Peace Strength with the least possible delay, that is, within three or four days of the declaration of war. This is the object to work up to in the Scheme for Mobilization.

If, after careful study, and taking into consideration the improvement that is sure to come in the position of Militia recruiting, you consider that your units will not be able to move towards their war station on the third or fourth day of mobilization, please advise the General Staff at Ottawa of that fact and of what time you estimate that your Division will be on the move to its War Station.

Section 2: General Instructions for Offensive Action

All training and organization in Peace and all arrangements during the Precautionary Period will lead up to a general Limited Offensive against the United States.

Pacific Command. The field troops of the Pacific Command to advance into and occupy the strategic points including Spokane, Seattle, and Portland, Oregon, bounded by the Columbia River. . . .

Prairie Command . . . should converge towards Fargo in North Dakota . . . and then continue a general advance in the direction of Minneapolis and St. Paul. The occupation of Minneapolis and St. Paul would cut most of the lines leading to Duluth . . . and would have a tendency to protect our railway communications through the Kenora and Rainy River Districts. . . .

Great Lakes Command . . . will, generally speaking, remain on the defensive, but rapid and well organized raids should be made across the Niagara Frontier, the St. Clair Frontier, the Detroit Frontier and the St. Mary's Frontier, with sufficient troops to establish bridgeheads. . . .

Quebec Command . . . will take the offensive on both sides of the Adirondack Mountains with a view of converging . . . in the vicinity of Albany, N.Y. . . .

Maritime Command . . . will make an offensive into the State of Maine....

DOCUMENT 2

Extracts from a Statement by the Prime Minister of Canada, W. L. Mackenzie King, at a Meeting of the Imperial Conference, 17 October 1923. (King Papers)

First, let me say how gratifying it was to hear what the First Lord of the Admiralty said in regard to the point of view of the Admiralty, the change in the point of view of the Admiralty, in respect of the Dominion navies. I think that changed point of view indicates perhaps better than anything else what we in the Dominions have most in mind in seeking co-operation rather than centralization in these matters of defence. . . . I do not think it would be possible for the Dominions, whether in relation to Naval, Military, or Air Forces, to concur in any policy in the nature of highly centralized policy. The question in the end comes back to taxation. All these matters in the last analysis are matters of taxation, and those of us who are really interested in the defence of the Empire have to ask ourselves, above every other question: How can the taxes be raised for the purposes for which we require them? I was a member of Sir Wilfrid Laurier's Government at the time the naval policy was introduced, and I know that the reason we held so strongly to the view of Dominion naval services was that we felt that, if anything in the nature of contributions were requested, if anything in the nature of centralization of organization was expected, we could never expect the Dominion to respond, as we felt sure it would were the people to feel that the naval service of the Dominion was the natural outgrowth of their national standing and national status. If that is understood and appreciated, I think it should give the key to the whole situation as to what may be possible in the future and the lines on which we should proceed. . . .

In matters which affect the honour and integrity and the common interest of the community of nations, Canada, I know, is ready to do her share and to do it well, but while the British Empire is a community of nations, a sort of League of Nations, a League within the world League, it is a community of "nations" and, as such, the national interest cannot be stressed too strongly in our Parliaments when we deal with the questions that come before us. The more we are in a position to lay emphasis on the national status which has been attained, the more easily will we be able to accomplish the aims we have in view. . . .

There is one other point that I think at this moment I ought to make quite clear here. It goes back to what I said on the first day, and in the remarks of the First Lord of the Admiralty it seems to me that he has kept this in mind throughout, that is, that we at this table cannot be too careful not to assume powers which we have not got. We have no right, as I see it, to regard ourselves as a Cabinet shaping policy for the British Empire. We are here as the representatives of Governments, deriving whatever power we have from that circumstance and that fact alone. It is easy to use words and phrases, but there is grave danger of very critical situations arising out of them when it comes to satisfying the expectations that are raised thereby. The word "Oceanic Commonwealth" is, for example, a fine word; it is a splendid word; but if the effect of its use is to convey to the minds of all who are present here that we sitting at this table are shaping the policy of that Oceanic Commonwealth, as a single Cabinet entrusted with any such powers, I am sure, when we get back to our Dominions, we will find that a different conception of our functions and duties has been entertained [than] by those present. Certainly when I get back to Canada I would find that the people there would say very quickly: "Well, Mr. King, we are glad you enjoyed your stay in London, but evidently you got carried away with it; you have forgotten entirely our conception of your duty at that Conference, which was to represent Canada, present her point of view, receiving at the same time the points of view of the other Governments as far as you were able, not questioning the community of interests or our desire to serve it."

The people of the Dominion have never given to me or to my colleagues any authority to say how far Canada is to be committed by what happens somewhere else, say in Egypt or in Africa. If they thought that, by using the words, "one defence of the Empire," we were committing Canada to responsibility as respects international complications and international difficulties that may arise in other quarters of the British Empire, there would be a feeling of alarm and concern that it would be almost impossible to describe. The man whom I think it is well to be on the look-out for, the real enemy, is the one who is watching for weapons with which he can defeat us, and I for my part do not wish to put into the hands of any person, if there are such in the Dominion, who wishes to criticize the British connection and our position within the British Empire, a weapon that may be used effectively against me in my desire to see the Empire maintained and developed. I should feel that the most serious impression that could be conveyed to Canada at the present time—I am not speaking of the other Dominions—but the most serious impression that could be conveyed to Canada certainly would be that the aim and object of this Conference was in some way to commit the Dominions to responsibilities as respects matters over which their Parliaments have no control. It would be making for disunion, not for union. . . .

It is important, I think, from the point of view of the British Empire, that when we are trying to people our country, particularly our Canadian West, with numbers of new immigrants, to build up a strong population there, we should not do anything which will create in their minds the idea that because they are settling in the part of North America which is British they are running risks and incurring obligations with respect to situations arising in parts remote from America, which they would not have if they were south of the line. . . .

What I have said about one foreign policy, and am saying about a single policy of defence, relates to the care with which we use particular terms and phrases, to be sure that when an expression is used we all mean by it the same thing. For example, if I may use Mr. Bruce's expression of the other day, that the British Empire is one and indivisible. I can use that expression, but I have to be very careful to make clear just what I mean by it, just what the impression is that I am seeking to convey. We believe that the Empire is one and indivisible, it may be said also of the Godhead that it is one and indivisible; so much depends upon what it is that it is meant to emphasize. There are aspects of imperial relationships of which account must be taken as respects the separate character of its parts. It is not true that in all particulars the Empire is indivisible; it is divisible, and very distinctly divisible. It is divisible geographically, racially, politically, and in a thousand ways, and we have to take account of all these divisions. . . .

In conclusion . . . may I say I do take strong exception to the publication in any of the Dominions of any memorandum prepared by the Admiralty, or by any other Department of the British Government, without the full sanction and authority, in the first instance, of the Governments of those Dominions. I do that for this reason. It is a fundamental principle in any theory of self government. If the people of Canada—I do not care for how trivial a reason—were to get the impression that in some way or other the British Admiralty or any other Department of the British Government were trying to appeal over the heads of the Canadian Government to the electorate, there would be produced a political situation which it would be very difficult to cope with, and I do not know of anything that would bring about such a situation more quickly than the publication of an Admiralty memorandum. One simply has to suggest carrying the procedure to other Departments to see what it really signifies. If an Admiralty memorandum, on a matter of defence, why not also a memorandum from the War Office on the Militia? Why not a memorandum from the Treasury as to finance? . . . I am quite prepared to agree that we cannot get too much in the way of information. . . . But we want it given to the Minister who is responsible, and we want our Cabinet to have the right to consider its significance. Then we will decide whether, in the interest of Canada, or in the interest of the British Empire, it is wise to give any particular memorandum publicity. I believe we shall be on safe lines so long as we remember that it is Governments that are conferring here; in whatever we do, whether it relates to foreign policy, defence, or anything else, it is all-important that Governments should speak to Governments, not that the individuals here should try to work out a single defence policy for the Empire, but that we should make it possible for our own Cabinets to give full consideration to whatever in the way of statement is to be given to Parliament and the people. Perhaps it is a little difficult to appreciate here just how jealous, in a very proper way, all members of a Cabinet are as to having the right to have their voices heard when a policy of large import is being considered. They have their problems. Our Ministers from the prairies and our Ministers from the manufacturing districts are as much concerned in having a say in the shaping of naval policy as are the Ministers who come from the provinces of British Columbia and Nova Scotia, which border on the sea; and I should hesitate in their absence in any way to try and commit any of my colleagues without their having an opportunity of having their voices heard. . . .

DOCUMENT 3

"Military Aviation Policy" (P.C. 395, 18 February 1920)

The Committee of the Privy Council have had before them a report, dated 29th November, 1919, from the Honourable Arthur L. Sifton, Chairman of the Air Board, stating that the Board has had under consideration the general principles which should underlie the organization of an Air Force in Canada and, in accordance with the decisions reached, submitting the following observations and recommendation:

If Canada is again obliged to engage in war, it will be necessary for her to rely upon an air force as well as upon land and sea forces, and the longer the period intervening before the commencement of such a war, the greater will probably be the importance of the air force by comparison with these other forces.

The maintenance in the air of aircraft is and will remain expensive, and it is consequently essential that every hour of flying done with a view to war strength should tend directly to serve that purpose. Casual and superficial training must be rigidly avoided.

War strength in the air depends not only upon very expensive and highly technical equipment, but upon the exercise both in the air and on the ground of a high degree of special skill. The equipment, unlike artillery equipment, very rapidly deteriorates even if unused. The skill, unlike almost all other military skill, is capable in a large measure of useful exercise in peace.

War flying requires a mental and physical condition seldom found in men much beyond their youth, and there should be very few men in a military air force who are beyond the average efficient age for war flying.

In an exclusively military air force, flying not yielding a high return in military preparedness would be almost impossible to prevent, and the profession of a military air force officer would be a "blind alley" profession from which he must be compelled to retire at a comparatively early age. Further, a professional military air force must, by reason of its cost, be so small as to be almost negligible in war, since war strength in the air will, as in other branches, depend primarily upon numbers. These difficulties and objections weigh so strongly against a purely military air force as to practically exclude resort to it.

Some, but not all of them might be met by the employment of air force officers and airmen on useful civil duties, such as mail carrying and surveying, but these duties can be as well or better carried on as civil services, and certainty on the point of the primary or ultimate purpose of an organization always results in confusion and uncertainty.

It follows, therefore, that war strength in the air must ultimately depend upon civil or commercial air strength; that most of the members of a war air force must normally pursue peaceful occupations (preferably, but not necessarily, in connection with air navigation), that war formations should exist only upon paper and not in the form of embodied units, and that war training should be periodic, intensive and widespread.

Such war training, which must include instruction in the use of many types of machines and complicated and various technical equipment, should be carried on at well organized and thoroughly equipped training stations. At least a small part of the staff at such stations would necessarily be continuously employed, but the size of this professional nucleus must be kept within the narrowest possible limits, partly on account of the expense involved not only for the pay but also for the pension of its members, and partly because it cannot in Canada be made large enough to offer to the best type of young man a sufficiently attractive career.

In peace even the instructional and administrative personnel at the training stations should consequently, with the fewest exeptions, be civilians temporarily assuming military duty. It is obvious that this would result in a lower peace efficiency than if a more numerous permanent professional military personnel were relied upon, but peace efficiency is not the primary consideration. A war organization so constituted as to be comparatively inefficient in peace but reasonably efficient in war is very greatly to be preferred to a war organization which shows a high degree of efficiency in peace but breaks down when it is called upon for war service.

It is the opinion of the Governor in Council that, once trained, both officers and airmen would retain their efficiency if they underwent further training during one month in every twenty-four, or in other words, that the air force as a whole would be maintained in a sufficient state of efficiency if one twenty-fourth of its total authorized non-professional strength was always on duty.

It is not possible to define with definiteness the number of professional military officers and airmen whose employment would be required for the maintenance of a reasonably efficient peace administration, but it is thought that this should not exceed twelve to each training station, with an even smaller number at headquarters.

There are other uncertain factors to be considered in making an estimate of the annual expense involved in keeping trained personnel in a reasonable state of efficiency. The expenditure on stations and equipment for use only in war will, of course, depend upon strategical considerations and upon policy. The cost of the recruitment of all ranks of the air force generally will depend upon the development of aviation generally.

For the purpose of the initial constitution of an air force in Canada, there are understood to be in Canada more than 12,000 officers and airmen who have served overseas with the Royal Air Force, and a large additional number who have served only in Canada.

In view of the considerations above set forth, and for the purpose of laying a foundation for the organization of a Canadian Air Force on the general lines indicated, the Minister, at the instance of the Air Board, recommends that Your Excellency in Council

(a) Authorize the publication of an invitation to former officers and airmen of the Royal Air Force to offer their services as members of the Canadian Air Force, on the footing that they will, in peace, not ordinarily be called upon for active duty for more than five weeks in any two years (including the time spent travelling to and from training centres), that they will receive pay only for the time so spent on active duty, and that the term of enlistment of airmen will be four years.

(b) Authorize steps to be taken looking towards the administration of the Canadian Air Force through provincial Air Force Associations, of which the Lieutenant Governor of each province be asked to act as Honorary President, the duties of each such Association being, among other things, to maintain the paper war formations of the Canadian Air Force in its province, to keep a roster of the officers and airmen belonging to them, and to select the individuals in turn for their tour of training, each association to receive a small grant to meet the cost of a secretary and office accommodation.

(c) Authorize negotiations to be entered into with the Air Ministry looking to an arrangement whereby officers of the Canadian Air Force who are also on the Reserve of the Royal Air Force will be released from their obligations in the latter capacity insofar as these might interfere with any duties they may be required to perform with the former.

The Committee, concurring in the foregoing, submit the above recommendations for Your Excellency's approval, and advise that the requisite authority be granted accordingly.

DOCUMENT 4

A. Draft Order-in-Council, 24 October 1932. (McNaughton Papers)

The undersigned has the honour to report:—

(1) That in accordance with the provisions of The National Defence Act, R.S., 1927, c. 136, s. 6: "The Governor in Council may make such orders and regulations as are deemed necessary or advisable for the proper and efficient administration and organization of the Department";

(2) that by Order-in-Council P.C. 1252 dated 20th June, 1922, Your Excellency "in order to facilitate the co-ordination of the several Departments and Services concerned" was pleased to constitute the Defence Council "To advise the Minister on all matters of Defence including or relating to the Minister on all matters of Defence including or relating to the Militia, the Military, Naval and Air Services of Canada, and on all matters referred to it by the Minister";

(3) that by Order-in-Council P.C. 163 dated 26th January, 1923, it was provided that the duties of the Defence Council as such were to be "solely of an advisory nature";

(4) that consequent on the provisions of the Consolidated Revenue and Audit Act, 1931, R.S., c. 178, there is need for the reconstitution of the Defence Council so as to provide for representation thereon of the Financial Branch of the Department the head of which is now responsible to the Comptroller of the Treasury;

(5) that it is also necessary to re-arrange and organize the duties and responsibilities to the Minister of the several officers presently members of the Defence Council so as better to provide for the efficient organization and administration of the Department, more particularly as regards the co-ordination of the respective functions and duties of the sea, land and air forces;

the undersigned has, therefore, the honour to recommend that Orders-in-Council P.C. 1252 dated 20th June, 1922, and P.C. 163 dated 26th January, 1923, shall be and the same are hereby cancelled and the following substituted:

His Excellency the Governor-General in council on the recommendation of the Minister of National Defence, and pursuant of the provisions of the National Defence Act, the Militia Act, the Naval Service Act, the Aeronautics Act and otherwise, is pleased to order that a Council composed as follows and to be styled "The Defence Council" shall be and the same is hereby created:—

I. *President*
The Minister of National Defence
Service Members:
The Chief of Staff
The Senior Naval Officer
The Senior Air Officer
The Adjutant-General
The Quartermaster-General
Civil Members
the Deputy Minister
The Financial Superintendent, National Defence
Secretary
An officer to be named from the Branch of the Deputy Minister, Department of National Defence.

II. The duties of the Defence Council shall be to consider such matters as are referred to it by the Minister of National Defence and to advise thereon, and it is further ordered that the duties of the several officers, members of Defence Council, shall be as follows:—

Service Members

III. *The Chief of Staff*

The Chief of Staff is the senior Service appointment in the Defence Forces. He shall be selected from among the combatant officers of the Canadian Militia, the executive officers of the Royal Canadian Navy and the flying officers of the Royal Canadian Air Force permanently employed and shall hold office during pleasure.

In concert with the senior officers of the several Services he shall be responsible for the consideration of questions of defence as a whole and for the co-ordination of the sea, land and air forces.

He shall be responsible for defence policy, intelligence and operations, and he shall issue the Minister's instructions in respect thereto.

When the Chief of Staff is an officer of the Land Forces, he shall, in addition, discharge the duties prescribed for the Chief of the General Staff and similarly with respect to the Sea and Air Forces.

When the Chief of Staff is an officer of the Sea or Air Forces a Chief of the General Staff for the Land Forces shall be appointed who will be a member of Defence Council and who will discharge in relation to the Land Forces and subject to the functions assigned to the Chief of Staff the duties prescribed.

IV. *The Senior Naval Officer*

The Senior Naval Officer is the senior appointment in the Naval Service. He shall be selected from among the officers of the executive branch and shall hold office during pleasure. He shall be responsible for the efficiency and training of the Sea Forces; for their vessels and technical naval equipment; and for the conduct of naval operations.

V. *The Senior Air Officer*

The Senior Air Officer is the senior appointment in the Air Services. He shall be selected from among the flying officers of the Royal Canadian Air Force permanently employed and shall hold office during pleasure. He shall be responsible for the efficiency and training of the Air Forces; for their aircraft and technical air equipment; and for the conduct of flying operations.

VI. In the consideration of questions of defence and in their arrangement therefore, the Chief of Staff and the Senior Naval Officer, the Senior Air Officer and the Chief of the General Staff, as the case may be, shall individually and collectively be responsible that the particular requirements of a single Service are subordinated to the main object of national defence which the three Services have in common.

VII. *The Adjutant-General*

The Adjutant-General shall discharge in relation to the Air Force the same duties and functions as are prescribed for him in relation to the Militia.

VIII. *The Quartermaster-General*

The Quartermaster-General, save as regards aircraft and technical air equipment, responsibility for which is vested in the Senior Air Officer, shall discharge in relation to the Air Force the same duties and functions as are prescribed for him in relation to the Militia.

IX. The Adjutant-General and the Quartermaster-General shall be responsible for all services within their respective duties which are miantained jointly for the land, sea, and air forces, and for those services and functions which in future are combined.

With a view to economy in administration and to the equalization of conditions of service they are directed in concert with the Senior Naval Officer and the Senior Air Officer, as from time to time seems advisable, to submit proposals for the combination of services which can be effected with advantage.

X. *Deputy Minister*

Under the provisions of the Interpretation Act, R.S., C. 1, s. 31 (m) the Deputy Minister will in the absence of the Minister act for him in all matters of ordinary business.

Under the provisions of the Civil Service Act, R.S., c. 22, s. 7, the Deputy Minister "shall subject to the directions of the head of the Department oversee and direct the officers, clerks and employees of the Department, have general control of the business thereof, and perform such other duties as are assigned to him by the Governor-in-Council."

In accordance with the statutory provisions above quoted the Minister has directed:—

(i) that the Deputy Minister shall in particular be charged with the following—

(*a*) general control of the civil administration of the Department and of the conduct of official business;

(*b*) all financial matters pertaining to the Department other than those assigned to the Financial Superintendent under the direction of the Comptroller of the Treasury;
(*c*) receipt, registration, distribution and custody of all official letters, telegrams, etc. received in the Department;
(*d*) parliamentary and legal business including proposals for legislation and submissions to the Governor in Council;
(*e*) formal communications to Departments of State, public offices and the outside public;
(*f*) circulation of news and official publications in the public press;
(*g*) contracts for the purchase of stores, equipment and supplies of whatever nature;
(*h*) control of printing and stationery.

XI. *Financial Superintendent*

(1) Under the provisions of the Consolidated Revenue and Audit Act, 1931, R.S., c. 178, and subject to the directions of the Comptroller of the Treasury, the Financial Superintendent is charged with—
(*a*) accounting for the expenditure and revenue of the Department of National Defence;
(*b*) the custody of funds, the control of expenditure in accordance with the Law and the payment of accounts;
(*c*) the oversight and direction of the officers, clerks, and employees engaged in this work.

(2) In concert with the heads of Branches, Directorates and Divisions, he will carry out—
(*d*) the compilation and consolidation of Parliamentary Estimates for submission to the Deputy Minister;
(*e*) the classification of expenditure;
(*f*) the allocation of funds and the supervision of the progress of liabilities and expenditure.

(3) He shall be responsible for—
(*g*) the financial consideration of proposals involving expenditure and for advice thereon;
(*h*) financial relations and adjustments with other Governments and Departments;
(*i*) the payment of the Defence Forces, the civil officers, clerks and employees of the Department;
(*j*) the audit of stores accounts of whatever nature;
(*k*) the custody of all financial records and documents relating to to the foregoing;
(*l*) the annual reports on Expenditure, Revenue and Stores Audit.

XII. *Secretary, Defence Council*

The Secretary, Defence Council, is responsible for the preparation of all papers for consideration and for the communication to the executive officers concerned of the decisions reached by the Minister.

All Regulations, Orders and Instructions inconsistent with the foregoing and with the several Acts of Parliament in question are hereby cancelled.

B. Memorandum in Explanation of the Draft Order-in-Council, 24 October 1932. (McNaughton Papers)

I. The constitution of the Defence Council proposed differs from that previously in force as follows:—

(*a*) There is no Vice-President. This appointment was previously held by the Deputy Minister with the result that he was considered, erroneously no doubt, to have had some undefined position of control in matters of policy over the heads of the Fighting Services.

It is essential that in matters of policy as distinguished from routine civil administration, that the heads of the Fighting Services should not be required to present their advice through and to take their instructions from a civil servant who has not had the benefit of the special training and professional experience in these matters which a senior officer of the Fighting Services who is selected for appointment as Chief of Staff may be presumed to possess.

Experience with Ministers and Governments since the war has emphasized that in policy matters they invariably and rightly insist on direct advice from their professional advisers, and that whenever an acute situation has arisen the Deputy Minister has only functioned in his proper role as an administrative officer.

To give the Deputy Minister a position of dominance over the Services is to set up an organization analagous to the Secretary-at-War which developed in England with disastrous consequences in the period preceding the Crimean War, and which was done away with in 1856 in the re-organization then undertaken.

It has been amply borne out by experience that to be effective the civil control of the armed forces which is essential must be exercised directly by a member of the Cabinet and not through a civil servant.

The duties of the Deputy Minister, defined by Statute and Regulations, correspond almost exactly to those assigned in England to the Under-Secretary of State for War, and this latter officer is the junior member of the Army Council.

(*b*) The appointment of Chief of Staff to co-ordinate the three Fighting Services has been revived. The situation in Canada is that we have a very large land force; a small but growing Air Force; and a very small Navy which is unlikely to expand into a High Seas Fleet.

The Air Force has been closely related to the Militia since its inception following the war, but the Navy, beginning in another Department of State and even after its incorporation in the Department of National Defence in 1923, has remained substantially separate and its senior officers have resisted co-ordination to the loss of efficiency in defence as a whole and against the dictates of economy in administration. It is important that a trend towards consolidation should be established, particularly as the role of the Canadian Navy in defence is in intimate co-operation with the Land and Air Forces and not as an independent force on the high seas.

The duties assigned to the Chief of Staff, who may be an officer either of the Land, Sea or Air Forces, according to circumstances, is co-ordination in the sphere of defence policy. Interference in technical Naval and Air duties is not contemplated, and on these matters the Naval and Air positions are safeguarded by leaving the respective senior officers with the right of access to the Minister whenever they feel it to be necessary.

(*c*) The appointment of a Senior Naval Officer has been substituted for that of the Chief of the Naval Staff.

The new title is more properly related to the functions to be discharged. For as a small naval force with no independent role it is misleading and out of proportion to set up a Chief of the Naval Staff. The continuance of this title would tend to the maintenance of the existing separatism in policy which it is the intention that the new organization should correct.

(*d*) The term Senior Air Officer has been substituted for Director of the Air Force.

The title is analagous to that proposed for the corresponding Naval officer.

The term Director is unsuitable for the reason that it connotes a lesser responsibility than is in fact intended.

The Director of the Air Force was previously an Associate Member of Defence Council, but this titular classification of membership adopted in 1923 has proved unsatisfactory in that it indicated that some of the members of Defence Council were of lower status than others, which is in fact not the case, as all members have an equal right of access to the Minister. The distinction therefore is not continued.

(*e*) The Adjutant-General and the Quartermaster-General remain on the Defence Council. Their previous classification as Associate Members, which had no real meaning, is abolished.

(*f*) The Deputy Minister is put at the head of the Civil as distinguished from the Service Members.

(*g*) The Financial Superintendent is added to the Civil members of Defence Council for the reasons stated in para. 4 of the preamble to the draft Order-in-Council.

The corresponding officials in the United Kingdom are members of the Army Council, Air Council, or Board of Admiralty. Having regard to the new Canadian legislation, the Financial Superintendent's duties can no longer be properly performed in subordination to the Deputy Minister. In financial matters the Financial Superintendent must have access to the Minister if he feels the necessity, and he must for the proper discharge of his duties and responsibilities, correspond on terms of equality with the senior Service officers.

(*h*) The duties of the Secretary remain as previously in force.

II. The provision that the Defence Council shall be advisory to the Minister, first enunciated in P.C. 163 dated 26th January, 1923, is made explicit.

In this respect the Defence Council differs from the Army Council and Board of Admiralty in the United Kingdom in that the latter have a certain corporate existence created by statutes of long standing. The tendency of new legislation in England is away from this to a clear responsibility being vested in the Minister as in Canada, except that in England the Prime Minister himself consults directly with the professional heads of the Services in matters of defence policy; this is in consequence of the fact that defence matters, even in peace, are relatively more insistent on the attention of the Prime Minister of England than they need be on the Prime Minister of Canada.

III. The duties assigned to the Chief of Staff comprise the broad questions of defence policy, intelligence and operations; the co-ordination of the Services; and the issue of the Minister's instructions in respect thereto.

In the interest of economy and efficiency it is essential that the Services should be co-ordinated in these matters, and experience has shown that no progress will be made until responsibility therefor is imposed on a selected individual.

The provisions in respect to the discharge of the additional duties of Chief of the General Staff of the Land Forces are practical for a Land Force officer, but in view of the size of the Land Forces, their complexity and wide distribution, when the office of Chief of Staff is filled by a Naval or more probably by an Air Officer, it would be necessary to have an additional Land Force officer as Chief of the General Staff unless in the meanwhile the Land Forces should be decreased as the Air Force increases.

IV. In technical naval matters the Senior Naval Officer will be responsible, and he will, if he sees the necessity, have direct access to the Minister.

V. The situation in respect to the Senior Air Force Officer is the same as for the Senior Naval Officer.

VI. This provision for individual and collective responsibility is a paraphrase of the warrant issued to the Chiefs of Staff in England and signed by the Prime Minister. This instruction developed out of the Court of the Committee of Inquiry into the correlation of National Defence, presided over by the Marquess of Salisbury. The wording of the instruction is said to have been drafted by Lord Balfour who was a member of the Committee.

VII.
and
VIII. The duties of the Adjutant-General and the Quartermaster-General in respect to the Air Force are as at present in effect.

IX. This is a direction to bring about further consolidation of the administrative services and departments in the interests of efficiency and economy.

It is considered that a definite mandate to proceed in this consolidation is necessary as heretofore very limited progress has been made particularly in matters concerning the Naval Service.

X. The duties prescribed for the Deputy Minister are a proper presentation of the position under existing Defence and Civil Service legislation.

As noted under Para. 1 the Deputy Minister is no longer shown as Vice President of the Defence Council as this appointment has created a misleading impression that the heads of the Fighting Services were his subordinates.

In framing the definition of the duties of the Deputy Minister it was also necessary to take account of his altered position in respect to finance which has been brought about by the Consolidated Revenue and Audit Act of 1931. Para. (ii) (b) has been worded accordingly.

XI. The duties prescribed for the Financial Superintendent correctly reflect the situation under existing Statutes including the Consolidated Revenue and Audit Act, 1931.

For the reason stated in para. 1 (g), it is considered expedient that the Financial Superintendent should now be accorded the status of a member of Defence Council, in equality with the senior officers of the Fighting Services.

The draft has been discussed with the Financial Superintendent and with the Comptroller of the Treasury who are satisfied with the wording proposed.

DOCUMENT 5

Extracts from Memorandum by the Chief of the General Staff for the Minister of National Defence, 1 June 1933. (McNaughton Papers)

Vote 83—Administration: $321,000

This vote provides for

(*a*) the pay and necessary travelling expenses of military officers holding staff appointments.
(*b*) the stationery for the military branches at Defence Headquarters, Ottawa, and for the printing of General and Militia Orders, Militia Lists, etc.
(*c*) a small grant of $1,500 for the purchase of books of reference and other incidental expenses of the departmental library.

(*a*) The military staffs have already been reduced to a minimum and are now below requirements.
(*b*) The allotment for printing and stationery stands at $35,000 which is $6,000 below that of last year. A further saving of $2,500 will be effected by publishing Militia Orders monthly in place of weekly, and by reducing the issue of text books and military manuals required for instruction.
(*c*) A reduction of $500 in the appropriation for the Library will be made by curtailing the purchase of reference books and postponing the binding of periodicals retained for reference.

Vote 84—Cadet Services: $300,000

Owing to the fact that the money is provided in the Cadet Vote to cover charges incurred in a school year commencing in the previous September and ending in June, the amount voted is already fully compromised and, in consequence, no reduction is possible without breaking agreements between the Government of Canada and the various School Boards and Teachers throughout the Country.

The policy in this matter has been reconsidered and, in view of the urgent necessity for economy, it is recommended that the training of Junior Cadets be discontinued, and that all concerned be notified not later than 15th June, 1933, to this effect so that no commitments in connection therewith will be made for the school year commencing September 1933.

If this is approved the vote for Cadet Services in the financial year 1934–35 will be reduced from $300,000 to $100,000, a saving of $200,000.

Vote 85—Contingencies: $35,000

The 10% reduction proposed by Treasury Board can be effected with a net saving of $3,500.

Vote 86—Engineer Services and Works: $297,500

The vote is required for the ordinary repairs and upkeep charges in connection with military buildings, rifle ranges, camps, fortifications, etc., and for any minor necessary construction not undertaken by the Public Works Department.

Ever since the War the vote has been inadequate to requirements. In 1913–14 it was $1,423,000; the present estimate is $297,000. The result is that through lack of repair and replacement many military properties are now in bad repair and any further curtailment in the funds voted for the purpose will result in the loss of valuable property which will have to be replaced at large capital outlay. The present estimate is $30,000 less than that for last year and no further reduction can be recommended.

Vote 87—General Stores: $667,800

This vote is to cover the cost of clothing, equipment and ammunition for the militia, and has been reduced to minimum requirements. To do this it has been necessary to order the Arsenal at Quebec to close for a period during which the employees will receive no wages.

The vote has been greatly reduced during recent years with the result that the reserves remaining from war stocks have been used up. Further, large stocks of clothing, blankets and camp equipment have been handed over to unemployment relief.

Vote 88—Non-Permanent Active Militia: $1,994,000

The estimate for this service was based on the minimum required to train one fifth of the Peace establishment of Non-Permanent Active Militia for a maximum period one third that authorized by Law. This is considered to be the minimum number and the minimum training necessary to provide against internal disorder.

The reduction proposed will necessitate the stoppage of all training; the closing of many armouries, and the disbanding of many units; the full consequence of this cannot be foreseen but might probably result in the disintegration of the present very fine organization which is kept going by the voluntary and largely unpaid efforts of devoted Militia officers throughout the Country. If this transpires there would be an immediate necessity to provide a much more expensive organization to take the place of our traditional Militia.

The estimate of $1,994,000 submitted represents a small increase over last year and was arrived at by the Hon. the Minister of National Defence after mature consideration and discussion with a view to setting a figure as low as practical.

Vote 89—Permanent Force: $4,910,034

It is essential that in the interest of law and order the Permanent Force should be maintained at present strength. It is broken up into small detachments scattered throughout the Dominion, and it is on the moral and physical force of these small groups that the police depend in the first instance in cases of emergency. The function of the Permanent Force is to act at once and so give time for the N.P. troops to assemble. For this purpose the widely separated detachments must be self contained and strong enough to make their presence felt. The reduction suggested would mean a decrease in the strength of 560 men in a force of 3,575.

Alternatively a substantial reduction in pay would have to be effected. I cannot recommend that this is a time to precipitate the discontent and unrest which would probably follow, but it would be practicable to make certain reductions in rates in the case of new enlistments and re-engagements. I estimate that 600 will be taken on or re-engaged during the balance of the current year, and that an average saving of approximately $50.00 per man might be made, resulting in a net saving of $30,000, which would increase progressively in subsequent years.

I must report, however, that it is my considered opinion that the Permanent Force is already under strength for its responsibilities in relation to the maintenance of law and order quite apart from its other duties, and that any savings which can be made as I have indicated should be devoted to increasing the strength. The alternative is to expend far greater sums increasing the Police Forces of the Dominion.

As in the case of the Non-Permanent Militia, the figures for the estimates for the Permanent Force were fixed by the Hon. the Minister of National Defence after full discussion and mature consideration and represent the absolute minimum requirement.

Vote 90—The Royal Military College: $358,150

The reduction of $24,120 proposed by the Treasury Board can be made . . .

CHRONOLOGY OF EVENTS, 1918–1935

1918	
11 November	Armistice
1919	
18 January	First Plenary Session, Peace Conference, Paris
15 May to 25 June	Winnipeg General Strike
23 June	Signing of Treaty of Versailles
25 June	Air Board of Canada constituted
8 November	Jellicoe Mission arrives
15 November	Lt.-Gen. Sir A. W. Currie Inspector-General
1920	
10 July	Meighen Ministry takes office Hugh Guthrie Minister of Militia and Defence C. C. Ballantyne Minister of the Naval Service
1 August	Maj.-Gen. J. H. MacBrien Chief of the General Staff
1921	
1 January	Captain Walter Hose Director of Naval Staff
20 June to 5 August	Imperial Conference, London
13 July	Anglo-Japanese Treaty expires
12 November to 6 February 1922	Conference on the Limitation of Armaments, Washington, D.C.
29 December	King Ministry takes office G. P. Graham Minister of Militia and Defence, and Minister of the Naval Service
1922	
16 September	Churchill's appeal to Dominions for help at Chanak

1923	
1 January	Department of National Defence proclaimed in force by Order-in-Council G. P. Graham Minister of National Defence Maj.-Gen. J. H. MacBrien Chief of Staff (superseding Chief of the General Staff)
28 April	E. M. Macdonald Minister of National Defence
1 October to 8 November	Imperial Conference, London
1924	
1 April	K.R. & O. for Royal Canadian Air Force
1 April	G. J. Desbarats Deputy Minister, Department of National Defence (superseding Deputy Minister of Militia and Defence, and Deputy Minister of the Naval Service)
1926	
7 October	J. L. Ralston Minister of National Defence
19 October to 23 November	Imperial Conference, London
1927	
1 May	Maj.-Gen. J. H. MacBrien resigns as Chief of Staff
4 May	Maj.-Gen. H. C. Thacker Chief of the General Staff (superseding Chief of Staff)
1928	
7 March	Director of Naval Service superseded by Chief of Naval Staff
31 December	Maj.-Gen. A. G. L. McNaughton Chief of the General Staff
1930	
7 August	Bennett Ministry takes office D. M. Sutherland Minister of National Defence
1 October to 14 November	Imperial Conference, London
1931	
18 September	Mukden Incident
1932	
2 February	L. R. Laflèche Deputy Minister of National Defence World Disarmament Conference convenes at Geneva
8 October	Unemployment relief projects of Department of National Defence authorized

1933

30 January	Hitler becomes Chancellor of the German Reich

1934

1 July	Captain Percy Nelles Chief of Naval Staff
17 November	Grote Stirling Minister of National Defence
5 December	Wal Wal Incident

1935

1 July	Maj.-Gen. E. C. Ashton Chief of the General Staff
3 October	Italy invades Ethiopia
23 October	King Ministry takes office Ian Mackenzie Minister of National Defence

NOTE ON THE SOURCES

The major published sources, apart from the books and monographs cited in the References, are: the Debates of the House of Commons and the Senate of Canada; the Annual Departmental Reports of the Department of Militia and Defence, the Department of the Naval Service, and (after 1922) the Department of National Defence; the *Canadian Defence Quarterly* (after 1924).

The unpublished sources include collections of papers, personal and institutional. I believe I am the first scholar, other than scholars retained for the writing of official history, to have enjoyed the privilege of access to the files of the Armed Forces. To all the materials of the period in the custody of the Naval Historian and the Air Historian, I was granted access with no conditions whatsoever. To all the materials of the period in the custody of the Army Historical Section (including the official papers of General A. G. L. McNaughton), I was granted access on the condition that any extracts that I wished to publish had to be authorized by the Director. In no instance did this procedure result in the withholding of any material that I considered necessary for inclusion in my study.

As well as these military materials, I have used the private papers of all of the Prime Ministers of the period; several of its Cabinet Ministers; public servants; and other influential persons. (I was not able to obtain access to the Ralston Papers, deposited at the Public Archives of Canada.) These collections are listed below; in each case the collection is cited by its name as this appears in the References, followed by the name or location of its present custodian.

Prime Ministers

Bennett Papers (Bonar Law-Bennett Library, University of New Brunswick, Fredericton, N.B.)
Borden Papers (Public Archives of Canada, Ottawa; microfilm copy at the Main Library, University of Toronto)
King Papers (Literary Executors of W. L. Mackenzie King)
Meighen Papers (P.A.C.)

Cabinet Ministers and Members of Parliament

Fielding Papers (Provincial Archives, Halifax, Nova Scotia)
Foster Papers (P.A.C.)

Gouin Papers (P.A.C.)
Rowell Papers (P.A.C.)
Woodsworth Papers (P.A.C.)

Public Servants and Military Officers

Christie Papers (Department of External Affairs, Ottawa)
MacBrien Papers (J. R. MacBrien, Esq., Toronto)
McNaughton Papers (Historical Section, Army Headquarters, Ottawa)
Massey Papers (Rt. Hon. Vincent Massey, C.H.)
Pope Papers (P.A.C.)

Armed Forces

Army Records (Historical Section, Army Headquarters, Ottawa; Central Registry, Department of National Defence, Ottawa; Public Archives Record Centre, Ottawa
Air Force Records (Historical Section, R.C.A.F., Ottawa; C.R.; P.A.R.C.)
Navy Records (Office of the Naval Historian, Ottawa; C.R.; P.A.R.C.)

Institutional

League of Nations Society in Canada (P.A.C.)
Legion Records (Dominion Command, Royal Canadian Legion, Ottawa)

Other

Dafoe Papers (P.A.C.)
Willison Papers (P.A.C.)
Wrong Papers (Main Library, University of Toronto)

REFERENCES

INTRODUCTION: VIEWS FROM A FIRE-PROOF HOUSE

1. Canada, H.C. *Debates*, 1920, vol. IV, p. 3646.
2. *Ibid.*, 1938, vol. III, p. 3179.
3. League of Nations, *Records of the First Assembly (1920)*, p. 379.
4. Loring Christie to Sir Robert Borden, 12 Dec. 1920. Borden Papers.
5. Arthur Meighen to N. W. Rowell, 10 Jan. 1921. Rowell Papers.
6. Diary of Sir George Foster, 7 April 1919.
7. Archer Martin to Mackenzie King, 14 Sept. 1923. King Papers.
8. P. C. Larkin to King, 12 March 1926. *Ibid.*
9. *The Memoirs of Herbert Hoover: The Cabinet and the Presidency, 1920–1933* (New York, 1951), p. v.
10. Martin to King, 14 Sept. 1923. King Papers.
11. Imperial Conference, 1923, Stenographic Notes of Proceedings, 4th meeting, 8 Oct. 1923. King Papers.
12. League of Nations, *Records of the Fifth Assembly (1924)*, p. 221.
13. Hoover, *Memoirs*, p. v.
14. Martin to King, 14 Sept. 1926.
15. J. Castell Hopkins, *The Canadian Annual Review, 1918* (Toronto, 1919), p. 323.
16. Sir Clifford Sifton, "Immigration," in *Addresses delivered before the Canadian Club of Toronto, 1921–2* (Toronto, 1923), pp. 185–6.
17. King to Aneuran Williams, 18 Feb. 1920. King Papers.
18. League of Nations, *Records of the Sixth Assembly (1925)*, pp. 88–9.
19. Canada, H.C. *Debates*, 1928, vol. II, p. 1960.
20. Quoted in G.P. deT. Glazebrook, *Canada at the Paris Peace Conference* (Toronto, 1942), p. 148.
21. Memorandum by Borden, 13 March 1919. Borden Papers.
22. W. F. Fielding to King, 15 Sept. 1922. King Papers.
23. League of Nations, *Records of the Third Assembly (1922)*, p. 23.
24. Fielding to King, 15 Sept. 1922. King Papers.
25. League of Nations, *Records of the Fourth Assembly (1923)*, Seventh Meeting of First Committee, 19 Sept., p. 27.
26. Sir Lomer Gouin to King, 1 Oct. 1923. King Papers.
27. Canada, H.C. *Debates*, 1919 (Special Session), p. 102, p. 103.
28. Christie, "Notes on the League of Nations Meeting of March, 1926," 14 April 1926. Borden Papers.
29. Canada, H.C. *Debates*, 1923, vol. IV, p. 4001.
30. Diary of Sir Joseph Pope, 11 Dec. 1920.

31. O. D. Skelton to Mackenzie King, no date. King Papers.
32. Skelton, "Notes on the Protocol of Geneva," no date. *Ibid.*
33. Sir Clifford Sifton to J. W. Dafoe, 19 Nov. 1920. Dafoe Papers.
34. Sifton to Dafoe, [no date] 1925. *Ibid.*
35. R. MacGregor Dawson, *William Lyon Mackenzie King: A Political Biography* (Toronto, 1958), p. 403.
36. *Montreal Star*, 20 Oct. 1925.
37. Toronto *Daily Mail and Empire*, 23 Sept. 1922.
38. Quoted in Dawson, *Mackenzie King*, p. 90.
39. R. B. Pugh, "The Colonial Office, 1801–1925," in E. A. Benians, Sir James Butler, and C. E. Carrington, eds., *The Cambridge History of the British Empire*, vol. III, *The Empire-Commonwealth, 1870–1919* (London, 1959), p. 768.
40. Quoted in J. W. Pickersgill, *The Mackenzie King Record*, vol. I, *1939–1944* (Toronto, 1960), p. 41.
41. Dafoe to G. M. Wrong, 9 Jan. 1920. Wrong Papers.
42. *Ibid.*
43. Christie to Borden, 30 Nov. 1925. Borden Papers.
44. United Kingdom, H.C. *Debates*, 1921, vol. 149, coll. 27–8.
45. "Notes of Meetings of Representatives of the United Kingdom, the Dominions, & India, held in London in June and July, 1921," 20 June 1921. King Papers.
46. *Ibid.*, 22 June 1921.
47. Dafoe to Sifton, 30 March 1922. Dafoe Papers.
48. "Notes of Meetings . . .", 20 June 1921. King Papers.
49. *Ibid.*, 11 July 1921.
50. *Ibid.*, 12 July 1921.
51. *The Times*, 8 Feb. 1923.
52. Philip Kerr to Vincent Massey, 17 Nov. 1922. Massey Papers.
53. Canada, H.C. *Debates*, 1923, vol. I, p. 29.
54. Quoted in Sir Charles Petrie, *Life and Letters of Sir Austen Chamberlain*, vol. II (London, 1940), p. 251.
55. Christie to Kerr, 8 Nov. 1925. Christie Papers.
56. Borden to Christie, 16 April 1926. *Ibid.*
57. Meighen to Christie, 13 Jan. 1926. *Ibid.*

I. THE STRANGE SIBERIAN INTERLUDE

1. Leonid I. Strakhovsky, "The Canadian Artillery Brigade in North Russia, 1918–1919," *Canadian Historical Review*, vol. XXXIX, no. 2, June, 1958, pp. 125–46; Gaddis Smith, "Canada and the Siberian Intervention, 1918–1919," *American Historical Review*, vol. LXIV, no. 4, July, 1959, pp. 866–77.
2. "Canadians in Siberia," *Hamilton Daily Times*, 12 Dec. 1918.
3. "An Amazing Episode," *Farmers' Sun*, 11 Dec. 1918.
4. T. A. Crerar to Sir Thomas White, 22 Nov. 1918. Borden Papers.
5. White to Crerar, 26 Nov. 1918 (telegram). *Ibid.*
6. Crerar to White, 28 Nov. 1918 (telegram). *Ibid.*
7. Maj.-Gen. A. Knox to Troopers [Canadian Overseas Ministry of Militia, London], 24 Nov. 1918 (telegram). Army Records (Siberian E.F., 1919, Folder 17).
8. Maj.-Gen. J. H. Elmsley to Troopers, 28 Nov. 1918 (telegram). *Ibid.*
9. N. W. Rowell to Sir Robert Borden, 27 Nov. 1918 (telegram). Rowell Papers.
10. Borden to Rowell, 2 Dec. 1918 (telegram). Borden Papers.

11. White to Borden, 3 Dec. 1918 (telegram). *Ibid.*
12. Borden to White, 7 Dec. 1918 (telegram). *Ibid.*
13. C.G.S. (Ottawa) to War Office, 4 Dec. 1918 (telegram). *Ibid.*
14. Text repeated in White to Borden, 6 Dec. 1918 (telegram). *Ibid.*
15. War Office to S.G.S. (Ottawa), 6 Dec. 1918 (telegram). *Ibid.*
16. Secretary of State for the Colonies to the Governor-General of Canada, 12 Dec. 1918 (telegram). *Ibid.*
17. Army Records (H.Q.C. 2514).
18. White to Borden, 7 Dec. 1918 (telegram). Borden Papers.
19. Borden to White, 9 Dec. 1918 (telegram). *Ibid.*
20. Borden to White, 9 Dec. 1918 (telegram). *Ibid.*
21. White to Maj.-Gen. S. C. Mewburn, 10 Dec. 1918. *Ibid.*
22. Mewburn to Troopers, 22 Dec. 1918 (telegram). *Ibid.*
23. Elmsley to Knox, 21 Dec. 1918. Army Records (Siberian E.F., Folder 17).
24. Knox to Elmsley, 26 Dec. 1918. *Ibid.*
25. War Office to C.G.S. (Canada), 4 Jan. 1919 (telegram). Borden Papers.
26. Memorandum by Maj.-Gen. W. G. Gwatkin, 5 Jan. 1919. Army Records (H.Q.C., 2514).
27. Memorandum by Maj. E. Bristol, 7 Jan. 1919. Borden Papers.
28. Elmsley to War Office, 9 Jan. 1919 (telegram). *Ibid.*
29. C.G.S. (Ottawa) to War Office, 10 Jan. 1919 (telegram). *Ibid.*
30. War Office to C.G.S. (Ottawa), 11 Jan. 1919 (telegram). *Ibid.*
31. Col. Morrisey to Elmsley, 14 Jan. 1919 (telegram). Army Records (Siberian E.F., Folder 9).
32. Knox to deputy, Vladivostok, 17 Jan. 1919 (telegram). *Ibid.* (Folder 17).
33. Lash to Mewburn, 19 Jan. 1919 (telegram), *Ibid.* (H.Q.C. 2514).
34. White to Borden, 24 Jan. 1919 (telegram). Borden Papers.
35. Borden to White, 28 Jan. 1919 (telegram). *Ibid.*
36. Borden to the Duke of Devonshire, 13 Feb. 1919; Borden to White, 17 Feb. 1919 (telegram). *Ibid.*
37. Borden to White, 17 Feb. 1919 (telegram). *Ibid.*
38. *Ibid.*
39. Winston Churchill to Borden, 17 March 1919. *Ibid.*
40. Elmsley to Gwatkin, 27 April 1919 (telegram). Army Records (H.Q.C., 2514).
41. Gwatkin to Mewburn, 1 May 1919. *Ibid.*
42. Gwatkin to Sir Henry Wilson, 12 Feb. 1919 (telegram). *Ibid.*
43. Captain J. K. Nesbitt, "The Syren Party." Army Records.
44. Borden to Churchill, 18 May 1919. Borden Papers.
45. Borden to Lloyd George, 18 May 1919. *Ibid.*
46. Mewburn to Borden, 26 May 1919. *Ibid.*

II. THE POLITICS OF RE-ESTABLISHMENT

1. Quoted in Clifford H. Bowering, *Service: The Story of the Canadian Legion, 1925–1960* (Ottawa, 1960), pp. 3–4.
2. Quoted in Gaddis Smith, "Canadian External Affairs during World War I," in Hugh L. Keenleyside, *et al., The Growth of Canadian Policies in External Affairs* (Durham, N.C., 1960), p. 46.
3. Bowering, *Service*, p. 4.
4. S. J. Gothard to Sir Robert Borden, 20 Dec. 1919. Borden Papers.
5. Minutes of a meeting of the Executive Committee, Dominion Command, G.W.V.A., Ottawa, 31 Aug. 1919. Legion Records.

6. Minutes of a meeting of the Executive Committee, Dominion Command, G.W.V.A., Ottawa, 1 Dec. 1918. *Ibid.*
7. Proceedings of the Fourth Annual Convention, G.W.V.A., Montreal, 22 March 1920. *Ibid.*
8. Report of the Fifth Convention, G.W.V.A., Port Arthur, 17 Oct. 1921. *Ibid.*
9. *Ibid.*, 19 Oct. 1921.
10. Sir Arthur Currie to T. W. Kinder, 4 Oct. 1921. Currie Papers.
11. J. Castell Hopkins, *The Canadian Annual Review, 1917* (Toronto, 1918), p. 537.
12. *What is the Great War Veterans' Association of Canada?* (Ottawa, 1917), pp. 13–14.
13. Minutes of a meeting of the Executive Committee, Dominion Command, G.W.V.A., Ottawa, 8 June 1919. Legion Records.
14. Report of the Fifth Convention, G.W.V.A., Port Arthur, 19 Oct. 1921. *Ibid.*
15. Gothard to Borden, 20 Dec. 1919. Borden Papers.
16. Quoted in D. C. Masters, *The Winnipeg General Strike* (Toronto, 1950), p. 4.
17. Memorandum by Brig.-Gen. H. D. B. Ketchen, 10 Feb. 1919. Army Records.
18. Quoted in Masters, *The Winnipeg General Strike*, p. 61.
19. Minutes of a meeting of the Executive Committee, Dominion Command, G.W.V.A., Ottawa, 1 Dec. 1918. Legion Records.
20. Report of Proceedings of the Dominion Convention of the Great War Veterans Association of Canada, Vancouver, 3 July 1919. *Ibid.*
21. Sir Thomas White to Borden, 16 April 1919 (telegram). Borden Papers.
22. Borden to White, 29 April 1919 (telegram). *Ibid.*
23. White to Borden, 16 May 1919 (telegram). *Ibid.*
24. Lord Milner to Borden, 23 July 1919 (telegram). *Ibid.*
25. Canada, H.C. *Debates*, 1919 (first session), vol. I, p. 3863.
26. *Ibid.* (second session), vol. II, p. 1789.
27. Report of Proceedings of the Dominion Convention of the G.W.V.A., Vancouver, 2 July 1919. Legion Records.
28. Quoted in J. Castell Hopkins, *The Canadian Annual Review, 1919* (Toronto, 1920), p. 620.
29. Canada, *Journals of the House of Commons*, vol. 56, Appendix, p. 411.
30. *Ibid.*, pp. 157–8.
31. *Ibid.*, p. 418.
32. *Ibid.*, p. 976.
33. *Ibid.*, p. 455.
34. *Ibid.*, pp. 39, 48, 56.
35. Diary of Sir George Foster, 10 Nov. 1919.
36. *Ibid.*, 8 Dec. 1919.
37. *Ibid.*, (no day date) Jan. 1920.
38. Proceedings of the Fourth Annual Convention, G.W.V.A., Montreal, 24 March 1920. Legion Records.
39. Quoted in J. Castell Hopkins, *The Canadian Annual Review, 1920* (Toronto, 1921), p. 453.
40. Diary of Sir George Foster, 3 April 1920.
41. Canada, H.C. *Debates*, 1920, vol. II, p. 1083.
42. Diary of Sir George Foster, 11 April 1920.
43. *Ibid.*, 18 April 1920.
44. Report of the Fifth Convention, G.W.V.A., Port Arthur, 21 Oct. 1921. Legion Records.

45. *Ibid.*
46. *Ibid.*
47. *Ibid.*
48. *Ibid.*, 22 Oct. 1921.

III. THE MILITARY AND ITS MISSIONS

1. "The Objects of Military Organization in Canada," no date. Army Records, S. 3500.
2. Big.-Gen. H. D. B. Ketchen to the Secretary, Militia Council, 14 May 1919. *Ibid.* (959.009 D31).
3. G.O.C., M.D. No. 11 to Adjutant-General, Ottawa, 5 June 1919 (telegram). *Ibid.* (322.009 D806).
4. Lt.-Col. H. E. Boak to Col. J. I. McLaren, 29 Dec. 1920. *Ibid.* (325.009 D272).
5. Memorandum, M.D. No. 2. No date; probably *c.* 30 Dec. 1920. *Ibid.*
6. "Situation Report, Week Ending 12 February 1921." *Ibid.*
7. "Appreciation of Situation." No date; probably Dec. 1921. *Ibid.*
8. Major A. W. Duffus (R.C.M.P.) to the Commissioner, R.C.M.P., Ottawa, 26 Jan. 1922. *Ibid.*
9. Col. J. Sutherland Brown to G.O.C., M.D. No. 2, 8 Aug. 1919. *Ibid.*
10. Canada, H.C. *Debates*, 1919, vol. IV, p. 3966.
11. *Ibid.*, pp. 3968–9.
12. *Ibid.*, pp. 3969–70.
13. *Ibid.*, p. 3973.
14. *Ibid.*, pp. 3975–6.
15. Mackenzie King to E. M. Macdonald, 7 July 1923. King Papers.
16. King to George P. Graham, 20 July 1923. *Ibid.*
17. 14–15 George V, c. 57.
18. Chief of the General Staff to District Officers Commanding, 15 Aug. 1931. Army Records 169.009. (D223).
19. Adjutant-General to District Officers Commanding, 27 March 1934. *Ibid.*
20. Maj.-Gen. E. C. Ashton to Maj.-Gen. A. G. L. McNaughton, 5 April 1935. McNaughton Papers (Folder 359, vol. II).
21. "The Re-organization of the Non-Permanent Active Militia of Canada," 29 Jan. 1931. Army Records (S. 5902, I.)
22. Quoted in G. R. Stevens, *Princess Patricia's Canadian Light Infantry, 1919–1957* (Griesbach, Alberta), p. 6.
23. "Extracts from Testimony Before the Otter Committee, M.D. No. 1, London, Ontario, 1 Dec. 1919." Army Records (462–16–1, II).
24. Report of the Fifth Convention, G.W.V.A., Port Arthur, 19 Oct. 1921. Legion Records.
25. "The Objects of Military Organization in Canada," no date. Army Records (S. 3500).
26. Gen. Sir W. G. Gwatkin to Deputy Minister, Department of Militia and Defence, 20 Nov. 1918. *Ibid.* (H.Q.C., 2862, I).
27. Memorandum by Gwatkin for Deputy Minister, 31 Jan. 1919. *Ibid.*
28. Maj.-Gen. Sir Eugène Fiset to Gwatkin, 5 Feb. 1919. *Ibid.*
29. Resolution of the G.W.V.A. Parkdale Branch, 13 Jan. 1920. Transmitted with covering letter to Maj.-Gen. S. C. Mewburn, Minister of Militia and Defence, 16 Jan. 1920. *Ibid.*
30. Memorandum by the Director of Military Operations and Intelligence for the Chief of Staff, 7 May 1927. *Ibid.* (3067–I).

31. Memorandum by the Director of Military Operations and Intelligence for the Chief of Staff, 11 Nov. 1927. *Ibid.* (H.Q. S. 3496, II).

32. Chief of the General Staff to Officers Commanding Military Districts, 12 April 1921. Army Records (H.Q. S. 3496, I).

33. Col. J. Sutherland Brown to Brig.-Gen. H. C. Thacker, 28 April 1921. *Ibid.*

34. Brig.-Gen. D. M. Ormand to Maj.-Gen. J. H. MacBrien, 19 May 1921. *Ibid.*

35. MacBrien to Ormond, 25 May 1921. *Ibid.*

36. Brig.-Gen. W. A. Griesbach to MacBrien, 24 May 1921. *Ibid.*

37. Director of Military Operations and Intelligence to Officers Commanding Military Districts, 16 Jan. 1922. *Ibid.*

38. Director of Military Operations and Intelligence to Officers Commanding Military Districts, 9 Nov. 1923. *Ibid.*

39. Col. J. P. Landry (C.O. M.D. No. 5) to National Defence Headquarters, 24. Dec. 1923. *Ibid.* (H.Q. S. 3496, II).

40. Col. C. J. Armstrong (C.O. M.D. No. 4) to National Defence Headquarters, 28 Dec. 1923. *Ibid.*

41. Col. D. M. Ormond (C.O. M.D. No. 12) to National Defence Headquarters, 27 Dec. 1923. *Ibid.*

42. Ketchen (C.O. M.D. No. 10) to Chief of Staff, Department of National Defence, Ottawa, 28 Dec. 1923. *Ibid.*

43. "Air Policy," *Canadian Defence Quarterly*, vol. I, no. 1, Oct. 1923, p. 60.

44. Brown, "Military Policy of Canada, 1905–1924, and Suggestions for the Future," *ibid.*, vol. I, no. 4, July 1924, p. 21.

45. Memorandum by the Director of Military Operations and Intelligence for the Chief of Staff, Department of National Defence, 11 Nov. 1927. Army Records (H.Q. S. 3496, II).

46. Col. R. O. Alexander (C.O. M.D. No. 10) to Col. H. H. Matthews, 24 July 1928. *Ibid.*

47. Mathews to Alexander, 10 Aug. 1928. *Ibid.*

48. Matthews to McNaughton, 26 Jan. 1929. *Ibid.*

49. Matthews to Officers Commanding Military Districts, 28 May 1931. *Ibid.*

50. Quoted in memorandum by McNaughton, 28 May 1935. *Ibid.* (112.3M-2009. D7).

51. McNaughton to Officers Commanding Military Districts, 24 Oct. 1933. *Ibid.* (H.Q. S. 3496, II).

52. Quoted in R. MacGregor Dawson, *William Lyon Mackenzie King: A Political Biography* (Toronto, 1958), p. 410.

53. Memorandum by Private Secretary, Minister of Militia and Defence, for Chief of the General Staff, 18 Sept. 1922. Army Records (S. 3948, I).

54. Brown, "Memorandum for the Honourable the Minister," 18 Sept. 1922. *Ibid.*

55. King Papers.

56. *Ibid.*

57. *Ibid.*

58. MacBrien, "General Organization for War," 4 Oct. 1926. Army Records (S. 5076).

59. Memorandum by Chief of Staff, Department of National Defence, for Director of Military Operations and Intelligence, 14 Oct. 1926. *Ibid.* (S. 3067, I).

60. *Ibid.*

61. Memorandum by the Director of Military Operations and Intelligence, for the Chief of Staff, Department of National Defence, 15 Oct. 1926. *Ibid.*

62. Memorandum by the Director of Military Operations and Intelligence, for the Chief of Staff, Department of National Defence, 7 May 1927. *Ibid.*

63. Memorandum by McNaughton to the Director of Military Operations and Intelligence, 25 Oct. 1926. *Ibid.* (S. 3498, I).
64. "Memorandum re Mobilization of an Expeditionary Force for Service in China," 26 Jan. 1927. *Ibid.*
65. Memorandum by Chief of Staff, Department of National Defence, for Director of Military Operations and Intelligence, 8 Feb. 1927. *Ibid.*
66. Memorandum by Director of Military Operations and Intelligence, for Chief of the General Staff, 23 Jan. 1930. *Ibid.*
67. Memorandum by the Chief of the General Staff for the Minister of National Defence, 11 Jan. 1932. *Ibid.* (S. 3498, II).
68. Defence Scheme No. 4, "Organization, Mobilization and Despatch of a Contingent." March 1932. *Ibid.* (112.3M2009, D64).
69. Quoted in W. R. P. Bridger, "Education and the Royal Military College of Canada," *Canadian Defence Quarterly*, July 1931, vol. VIII, no. 4, p. 448.
70. *Report of the Department of Militia and Defence, 1921*, p. 80. Sessional Papers vol. LVIII, no. 9, 1922.
71. *Ibid.*, p. 86.
72. *Ibid.*, p. 97.
73. *Ibid.*, *1920*, p. 62. Sessional Papers, vol. LVII, no. 9, 1921.
74. Bridger, "Education and R.M.C.," p. 451.
75. *Report of the Department of Militia and Defence, 1921*, p. 86.
76. *Ibid.*, *1920*, p. 67.
77. Lt.-Gen. Maurice A. Pope, *Soldiers and Politicians* (Toronto, 1962), p. 98.
78. *Ibid.*, p. 74.
79. *Ibid.*, p. 76.
80. *Ibid.*, p. 53.
81. F. R. Scott, "The Collective System." Report of the First Study Conference, Canadian Institute of International Affairs, Montreal, 19–20 May, 1934, p. 12.
82. Lt.-Col. K. Stuart to F. R. Scott, 17 Sept. 1934. McNaughton Papers (C.G.S., Folder 17).
83. McNaughton, "Memorandum for the Minister," 18 Jan. 1929. *Ibid.* (C.G.S., Folder 79).
84. Scott, "The Collective System," p. 12.
85. McNaughton, "Memorandum for the Minister," 18 Jan. 1929. McNaughton Papers (C.G.S., Folder 17).
86. Lt.-Col. H. D. G. Crerar to Col. W. W. Torr, 13 Jan. 1936. Army Records. (000.8 D.3).
87. J. L. Ralston to King, 7 May 1927. King Papers.
88. King to Ralston, 28 Sept. 1927. *Ibid.*
89. L.A.G.O.R., "Food for Thought," *Canadian Defence Quarterly*, Jan. 1925, vol. II, no. 2, pp. 105–6.
90. Lt.-Col. G. R. Pearkes, "A Short Outline of the Growth of the Intelligence Services," *ibid.*, vol. II, no. 3, April 1925, p. 279.
91. Col. T. V. Anderson, "Qualifying for Promotion in the Permanent Force," *ibid.*, vol. II, no. 4, July 1925, p. 326.
92. John C. Cairns, *International Journal*, vol. XVI, no. 2, spring 1961, p. 195.
93. *Canadian Defence Quarterly*, vol. X, no. 2, Jan. 1933, p. 135.
94. *Ibid.*, p. 135.
95. *Ibid.*, vol. I, no. 3, April 1924, pp. 122.
96. *Ibid.*, vol. VII, no. 1, Oct. 1929, pp. 1–2.
97. *Ibid.*
98. *Ibid.*, vol. VII, no. 2, Jan. 1930, pp. 144–5.
99. *Ibid.*
100. *Ibid.*, vol. VII, no. 2, Jan. 1930, p. 192.
101. *Ibid.*, vol. VII, no. 3, April 1930, pp. 281–2.

102. Cptn. E. L. M. Burns, "Dialogue of a Soldier and a Pacifist," *ibid.*, vol. II, no. 1, Oct. 1924, p. 23.
103. Editorial, *ibid.*, vol. VIII, no. 4, July 1931, p. 435.
104. McNaughton Papers (C.G.S., Folder 17).
105. Stuart to Scott, 17 Sept. 1934. *Ibid.*
106. Scott, "The Collective System," p. 12.
107. McNaughton to R. B. Bennett. McNaughton Papers (C.G.S., Folder 17).
108. Lt.-Col. E. L. M. Burns, "The Defence of Canada," *Canadian Defence Quarterly*, vol. XIII, no. 4, July 1936, p. 379.
109. Pope to Crerar, 6 Sept. 1936, Army Records (000.8. D5).
110. Minutes of the Fifth Meeting of the Conference of Defence Associations, Ottawa, Nov. 13–14, 1936. Army Records.
111. Massey to Skelton, 23 Feb. 1929. Massey Papers.
112. Crerar to Pope, 11 April 1936. Army Records (000.8 D5).
113. Col. C. F. Hamilton, "Lieut.-General Sir Willoughby Gwatkin: An Appreciation," *Canadian Defence Quarterly*, vol. II, no. 3, April 1925, p. 229.
114. D.D.M.K., "News Value," *Canadian Defence Quarterly*, vol. II, no. 3, April 1925, pp. 224–5.
115. Quoted in Margaret Stewart and Doris French, *Ask No Quarter: A Biography of Agnes Macphail* (Toronto, 1959), p. 89.
116. Canada, H.C. *Debates*, 1931, vol. III, p. 3113.
117. *The Canadian Club Yearbook, 1919–1920* (Ottawa, 1921), p. 91.
118. *Quebec Chronicle*, 23 April 1924.
119. J. A. E. Woodhouse, "Some Notes on the Naval Service of Canada, 1927." Naval Records.
120. F.H.U., "Canada and War," *Canadian Forum*, May 1933, p. 286.
121. F. H. Underhill, "Canada and the Next War," Addresses and Outlines of Addresses Given at the Canadian Institute on Economics and Politics, 1934 (mimeographed, 1934), pp. 38–9.
122. Escott Reid, "On War Guilt and Preparedness," *Trinity University Review*, March 1927, pp. 12–13.
123. Brooke Claxton, "Canadian Defence and Security," *McGill News*, Dec. 1934, p. 28.
124. Quoted in George H. Ford, ed., *The Pickersgill Letters* (Toronto, 1948), p. 37.
125. League of Nations Society in Canada, *Report of Annual Meeting, 1934*, inside back cover.
126. Quoted in *ibid.*, pp. 112–13.
127. Canada, Senate *Debates*, 1934, p. 329.
128. League of Nations Society in Canada, *Report of Annual Meeting, 1934*, pp. 87–8.
129. Salvador de Madariaga, *Disarmament* (New York, 1929), pp. 10–11.
130. League of Nations Society in Canada, *Report of Annual Meeting, 1934*, p. 82.
131. Canada, Senate *Debates*, 1934, p. 242.
132. Vincent Massey to George Drew, 21 May 1934. Massey Papers.
133. Toronto *Star*, 12 June 1934.
134. Lt.-Col. George A. Drew, "Salesmen of Death: The Truth about War Markets," *Maclean's Magazine*, 1 Aug. 1931.
135. Master General of the Ordnance to Chief of the General Staff, 26 May 1936. Army Records (H.Q.C. 72–32–1, vol. V).
136. Canada, H.C. *Debates*, 1932, vol. I, p. 575.
137. *Ibid.*, p. 761.
138. *Ibid.*, p. 781.

139. *Ibid.*, 1935, vol. II, pp. 1547–9.
140. Quoted in *ibid.*, p. 1547.
141. *Ibid.*, p. 1558.
142. de Madariaga, *Disarmament*, pp. 11–12.
143. Quoted in H.C. *Debates*, 1928, vol. III, p. 3329.
144. *Ibid.*, 1927, vol. II, p. 2207.
145. *Ibid.*, 1935, vol. II, pp. 1548–9.
146. League of Nations Society in Canada, *Report of Annual Meeting, 1934*, p. 76.
147. W. L. Grant, "Is Canada Treating the League of Nations Seriously?" *Saturday Night*, 31 Dec. 1932.
148. McNaughton to Sir George Perley, 3 Jan. 1933. McNaughton Papers (C.G.S., 5).
149. Escott Reid, " 'Lest We Forget' What?" *Saturday Night*, 4 May 1935.
150. *Canadian Defence Quarterly*, vol. IX, no. 1, Oct. 1931, pp. 4–5.
151. A. R. M. Lower to Deputy Minister, Department of National Defence, 27 Jan. 1935. Navy Records.
152. Draft reply by Comm. Percy Nelles, for Deputy Minister, Department of National Defence, 4 Feb. 1935. *Ibid.*
153. Minute by McNaughton, on draft reply by Nelles, 4 Feb. 1935. *Ibid.*
154. Minutes of Second Meeting of Conference of Defence Associations, Ottawa, 17 and 18 Nov. 1933. *Ibid.*
155. Minutes of the First Meeting of Conference of Defence Associations, Ottawa, 18 and 19 Nov. 1932. *Ibid.*
156. *Ibid.*
157. Minutes of the Second Meeting of the Conference of Defence Associations, Ottawa, 17 and 18 Nov. 1933. *Ibid.*
158. Minutes of the Fifth Meeting of the Conference of Defence Associations, Ottawa, 13 and 14 Nov. 1936. Army Records.
159. *Ibid.*
160. *Ibid.*
161. *Ibid.*
162. G. M. LeFresne, "The Royal Twenty-Centers: The Department of National Defence and Federal Unemployment Relief, 1932–1936" (M.A. thesis, Royal Military College, 1962), pp. 11–12.
163. Memorandum by McNaughton, 20 Feb. 1933. McNaughton Papers (C.G.S., Folder 301, vol. I).
164. McNaughton to J. W. McConnell, 15 April 1933. *Ibid.*
165. McNaughton to H. H. Stevens, 26 June 1933. *Ibid.* (vol. II).
166. McNaughton to W. M. Dickson, 1 June 1933. *Ibid.* (Folder 333).
167. Memorandum by McNaughton, 3 Oct. 1933. *Ibid.* (301, vol. III).
168. Memorandum by McNaughton, 29 May 1934. *Ibid.* (333).
169. McNaughton to R. K. Finlayson, 22 June 1934. *Ibid.* (348).
170. Memorandum by McNaughton, 18 July 1934. *Ibid.* (301, vol. IV).
171. Memorandum by McNaughton, 29 May 1934. *Ibid* (333).
172. Memorandum by H. J. Barber, "Re Wage Scheme for Unemployment Camps in Canada." No date (probably Oct. 1934). *Ibid.*, 301 (vol. V).
173. Memorandum by McNaughton, 16 Oct. 1934. *Ibid.*
174. Joseph Pelletier to W. A. Gordon, 24 April 1933. *Ibid.* (301, vol. II).
175. Canada, H.C. *Debates*, 1935, vol. IV, p. 4052.
176. McNaughton to Pelletier (draft reply), 2 May 1933. McNaughton Papers (301, vol. II).
177. Dickson to Percy R. Bengough, 22 Jan. 1935. *Ibid.* (359, vol. II). Drafted by McNaughton.

178. Quoted in LeFresne, "The Royal Twenty-Centers," p. 103.
179. *Final Report of the Unemployment Relief Scheme for the Care of Single, Homeless Men Administered by the Department of National Defence, 1932–1936* (Ottawa, 1937), vol. I, p. 2.
180. Minutes of Third Meeting of Conference of Defence Associations, Ottawa, 16 and 17 Nov. 1934. Navy Records.
181. Margaret A. Ormsby, *British Columbia: A History* (Toronto, 1958), p. 445.
182. Bennett to Gordon Sloan, 25 Feb. 1934 (telegram). McNaughton Papers (C.G.S., 359, vol. I).
183. McNaughton to Miss A. E. Millar, 9 March 1934. *Ibid.*
184. T. D. Pattullo to Bennett, 17 Dec. 1934 (telegram). *Ibid.*
185. Bennett to Pattullo, 28 Dec. 1934 (telegram). *Ibid.*
186. Bennett to Pattullo, 2 Jan. 1935 (telegram). *Ibid.*
187. Pattullo to Bennett, 3 Jan. 1935 (telegram); Bennett to Patullo, 5 Jan. 1935 (telegram). *Ibid.*
188. McNaughton to Ashton, 10 Jan. 1935. *Ibid.*
189. Ashton to Secretary, Department of National Defence, Militia Services, 5 Jan. 1935. *Ibid.* (359, vol. II).
190. Ashton to McNaughton, 16 March 1935. *Ibid.*
191. Memorandum by McNaughton, 20 March 1935. *Ibid.*
192. Ashton to McNaughton, 16 March 1935. *Ibid.*
193. Pattullo to Perley, 25 March 1935 (telegram). *Ibid.*
194. Memorandum by McNaughton, 26 March 1935. *Ibid.*
195. Pattullo to Perley, 27 March 1935 (telegram). *Ibid.*
196. Perley to Pattullo, 27 March 1935 (telegram). *Ibid.*
197. Pattullo to Perley, 27 March 1935 (telegram). *Ibid.*
198. Perley to Pattullo, 28 March 1935 (telegram). *Ibid.* Memorandum by McNaughton, 28 March 1935. *Ibid.*
199. Ashton to McNaughton, 25 March 1935. *Ibid.*
200. *Ibid.*
201. Memorandum by McNaughton, 4 April 1935. *Ibid.*
202. Ashton to McNaughton, 5 April 1935. *Ibid.*
203. Memorandum by McNaughton, 18 April 1935. *Ibid.*
204. MacBrien to Grote Stirling, 18 April 1935 (telegram). *Ibid.*
205. Memorandum by McNaughton, 19 April 1935. *Ibid.*
206. Memorandum by McNaughton, "Situation in Vancouver, B.C.," 19 April 1935. *Ibid.*
207. Memorandum by McNaughton, 19 April 1935. *Ibid.* (359, vol. III).
208. Memorandum by McNaughton, 20 May 1935. *Ibid.* (359, vol. IV).
209. British Columbia Provincial Police Report of Meeting held by Arthur Herbert Evans, Victoria B.C. 19 Dec. 1935. Army Records (322.009. D743).
210. LeFresne, "The Royal Twenty-Centers," pp. 113–4.
211. Canada, H.C. *Debates*, 1935, vol. IV, pp. 3900–01.
212. C. P. Stacey, *The Military Problems of Canada* (Toronto, 1940), p. 95.

IV. THE NAVY AND THE NATION

1. *Robert Laird Borden: His Memoirs* (Toronto, 1938), vol. II, p. 841.
2. Quoted in *ibid.*, pp. 842–3.
3. Sir Robert Borden to Lord Milner, 18 April 1919. Borden Papers.
4. Minutes of the Naval Committee, 13 March 1919. Navy Records.
5. Occasional Paper No. 2, "Proposals for Canadian Naval Expansion," 3 July 1919. *Ibid.*

6. Gilbert Norman Tucker, *The Naval Service of Canada*, vol. I (Ottawa, 1952), pp. 308–9.
7. Quoted in J. Castell Hopkins, *The Canadian Annual Review, 1919* (Toronto, 1920), p. 195.
8. Quoted in *ibid.*, p. 196.
9. Henri Bourassa, *La Mission Jellicoe: Nouvelle poussée d'imperialisme* (Montreal, 1920), p. 14.
10. Borden, *Memoirs*, vol. II, pp. 1014–5.
11. Borden Diary, entry for 28 Nov. 1919.
12. Enclosed with Gordon B. Jackson (Secretary, Dominion Headquarters, Navy League of Canada) to C. C. Ballantyne, 8 Nov. 1920. Naval Records (N.S. 1080–206–IV).
13. *Victoria Colonist*, 9 March 1919.
14. Bourassa, *La Mission Jellicoe: Nouvelle poussée d'imperialisme*, pp. 30–31.
15. Admiral Sir Charles Kingsmill, "Memorandum for the Minister," 16 May 1918. Naval Records (N.S. 1080–206–I).
16. Kingsmill, "Memorandum for the Minister," 31 May 1918. *Ibid.*
17. Kingsmill to G. J. Desbarats, 16 Jan. 1920. *Ibid.* (N.S. 1080–206–III).
18. Ballantyne to S. F. Tolmie, 29 Nov. 1919. *Ibid.*
19. Ballantyne to Æmilius Jarvis, 21 Nov. 1919. *Ibid.*
20. Borden Diary, 29 Nov. 1919.
21. *Montreal Gazette*, 11 Aug. 1920.
22. J. A. E. Woodhouse, "Some Notes on the Naval Service of Canada," 1927. Naval Records.
23. *Ibid.*
24. *Ibid.*
25. Quoted in Sir Reginald Bacon, *Life of John Rushworth, Earl Jellicoe* (London, 1936), p. 419.
26. Borden diary, entry for 28 Dec. 1919.
27. Sir George Foster to Borden, 25 March 1920. Borden Papers.
28. Ballantyne to Borden, 12 April 1920. *Ibid.*
29. Rear-Adm. Walter Hose, "The Early Years of the Royal Canadian Navy," unpublished text of address to the R.C.N. Golden Jubilee Dinner, 19 Feb. 1960, pp. 8–9.
30. *Ibid.*, p. 9
31. Canada, H.C. *Debates*, 1920, vol. I, p. 707.
32. "Empire Naval Policy and Co-operation," Feb. 1921. King Papers.
33. J. S. Willison to Sir Campbell Stuart, 7 Dec. 1920. Willison Papers.
34. Willison to Arthur Meighen, 18 April 1921. *Ibid.*
35. Ballantyne to Meighen, 29 April 1921. Meighen Papers.
36. Grattan O'Leary to Willison, 22 May 1921. Willison Papers.
37. Ballantyne to Bennett, 16 Jan. 1928. Bennett Papers.
38. Conference of Prime Ministers and Representatives of the United Kingdom, the Dominions, and India, held in June, July and August, 1921, *Summary of Proceedings and Documents*, Cmd. 1474, p. 6.
39. Canada, H.C. *Debates*, 1922, vol. II, p. 1737.
40. Hose, R. M. Stephens, Desbarats, "Memo. to the Minister," 28 Feb. 1922. Navy Records (1078–2–4).
41. Canada, H.C. *Debates*, 1922, vol. II, pp. 1739–40.
42. Woodhouse, "Some Notes on the Naval Service of Canada," 1927. Navy Records.
43. Hose to Cptn. H. E. Holme, 10 Aug. 1922. *Ibid.*
44. Canada, H.C. *Debates*, 1922, vol. II, p. 1745.
45. Meighen to John W. Regan, 19 May 1922. Meighen Papers.

46. Jarvis to King, 9 May 1922. King Papers.
47. Admiralty Memorandum, Aug. 1922. Quoted in O. D. Skelton, "The Imperial Conference, October 1923. Preliminary Notes," no date. *Ibid.*
48. P. C. Larkin to King, 5 March 1923; Larkin to King, 19 March 1923. *Ibid.*
49. L. S. Amery to King, 4 July 1923. *Ibid.*
50. King to Amery, 17 July 1923. *Ibid.*
51. Committee of Imperial Defence, "Empire Naval Policy and Co-operation. Canada," 1923. King Papers.
52. O. D. Skelton, "Canada and Foreign Policy," *The Canadian Club Yearbook, 1921–22* (Ottawa, 1922), pp. 58–69.
53. Quoted in R. MacGregor Dawson, *William Lyon Mackenzie King: A Political Biography* (Toronto, 1958), p. 454.
54. O. D. Skelton, *Life and Letters of Sir Wilfrid Laurier,* vol. II (Toronto, 1921), pp. 325–6.
55. "Memorandum for Mr. King re Imperial Defence Resolutions, 1923," no date. King Papers.
56. Skelton, "Imperial Conference, 1923: Naval Defence," no date. *Ibid.*
57. Skelton, "The Imperial Conference, October, 1923. Preliminary Notes," no date. *Ibid.*
58. Martin to King, 14 Sept. 1923. *Ibid.*
59. Raoul Dandurand to King, 12 Sept. 1923. *Ibid.*
60. J. W. Dafoe to Sir Clifford Sifton, 12 Sept. 1923. Quoted in Ramsay Cook, "J. W. Dafoe at the Imperial Conference, 1923," *Canadian Historical Review,* vol. XLI, no. 1, March 1960, p. 21.
61. Quoted in *ibid.* pp. 23–24.
62. L. S. Amery, *My Political Life,* vol. II, *War and Peace, 1914–1929* (London, 1953), p. 276.
63. King Papers.
64. *Ibid.*
65. Quoted in Cook, "Dafoe at the Imperial Conference, 1923," p. 28.
66. Dawson, *Mackenzie King,* p. 467.
67. Amery to King, 27 Oct. 1923. King Papers.
68. King to Amery, 7 Nov. 1923. *Ibid.*
69. Quoted in Dawson, *Mackenzie King,* p. 468.
70. Imperial Conference, 1923, *Summary of Proceedings* (Ottawa, 1924), pp. 15–16.
71. Quoted in Dawson, *Mackenzie King,* p. 480.
72. King to the Duke of Devonshire, 12 Jan. 1924 (telegram). King Papers.
73. Amery, *My Political Life,* p. 275.

V. THE EARLY YEARS OF THE R.C.A.F.

1. "Air Board, C.A.F. and R.C.A.F., 1919–1939," Unpublished manuscript. Air Force Records.
2. Air Force Records. (N.S. 15–24–2, I).
3. Ministry of Overseas Military Forces to Department of Militia and Defence, 20 Feb. 1919. *Ibid.*
4. "Memorandum on Proposed Air Board," 2 April 1919. *Ibid.*
5. R. M. Stephens to Director of the Naval Service, 4 April 1919. *Ibid.*
6. Stephens to Director of the Naval Service, 4 April 1919. *Ibid.*
7. Minutes of the Naval Committee, 6th meeting, 9 April 1919. *Ibid.*
8. Memorandum by Sir Willoughby Gwatkin, 10 April 1919. *Ibid.*
9. Memorandum by Stephens, "Remarks on the Proposed Air Board Bill," 10 April 1919. *Ibid.*

10. Memorandum by Stephens, "Remarks on Canadian Air Policy," 10 April 1919. *Ibid.*
11. Memorandum for the Deputy Minister, by Stephens, 24 April 1919. *Ibid.*
12. Memorandum, unsigned, undated. *Ibid.*
13. Canada, H.C. *Debates*, 1919, vol. II, pp. 1864–5.
14. *Ibid*, p. 2051.
15. Maj. C. MacLauren to the President, the Aero Club of Canada, 11 June 1919. Air Force Records (N.S. 15–24–2).
16. Memorandum by A. L. Sifton, "The Permanent Organization of the Air Board," 17 March 1920. *Ibid.*
17. Arthur Meighen to C. C. Ballantyne, 4 July 1919. *Ibid.*
18. Ballantyne to Meighen, 7 July 1919. *Ibid.*
19. Memorandum by Sifton, "The Permanent Organization of the Air Board," 17 March 1920. *Ibid.*
20. Lt.-Col. R. Leckie to Maj. D. MacLaren, 26 April 1920. *Ibid.* (889–2–11).
21. "Aerial Expansion—with Particular Reference to Canada." Air Ministry Memorandum, April 1919. *Ibid.* (N.S. 15–24–2, II).
22. Occasional Paper No. 24, "Remarks on a Canadian Naval Air Force," Naval War Staff, Ottawa, 26 Jan. 1920. Naval Records.
23. Memorandum by R. M. Stephens to the Director of the Naval Service, 19 Dec. 1919. Air Force Records (N.S. 15–24–2, II).
24. Stephens to E. F. Newcombe, 14 Jan. 1920. *Ibid.*
25. Newcombe to Stephens, 23 Jan. 1920. *Ibid.*
26. *Report of the Air Board for the Fiscal Year Ending March 31, 1920* (Ottawa, 1920), p. 7.
27. Quoted in "Air Board, C.A.F. and R.C.A.F.," Air Force Records.
28. Canada, H.C. *Debates*, 1920, vol. V, pp. 4553–54.
29. *Ibid.*, p. 4556.
30. *Ibid.*, p. 4556.
31. Minutes of Meeting of Delegates of Provincial Executive Committees of the Canadian Air Force Association, Winnipeg, 3 July 1920. Air Force Records.
32. *Ibid.*
33. Col. J. A. Glen to Lt.-Col. R. Leckie, 4 Feb. 1920. Air Force Records (889–2–11).
34. Glen to Biggar, 19 Feb. 1920. *Ibid.*
35. Glen to Leckie, 20 Feb. 1920. *Ibid.*
36. Leckie to MacLaren, 16 March 1920. *Ibid.*
37. Leckie to MacLaren, 24 March 1920. *Ibid.*
38. Leckie to Glen, 9 April 1920. *Ibid.*
39. Canada, H.C. *Debates*, 1920, vol. V, p. 4555.
40. *Ibid.*, p. 4555.
41. Minutes of Meeting of Delegates of Provincial Executive Committees of the Canadian Air Force Association, Winnipeg, 3 July 1920. Air Force Records.
42. *Report of the Air Board for the Year 1921* (Ottawa, 1922), pp. 11–12.
43. Air Comm. K. C. Tylee to Gen. Sir Willoughby Gwatkin, 2 Feb. 1921. Air Force Records (3762).
44. Lloyd Harris and R. W. Leonard to Hugh Guthrie, 3 Feb. 1921. Meighen Papers.
45. Arthur Meighen to Lloyd Harris, 7 Feb. 1921. *Ibid.*
46. Harris to Meighen, 8 Feb. 1921. *Ibid.*
47. Memorandum, 16 March 1921. Air Force Records (3762).
48. Wg. Cdr. J. S. Williams to the Secretary, the Air Board, 9 June 1921. *Ibid.*
49. Meighen to Thomas H. Spence, 19 Nov. 1921. Meighen Papers.
50. "Air Board, C.A.F. and R.C.A.F., 1919–1939."

51. Gwatkin to Sir Hugh Trenchard, 14 Dec. 1921. Air Force Records (601–4B–8).
52. Gwatkin to George P. Graham, 20 March 1922. *Ibid.* (C. 3803).
53. Gwatkin to Maj.-Gen. J. H. MacBrien, 6 April 1922. *Ibid.* (C. 3802).
54. Gwatkin to MacBrien, 24 March 1922. *Ibid.*
55. *Report of the Air Board for the Year 1922* (Ottawa, 1923), p. 11.
56. Canada, H.C. *Debates*, 1922, vol. II, pp. 1724–5.
57. *Ibid.*, p. 1728.
58. *Ibid.*, p. 1732.
59. *Report of the Air Board for the Year 1922* (Ottawa, 1923), p. 12.
60. Wg. Cdr. W. G. Barkey to Director, C.A.F., 5 Jan. 1923. Air Force Records (3762).
61. Wg. Cdr. J. L. Gordon to Barkey, 10 Jan. 1923. *Ibid.*
62. Memorandum by Wg. Cdr. W. Stedman, 30 May 1922. *Ibid.* (C. 3756).
63. Gwatkin to MacBrien, 31 May 1922. *Ibid.*
64. MacBrien to Gwatkin, 1 June 1922. *Ibid.*
65. Gwatkin to MacBrien, 5 June 1922. *Ibid.*
66. MacBrien to Gwatkin, 5 June 1922. *Ibid.*
67. "Submission by the Chairman of the Air Board to the Governor General in Council," 15 Nov. 1922. *Ibid.*
68. "Memorandum for the C.G.S. by Director, R.C.A.F.," 5 Aug. 1927. *Ibid.* (895–1–I).
69. Canada, H.C. *Debates*, 1929, vol. III, p. 3210.
70. *Ibid.*, p. 3210.
71. *Ibid.*, p. 3221.
72. "Air Requirements of the Dominions—Canada." Memorandum by the Air Staff, R.A.F., October 1923. Air Force Records (3762).
73. King Papers.
74. *Ibid.*
75. *Ibid.*
76. *Ibid.*
77. *Imperial Conference 1923, Summary of Proceedings* (Ottawa, 1924), p. 15.
78. "The Approach towards a System of Imperial Air Communications," Memorandum prepared for the Imperial Conference, 1926, by the Secretary of State for Air. King Papers.
79. Memorandum. *Ibid.*
80. King Papers.
81. *Ibid.*
82. Sir Samuel Hoare to King, 9 Nov. 1926. *Ibid.*

VI. CHAINS OF COMMAND

1. Quoted in Arthur J. Marder, *From the Dreadnought to Scapa Flow: The Royal Navy in the Fisher Era, 1904–1919,* Vol. I, *The Road to War, 1904–1914* (London, 1961), p. 24.
2. Sir Arthur Currie to Arthur Meighen, 5 Aug. 1920. Meighen Papers.
3. Currie to Hugh Guthrie, 5 Aug. 1920. *Ibid.*
4. Cptn. Walter Hose to Gen. Sir Willoughby Gwatkin, 24 Aug. 1921. Air Force Records (C. 3801).
5. Minutes of the Defence Committee, 15 Dec. 1921. *Ibid.*
6. Sir Eugène Fiset to Mackenzie King, 15 Dec. 1921. King Papers.
7. *Ibid.*
8. Currie to King, 19 Dec. 1921. *Ibid.*

9. Canada, H.C. *Debates*, 1922, vol. I, p. 7.
10. Currie to Brig.-Gen. R. Brutinel, 14 March 1922. Army Records.
11. General Sir Willoughby Gwatkin to Sir Hugh Trenchard, 14 Dec. 1921. Air Force Records (601–4B–8).
12. Minutes of the Air Board, meeting no. 219, 16 Jan. 1922. Air Force Records.
13. *Ibid.*, meeting no. 216, 9 Jan. 1922.
14. George P. Graham to G. J. Desbarats, 14 Feb. 1922. Naval Records.
15. O. M. Biggar to Graham, 15 Feb. 1922. Air Force Records (C. 3801).
16. Graham to Biggar, 24 Feb. 1922. *Ibid.*
17. Canada, H.C. *Debates*, 1922, vol. I, pp. 657–8.
18. *Ibid.*, p. 666.
19. *Ibid.*, p. 738.
20. *Ibid.*, p. 739.
21. *Ibid.*, p. 738.
22. *Ibid.*, p. 739.
23. *Ibid.*, p. 740.
24. *Ibid.*, p. 665.
25. *Ibid.*, p. 666.
26. *Ibid.*, p. 668.
27. *Ibid.*, p. 669.
28. *Ibid.*
29. "Notes by the Director of the Naval Service," Jan. 1923. Naval Records.
30. Hose, "Memorandum for the Deputy Minister," 17 Jan. 1923. *Ibid.*
31. Hose, "Memorandum for the Deputy Minister," 19 Jan. 1923. *Ibid.*
32. "Notes by the Director of the Naval Service," Jan. 1923. *Ibid.*
33. Fiset to Graham, 17 Oct. 1922. King Papers.
34. Graham to King, 26 Oct. 1922. *Ibid.*
35. "Notes by the Director of the Naval Service," Jan. 1923. Naval Records.
36. Interview with Adm. Hose, 22 April 1963.
37. Col. J. Sutherland Brown to Chief of Staff, 8 June 1923. Army Records (500.009(D59)).
38. Chief of Staff to Minister of National Defence, 28 June 1923. *Ibid.*
39. Memorandum by Chief of Staff for Minister of National Defence, 10 Sept. 1923. *Ibid.*
40. George P. Graham to Judge-Advocate General, 26 Jan. 1923. Naval Records.
41. Memorandum by Judge-Advocate General, "Organization—Department of National Defence," 31 Jan. 1923. *Ibid.*
42. Director of the Naval Service, "Memorandum for the Minister," 7 March 1923. *Ibid.*
43. Hose, "Memorandum for the Deputy Minister," 9 April 1923. *Ibid.*
44. R. MacGregor Dawson, *William Lyon Mackenzie King: A Political Biography* (Toronto, 1958), p. 450.
45. E. M. Macdonald, *Recollections Political and Personal* (Toronto, n.d.), pp. 408–09.
46. Hose to G. J. Desbarats, 2 Feb. 1924. Naval Records.
47. Memorandum by the Chief of Staff for the Deputy Minister, Department of National Defence, 17 Feb. 1925. *Ibid.*
48. Memorandum by the Deputy Minister for the Chief of Staff, Department of National Defence, 16 Feb. 1925. *Ibid.*
49. Memorandum by the Chief of Staff for the Deputy Minister, Department of National Defence, 17 Feb. 1925. *Ibid.*
50. Memorandum by the Deputy Minister for the Chief of Staff, Department of National Defence, 11 March 1925. *Ibid.*

51. Memorandum by the Chief of Staff for the Deputy Minister, Department of National Defence, 17 March 1925. *Ibid.*

52. Memorandum by the Director of the Naval Service for the Deputy Minister, Department of National Defence, 20 March 1925. *Ibid.*

53. Memorandum by the Chief of Staff for the Minister, Department of National Defence, 3 April 1925. *Ibid.*

54. Memorandum by the Chief of Staff for the Minister, Department of National Defence, 11 Dec. 1925. *Ibid.*

55. Memorandum by the Director of the Naval Service for the Minister, Department of National Defence, 10 Feb. 1926. *Ibid.*

56. Minute by MacBrien on memorandum by the Director of the Naval Service for Chief of Staff, Department of National Defence, 22 Feb. 1926. *Ibid.*

57. Memorandum by the Chief of Staff, Department of National Defence, for the Minister, 5 June 1926. MacBrien Papers.

58. Chief of Staff, Department of National Defence, to Chief of the Imperial General Staff, 26 Jan. 1927 (telegram). *Ibid.*

59. "Prefer to Follow Julius Caesar," *Halifax Citizen*, 25 Jan. 1929.

60. Chief of the General Staff to District Officer Commanding, M.D. No. 11, 13 Dec. 1928 (telegram). McNaughton Papers.

61. Hose, "Position of the Chief of the Naval Staff in the Department of National Defence." Navy Records.

62. *Ibid.*

63. *Ibid.*

64. Chief of the Naval Staff to the Under Secretary of State for External Affairs, 7 Jan. 1932. Quoted in *ibid.*

65. Hose to R. B. Bennett, 21 Jan. 1932. Quoted in *ibid.*

66. Bennett to Hose, 21 Jan. 1932. Quoted in *ibid.*

67. Lt.-Col. H. D. G. Crerar to McNaughton, 24 April 1932. McNaughton Papers.

68. "Memorandum to the Honourable the Minister," by the Chief of the Naval Staff, Comm. Percy W. Nelles, 28 Nov. 1934. Naval Records.

69. "Memorandum to the Honourable the Minister," by the Acting Chief of the Naval Staff, 14 March 1934. *Ibid.*

70. "Memorandum for the Honourable the Minister—Co-ordination of Services, Department of National Defence," by the Acting Chief of the Naval Staff, 9 April 1934. *Ibid.*

71. "One Chief of Staff to the Department of National Defence," by Nelles, 28 Nov. 1934. *Ibid.*

VII. DEPRESSION AND DEPLETION

1. Comm. Walter Hose to Mackenzie King, 19 May 1926. King Papers.

2. 12th meeting, Plenary Session, Imperial Conference, 15 Nov. 1926. *Ibid.*

3. J. A. E. Woodhouse, "Some Notes on the Naval Service of Canada," 1927. Navy Records.

4. *Ibid.*

5. C. C. Ballantyne to R. B. Bennett, 16 Jan. 1928. Bennett Papers.

6. R. Dandurand to King, 8 Nov. 1928. King Papers.

7. Memorandum by the Chief of the Naval Staff, "Present Naval Requirements," 26 Aug. 1930. Army Records (112–I. D70).

8. Minutes of Defence Council, 29 Aug. 1930. *Ibid* (112.1.D77).

9. *Ibid.*

10. Memorandum by Maj. Gen. A. G. L. McNaughton, 1 June 1933. McNaughton Papers (C.G.S., 64A).

11. Memorandum by McNaughton, 1 June 1933. Navy Records.
12. Memorandum by Hose, 1 June 1933. *Ibid.*
13. *Ibid.*
14. "Policy Regarding Naval Defence which would be affected by Reductions in the Service," 1 June 1933. *Ibid.*
15. "Observations by A. G. L. McN.," 8 June 1933. McNaughton Papers (C.G.S., 64A).
16. "Treasury Board Meeting—Friday, 23rd June, 1933. Synopsis by C.N.S." Navy Records.
17. "Memorandum for the Honourable the Minister," 23 June 1933. *Ibid.*
18. "Treasury Board Meeting, 23 June 1933," *Ibid.*
19. *Ibid.*
20. Hose to Vice-Adm. The Hon. R. A. R. Plunkett-Ernle-Erle-Drax, 26 June 1933. *Ibid.*
21. "Memorandum by A. G. L. McNaughton on Conversation with Admiral Sir Rogers Keyes, 10 Sept. 1934." McNaughton Papers (C.G.S., 40).
22. "Note of a Discussion which took place at a meeting of the Ottawa branch of the Canadian Institute of International Affairs, 25 October 1934." *Ibid.*
23. "Service Notes," *Army, Navy & Air Force Gazette,* 14 Feb. 1935.
24. Minutes of Third Meeting of Conference of Defence Associations, 16 and 17 Nov. 1934. Navy Records.
25. *Ibid.*
26. *Ibid.*
27. "Notes by Lt.-Commander E. C. Sherwood on Proceedings at Conference of Defence Associations, Nov. 1934." *Ibid.*
28. Canada, H.C. *Debates,* 1931, vol. III, pp. 3113–4.
29. C. C. Walker to R.C.A.F. Liason Officer, Air Ministry, London. Air Force Records.
30. "Memorandum by Chief of the General Staff for Quartermaster-General," 23 March 1931. McNaughton Papers (C.G.S., 76).
31. Lt.-Col. H. H. Matthews to McNaughton, 28 Jan. 1932. *Ibid.* (C.G.S., 5).
32. Matthews to McNaughton, 3 Feb. 1932. *Ibid.*
33. Matthews to McNaughton, 9 Feb. 1932. *Ibid.*
34. Matthews to McNaughton, 17 Feb. 1932 (telegram). *Ibid.*
35. Matthews to McNaughton, 18 Feb. 1932 (telegram). *Ibid.*
36. Matthews to McNaughton, 19 Feb. 1932. *Ibid.*
37. McNaughton to Matthews, 20 Feb. 1932 (telegram). *Ibid.*
38. Matthews to McNaughton, 21 Feb. 1932 (telegram). *Ibid.*
39. Walker to R.C.A.F. Liaison Officer, Air Ministry, London, 1 March 1932. Air Force Records.
40. Canada, H.C. *Debates,* 1932, vol. I, p. 360.
41. W. G. Beeman to McNaughton, 27 Feb. 1932. McNaughton Papers (C.G.S., 5); Canada, H.C. *Debates,* 1932, vol. I, p. 595.
42. Canada, H.C. *Debates,* 1932, vol. I, p. 597.
43. *Ibid.*, p. 367.
44. Walker to R.C.A.F. Liaison Officer, Air Ministry, 1 March 1932. Air Force Records.
45. Walker to R.C.A.F. Liaison Officer, Air Ministry, 17 March 1932. *Ibid.*
46. Walker to R.C.A.F. Liaison Officer, Air Ministry, 31 March 1932. *Ibid.*
47. Sqn. Ldr. T. A. Lawrence to Oliver Villiers, 29 March 1932. *Ibid.*
48. Memorandum for the Chief of the General Staff by the Deputy Minister, Department of National Defence, 19 Dec. 1932. McNaughton Papers (C.G.S., 65).
49. Memorandum for the Deputy Minister, Department of National Defence, by the Chief of the General Staff, 21 Dec. 1932. *Ibid.*

50. Memorandum for the Minister of National Defence, by the Chief of the General Staff, 6 Feb. 1933. *Ibid.*
51. Memorandum by the Senior Air Officer, R.C.A.F., for the Minister of National Defence, 24 Feb. 1933. *Ibid.*
52. Memorandum by the Chief of the General Staff, 18 April 1933. *Ibid.*
53. Memorandum by the Senior Air Officer, R.C.A.F., for the Chief of the General Staff, 23 May 1933. *Ibid.*
54. Chief of the General Staff to Deputy Minister, Department of National Defence, 17 June 1933. *Ibid.*
55. Memorandum by Gp. Cptn. G. O. Johnson, A/Senior Air Officer, R.C.A.F., for the Chief of the General Staff, 27 Oct. 1933. Air Force Records (C3762).
56. Memorandum by Johnson, 2 March 1934: "Service Aircraft in the R.C.A.F." *Ibid.*
57. Canada, H.C. *Debates*, 1934, vol. II, p. 1553.
58. Gp. Cptn. G. M. Croil, Senior Air Officer, R.C.A.F., to the Chief of the General Staff, 15 May 1934. Air Force Records (C 3762).
59. "The Defence of Canada," Memorandum by the Chief of the General Staff, 28 May 1935. Army Records (112.3M2009.D7).
60. Arthur Meighen to King, 22 Oct. 1921. Meighen Papers.
61. Meighen to King, 25 Oct. 1921. *Ibid.*
62. King to P. C. Larkin, 27 Nov. 1922. King Papers.
63. Meighen Papers.
64. C. C. Ballantyne to Meighen, 26 Dec. 1922. *Ibid.*
65. Meighen to Ballantyne, 27 Dec. 1922. *Ibid.*
66. "Summary of Naval, Military and Air Defence Services, 1867–1927," Army Historical Section, 10 May 1927. Desbarats Papers.
67. *Ibid.*
68. King to E. M. Macdonald, 20 Feb. 1924. King Papers.
69. "Summary of Naval, Military and Air Defence Services, 1867–1927," Desbarats Papers.
70. Canada, H.C. *Debates*, 1927, vol. II, p. 2203.
71. *Ibid.*, p. 2246.
72. *Ibid.*, pp. 2247–53.
73. *Ibid.*, p. 2206.
74. *Ibid.*, 1928, vol. III, p. 3335.
75. "Memorandum on Deficiencies in Equipment," Sept. 1930. Army Records (112.I.D.70).
76. "The Re-Organization of the Non-Permanent Active Militia of Canada," 29 Jan. 1931. *Ibid.* (5902–I).
77. Canada, H.C. *Debates*, 1931, vol. III, p. 2896.
78. *Ibid.*, p. 2898.
79. William H. Price to Bennett, 2 May 1931. Bennett Papers.
80. Quoted in R. H. Roy, *Ready for the Fray: The History of the Canadian Scottish Regiment, 1920–1958* (Vancouver, 1958), p. 44.
81. Quoted in *ibid.*
82. *Ibid.*, p. 61.
83. R. W. Queen-Hughes, *Whatever Men Dare: A History of the Queen's Own Cameron Highlanders of Canada, 1935–1960* (Winnipeg, 1960), pp. 3–6.
84. Quoted in Arnold Warren, *Wait for the Waggon: The Story of the Royal Canadian Army Service Corps* (Toronto, 1961), pp. 129–30.
85. Quoted in *ibid.*, pp. 141–2.
86. Waldo E. L. Smith, *What Time the Tempest: An Army Chaplain's Story* (Toronto, 1953), pp. 1–4.
87. George Drew to Bennett, 28 May 1931. Bennett Papers.

88. Drew to D. M. Sutherland, 3 Dec. 1931. *Ibid.*
89. McNaughton to Lord Byng, 10 April 1931. Army Records (001.D2).
90. Canada, H.C. *Debates*, 1931, vol. III, pp. 2801–2.
91. "Memorandum regarding Dominion Arsenals at Quebec and Lindsay," Feb. 1919. Army Records (114.1 [D7]B2—Arsenals).
92. Memorandum by the Chief of the General Staff, 12 May 1930. *Ibid.* (H.Q.C. 72–32–1, vol. I).
93. Quoted in J. W. Pickersgill, *The Mackenzie King Record*, I, (Toronto, 1960), p. 359.
94. Col. C. P. Stacey, *Six Years of War* (Ottawa, 1955), p. 22.
95. Beeman to McNaughton, 27 Feb. 1932. McNaughton Papers (C.G.S., 5).
96. "Reconstituted version of R. B. Bennett's speech to the Conference of Defence Associations, Ottawa, 17 November 1934." Army Records (112.3M2009.-D66).
97. "Memorandum of conversation between Gen. A. G. L. McNaughton and Sir Maurice Hankey, Ottawa, between 22 December 1934 and 26 December 1934." *Ibid* (112.3M2.D462).
98. Memorandum by McNaughton, 18 July 1934. McNaughton Papers (C.G.S., 301, vol. IV).
99. McNaughton to Bennett, 5 April 1935. Army Records (014.014.D1).
100. "The Defence of Canada," Memorandum by McNaughton, 5 April 1935 (revised 28 May 1935). *Ibid.* (112.3M2009.D7).
101. Canadian Advisory Officer to Secretary of State for External Affairs, 22 May 1935 (telegram). Bennett Papers.

INDEX

(Officers and titled people are listed under the highest rank and title attained during the period 1918–1935.)